Real-Time Java™ Progamming

Real-Time Java™
Programming
with Java RTS

Eric J. Bruno
Greg Bollella

PRENTICE
HALL

Upper Saddle River, NJ • Boston • Indianapolis • San Francisco
New York • Toronto • Montreal • London • Munich • Paris • Madrid
Capetown • Sydney • Tokyo • Singapore • Mexico City

The publisher offers excellent discounts on this book when ordered in quantity for bulk purchases or special sales, which may include electronic versions and/or custom covers and content particular to your business, training goals, marketing focus, and branding interests. For more information, please contact: U.S. Corporate and Government Sales, (800) 382-3419, corpsales@pearsontechgroup.com.

For sales outside the United States please contact: International Sales, international@pearsoned.com.

Visit us on the Web: informit.com/ph

Library of Congress Cataloging-in-Publication Data
Bruno, Eric J., 1969-
    Real-time Java programming with Java RTS / Eric J. Bruno, Greg Bollella.
        p.   cm.
    Includes bibliographical references and index.
    ISBN 978-0-13-714298-9 (pbk. : alk. paper) 1. Java (Computer program language)
2. Real-time programming. 3. Application program interfaces (Computer software)
I. Bollella, Gregory. II. Title.

    QA76.73.J38B823 2009
    005.2'739—dc22

                                                2009015739

ISBN-13: 978-0-13-714298-9
ISBN-10:   0-13-714298-6
Text printed in the United States on recycled paper at R.R. Donnelley in Crawfordsville, Indiana.
First printing, May 2009

To my parents, Joseph and Sandra

—EJB

To Melinda

—GB

Contents

Preface

*"To achieve great things, two things are needed: a plan,
and not quite enough time."*

—Leonard Bernstein

As this book is being written, the age of real-time programming, especially with Java, has only begun. In the near future, however, we predict that real-time Java—namely, the Java Real-Time System (Java RTS) from Sun Microsystems—will be used predominantly in real-time application areas, such as software in the financial world, critical control systems, manufacturing lines, military and other government systems, and so on. This prediction arrives in the shadow of a time when Java was once considered "too slow" to be used in the development of mission-critical and other enterprise systems.

However, just as Java had proven quickly to the world that it could perform well enough for even the most demanding enterprise systems, Java RTS is actively proving itself in the real-time space. Gone is the *necessity* for complicated, specialized, real-time languages and operating environments; Java RTS brings all of the productivity and familiarity of the Java language to systems with real-time requirements. Literally decades of research, knowledge, and advancement found in the real-time discipline is now at the fingertips of every Java developer, requiring little more understanding than that of a new library of classes.

It was in the late '90s that Greg Bollella had the idea for a real-time version of Java while in Chicago on a business trip. Soon after, JSR-001 was started and the specification was in its early stages. The specification was led by Greg, and involved many of the best minds involved in real-time scheduling theory, microprocessor design, embedded systems design, and language design. In the end, a specification was finalized that defines how Java is to behave in the real-time space, and Java RTS was built to conform to it and make it a reality.

Defining "Real-Time"

Although the first chapter of this book discusses and defines real-time systems thoroughly, it's best to set the stage early and agree upon a precise definition. With *real-time programming*, the overall goal is to ensure that a system performs its tasks, in response to real-world events, before a defined deadline. Regardless of whether that deadline is measured in microseconds or days, as long as the task is required to complete before that deadline, the system is considered real-time. That simple definition is the foundation for an entire discipline in computer science, with years of research and development within both academia and industry.

To put it differently, the time delay from when a real-world event occurs (such as an object passing over a sensor, or the arrival of a stock market data-feed tick) to the time some code finishes processing that event should be bounded. The ability to meet this deadline must be predictable and guaranteed, all the time, in order to provide the determinism needed for a real-time system.

Meeting the requirements for real-time systems can be so demanding that dedicated programming languages, operating systems, frameworks, and scheduling algorithms have been created. Distinct areas of study, sets of tools, and even entire companies have been formed to solve real-time problems. It is precisely for these reasons that the Sun Java Real-Time System has been created.

The Real-Time Specification for Java

The Java Real-Time System from Sun is a 100%-compatible implementation of the *Real-Time Specification for Java* (RTSJ). The RTSJ is also known as JSR-001; the very first Java specification request (JSR) for which the entire Java Community Process (JCP) was created. Real-time Java is the first of many firsts, and has paved a way for not only what it was intended (real-time programming in Java), but also for the foundation of Java's growth in terms of language features through the creation of the JCP.

The RTSJ is a standard that defines how Java applications are to behave in a real-world environment. It was created by experts in many disciplines (i.e., embedded systems design, language design, operating system design, processor design, real-time scheduling theory, and so on), from many companies, from all around the world—a truly global effort. The number one goal, other than defining how real-time behavior could be achieved with Java, was to not *change* the Java language at all. Meeting this goal was important to ensure that Java, as the thousands of developers know it today, can be used in a real-time context, with no compromise.

In order for an implementation of Java to call itself "real-time," it *must* conform to the RTSJ. Anything else is non-standard, as defined by the Java community as a whole. This ensures that developing a real-time application in Java will work with any RTSJ-compliant JVM, and will behave as defined in a real-time environment, without the need for specialized extensions or hardware. Anything else would violate the very principles Java was founded upon. Java RTS is compliant with the RTSJ, and is therefore standards-based.

This Book's Focus and Audience

Although other books have been written about the RTSJ, this book focuses on Java RTS, its APIs, and what it takes to build real-time applications in Java. The intent is to provide you with practical knowledge and examples of how to build real-time applications with Java. Wherever possible, key teachings will be presented through the use of actual working code examples, as well as visual diagrams to make complicated concepts clear.

Although Java RTS is the focus, all of the knowledge gained from this book will be RTSJ-compliant by default. An understanding of the RTSJ is not a prerequisite for this book, but it's highly recommended that you read this specification since it's the basis for the material presented herein. You can find the latest specification and related material at http://www.rtsj.org.

This book's primary audience is comprised of architects and developers (of all levels) who need to build an application with time-critical code. There are different types of developers that this book targets:

- Java developers who are currently building applications with real-time requirements with or without Java RTS
- Java developers who are interested in learning the Java RTS APIs for future projects
- Non-Java real-time application developers who wish to use Java for real-time application development
- Architects and developers who wish to use Java RTS in order to deploy on a general-purpose operating system (as opposed to a specialized operating system, platform, or language)

To each of these developers, Java RTS and the RTSJ represent freedom from specialized hardware, operating systems, and languages. When this freedom is coupled with Java's productivity gains and large developer community, Java RTS represents a wise business choice as well, and a potentially huge savings in money.

Structure of the Book

This book has been broken down into three main sections:

Part I—Real-Time Computing Concepts: The first part lays the groundwork for using Java RTS. It clearly defines the concept of real-time in the computing world, and discusses many of the theories of real-time application design and development.
This includes Chapters 1 through 4.

Part II—Inside Java RTS: The second part dives deep into the Java RTS APIs, providing ample code samples to illustrate the inner workings and use of Java RTS. You'll gain a deeper understanding of the RTSJ principals, as applied to real problems.
This includes Chapters 5 through 10.

Part III—Using Java RTS: The third and final part discusses a comprehensive case study where Java RTS has been used to solve actual real-time system problems, as well as tools used to develop and debug Java RTS applications.
This includes Chapters 11 and 12.

The chapter breakdown of this book is as follows:

Chapter 1—Real-Time for the Rest of Us: This chapter provides a thorough definition of real-time systems, and then compares them to high-performance systems and those with high-throughput requirements. Other key terms, such as predictability, jitter, latency, and determinism are defined and explored. The second half of this chapter contains a high-level discussion of real-time scheduling. Analogies, descriptions, and visuals will be used to bring the concepts down to earth; at a level where the average programmer should be comfortable.

Chapter 2—Real-Time and Java SE: This chapter explores the use of standard Java in real-time environments. Issues that arise, such as the execution of the Java garbage collector, and the just-in-time compiler, will be discussed as sources of trouble. The chapter discusses, in detail, garbage collection in Java

SE 6 and the forthcoming Java SE 7, and concludes with an overview of real-time garbage collection algorithms.

Chapter 3—The Real-Time Specification for Java: The RTSJ defines how Java should behave in the real-time space. In fact, the RTSJ was the first Java Specification Request (JSR), and a big reason why the Java Community Process (JCP) was formed. The specification, led by Greg Bollella, included experts from around the globe, from both academia and industry, and is known today as a standard for real-time Java development. This chapter provides a brief overview of the RTSJ.

Chapter 4—The Sun Java Real-Time System: This chapter begins our exploration of real-time Java with a discussion of Java RTS, Sun's product that implements the RTSJ. Reading this chapter will help you get up and running with a working Java RTS system on either Solaris or Linux.

Chapter 5—Threads, Scheduling, and the New Memory Models: As the first chapter to dive deep into the Java RTS APIs, the focus of the chapter is on the new threading models available to you, along with the different memory models introduced with the RTSJ.

Chapter 6—Synchronization: This chapter explores how thread synchronization is changed in Java RTS. It also dives into the internals to examine some of the enhancements made in the Java VM to minimize latency when synchronizing multiple threads' access to shared resources.

Chapter 7—The Real-Time Clock API: Java RTS provides support for high-resolution timers, and deterministic timer objects. In this chapter, we'll examine the real-time Clock API, and how timer objects can be created for deterministic operation.

Chapter 8—Asynchronous Events: Java RTS gives you more control over how work is scheduled in a system. This chapter examines the classes that are available to you to control how events are handled in your real-time application.

Chapter 9—Asynchronous Transfer of Control and Thread Termination: In this chapter, we'll explore the fine-grained control Java RTS provides for schedulable objects in terms of transferring control from one method to another, and terminating tasks.

Chapter 10—Inside the Real-Time Garbage Collector: This chapter dives deep into the inner workings of the real-time garbage collector, and describes how it operates. Having a solid understanding of how the RTGC works, how it affects your system, and how it can be tuned will help you build more efficient Java RTS applications.

Chapter 11—An Equities Trading System: This chapter explores the use of Java RTS in a financial application that closely mimics those used by traders, investment banks, and exchanges in the world of finance. In the world of investing, banking, and finance, latencies due to garbage collection introduce the risk of missing important market events. The resulting delays translate directly to lost money in these markets.

Chapter 12—Java RTS Tools: Here, we discuss the tools available to develop and debug Java RTS applications.

Staying Up-to-Date

No book is ever complete, and important technologies such as Java RTS aren't static—they constantly evolve. Check the web site, http://www.ericbruno.com/realtime, for updates and extra content, as well as the complete code for the samples and many of the case studies. We'll also keep you up to date on changes to the RTSJ, as well as to Sun's implementation, Java RTS.

Acknowledgments

"Better late than never, but never late is better."

—Unknown

THIS journey began with a short lecture on Java RTS, given by Greg Bollella in August 2006 in Menlo Park, California. I was attending this lecture as part of a broader Sun training session, but Greg's lecture was the high point for me. I had done development work on real-time systems in the past, but never with Java. Greg's discussion of deadlines, predictability, Java's garbage collection, and so on intrigued me, and began my feverish interest in the topic.

Attending this lecture with me was Craig Ellis (my manager at the time), who promptly gave me and two of my peers the task of building a proof-of-concept application that we would use to demonstrate Java RTS to others. Therefore, my very first round of thanks goes out to Greg Bollella, Craig Ellis, Jim Clarke, and Jim Connors. Jim, Jim, and myself (who some call the "Three Amigos") conceived, designed, and built the equities trading system used in Chapter 11 of this book. Without the actions of these four people, the seeds for this book would not have been planted. Again, a sincere *thank you!*

And finally, a big thank you goes to my wife, Christine, and our children, Brandon and Ashley, for being patient with me (and my grumpiness) as I focused on this book. It took a full year of research before I completed the first chapter, and although I tried to impact family time as little as possible, I know there were times when I was preoccupied. You guys are the best! I thank God that it's complete.

—Eric J. Bruno, March 2009

Eric did the vast majority of the actual work on this book, so my thanks to him. He also kept me on task when numerous other professional responsibilities loomed and threatened to pull me away. Peter Dibble and Andrew Wellings have also published books on programming and using implementations of the Real-Time Specification for Java (RTSJ). These books have been of immense help to the RTSJ community in general and help for Eric and me. So, I add my personal thanks to Peter and Andy. Working on this book did take time away from other responsibilities at Sun, so my personal thanks to everyone on the Java RTS team, engineers, sales, marketing, and management for accommodating my sometimes erratic attendance at meetings.

My wife, Melinda, and daughter, Allie, also helped the effort by pitching in when needed and putting up with my erratic schedule. Thanks to them.

—Greg Bollella, March 2009

Of course, it doesn't end there. The authors would like to thank Greg Doench, Michelle Housley, Noreen Regina, and others at Pearson for guiding the book project along, even when we blew past some important milestones. Also, we appreciate the encouragement we received from Vineet Gupta, Lino Persi, Dave Hofert, Dave Therkelsen, Tony Printezis, Gail Yamanaka, Gary Collins, Craig Ellis, Jim Connors, Jim Clarke, Ranbir Mazumdar, Steve Lipetz, Brent Loschen, Robert Rogers, Kevin Smith, Tom Harris, Dan Green, Scott Stillabower, Sekar Srinivasan, Tom Stanton, Greg Conk, Mike Genewich, James Allen, Jim Lipkis, Tom Karbowski, Dave Clack, Andy Gilbert, and our families.

Continuing onward, we need to thank the Java RTS technical team who put the bits together and also answered our many questions: Bertrand Delsart, Romain Guider, David Holmes, Olivier Lagneau, Carlos Lucasius, Frederic Parain, and Roland Westrelin.

Also, a big round of thanks goes to those who reviewed the manuscript and offered many excellent corrections and suggestions: David Holmes, Bertrand Delsart, Tony Printezis, Peter Dibble, and Michael Thurston. Without you, this book would not be nearly as complete.

Finally, none of this would have been possible without the work environment that Sun Microsystems offers its employees. We're proud to work for a company that focuses on customers, the technology needed to solve problems, and its employees who work hard to serve both. To Sun and its dedicated employees around the world: *Thank you!*

About the Authors

Eric J. Bruno, systems engineer at Sun Microsystems, specializes in Java RTS in the financial community. He is contributing editor for *Dr. Dobb's Journal*, and writes its online Java blog. Prior to Sun, Eric worked at Reuters where he developed real-time trading systems, order-entry and routing systems, as well as real-time news and quotes feeds, in both Java and C++.

Greg Bollella, Ph.D., distinguished engineer at Sun Microsystems, leads R&D for real-time Java. He was specification lead for JSR-001, the Real-Time Specification for Java (RTSJ), and led the Real-Time for Java Expert Group under the Java Community Process. He has written multiple books, articles, and professional papers about real-time computing. He has a Ph.D. in computer science from the University of North Carolina at Chapel Hill, where he wrote a dissertation on real-time scheduling theory and real-time systems implementation.

Part I

Real-Time Computing Concepts

Real-Time for the Rest of Us

"Let him who would enjoy a good future waste none of his present."

—Roger Babson

THERE are many misunderstandings about what real-time is, even amongst seasoned enterprise Java developers. Some confuse it with high-performance, or fast, computing; others think of dynamic applications such as instant messaging. Neither one is necessarily an example of a real-time system. Therefore real-time does not always equal "real fast," although good performance is often desirable and achievable. In fact, real-time is often orthogonal with high-throughput systems; there's a trade-off in throughput in many cases. The best way to avoid all of this confusion is to think of it this way: application performance and throughput requirements can be solved with faster, or additional, hardware; real-time requirements, in general, cannot.

This chapter will define real-time computing, and will explain why throwing hardware at a real-time requirement will almost never do any good. We'll discuss the qualities of a real-time system, define key terms used in the discipline, and examine tools, languages, and environments available to real-time developers outside of the Java world. By the end of this chapter, you'll have a good real-time foundation to build upon.

Qualities of Real-Time Systems

The goal of a real-time system is to respond to real-world events before a measurable deadline, or within a bounded time frame. However, a real-time system is also about precision. The measured speed of a system's response to an event is important, but what's also important is the system's ability to respond at precisely the right moment in time. Access to a high-resolution timer to perform actions on precise time periods is often a requirement. These two qualities together best define a real-time application's acceptable behavior: the ability to respond to an event before a deadline, and accurately perform periodic processing, regardless of overall system load. Before we go any further, it's important to examine the term deadline a little more closely, as well as some other terms often used in the context of real-time systems.

The term *deadline* can have one of two meanings. First, it can be a deadline *relative* to an event, such as a notification or message in some form. In this case, the system must respond to that event within a certain amount of time of receiving that event, or from when that event originally occurred. One example of a relative deadline is an elevator as it passes over a sensor indicating that it's almost at the floor it's meant to stop at. The real-time software within the elevator must respond to that event within milliseconds of passing the sensor, or it won't be able to stop at the intended floor. The occupants of an elevator that skips stops are certain to consider this an error.

> **Relative Deadline (D_i):** the amount of time *after* a request is made that the system needs to respond.

> **Absolute Deadline (d_i):** the precise point in time that a task must be completed, regardless of task start time, or request arrival.

Often, with an *absolute* deadline, a real-time system checks for a particular system state on a regular interval. Some examples of this are an aircraft flight control system, or a nuclear power plant's core temperature monitoring system. In both of these cases, critical data is continuously polled, such as altitude, or core temperature. Failing to monitor these values at precise points in time can cause these systems to go into a bad state with potentially catastrophic results.

Regardless of the type of deadline, relative or absolute, time is still a main component in proper system behavior. It's not enough that an elevator's software knows and responds to a floor sensor; it must do so within a deadline in order to behave correctly. Also, a flight control system must be able to move an aircraft's control surfaces at the precise time, in reaction to the most recent and accurate set of data, in order to fly the aircraft correctly (without crashing!).

For example, let's say we have a system requirement to send a response to a request within one millisecond. If the system responds within 500 microseconds every time, you may think the requirement has been met. However, if the request is delayed, outside the system under measurement, the response will not have been sent at the right moment in time (even if it's sent within one millisecond). Remember, we're talking about "real" time here; the one-millisecond requirement applies to when the originating system sent the original request.

Figure 1-1 illustrates the problem. Here you see that the system in question has responded to the request within one millisecond, but it was at the wrong time because the request was delayed in delivery. A real-time system must adhere to the end-to-end deadline.

In a real-time system, the time delay from when a real-world event occurs (such as an object passing over a sensor, or the arrival of a stock market data-feed tick) to the time some code finishes processing that event should be reasonably bounded. The ability to meet this deadline must be predictable and guaranteed, all the time, in order to provide the determinism needed for a real-time system.

What Is "Bounded"?

When we use the term *bounded* in relation to a *bounded amount of time*, what we really imply is a reasonable amount of time for the system to respond. In other words, saying that the elevator responds to sensor events within a ten-year bounded timeframe is unreasonable. It must do so according to a time requirement that allows it to function properly. Therefore, when we use the term bounded, it's relative to the proper operation of the time-critical event we're describing.

When discussing real-time systems, the basic element of execution is often referred to as a job, or task. (For a more accurate definition of jobs and tasks in real-time systems, see the note on Jobs and Tasks in Real-Time Systems). There can be one or more tasks in a given system, and therefore tasks can either be

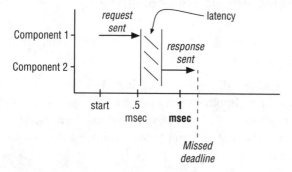

Figure 1-1   The response time was good, but the deadline was missed. This is not a real-time system.

running or waiting. On a uniprocessor machine, only one task can be running at a single point in time, as opposed to multiprocessor machines that can execute more than one task at a time.

Note: Jobs and Tasks in Real-Time Systems   At this point in the discussion, it's fair to accurately define the terms *job* and *task* as used in discussions of real-time scheduling theory. Formally speaking, a job is any unit of work that can be scheduled and processed, while a task is a group of related jobs that work together to achieve some function. In this classic definition, a task contains related jobs, where those jobs have real-time constraints.

However, to keep the discussions light and simple in this book we will not distinguish between tasks and jobs; a unit of schedulable work will simply be referred to as a task. Therefore, in this book, a task represents a thread of execution and is synonymous with an OS thread.

Regardless, discussions often revolve around the arrival of a system event, or the start of task execution, which can sometimes be one and the same. To clarify, we say that a task can be in one of the three main states:

Eligible-for-Execution: the task is eligible (ready) to execute.

Executing: the task is currently executing (running) on a processor.

Blocked: the task is neither executing, nor eligible to begin executing. It's blocked for some reason, and this reason is usually stated as part of the state; i.e., blocked-for-IO, blocked-for-release-event, and so on.

With these task states defined, we can begin to discuss how tasks are scheduled in a real-time system. First, the following definitions must be stated:

Release Time (r_i): sometimes called *arrival time*, or *request time*, this is the time that a task becomes ready to execute.

Start Time (s_i): the time that a task begins executing. As stated above, these concepts may be combined for simplification in many discussions. For example, a task may be started because of a request, or it may be started as part of a predefined schedule. This book shall attempt to separate these concepts when necessary to avoid confusion.

Finish Time (f_i): the time when a task is complete.

Task Completion Time ($C_i = f_i - r_i$): the amount of time a particular task takes to complete its processing by subtracting the task's arrival time from its finish time. This is also referred to as the cost of task execution.

Lateness (L_i): the difference between the task finish time and its deadline; note that this value is negative if a task completes before its deadline, zero if it completes at its deadline, and positive if it completes after its deadline.

These terms and their associated abbreviations will be used throughout the book. To further clarify them, and to gain a better understanding of real-time systems, let's explore the factors that affect a system's ability to meet its deadlines.

Predictability and Determinism

Other important qualities of a real-time system are that of *predictability* and *determinism*. A real-time system must behave in a way that can be predicted mathematically. This refers to the system's deadline in terms of relative and absolute time. For instance, it must be mathematically predictable to determine if the amount of work to be done can be completed before a given deadline. Factors that go into this calculation are system workload, the number of CPUs (or CPU cores) available for processing, running threads in the real-time system, process and thread priorities, and the operating system scheduling algorithm.

Determinism represents the ability to ensure the execution of an application without concern that outside factors will upset the execution in unpredictable ways. In other words, the application will behave as intended in terms of functionality, performance, and response time, all of the time without question. In many respects, determinism and predictability are related, in that one results in the other. However, the important distinction is that a deterministic system puts the control of execution behavior in the hands of the application developer. Predictability is then the result of proper programming practice on a system that enables such behavior. This book will explore the statement "proper programming practice" in relation to real-time applications written in Java because using a real-time language or operating system is never enough—discipline is also required.

Another aspect of deterministic application behavior is that it's fixed, more or less. This means that unforeseen events, such as garbage collection in Java, must never upset a real-time application's ability to meet its deadlines, and hence become less predictable. A real-time system such as an anti-lock brake system, or an airplane's flight-control system, must always be 100% deterministic and predictable or human lives may be at stake.

Many practical discussions of real-time systems and their requirements involve the terms latency and jitter. Let's examine these now, and form precise definitions that we'll use in our discussion going forward.

Identifying Latency

Much of the discussion so far has been about responding to an event before a deadline. This is certainly a requirement of a real-time system. *Latency* is a measure of the time between a particular event and a system's response to that event, and it's quite often a focus for real-time developers. Because of this, latency is often a key measurement in any real-time system. In particular, the usual focus is to minimize system latency. However, in a real-time system the true goal is simply to *normalize* latency, not minimize it. In other words, the goal is to make latency a known, reasonably small, and consistent quantity that can then be predicted. Whether the latency in question is measured in seconds, or microseconds, the fact that it can be predicted is what truly matters to real-time developers. Nonetheless, more often than not, real-time systems also include the requirement that latency be minimized and bounded, often in the sub-millisecond range.

To meet a system's real-time requirements, all sources of latency must be identified and measured. To do this, you need the support of your host system's operating system, its environment, network relationship, and programming language.

Identifying Jitter

The definition of *jitter* includes the detection of irregular variations, or unsteadiness, in some measured quantity. For example, in an electronic device, jitter often refers to a fluctuation in an electrical signal. In a real-time system, jitter is the fluctuation in latency for similar event processing. Simply measuring the latency of message processing for one event, or averaging it over many events, is not enough. For instance, if the average latency from request to response for a certain web server is 250 milliseconds, we have no insight into jitter. If we look at all of the numbers that go into the average (all of the individual request/response round-trip times) we can begin to examine it. Instead, as a real-time developer, you must look at the distribution and standard deviation of the responses over time.

Other Causes of Jitter

Jitter can also be caused by the scheduling algorithm in your real-time system. For instance, in a system with many real-time periodic tasks, a particular task can finish anywhere within its time period. If it sometimes finishes early in its period (well before the deadline), but other times it finishes just before the period end, it has jitter. In some systems, there are control algorithms that cannot tolerate this.

For example, say we have a task with a 100-millisecond period, where the execution cost is 10 milliseconds, and the worst-case latency is always less than 1 millisecond. In a complex system, this task can finish anywhere from the period boundary + 10 milliseconds processing time + 1 millisecond latency, to the period boundary + 100 milliseconds (start of next period). One solution to this problem, the one proposed by the Real-Time Specification for Java (RTSJ) in particular, is to set the deadline to 12 milliseconds.

The chart in Figure 1-2 shows a sampling of latency data for a web server's request/response round-trip time. You can see that although the average of 250 milliseconds seems pleasing, a look at the individual numbers shows that some of the responses were delivered with up to one-second latency. These "large" latency

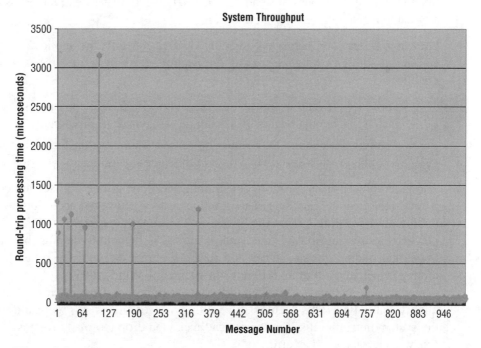

Figure 1-2 The average response time measurement of a transaction can cover up latency outliers.

responses stand out above most of the others, and are hence labeled *outliers*, since they fall outside of the normal, or even acceptable, response time range.

However, if the system being measured is simply a web application without real-time requirements, this chart should not be alarming; the outliers simply aren't important, as the average is acceptable. However, if the system were truly a real-time system, these outliers could represent disaster. In a real-time system, *every* response must be sent within a bounded amount of latency.

Hard and Soft Real-Time

In the real-time problem domain, discussions often involve the terms *hard real-time* and *soft real-time*. Contrary to what many people assume, these terms have nothing to do with the size of the deadline, or the consequence of missing that deadline. It's a common misconception that a hard real-time system has a smaller, or tighter, deadline in terms of overall time than a soft real-time system. Instead, a hard real-time system is one that cannot miss a single deadline or the system will go into an abnormal state. In other words, the correctness of the system depends not only on the responses it generates, but the time frame in which each and every response is delivered. A soft real-time system is one that may have a similar deadline in terms of time, but it instead has the tolerance to miss a deadline occasionally without generating an error condition.

For example, let's compare a hypothetical video player software application to an automated foreign exchange trading application. Both systems have real-time qualities:

- The video player must retrieve and display video frames continuously, with each frame being updated by a deadline of, say, one millisecond.
- A foreign exchange trade must be settled (moneys transferred between accounts) within exactly two days of the trade execution.

The video player has a far more constraining deadline at one millisecond compared to the two-day deadline of the trading system. However, according to our definition, the trading system qualifies as a hard real-time system, and the video player as a soft real-time system, since a missed settlement trade puts the entire trade, and trading system, into a bad state—the trade needs to be rolled back, money is lost, and a trading relationship strained. For the video player, an occasional missed deadline results in some dropped frames and a slight loss of video quality, but the overall system is still valid. However, this is still real-time since the system must not miss too many deadlines (and drop too many frames) or it, too, will be considered an error.

Additionally, the severity of the consequence of missing a deadline has nothing to do with the definition of hard versus soft. Looking closer at the video player software in the previous example, the requirement to match audio to the corresponding video stream is also a real-time requirement. In this case, many people don't consider the video player to be as critical as an anti-lock brake system, or a missile-tracking system. However, the requirement to align audio with its corresponding video is a hard real-time constraint because not doing so is considered an error condition. This shows that whereas the consequence of a misaligned video/audio stream is minimal, it's still a hard real-time constraint since the result is an error condition.

Therefore, to summarize hard and soft real-time constraints, a hard real-time system goes into a bad state when a *single* deadline is missed, whereas a soft real-time system has a more flexible deadline, and can tolerate occasional misses. In reality, it's best to avoid these terms and their distinction and instead focus on whether a system has a real-time requirement at all. If there truly is a deadline the system must respond within, then the system qualifies as real-time, and every effort should be made to ensure the deadline is met each time.

Isochronal Real-Time

In some cases, the requirement to respond to an event before a deadline is not enough; it must not be sent too early either. In many control systems, responses must be sent within a window of time after the request, and before the absolute deadline (see Figure 1-3). Such a system has an *isochronal real-time* requirement.

Although clearly distinct from a hard real-time task that needs to complete any time before its deadline, in most cases isochronal real-time tasks are simply classified as hard real-time with an additional timing constraint. This certainly makes it easier to describe the tasks in a system design. However, this added constraint does make a difference to the real-time task scheduler, which is something we'll explore later in this chapter.

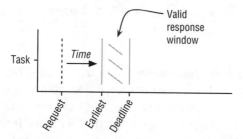

Figure 1-3 Isochronal real-time: the deadline must be met, but a response must not be sent too early, either.

Real-Time Versus Real Fast

Application or system performance is a relative measurement. When a system is said to be fast or slow, it's usually in comparison to something else. Perhaps it's an older system, a user expectation, or a comparison to an analogous real-world system. In general, performance is more of a relative measurement than a precise mathematical statement. As discussed earlier in this chapter, real-time does not necessarily equal real fast.

Instead, whereas the objective of fast computing is to minimize the average response time of a given set of tasks, the objective of real-time computing is to meet the individual time-critical requirement of each task. Consider this anecdote: there once was a man who drowned in a river with an *average* depth of 6 inches [Buttazzo05]. Of course, the key to that sentence is the use of the average depth, which implies the river is deeper at some points. A real-time system is characterized by its deadline, which is the maximum time within which it must complete its execution, not the average.

However, the *goals* of most real-time systems are to meet critical deadlines *and* to perform optimally and efficiently. For example, a system with sub-millisecond deadlines will most likely require high-performance computer hardware and software. For this reason, real-time systems programming is often associated with high-performance computing (HPC). However, it's important to remember that high-performance does not imply real-time, and vice versa.

Real-Time Versus Throughput

Another area of system performance that is often confused with real-time is that of system throughput. Throughput is often used to describe the number of requests, events, or other operations, that a software system can process in any given time frame. You often hear of software positively characterized with terms like "messages-per-second," or "requests-per-second." A system with high throughput can give its operators a false sense of security when used in a real-time context.

This is because a system with high throughput is not necessarily a real-time system, although it is often misunderstood to be. For instance, a system that supports thousands of requests per second may have some responses with up to a second of latency. Even though a majority of the requests may be handled with low latency, the existence of some messages with large latency represents outliers (those outside the normal response time). In other words, with this example, most requestors received their responses well within the one-second window. However, there were some that waited the full second for their response. Because the degree of, and the amount of, these outliers are unpredictable, high-throughput systems are not necessarily real-time systems.

Typically, real-time systems exhibit lower average throughput than non-real-time systems. This engineering trade-off is well known and accepted in the real-time community. This is due to many factors that include trade-offs as to how tasks are scheduled and how resources are allocated. We'll explore these factors in relation to Java RTS throughout this book.

Task Completion Value

In a modern computing system, the basic element of execution is called a thread, or a task. A process is defined as an application launched by the user (either explicitly through a command, or implicitly by logging in) that contains one or more threads of execution. Regardless of how each task begins executing, the basic unit of execution is a thread. To simplify things going forward, the thread will be the focus of the discussion.

The value, or usefulness, that a task has to any running system is usually dependent upon when it gets its work done, not just that the work is done properly. Even non-real-time systems have this quality. For example, the chart in Figure 1-4 shows that the value of tasks in a non-real-time system usually increases as more of them are completed over time. This is evidence of the throughput quality of non-real-time systems, as explained in the previous section.

For a soft real-time system, the value of task completion rapidly decreases once the task's deadline passes. Although the correct answer may have been generated, it gets more and more useless as time passes (see Figure 1-5).

Contrast this to a hard real-time system, where the task has zero value after the deadline (see Figure 1-6).

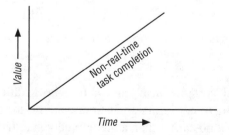

Figure 1-4 In a non-real-time system, the perceived value of task completion is directly proportional to the total number completed over time.

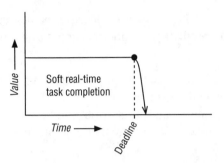

Figure 1-5   In a soft real-time system, the value of task completion, after the deadline, decays over time.

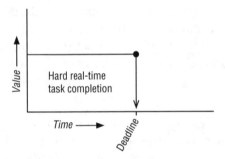

Figure 1-6   The value of task completion in a hard real-time system is zero the moment the deadline passes.

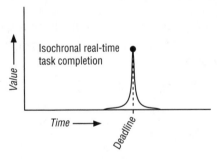

Figure 1-7   The value of task completion in a firm, isochronal, real-time system is zero if it completes early, or late.

The discussion so far assumes that task completion anytime before the deadline is acceptable. In some cases, as with firm, or isochronal, real-time systems, the task must complete before the deadline, but no earlier than a predefined value. In this case, the value of task completion before *and* after the deadline is, or quickly goes to, zero (see Figure 1-7).

Of course, these graphs are only general visual representations of task completion value in non-real-time and real-time systems; actual value is derived on a case-by-case basis. Later in this chapter, we'll examine this in more detail as task cost functions are used to calculate efficient real-time scheduling algorithms.

Real-Time Computing

Now that you have an understanding of what real-time is and what it means, it's time to expand on it. *Real-time computing* is the study and practice of building applications with real-world time-critical constraints. Real-time systems must respond to external, often physical, real-world events at a certain time, or by a deadline. A real-time system often includes both the hardware and the software in its entirety. Traditionally, real-time systems were purpose-built systems implemented for specific use; it's only recently that the real-time community has focused on general-purpose computing systems (both hardware and/or software) to solve real-time problems.

Today, the need for specialized, dedicated, hardware for real-time systems has mostly disappeared. For instance, modern chipsets include programmable interrupt controllers with latency resolution small enough for demanding real-time applications. As a result, support for real-time requirements has moved to software; i.e., specialized schedulers and resource controllers. Algorithms that were once etched into special circuitry are now implemented in software on general-purpose computers.

This is not to say that hardware support isn't needed in a real-time system. For example, many real-time systems will likely require access to a programmable interrupt controller for low-latency interrupts and scheduling, a high-resolution clock for precise timing, direct physical memory access, or a high-speed memory cache. Most modern computer hardware, including servers, workstations, and even desktops and laptops, support these requirements. The bottom line is whether the operating system software running on this hardware supports access to these hardware facilities.

The operating system may, in fact, support real-time tasks directly through its scheduling implementation, or may at least allow alternative scheduling algorithms be put in place. However, many general-purpose operating systems schedule tasks to achieve different goals than a real-time system. Other factors, such as overall system throughput, foreground application performance, and GUI refresh rates, may be favored over an individual task's latency requirements. In fact, in a general-purpose system, there may be no way to accurately specify or measure an application's latency requirements and actual results.

However, it *is* still possible to achieve real-time behavior, and meet real-time tasks' deadlines, on general-purpose operating systems. In fact, this is one of the charter goals that Java RTS, and the RTSJ, set out to solve: real-time behavior in Java on general-purpose hardware and real-time operating systems. In reality, only a subset of general-purpose systems can be supported.

The remainder of this chapter provides an overview of the theory and mechanics involved in scheduling tasks in a real-time system. To be clear, real-time scheduling theory requires a great deal of math to describe and understand thoroughly. There is good reason for this: when a system has requirements to meet every deadline for actions that may have dire consequences if missed, you need to make assurances with the utmost precision. Characterizing and guaranteeing system behavior with mathematics is the only way to do it. However, we'll attempt to discuss the subject without overburdening you with deep mathematical concepts. Instead, analogies, descriptions, and visuals will be used to bring the concepts down to earth, at a level where the average programmer should be comfortable. For those who are interested in the deeper math and science of the subject, references to further reading material are provided.

The Highway Analogy

One simple way to describe the dynamics of scheduling tasks in a real-time system is to use a highway analogy. When driving a car, we've all experienced the impact of high volume; namely, the unpredictable amount of time spent waiting in traffic instead of making progress towards a destination. This situation is strikingly similar to scheduling tasks in a real-time system, or any system, for that matter. In the case of automobile traffic, the items being scheduled are cars, and the resource that they're all sharing is road space. Comparatively, a computer system schedules tasks, and the resource they share is CPU time. (Of course, they also share memory, IO, disk access, and so on, but let's keep it simple for now.)

In the highway analogy, the lanes represent overall computer resources, or time available to process tasks. More capable computers can be loosely described as having more lanes available, while less capable systems have fewer. A car is equivalent to a task that has been released (eligible for execution). Looking at Figure 1-8, you can see tasks "traveling" down individual lanes, making forward

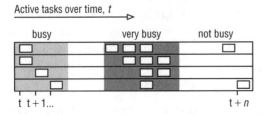

Figure 1-8   As with cars on a highway, when there are more tasks executing, the system slows down, and execution times become unpredictable.

progress over time. At moments when more tasks share the highway, the entire system is considered to be busy, and usually all tasks will execute slower. This is similar to the effects that high volumes of cars have on individual car speeds; they each slow down as they share the highway. Since, in this scenario, all tasks share the resources (the highway) equally, they are all impacted in a similar, but unpredictable, way. It's impossible to deterministically know when an individual task will be able to complete.

In the real world, engineers designing road systems have come up with a solution to this problem: a dedicated lane.

The Highway Analogy—Adding a Priority Lane

Figure 1-9 proposes a specialized solution to this problem: a dedicated high-priority lane (sometimes called a carpool, or HOV lane, on a real highway). We refer to it as specialized because it doesn't help all tasks in the system (or all cars on the highway), only those that meet the requirements to enter the high-priority lane. Those tasks (or cars) receive precedence over all others, and move at a more predictable pace. Similarly, in a real-time system, dedicating system resources to high-priority tasks ensures that those tasks gain predictability, are less prone to traffic delay, and therefore complete more or less on time. Only the normal (lower-priority) tasks feel the effects of high system volume.

This analogy goes a long way towards describing, and modeling, the dynamics of a real-time system. For instance:

- Tasks in the high-priority lane gain execution precedence over other tasks.
- Tasks in the high-priority lane receive a dedicated amount of system resources to ensure they complete on time.
- When the system is busy, only normal tasks feel the impact; tasks in the high-priority lane are almost completely unaffected.

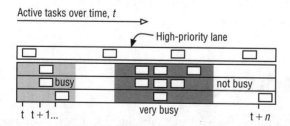

Figure 1-9   Introducing a high-priority lane to a highway ensures that the cars in that lane are less susceptible to traffic, and therefore travel more predictably towards their destinations.

- Overall, the system loses throughput, as fewer lanes are available to execute tasks.
- Tasks only enter the high-priority lane at certain checkpoints.
- Some system overhead is required at the checkpoints. Just as cars need to cautiously (and slowly) enter and exit a carpool lane, tasks are slightly impacted.
- Tasks may be denied access to the high-priority lane if their entry would adversely affect the other tasks already running.

Additionally, metering lights are used at the on-ramps to many highways. These lights control the flow of additional cars (analogy: new tasks) onto the highway to ensure the cars already on the highway are impacted as little as possible. These lights are analogous to the admission control algorithm of the scheduler in real-time system.

Most importantly, this analogy shows that there's no magic involved in supporting a real-time system; it, too, has its limits. For instance, there's a limit to the number of high-priority tasks that can execute and meet their deadlines without causing all tasks to miss their deadlines. Also, because of the need to dedicate resources to real-time tasks, the added checkpoints for acceptance of real-time tasks, the need to more tightly control access to shared resources, and the need to perform additional task monitoring; the system as a whole will assuredly lose some performance and/or throughput. However, in a real-time system, predictability trumps throughput, which can be recovered by other, less-complicated, means.

As we explore the details of common scheduling algorithms used in actual real-time systems, you will also see that simply "adding more lanes" doesn't always resolve the problem effectively. There are practical limits to any solution. In fact, in some cases that we'll explore, adding processors to a computer can cause previously feasible schedules to become infeasible. Task scheduling involves many system dynamics, where the varying combination of tasks and available resources at different points in time represents a difficult problem to solve deterministically. However, it *can* be done. Let's begin to explore some of the common algorithms used, and the constraints they deal with.

Real-Time Scheduling

A task by itself represents a useless body of instructions. For a task to be useful and meaningful, it must be processed, and it therefore must have scheduled execution time on a processor. The act of scheduling processor time to a task, or thread, and assigning it a free processor is often called *dispatching*. Real-time schedulers can schedule individual tasks for execution either offline (prior to the system entering its running state) or online (while the system is in an active, running state). Regardless of when it occurs, all scheduling work is done according to a predefined algorithm, or set of rules.

Scheduling Constraints

Many factors, or constraints, are taken into account when scheduling real-time tasks. Because each application—and hence each task—is different, these constraints may vary from system to system. However, they all generally fall into a subset of constraints that need to be considered. The first constraint is the amount of available resources; whether they're tasks in a computer or construction workers on a job, having what you need to complete a task is important. The second constraint is task precedence; to avoid chaos, and to ensure proper system behavior, certain tasks may need to be executed before others. The third constraint is timing; each task has its own deadline, some tasks execute longer than others, some may execute on a steady period, and others may vary between release times.

Each constraint contains many of its own factors that need to be considered further when scheduling tasks. Let's examine these constraints in more detail now, and how they may affect task scheduling.

Resources

Because we speak in terms of processors, tasks, and execution times, most people think of only the CPU as the main resource to be scheduled. This isn't always the case. For example, recalling the highway analogy above, cars represented tasks, and the road represented the processor. More realistically, in a real-time network packet switching system, tasks represent data packets, and the processor represents an available communication line. Similarly, in a real-time file system, a task is a file, and the processor is an individual disk platter/head combination. However, regardless of the actual physical work being done (sending a packet, writing a file, or executing a thread), we will refer to all of them as simply a task. Further, regardless of the actual component doing the work (a network card/communication link, a disk controller, or a CPU), we will refer to all of them as simply a processor.

It's easy to see how the availability of critical system resources, such as the processor, is important to a scheduling algorithm. After all, to execute a thread, there must be a CPU available to execute it. However, it goes beyond just the processor; other resources, such as shared objects that require synchronization across tasks, are to be considered. This may be something as abstract as a shared object in memory, or something more concrete such as a shared region of memory, or the system bus. Regardless, there is often a need to lock shared resources to avoid errors due to concurrent access. This effectively limits a resource to being updated atomically, by one task at a time. Since resource locking synchronizes access to a shared resource, one task may become blocked when attempting to access a resourced that is currently locked by another task.

In a real-time system, it's important to ensure that high-priority, hard real-time tasks continue to make progress towards completion. Resource locking is commonly a problem since priority inversion can cause tasks to execute out of order. In many general-purpose operating systems, resource locking can lead to priority inversion, resulting in unbounded latency for critical tasks, and missed deadlines in a hard real-time system. For instance, in Figure 1-10, we see three tasks, T1, T2, and T3, each with decreasing priority, respectively.

In this scenario, task T3 is released shortly after the system starts. Although it's the lowest-priority task in the system, it begins execution immediately because no other tasks have been released. Early in its execution, it acquires a lock on resource R1. At about time t + 1.5, task T1 is released and preempts the lower-priority task, T3. At time t + 3, task T2 is released but cannot execute because task T1 is still executing. At some point after t + 3, task T1 attempts to acquire a lock on R1, but blocks because it's already locked. Because of this, T2 gains execution precedence over T1 even though it has a lower priority. When T2 completes, T3 continues again until it releases R1, at which point T1 is finally able to resume.

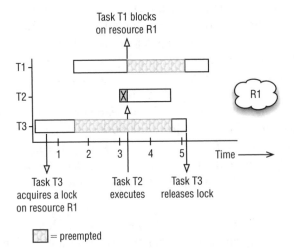

= preempted

Figure 1-10   Resource locking can lead to priority inversion. In a real-time system, this scenario must be controlled, or avoided.

In a general-purpose computer system, this may be a common and acceptable situation. In a real-time system, however, this violates the principal of task priority execution, and must be avoided. The time frame from shortly after t + 3, to shortly after t + 5, represents unbounded latency that adds an unknown amount of delay to the critical task, T1. As a result, real-time systems must implement some form of priority inversion control, such as priority inheritance, to maintain forward progress of critical tasks. This will be discussed later in the chapter; for now, let's continue our discussion on scheduling constraints.

Precedence

In many systems, real-time systems included, tasks cannot be scheduled in arbitrary order. There is often a precedence of events that govern which threads must be scheduled first. Typically, the threads themselves imply the ordering through resource sharing, or some form of communication, such as a locking mechanism. One example is a system where a task *T1* must wait for another task *T2* to release a lock on an object before it can begin execution. This act of *task synchronization* must be performed at the OS kernel level so as to notify the scheduler of the task precedence that exists.

In the example above the scheduler will block task *T1*, and will allow task *T2* to execute. When task *T2* completes its processing and releases its lock on the synchronized object that the two tasks share, the scheduler can dispatch task *T1*. The task precedence dictated by the synchronization in this example must be obeyed even if there are other processors in the system that are ready to execute waiting tasks. Therefore, in this example, regardless of the number of available processors, task *T1* will *always* wait for task *T2* to complete and hence release task *T1* to begin.

Notation: T2 < T1, or T2 → T1 for immediate task precedence

Task precedence can get complex, as a system with multiple tasks (each with its own dependencies) must be scheduled according to the precedence rules. Real-time system designers must understand task precedence fully before a system begins execution to ensure that real-time deadlines can be met. To do this, precedence relationships can be predetermined and represented by a graph, such as the one shown in Figure 1-11.

In this diagram, each node on the graph represents a task. The nodes at the top must execute and complete first before threads below them can execute. These rules are repeated at each level of the graph. For instance, the scheduler for the tasks represented in Figure 1-11 will begin by dispatching task *T2* to execute first. Once *T2* is complete, task *T1* will execute, while tasks *T3* and *T4* are blocked.

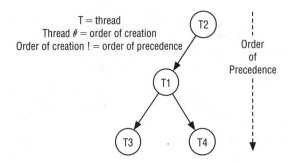

Figure 1-11   A directed acyclic graph helps to summarize task dependencies in a system.

Once *T1* completes, tasks *T3* and *T4* will be eligible to be dispatched. If there is more than one processor ready, both tasks *T3* and *T4* can be scheduled to run simultaneously—this graph does not indicate precedence between them.

Timing

Real-time tasks are labeled as such because they have time-related constraints, usually to do with a deadline for processing. As a result, schedulers are concerned with many time-related parameters to ensure that a task can complete on or before its deadline. For instance, schedulers need to consider the following, per task:

Deadline: of course, understanding the task's deadline (relative or absolute) and its value is critical to determining if it can be scheduled feasibly.

Period: many real-time tasks need to execute at regular time intervals. Others do not, and instead respond to events as they happen. The scheduler must distinguish each task's type (periodic, aperiodic, and sporadic), along with the timing characteristics that might apply. We'll discuss periodic tasks in the next section.

Release Time: important information when scheduling periodic tasks, to determine if a set of tasks can be scheduled feasibly.

The Variation in Releases Times: tasks vary slightly from period to period as to when they will actually be eligible for execution.

Start Time: some tasks will not be able to execute as soon as they are released (due to locks, higher-priority tasks running, and so on).

Execution Time: task cost functions need to know the best- and worst-case execution times for a task.

Other parameters are calculated as a result of scheduling a given set of tasks, such as:

Lateness: the difference between a task's actual completion time, and its deadline.

Tardiness: the amount of time a task executes after its deadline. This is not always equal to the lateness value, as a task may have been preempted by another task, which caused it to miss its deadline.

Laxity: the amount of time after its release time that a task can be delayed without missing its deadline.

Slack Time: same as laxity (above). However, this term is sometimes used to describe the amount of time a task can be preempted during its execution and still meet its deadline.

Scheduling Algorithms

The three constraint sets above are directly used in scheduling algorithms to determine a feasible schedule for a set of real-time tasks. Feeding into the algorithm as parameters are the set of tasks, T, to be scheduled; the set of processors, P, available to execute them; and the set of resources, R, available for all tasks in the system.

Scheduling algorithms differ in their criterion in determining when, and for how long, a task can execute on a processor. Real-time scheduling algorithms exist to ensure that regardless of system load—or the amount of threads eligible to be dispatched—the time-critical tasks of the system get ample processing time, at the right time, to meet their deadlines. Let's examine some of the high-level characteristics of real-time schedulers.

Preemptive Versus Non-Preemptive Scheduling

To understand scheduling algorithms, we need to agree upon some basic concepts. For instance, most operating systems allow a task to be assigned a priority. Higher-priority tasks, when ready to execute, will be given precedence over lower-priority tasks. An algorithm is said to be preemptive if a running task can be interrupted by another, higher priority task. However, there are scheduling algorithms in the real-time world that are non-preemptive [Liu00]. In this case, once a thread executes, it continues to do so until it completes its task.

Some algorithms allow a mixture of preemptive and non-preemptive tasks with classes of thread priorities, and specific support for real-time tasks. On a multi-processor system, this hybrid approach works well, since relatively long-running non-preemptive tasks do not prevent the system from performing other tasks, as long as there are more processors available than real-time tasks. The advantage to the real-time programmer is increased control over system behavior, which results in a more deterministic system overall.

Context Switching

In addition to the added determinism it provides, another reason to choose a non-preemptive scheduler is to avoid unforeseen *context switches*, which occur when one thread preempts another thread that's already running. The operating system must expend processor time executing code that saves the state of the already running thread, and then resets internal data structures and processor registers to begin execution of the preempting thread so that it can begin execution. This entire preemption process is summarized as *dispatching*, as mentioned earlier in this chapter. The time it takes a particular system to perform this preemption task is called *dispatch latency*, and can interfere with a system's ability to respond to an event by its deadline.

As a system becomes increasingly busy, with more threads competing for processing time, a considerable percentage of time can be spent dispatching threads, resulting in an additive effect in terms of dispatch latency. A system that spends more time dispatching threads than actually performing real work is said to be thrashing. Real-time systems must guarantee that even under high system load, thrashing due to context switches will not occur, or that it at least won't interfere with the high-priority threads performing real-time processing in the system. OS kernels with hybrid preemption/non-preemption support are useful in these cases, allowing real-time processing to be guaranteed on a general-purpose system.

Dynamic and Static Scheduling

One way to control context switching while still allowing preemption is through *static scheduling*. For instance, in a *dynamically scheduled* system, tasks are dispatched on the fly as the system is running, based upon parameters that may change over time (such as task priority). All decisions as to which task to schedule at each point in time are made while the system is running, and are based on the system state at certain checkpoints. This is a common scheduling algorithm used in many popular operating systems.

With static scheduling, however, the execution eligibility of a task never changes once it's assigned. The important scheduling parameters for each task, such as the priority, are determined when those tasks first enter the system based upon the state of the system and its current set of tasks. For instance, a static scheduling algorithm may assign a priority to a new task based on its period (defined below) relative to the periods of the other tasks in the system. In this way, a static scheduling algorithm can be used either offline or online (while the system is running).

Task Migration

Another important parameter to real-time task scheduling is the ability of a task to be executed by different processors in a multiprocessor system. For instance, in some systems, once a task begins execution on a particular processor, it cannot migrate to another processor even if it's preempted, and another processor is idle. In this type of system, task migration is not allowed.

However, many systems do allow tasks to migrate between available processors as tasks are preempted, and different processors become available. This type of system supports *dynamic task migration*, as there are no restrictions placed on tasks in relation to processors. Of course, there are systems that fall in between, which support *restricted task migration*. One example is a system with many processors, where certain tasks are restricted to a subset of total processors within the system. The remaining processors may be dedicated to a task, or small set of tasks, for example. Another example might be that on multiprocessor/multi-board systems, the OS might limit task migration to CPUs on the same board to take advantage of locality of reference.

An example of a common real-time operating system that supports restricted task migration is Solaris. Solaris allows you to define individual processor sets, assign physical processors (or processor cores) to the defined sets, and then dedicate a processor set to a particular application. That processor set will then execute only the threads (tasks) within that application, and no others. The tasks will be able to migrate across the physical processors within the set, but not the others.

Periodic, Aperiodic, and Sporadic Tasks

Earlier in this chapter, we discussed relative and absolute deadlines, and compared the differences using some examples. A task that is released at a regular time interval is often called a *periodic* task. An aperiodic task has no known period; external events are generated asynchronously at unknown, often random, time intervals. To be precise, with an aperiodic task, the time interval between releases varies, but is always greater than or equal to zero:

For aperiodic task, t_i: $\forall i \in N, (r_{i+1} - r_i) \geq 0$

In comparison, for a periodic task, the length of the time interval between any two adjacent releases is always constant:

For periodic task, t_i: $\forall i \in N, (r_{i+1} - r_i) = C$

Whether a thread is periodic or aperiodic can make a difference to the scheduler, as one is to do work on a known time interval, and the other is released when an event notification arrives—such as a network message—at unknown points in time. It's obvious that if all threads in a system were periodic, it would be easier to work out a schedule than if all threads were aperiodic.

A system with multiple aperiodic threads must be carefully planned and measured as unforeseen events, and combinations of events, can occur at any time. This situation may seem orthogonal to the real-time requirement of predictability, but with careful consideration of thread priorities, it's mathematically possible to schedule such a system. Later in this chapter, we'll examine how the most common scheduling algorithms handle aperiodic tasks through what's called a *sporadic server*.

A common example of a sporadic task in a hard real-time system is the autopilot control in an airplane's flight control system. The human pilot may switch the autopilot on, and subsequently off, at specific points in time during a flight. It's impossible to determine precisely when these points in time may occur, but when they do, the system must respond within a deadline. It would certainly be considered an error condition if, when the pilot switched off the autopilot, that the system took an unduly large amount of time to give the human pilot control of the aircraft.

A sporadic task is one where the length of the time interval between two adjacent releases is always greater than or equal to a constant (which itself is non-zero):

For sporadic task, t_i: $\forall i \in N, (r_{i+1} - r_i) \geq K$

Execution Cost Functions

When scheduling real-time tasks, it's necessary to have a mathematical basis upon which to make scheduling decisions. To do this, we need to take into account the following calculations of task execution cost:

Total completion time, $t_c = max(f_i) - min(a_i)$

This cost function calculates the overall completion time for a set of tasks by subtracting the time the last task finished from the time the first task started; note that these can be different tasks.

$$\text{Late task, late}(t_i) = \begin{cases} \textit{if } d_i > 0 \textit{ and } f_i > d_i \textit{ then 1 else 0} \\ \textit{if } D_i > 0 \textit{ and } C_i > D_i \textit{ then 1 else 0} \end{cases}$$

This function returns the value 1, indicating true, if the task's finish time exceeds its absolute deadline, or if the task's completion time exceeds its relative deadline, depending upon the type of deadline the task has.

Number of late tasks, $N_{late} = \displaystyle\sum_{i=1}^{n} late(t_i)$

This function calculates the total number of tasks that miss their deadline in a given real-time system with n tasks. Note: To simplify the equations and the discussion going forward, let's define a task's deadline, d_i, where d_i equals its absolute deadline d_i when a task has an absolute deadline, or $d_i = a_i + D_i$ when a task has a relative deadline.

Maximum lateness, $L_{max} = max(f_i - d_i)$: this function calculates the task with the maximum lateness (missed its deadline by the greatest amount of time) using d_i as we've just defined it. Note that this value can be negative (when all tasks finish before their deadlines), or positive.

Average response time, $R_{avg} = \dfrac{1}{n}\left(\displaystyle\sum_{i=1}^{n} C_i\right)$

This function calculates the average response time for a given real-time system by dividing the sum of all task completion times by the total number of tasks in the system.

Classification of Real-Time Schedulers

Let's look now at the common types of schedulers used in real-time systems. We've already explored some features of scheduling algorithms in general, such as preemption, static and dynamic scheduling, and support for aperiodic and periodic tasks. Real-time systems go further in breaking down task scheduling

For instance, real-time schedulers can be broken down into two overall categories:

Guarantee-Based: these algorithms are often static, often non-preemptive, and rigid to ensure that all tasks can complete their work by their given deadline. In dynamic systems, conservative measurements are typically used to ensure that the arrival of new tasks will not cause any existing tasks to miss their deadlines as a result. Often, these algorithms will err on the side of not allowing a new task to start if there is a chance it can disrupt the system. This is done to avoid a domino effect, where the introduction of a new task causes all existing tasks to miss their deadlines. This pessimistic approach can sometimes mean that tasks may be blocked from starting that would *not* have caused a problem in reality.

Best-Effort Based: these algorithms are dynamic, more optimistic, and less conservative, when it comes to new task arrival. These schedulers are typically used in systems with soft real-time constraints, such that a missed deadline due to new task arrival is generally tolerable. They are classified a "best-effort" because these schedulers almost always allow new tasks into the system, and will do their best to ensure that all tasks complete their processing on or close to their deadlines. This results in a very responsive, efficient, real-time system that is best suited for soft real-time tasks where hard guarantees are not needed.

Within both classifications, the different algorithms must be one of the following to be considered as real-time:

Feasible: sometimes called an heuristic algorithm, this scheduler searches for a feasible schedule whereby all tasks complete their work at or before their respective deadlines. A feasible schedule still guarantees the real-time behavior of the system. A schedule is deemed *infeasible* if one or more tasks within a real-time system miss a deadline.

Optimal: an optimal scheduling algorithm is one that will always find a feasible schedule (all tasks complete on or before their deadlines) if one exists. An optimal algorithm may not always produce the *best* schedule, but it will always produce a schedule that meets every task's deadline if one is possible.

To achieve a feasible schedule for tasks in a hard real-time system, there are three common approaches often used. These are:

Clock-Driven: sometimes called time-driven, this approach schedules task execution based on known time qualities of each task in the system before the system starts. Typically, all decisions are made offline, and scheduling activities are performed during well-known points in time while the system is running. The result is a guaranteed real-time schedule with predictable execution, where the scheduler operates with very little overhead. The time-based quality(s) used to make scheduling decisions vary among the different clock-driven algorithms often used.

Weighted Round-Robin: similar to round-robin schedulers used in time-sharing systems, this approach applies a different weight value to each task in the system based upon some criterion. Tasks with higher weight are given more execution time, or higher priority, resulting in their ability to complete their work sooner. This approach is only suitable in certain types of systems (such as those with very little interdependency amongst the individual tasks in the system).

Priority-Driven: sometimes called event-driven, scheduling decisions are made when important system events occur (such as the release of a task, the availability of a resource, an IO event, and so on) with the intent to keep resources as busy as possible. With this approach, tasks are given a priority, placed in priority-ordered queues when released, and are then dispatched at the earliest point in time that a processor is free. No task is unduly delayed when an idle processor exists (a trait that can be a liability in some cases). Algorithms within this scheduling class are further sub-classed as fixed-priority (where task priorities and execution orders remain constant during system execution), and dynamic-priority (where tasks' priorities can change, and all scheduling is done online while the system is running).

There are many different real-time scheduling algorithms in existence, each of which works best with certain types of systems. For instance, some schedulers analyze tasks offline, before the system begins to execute. This type of system requires all tasks be known before execution, and that no new tasks be introduced while the system is in a time-critical mode.

Other schedulers work while a system is online, and must contain additional logic to ensure that as new tasks enter the system, a new feasible schedule can be generated. In either offline or online scenarios, some schedulers work only with fixed-priority tasks, while others allow tasks' priorities to change while the system is running.

The dynamic-priority, online schedulers tend to be the most complex and least predictable, while static-priority schedulers tend to be best for hard real-time systems. Let's look at some common algorithms that fall into these categories, and examine their characteristics:

First-Come-First-Served (FIFO): sometimes referred to as a first-in-first-out (FIFO) schedule, this is a dynamic-priority algorithm that schedules tasks based on their release times (execution eligibility).

Earliest-Deadline-First Scheduler (EDF): in this dynamic preemptive scheduler, at any instant the executing task is the task with the closest deadline.

Shortest-Execution-Time-First Scheduler (SETF): in this non-preemptive scheduler, the task with the smallest execution time is scheduled first.

Least-Slack-Time Scheduler (LST): tasks are given higher priority based on their slack time. In this dynamic-priority algorithm, task slack time is calculated as the task's deadline minus the current point in time minus the time required to complete processing. The task with the smallest slack time is given highest priority. Slack times—and hence priorities—are recalculated at certain points in time, and tasks are subsequently rescheduled.

Latest-Release Time-First Scheduler (LRT): sometimes called reverse-EDF, tasks are scheduled backward, in the sense that release times are treated as deadlines, and deadlines are treated as release times. The scheduler works backwards in time and assigns tasks to processors based on their deadlines, working back to the start of execution. Think of it as reading from right to left. This scheduler performs all scheduling offline, before the system begins to execute.

Rate-Monotonic Scheduler (RM): the inverse of a task's period is called its *rate*. Used in systems with periodic tasks and static priorities, this fixed-priority preemptive algorithm assigns higher priorities to tasks with shorter periods (higher rates).

Deadline-Monotonic Scheduler (DM): in this static, fixed-priority preemptive scheduler, the task with the shortest relative deadline is scheduled first. In a real-time system, when each task's relative deadline equals its period, the RM and DM schedulers generate the same schedule.

In some systems, such as those that run both real-time and general-purpose applications together, a scheduling algorithm is used in conjunction with a partitioning scheme to achieve optimal system behavior. With this approach, tasks are partitioned, or grouped, based upon certain criteria. The partitioning scheme can be either fixed, or adaptive:

Fixed-Partition Scheduling: this is a dynamic, preemptive, scheduler that assigns time budgets, in terms of total processing time allowed, to different groups of tasks called partitions. Each partition, as a whole, is bounded not to exceed its total budget of processor time (i.e., 10% of the CPU).

Adaptive-Partition Scheduling: this is a dynamic, preemptive, scheduler where a percentage of the processor time (and sometimes system resources) are reserved for a particular group of tasks (partition). When the system reaches 100% utilization, hard limits are imposed on the non-real-time partition in order to meet the needs of the real-time tasks. When the system is less than 100% utilized, however, active partitions will be allowed to borrow from the budget reserved for other, non-active, partitions.

The intent of the Java Real-Time System is to hide this complexity from you. However, to truly appreciate its implementation, and to understand why your Java applications behave as they do within it, you should at least have a cursory understanding of the theory behind its implementation.

Both the RTSJ and Sun's Java RTS are meant to provide real-time behavior to Java applications even on general-purpose hardware with a real-time OS. However, this is a deviation from what has been classically accepted as a real-time system. In the past, you had to write code in a language designed for real-time applications and use dedicated, special-purpose hardware to run them on. Again, to gain a true appreciation of the real-time space, and the problems that Java RTS had to overcome, let's take a brief look at some common real-time languages and operating systems.

Multi-Core Processors and Scheduling

For the most part, modern operating systems treat individual processor cores as individual processors themselves. This is an accurate representation, as each core *is* a complete processor in its own right, capable of acting like an independent processor—albeit sometimes with a shared on-chip cache. Therefore, it's not required for the OS to treat individual cores any differently than individual processors.

However, some OS kernels do take special care in scheduling threads on separate cores as opposed to separate physical processors. Solaris 10, for instance, will schedule eligible threads to distribute them across physical processors first, then across the cores of individual processors [McDougall07]. For instance, on a system with two dual-core processors, Solaris will dispatch the first thread on core 1 of processor 1, and the second thread on core 1 of processor 2 (see Figure 1-12).

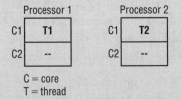

C = core
T = thread

Figure 1-12   The Solaris kernel attempts to balance threads across CPUs to help with heat dissipation.

continued

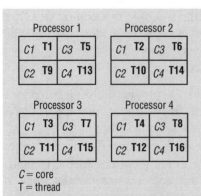

C = core
T = thread

Figure 1-13   Solaris kernel threads spread equally across all available cores. From this point onward, additional threads will be scheduled on the next available (free) core.

Threads 3 and 4 will be dispatched to core 2 of processor 1, and core 2 of processor 2, respectively. In this case, even though thread 2 could have been scheduled on core 1 of processor 1, this would upset the balance. The intent is to distribute running threads across physical processors *and* their cores evenly. For instance, on a system with four quad-core processors, with sixteen dispatched and running threads, the thread-to-processor/core distribution should look as shown in Figure 1-13.

This distribution of threads over available cores has little bearing on our real-time discussion, although it's important to know that it does occur.

Real-Time Operating Systems

To meet the needs of the most demanding real-time systems, specialized operating systems are available. Besides having the required features to support predictable task execution for time-critical applications, the real-time OS will also have its own real-time constraints. For example, core scheduling and other OS-specific functionality must behave in predictable, measurable, ways, with high efficiency and low latency. In other words, the OS and its scheduling activities must never contribute to unbounded task latency, or be unpredictable in any sense.

A real-time OS has thread schedulers built-in that support real-time systems. Most often, these operating systems allow programmers to control the computer hardware at the lowest level, including processor interrupts, physical memory access, and low-level input/output (I/O) processing. This is done so that the real-time application developer can remove as much of the non-deterministic behavior and end-to-end latency found in general-purpose operating systems.

Many real-time operating systems target embedded systems with dedicated functionality and limited hardware resources. This means that these systems are not meant to be general-purpose systems, and using a real-time OS proves to be a valuable tool in these cases. However, as mentioned before in this chapter, with the continuing advances in hardware capabilities at lower cost, the need for specialized hardware *and* operating systems has diminished significantly. A dedicated real-time OS comes at a high cost relative to the general-purpose operating systems available today. Many argue that the state of the industry has reached a point that this extra cost is no longer justified. However, recall that while adding additional, more powerful, hardware can help improve raw performance and throughput, it almost never makes an unpredictable system behave predictably.

Regardless, there are instances, such as with embedded systems, where a real-time OS continues to be the only option. While this book does not go into detail regarding real-time operating systems, it's important to know that they do exist and serve a specialized purpose. Real-time applications typically require the same set of services from the OS—such as disk IO, networking support, a file system, user IO, and so on—as general purpose applications do. However, the real-time application requires its OS to make guarantees that are both measurable and predictable.

RT-POSIX Operating System Extensions

With the intent to unify the real-time application and OS space, the Real-Time Portable Operating System based-on Unix (RT-POSIX 1003.1b) standard was created. POSIX is a standard that has been very successful and widely adopted in a wide-range of OS implementations, for both mission-critical and general-purpose computing. RT-POSIX defines an extension to it that addresses the needs of hard and soft real-time systems.

The standard defines a minimum set of features that a compliant OS must implement. Additional features can be implemented, provided that they do not conflict with or hereby negate the required features. For example, RT-POSIX-compliant operating systems must have the following traits:

Preemption: true task preemption must be supported using task priority rules that are strictly obeyed.

Priority Inversion Control: although it cannot guard well against deadlocks, priority inheritance ensures that lower-priority threads will never be able to block higher-priority threads due to classic priority inversion.

Periodic, Aperiodic, and Sporadic Threads: the POSIX standard requires only processes be implemented. For real-time applications, threads of different priority may need to run to perform a task. For this reason, the RT-POSIX standard requires the OS be able to schedule tasks down to the thread level, and that applications be able to create and destroy those threads. Underlying OS threads must be able to support the various types of task release events common to real-time applications. For instance, a thread should be able to specify its period and then rely on the OS to wake it up at precise time boundaries that match that period. Simply performing a call to "sleep" from within the task's code (as is done in a non-real-time OS) is not sufficient.

High-Resolution Timers: such timers should be made available to real-time applications, as well as the real-time OS itself so that it can dispatch threads with as little latency and jitter as possible. For example, an OS scheduler with a 10-millisecond tick size will, at best, experience up to 10 milliseconds latency during thread dispatch processing. In general, the larger the tick count, the higher the max latency and jitter values will grow. Both are qualities to be avoided in real-time systems. The RT-POSIX standard states that up to 32 timers per process must be supported, and that timer overruns (when a timer goes beyond its chosen duration) be recorded.

Schedulers: the kernel needs to support both deadline-monotonic and rate-monotonic deadline scheduling in order to support the common real-time scheduling algorithms such as weighted round-robin, fixed-priority, and earliest-deadline-first scheduling. The type of scheduler used can be defined down to the thread level, where two threads of the same process may be scheduled differently.

Scheduled Interrupt Handling: the ability to create a preemptable task that processes low lever device interrupts. This is sometimes called a software interrupt. In contrast, a general-purpose OS typically handles these events completely itself, making the data or status available through some other means.

Synchronous and Asynchronous IO: synchronous IO operations provide real-time tasks more control over IO-related tasks, such as file and network operations. Asynchronous IO allows the system to progress task execution while IO is occurring, or waiting to occur. For instance, a task that reads a network packet can process the packet's payload even while it waits for the next packet to arrive.

Inter-Task Communication: to facilitate predictable, low-latency, communication between tasks, queues should be provided at the OS level. This also ensures fast, consistent, and measurable performance, with support for message prioritization. These queues are sometimes made available to tasks both local to the system, and remote. Regardless, message delivery must be prioritized, and at least eight prioritized signals are supported per process.

Priority Inheritance: to guard against deadline misses due to priority inversion (where a lower-priority task's priority is raised above that of a higher-priority task) priority inheritance needs to be implemented at the kernel level, or at least emulated.

Resource Quotas: the ability to monitor and control the usage of system resources such as memory and processor time to ensure the system behaves in a predictable way even when under heavy load.

Memory Sharing: shared memory (between processes) and memory-mapped files must be supported.

Memory Locking: applications must be able to control the memory residency of their code sections through functions that will either lock all of its code, or only the portions specified.

Real-Time File System: file systems that ensure files are made up of contiguous disk blocks, pre-allocate files of fixed size to be used on-demand while the system is running, and offer sequential access, provide the most predictable behavior and timing characteristics.

Synchronization: OS primitives that support efficient resource sharing between tasks with priority inheritance, and ceiling priority (both of which are protocols to control or avoid thread priority inversion).

Further Reading

Much of the information for this chapter was gathered from papers and texts on the subject of real-time systems and scheduling theory. For readers who are interested, below is a list of reading material that will help build a complete foundation for real-time theory and practice:

[Buttazzo05] Buttazzo, Georgia C., *Hard Real-Time Computing Systems*. Springer, 2005.

[Klein93] Klein, Mark, et al., *A Practitioner's Guide to Real-Time Analysis*. Kluwer Academic Publishers, 1993.

[Layland73] Liu, C.L. and Layland, James W., *Scheduling Algorithms for Multiprogramming in a Hard Real-Time Environment*. Journal of the ACM, 1973 (Available at http://portal.acm.org/citation.cfm?id=321743).

[Liu00] Liu, Jane W. S., *Real-Time Systems*. Prentice Hall, 2000.

[McDougall07] Mauro, Jim, McDougall, Richard, *Solaris Internals*. Prentice Hall, 2007.

2

Real-Time and Java SE

"You may delay, but time will not."
—Ben Franklin

Can Java be used in a real-time context? Prior to the Real-Time Specification for Java (RTSJ), it was common wisdom of people in the classic real-time world, as well as those in the Java world, that it couldn't be done. Skipping to the last page of this story, Java RTS has proven that Java *can* be used for real-time. However, this chapter will step back and explore the question so that you can learn this for yourself.

To be precise, standard Java does have trouble operating in a real-time context. There are many sources of latency and jitter that remove the predictability and determinism needed for a real-time application. Some are inherent in the way the Java Virtual Machine (VM) implementers have interpreted the Java language specification; others are due to facilities built into the Java VM, such as the garbage collector and the just-in-time (JIT) compiler. This chapter will explore these factors, and more, and lay out the set of problems that needed to be solved by the RTSJ writers, and the Java RTS implementers alike.

Is Java a Real-Time Language?

The Java Standard Edition (Java SE) virtual machine has evolved into a general purpose, desktop- and server-based platform for high-throughput application performance. This is the result of Java's popularity in the server and web space, where performance is measured in requests per second. Java is not a choice for real-time

37

applications because most Java VMs are tuned to meet throughput requirements. As a result, the VM implementation is orthogonal to what a real-time application requires. It's also the result of early impressions that Java is a slow, interpreted language.

However, mainstream Java implementations are no longer slow; with the HotSpot Java VM from Sun, Java bytecode(s) is compiled to machine code and continually optimized as an application runs. Each release of the Java platform has improved upon this optimization. Garbage collection (GC) algorithms have also improved, and the Java VM has evolved to take advantage of today's computing resources, such as hyper-threading, multiple cores, and large amounts of RAM. As a result, Java has spread beyond its web application roots and has penetrated application spaces that were once the domain of C developers. Today, for example, Java is used in embedded devices, such as cell phones, printers, smart RFID readers, TV set-top boxes, robotics, parking meters, game terminals used in casinos, handheld devices, and so on.

Java continues this expansion today, moving into other areas once considered outside of Java's domain or capabilities. This includes distributed, mission-critical, and safety-critical applications; but what about real-time?

Sources of Unbounded Latency and Jitter

As Java caught the attention of real-time system designers, it became apparent that Java was not ideal in this space. Existing Java VMs simply were not designed for predictability and determinism. The garbage collector, for instance, is one source of trouble. Garbage collection (GC) can occur at any time, for any length of time, outside of the Java developer's control. This potential for uncontrolled latency makes it impossible to guarantee a system's behavior; it's non-deterministic. Attempts to pool objects or somehow control their lifetime to avoid GC are often in vain, as GC pauses may still occur. Besides, this extra effort and complicated code works against the benefits of using Java in the first place.

However, Java SE's real-time deficiencies go way beyond the garbage collector. The just-in-time (JIT) HotSpot compiler—the same one that compiles bytecode to machine code—is also non-deterministic. Since JIT compilation can occur when your code is executing, and can take an unknown length of time to complete, you cannot be guaranteed that your code will meet its deadlines all of the time. Even Java classes that have been JIT compiled are subject to re-optimization at any point in the future. Additionally, some of the performance optimizations the compiler makes (such as biased locking) counter real-time application behavior. Therefore the JIT compiler remains a source of jitter throughout your Java SE application's execution lifetime.

Lack of Strict Thread Priorities

Most importantly, standard Java provides no guaranteed way to prioritize threads and event handling. Regarding this, the original Java Language Specification (JLS) stated the following:

> Every thread has a priority. When there is competition for processing resources, threads with higher priority are generally executed in preference to threads with lower priority. Such preference is **not, however, a guarantee that the highest priority thread will always be running**, and thread priorities cannot be used to reliably implement mutual exclusion.

This statement was added to the JLS because of Java's write-once-run-anywhere requirement. In Java's early days, many operating systems didn't (and some still don't) guarantee thread priority obedience, or true thread preemption based on priority. Due to this, the Java VM cannot guarantee it either. Without the ability to prioritize an application's threads' execution above the execution of other threads in the system, you cannot build a real-time application.

This raises an important point: even if the execution of the garbage collector and the JIT compiler could be controlled by the Java application, real-time behavior still cannot be guaranteed in Java without the implementation of strict thread priority control. We stress this point because, all too often, developers blame GC and JIT solely for Java's real-time deficiencies. In reality, Java requires more than just a low-pause garbage collector, or a better JIT compiler, to be accepted in the real-time space. To be thorough, for use in real-time application development, the Java VM and its operating environment must be POSIX real-time compliant, and support the following:

- Strict thread priority control
- True thread preemption based on thread priority
- Thread priority inversion control
- Advanced resource locking with minimal wait states (limited critical sections)
- A low-pause garbage collector
- Control over code compilation (JIT, or otherwise)
- Synchronous and asynchronous event processing
- Access to physical memory
- Access to hardware interrupts, and the ability to schedule them
- The ability to lock code and the heap into memory
- Inter-thread communication and transfer of control

Certainly, you need more than a low-pause, or pause-less, garbage collector to achieve real-time behavior in Java. However, with that said, the garbage collector often becomes the single largest cause of jitter and latency in a Java application. To understand why this is so, and how to correct this, let's examine how garbage collection works in Java SE.

Garbage Collection

The activity of garbage collection, and the garbage collector itself, is a source of an unpredictable amount of latency in a Java application. In fact, it's often the largest culprit when it comes to latency and risk while a Java application is running. For example, if the garbage collector is activated just as an important thread in your application is calculating the trajectory needed to intercept an inbound missile, the resulting latency can have disastrous consequences.

Before you label the garbage collector as the enemy, it's wise to understand how it works. In fact, Java RTS includes a garbage collector that meets the requirements for most real-time applications. This chapter will explore the various garbage collection algorithms (mostly non-real-time, and some real-time) that exist today, as well as the various garbage collector implementations available with the Java SE platform. From theory to application, after reading this section, you'll gain an understanding and appreciation of the factors that garbage collector developers have to deal with. First, let's discuss why garbage collection exists at all, considering the lack of determinism inherent with its execution.

What, Exactly, Is Garbage Collection?

Many dynamic languages, such as C/C++, Pascal, and so on, require the programmer to manage memory explicitly. This includes memory allocation, deallocation, and all of the accounting that occurs in between. For instance, after some memory is allocated for use within an application, it's conceivable that it must be freed eventually. In the time frame between allocation and deallocation, the programmer must be sure to not lose track of the memory (thereby failing to ever free it), or the result will be a memory leak. Excessive memory leaks can lead to poor application performance, and even failure, over time. For simplicity, we'll refer to a region of allocated memory as an object.

Another common problem with explicit memory management is the attempt to access or use an object after it has been deallocated. A pointer, or reference, to an object that has had its underlying memory deallocated is called a dangling pointer, or dangling reference. Access through a dangling pointer within an application can result in undefined behavior, the accidental overwriting of other critical data, a security hole, or an abrupt application crash or exception.

Even if the deallocated memory is never accessed again, there is still a danger in that a dangling pointer in your code can result in a second attempt to deallocate the memory. This, too, can lead to an application crash or exception. Automatic memory management removes the likelihood that these issues will occur since it's no longer left up to each developer to account for memory allocations. In C++, the concept of smart pointers is one solution, and in other languages, such as Lisp, SmallTalk, and Java, a full-featured garbage collector tracks the lifetimes of all objects in a running program.

John McCarthy is a computer scientist who worked in the field of artificial intelligence in the early 1950s, and beyond. He announced the Lisp programming language in a paper he wrote in 1958 [McCarthy58], and invented the concept of garbage collection in 1959, mainly as part of Lisp [McCarthy59]. In short, a garbage collector works to reclaim areas of memory within an application that will never be accessed again. No longer is it the programmer's responsibility to allocate, and subsequently deallocate an object's memory. This eliminates many, if not all, of the potential memory-related errors outlined above. At the most fundamental level, garbage collection involves two deceivingly simple steps:

1. Determine which objects can no longer be referenced by an application. This is done by either direct means (such as with object reference counts), or indirect means (where object graphs are traced to determine live and dead objects).

2. Reclaim the memory used by dead objects (the garbage).

Of course, the work to reclaim dead objects takes time, and must be executed from time to time to ensure that enough free memory is consistently made available for the application threads to consume. We call application threads *mutator threads* since, from the collector's point of view, they change the heap. Complexities arise in determining when, for how long, and how often, garbage collection activities are to take place. This work directly impacts the performance and determinism of the running application, as it takes time to run the associated garbage collector logic.

There are many algorithms and approaches for garbage collection. The work can be performed in parallel to application threads (which is often referred to as concurrent GC), parallel to other GC-related activities (often referred to as parallel GC), or serially. Some of the GC work can be performed at object allocation time, or all of it can be deferred until free memory falls below a threshold percentage. Let's examine common GC algorithms, and which ones are available in Java SE today.

Common Garbage Collection Algorithms

Garbage collection has been the subject of much research and development since the 1950s, when it was first considered. However, a garbage collector's job is fairly straightforward: identify dead objects and reclaim their memory. Therefore, most algorithms share many of the same concepts. There are different strategies to getting this work done, which we'll explore here. Some of them overlap, they may be used together in many cases, and some of them are mutually exclusive. Most of them work on the principles of tracing and reachability.

In short, these concepts require heap memory to be swept, or traced, at certain intervals to determine which objects are live or dead through analysis of the running application's code. The trigger for this event can be time-based, threshold-based (free memory dips below a certain level), or allocation-based.

Tracing GC

A tracing garbage collector spends most of its time determining which objects are reachable. Those that are not reachable are simply discarded, and their memory regions made available for subsequent allocations. Reachability is determined through the application's active variables (local, global, and stack-based). If an object is referenced by an active variable directly, or through other objects reachable through an active variable, then that object is reachable (see Figure 2-1).

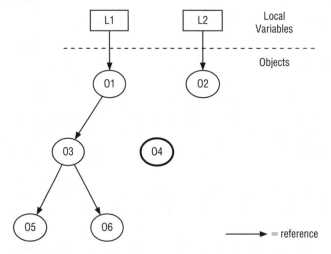

Figure 2-1   An object is reachable when a local, global, or stack-based variable references it, or references another object that references it.

This figure clearly shows that reachability is transitive; if a reachable object (i.e., object O3) references other objects (i.e., objects O5 and O6), those objects are also reachable, and so on. Objects O1 and O2 are special in that they're *root* objects; that is, they are referenced directly by an active local variable. This object reference graph shows that object O4 is not reachable through any active application references, and is therefore a dead object.

Reachability is most closely associated with scope, as opposed to object usage. For instance, an object may be considered reachable long after the last time it's used in the application code. This can occur when, say, a class method uses an object only at the beginning of its execution, but executes for quite a bit longer before exiting the method (and hence, the scope of the local variable). The sample code below illustrates how this definition of garbage is less than optimal, compared to semantic analysis of the code to prove that the object, stock, is not used after line 6. Unfortunately, the object referenced by stock isn't eligible for garbage collection until after the method waits for a specific length of time before sending the conflated update (via the sendConflatedUpdate method), even though it doesn't use the object anymore. This is because variable stock stays in scope the entire time.

```
1. public boolean sendConflatedData(String companyName
2.                                   long duration)
3. {
4.     // Set asynchronous listener to receive real-time updates
5.     Stock stock = equityLookup( companyName );
6.     setUpdateListener( stock.getSymbol(), this );
7.
8.     // Wait for a length of time (duration) and conflate all
9.     // received real-time data to send as a single update
10.    waitAndConflate( duration );
11.    sendConflatedUpdate();
12. }
```

To make matters more complex, the usage of an object may be contained within a conditional. If the conditional is true, the object will be used within that scope; otherwise, it will not. These are examples where a semantic garbage collector can be more optimal, as opposed to a syntactic garbage collector. For reasons of complexity, some garbage collectors are syntactic ones, operating only in situations where no semantic analysis is required. Syntactic GC uses scope to determine which objects are live or dead. However, today's advanced compilers help flag these situations as optimizations, where the objects will be cleaned up at safepoints before the object goes out of scope.

Tri-Color Scheme

With tracing collectors, objects are marked using a tri-color scheme, in theory. As the object graph is traversed from the roots, all objects are considered "white," or unmarked. As the root objects are checked, live objects are marked as "grey," since their children have not yet been checked for liveness. The collector then traverses the rest of the object graph recursively, from the roots. When a root object and all of its children have been determined to be live, they are marked as "black."

Although colors may not be used to track object state (sometimes a bit pattern is used), the tri-color scheme goes a long way towards describing how the algorithm works in theory, regardless of how it's implemented.

Stop-the-World and Concurrent GC

Some basic forms of garbage collection require that the application's memory not be mutable while GC is taking place. Basically this means that all application progress is halted, and it can do no useful work, while the collector is running, or *sweeping* active memory. In this *stop-the-world* GC implementation, the entire contents of memory are examined to determine which objects are reachable and not reachable. The pause is required to ensure that an object's reachability status doesn't change while the collector is still working. Additionally, it's imperative that no new objects be created during this phase, as its reachability status will not be known at the end of the sweep. Simply assuming these objects are live can result in floating garbage—dead objects that live beyond a GC cycle. This is something most GC designers try to avoid.

Modifications to this strategy enable the GC to either break its work down into smaller parts (thereby reducing pause times), or to remove stop-the-world pauses altogether by working concurrently with the running application. These are called incremental and concurrent garbage collectors, respectively.

By working incrementally, pauses still occur, but they're simply broken up into multiple smaller pauses over time. The drawbacks here include the risk that GC won't be able to keep up with the memory consumption of the application, and care must be taken to ensure that GC threads and mutator threads do not interfere with one another at critical points (such as object creation). Concurrent collectors synchronize with the application to ensure safe concurrent memory access with the application. Although the related complexity does require some overhead in terms of resources, this strategy allows the system to make best use of multi-core and multi-processor systems as GC threads and mutator threads can run together, on separate processors/cores. The end result is a far more efficient system overall on modern hardware.

Moving and Copying

All of the work involved with tracing, or sweeping, through memory to determine reachability has a point: to free unused memory. Again, this is a deceptively simple operation. For instance, the garbage collector can simply mark the area of memory consumed by each dead object in question as free, and subject to be used again in future allocation requests. This is, after all, a quick and efficient operation, and intuitively sounds like the approach to take. However, upon further examination, you'll see that it can lead to a very inefficient solution in terms of memory allocation.

As illustrated in Figure 2-2, this approach to freeing memory results in a very fragmented heap, with pockets of free space scattered between live objects. As new objects are created, they may or may not fit into these pockets of free space depending upon their size requirements.

If the free pockets are large enough for most allocations, they more than likely will not fit precisely into them, thereby leaving even smaller pockets of free space, which are too small to be useful. As time progresses, most of the system's free memory will consist of multitudes of very small regions of free memory. The result is what appears to be ample free memory in sum, but failed allocation requests because none of them are large enough on their own (see Figure 2-3).

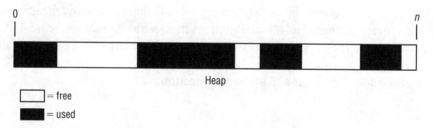

Figure 2-2   As objects are freed in place, the heap can become fragmented.

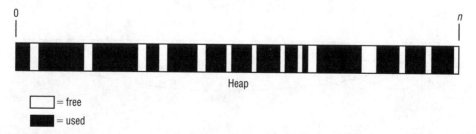

Figure 2-3   A fragmented heap **may** result in pockets of free space that are too small to be useful.

> **Note: Fragmentation**   It's important to note that fragmentation has little to do with the absolute size of free memory blocks, but instead is relative to the average object allocation size. We determine that memory is fragmented when free heap regions are smaller than the smallest average object size being created.

One solution is to allow objects to span multiple regions of free memory (free memory blocks), and to perform the accounting necessary to access the list of memory blocks as though they were contiguous. This is possible, but relatively expensive, and requires some overhead in terms of memory to track the lists of free memory blocks per object.

A better solution to this problem is one that's seemingly counter-intuitive—moving live objects to a region of memory so that they are adjacent to one another. Over time, all live objects are moved (a.k.a. swept) to one side of the heap, while all free space resides linearly on the other side (see Figure 2-4). This makes both the tasks of reclaiming dead objects, and allocating memory for new objects, faster and more efficient. For instance, dead objects are simply not moved, they're marked as free in-place. And since most (if not all) of the free memory is contiguous, allocating memory from this region involves the simple step of moving the free memory pointer over by the size of the object being allocated.

Although there is quite a bit of overhead in moving objects, this overhead is offset by the efficient reclaim and allocation times that result. Further refinement of this algorithm includes the addition of memory "spaces" where objects are alternately allocated from and moved to. The Java virtual machine uses a form of this type of collection, called generational garbage collection.

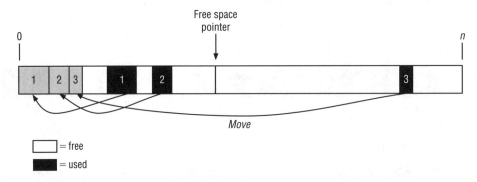

Figure 2-4   Live objects are moved to the left, leaving the right side for allocations.

Generational GC

Observation across many types of applications shows us that the most recently created objects are usually the most short-lived ones in the system. In other words, almost all objects have a very short lifetime within a running system. This observation has been used to help optimize garbage collection. To do so, the garbage collector maintains multiple areas of the heap, each broken down by object age. To keep the conversation simple at this point, let's concern ourselves with only two: a young generation of objects, and an old generation of objects (see Figure 2-5).

In this algorithm, all objects are initially created in the young generation area. When garbage collection work is performed, it takes place in either the young or old generation areas. Garbage collection in either area does not occur until free space in that region drops below a certain threshold. When GC does occur, objects in the young generation are traced, and survivors (those with active references) are marked. When an object in the young generation survives a certain number of collections, it's promoted to the old generation (i.e., moved there).

Old generation collections occur less frequently, but when they do, effort is made to move the longest-living objects together to result in a low-garbage density region of memory. This helps to improve GC times in the old generation area. Overall, generational garbage collectors tend to be very efficient for the following reasons:

- GC occurs on only a subset of the heap: either the young generation or the old generation, in this example. However, most implementations sub-divide these regions even further. This results in incremental GC cycles that are relatively fast.

- The young generation tends to be the smallest region (requiring less area to cover).

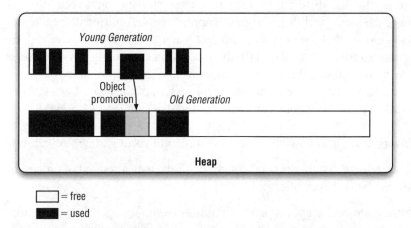

Figure 2-5   Generational garbage collection maintains objects by age.

- Most objects in the young generation are reclaimed and don't require a move operation.
- The old generation area grows slowly, and requires less-frequent GC cycles.

There are some interesting side effects from generational collection. Most notably, it's common for some unreachable objects to not get reclaimed when a GC cycle occurs. For instance, nepotism can occur, which is when a young object is referenced from an object in the old part of the heap that happens to be dead. Since the liveness of the old object is not determined during a young collection, the young object is not reclaimed. As a result, free memory can run low on these systems, and a full, or major, garbage collection cycle may need to take place, requiring more time to complete. Overall, however, generational collectors tend to be the most efficient, and therefore are the most commonly implemented in practice, including within Java SE.

Garbage Collection in Sun's Java SE 6 HotSpot

Sun's Java SE 6 HotSpot, the latest Java distribution available from Sun as of this writing, contains four main collectors: the serial collector, the parallel collector, the parallel-compacting collector, and the concurrent collector. All of them work with the same set of goals in mind: to be safe, comprehensive, and efficient. This translates to no dangling pointers or memory leaks, reclaiming dead objects soon after they become dead, and no long pauses.

Each collector has different performance characteristics and related behaviors, making each ideal for different types of applications. Additionally, each collector works to ensure that the heap does not get fragmented. This is achieved through either compaction or evacuation (both involve object copying). With compaction, objects are moved together in the same section of the heap, whereas with evacuation, they're moved to an entirely different section of the heap. Let's define some key measurements used when talking about garbage collection in Java:

Throughput: percentage of processing time **not** spent garbage collecting.

GC Overhead: the inverse of throughput, or the measurement of processor time used by the garbage collector.

Pause Time, or Latency: the length of time the application stops executing due to garbage collection activity. Note that this does not always equal GC overhead, as some collectors do their work concurrently with the application.

Footprint: the size of the collector in terms of memory used.

Promptness: the time from when an object becomes dead to when it is reclaimed.

Obviously, different Java applications have different requirements when it comes to garbage collection. For instance, interactive applications typically require good *average* pause times; web applications require high throughput; embedded applications require a small footprint; and real-time applications require bounded, deterministic, GC pause times all the time (not just on the average). Regardless of the application requirements and the performance characteristics of each collector, they all do their work according to their own timing. This is usually related to how consumed the heap is, or some threshold of free memory available at a given point in time.

Java Object Generations

Earlier in the chapter, we discussed generational garbage collection, where objects are grouped based on age, young and old. Java SE extends this technique, and maintains three main generations of objects within the heap: the *young generation*, the *old generation*, and the *permanent generation*. The young generation is further broken down in three subsets: the *Eden* space, and two survivor spaces alternately labeled *To* and *From* (see Figure 2-6).

The Java heap generations are directly related to the age of objects. For instance, most new objects are allocated directly in the young generation (Eden, to be

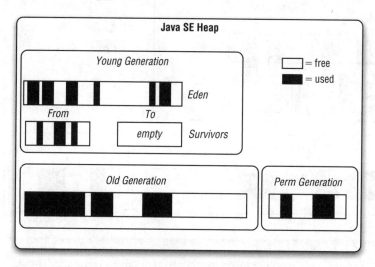

Figure 2-6 Java SE maintains multiple object generations to help ensure efficient Java VM operation.

precise), although occasionally some very large objects may be allocated directly to the old generation. Also, when a generational space fills up, objects may be moved directly to the old generation regardless of age. However, these cases are the exception rather than the rule, so we'll ignore them both for now. As objects age (survive successive young collections) they're moved from Eden to the survivor spaces, and eventually to the old generation. The permanent generation is used for internal Java VM metadata about the running application, its classes, and class methods. For the most part, we won't discuss this area in detail.

When a young generation object collection occurs, the following steps are taken:

1. Live objects in the Eden space are copied to the empty Survivor space (labeled *To* in Figure 2-6).

2. Additionally, live objects in the Survivor space labeled *From* are copied to the Survivor space labeled *To* (see Figure 2-7). This should explain why the survivor spaces are labeled as such. If a particular object has survived a specific number of young generation collections, it will be promoted (copied) to the old generation.

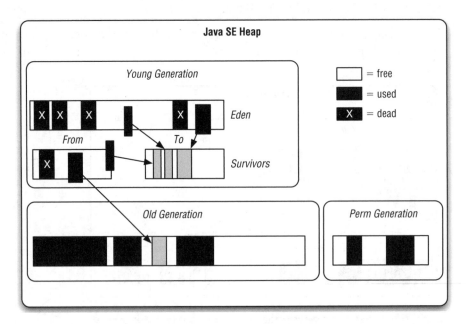

Figure 2-7   Surviving objects are moved to other memory areas (promoted) based on age.

3. The remaining objects in both the Eden and Survivor space labeled *From* are garbage, and can be reclaimed (no further work needs to be done). Remember, survivors were copied to either the *To* Survivor space, or the old generation. The implicit results of this are:

   a. Eden is now empty and available for new object allocations.

   b. The Survivor space labeled *From* is now empty.

   c. The roles (and hence the labels) of the Survivor spaces are swapped (see Figure 2-8).

Note: An object in the *From* space may be promoted directly to the old generation if it's too large for the *To* space, regardless of the number of collections it has survived.

In a typical system, young generation collection occurs frequently and quickly because this part of the heap is (intentionally) small. Often there are a lot of objects to reclaim at once, therefore the algorithm is written for speed. In Java SE, a young generation collection is often referred to as a *minor collection*, as it's considered to be of minor consequence to the running application's performance.

Objects that survive multiple young generation collections are promoted from the young generation to the old generation. Because they reside in a much larger portion of the heap, old generation objects collections are infrequent, but they can take longer. This is because the algorithm used works with a much larger portion of the heap, and is simply not tuned for speed. Instead, it's written to use the old generation space as efficiently as possible in terms of fragmentation and object allocation. An old generation collection is referred to as a *major collection* because it operates over a large portion of the heap, and can take longer than a young generation collection.

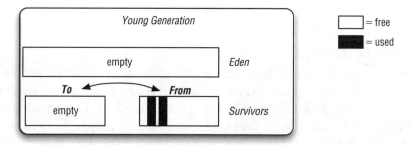

Figure 2-8   The young generation after the collection shown in Figure 2-7.

To aid in tracking and collecting the old generation, which encompasses a relatively large portion of the heap, the heap is broken down into sections of a specific size (usually 512 bytes) called *cards*. Each card is represented in a bitmap called a *card table*. Each entry in the table represents a card in the heap, and is used to track references to objects in the young generation from objects in the old generation. During an unconditional write barrier, when an old object is created (or updated) to reference a young object, its associated card table entry is marked (sometimes referred to as being "dirtied"). This helps the collector more efficiently discover which objects in the heap contain live objects.

Typically, many young generation collections (using the young generation collector) will occur before an old generation collection is needed. Occasionally, however, a young generation collection will be halted because the old generation is too full to promote survivors to it. Instead, the old generation collector will be used to sweep and collect objects across the entire heap (including the young, old, and permanent generations). This is referred to as a *full collection*, and usually results in relatively large application pauses.

One exception to this is when the concurrent mark-sweep collector is used for old generation collections (you do have choices here, which we'll discuss in the next section). In that case, the young generation collector is always used for young generation objects. Let's take a look at the different types of collectors available in Java SE, and how/when they're used.

Collectors

There are four main collectors available in Java SE: the *serial collector*, the *parallel-scavenging collector*, the *parallel-compacting collector*, and the *concurrent mark-sweep collector*. Different collectors can be used for different generations at the same time; they're not mutually exclusive. However, there are some limitations as to which collectors can be used for each generation—we'll examine those limitations in this section.

The Serial Collector

The serial collector executes in one thread (on a single CPU), which pauses the running application completely when it performs a collection. This is sometimes referred to as a *stop-the-world* collection (see Figure 2-9). Even if additional CPUs/cores are available to execute application threads, they're blocked during the entire GC operation.

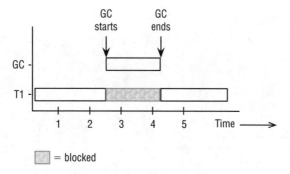

Figure 2-9   Even on a multi-CPU machine, application threads are stopped during serial GC.

The serial collector can operate on both the young and old generations. When collecting the young generation, work is performed as described in the previous section. The algorithm is efficient, and dead objects are left in place. When the serial collector operates on the old generation, it uses a different algorithm. Collections are done in three phases:

1. *Mark Phase*: live objects are marked.

2. *Sweep Phase*: the entire generation is swept to identify garbage.

3. *Sliding-Compact Phase*: live objects are moved to the beginning of the generation.

The sliding-compact phase moves all live objects to the beginning of the old generation, grouped closely together. This both eliminates fragmentation within the heap, and allows for faster allocation times as all of the free space is grouped together as well. We'll discuss object allocation in more detail in the next section. You can force the serial collector to be used with the following Java SE command-line parameter: -XX:+UseSerialGC.

The Parallel Scavenging Collector

The parallel collector only works with the young generation; the Java VM will default to the serial collector for the old generation. It works on the young generation almost exactly as the serial collector does. For instance, it uses the same algorithm, performs the same steps, and it will stop all application threads. However, it performs its work using multiple GC threads, where the threads can safely execute in parallel (to each other, not the application's threads) across multiple CPUs. The result is more efficient collection, with an increase in overall application throughput (see Figure 2-10).

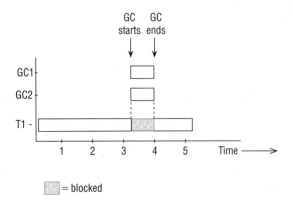

= blocked

Figure 2-10   The parallel collector performs work in parallel GC threads.

Although the application is still subject to old generation collections with long pause times, it will gain overall from the higher throughput young generation collections that occur most often. This assumes, of course, that multiple processors or cores are available to execute the GC threads in parallel. You can force the parallel collector to be used with the following Java SE command-line parameter: -XX:+UseParallelGC.

The Parallel-Compacting Collector

The parallel-compacting collector (available as of Java SE 5, update 6) is similar to the parallel collector, except that it can operate on the old generation as well as the young generation. In fact, for the young generation, it works identically to the parallel collector, as described previously.

For the old generation, collections are performed as with the serial collector, although portions are broken up and performed in parallel with additional GC threads. As with the serial collector, there are still three phases to old generation collection, although each phase is executed differently. In fact, the second phase is very different from the serial collector. The phases are as follows:

1. *Parallel Mark Phase*: the old generation is broken into three parts, or regions, to be executed by three threads in parallel. Each thread is assigned to one of the three regions, and live objects are marked within each in parallel. As each thread marks objects, it keeps track of each object's size and location, to be used in the next step.

2. *Summary Phase*: in this phase, portions of the generation's heap are examined as a whole, as such:

   a. Areas of the heap that contain a high density of live objects are identified.

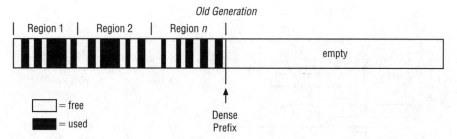

Figure 2-11 Results of the parallel-compacting collector in the old generation. Note: figure not to scale.

    b. Due to past collections, these areas will generally be located on the left side of the generation. A threshold point is identified somewhere in the middle, called the dense prefix.

    c. The space to the right of the dense prefix point is broken into regions that will be compacted (the rest will be ignored, as it's already compact).

  3. *Parallel Compact Phase*: the regions marked in the summary phase are assigned to threads, and are compacted in parallel. When complete, the generation will be dense with live objects on one side, but with a large, contiguous, block of free space on the other (see Figure 2-11).

When operating on either the young or old generation, the application will still experience stop-the-world pauses. However, overall throughput is increased for old generation collections, in addition to young generation collections, resulting in increased throughput over both the serial and parallel collectors. You can force this collector to be used (in a compatible Java VM) with the following Java SE command-line parameter: `-XX:+UseParallelOldGC`. In this case, the *old* in the command refers to the *old generation*, not an older software version.

The Concurrent Mark-Sweep Collector

The description of garbage collection so far illustrates that, for the most part, young generation collections are relatively quick, and impose only small pauses. However, old generation collections (major collections), and full collections impose much longer pauses. This can add latency to application response times, and can occur at unpredictable points in time. This is true of all the collectors we've examined so far.

Fortunately, the concurrent mark-sweep (CMS) collector offers a low-latency alternative to old generation collections. The CMS collector decreases latency by

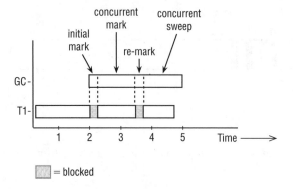

= blocked

Figure 2-12   While application pauses are much smaller, the CMS collector performs more work overall.

eliminating, or significantly reducing, the stop-the-world pauses during collection. As illustrated in Figure 2-12, it performs most of its work in parallel with the application.

The CMS collector only operates on the old generation; the parallel collector performs young generation collections. Like the other collectors, the CMS collector works in phases:

1. *Initial Mark Phase*: during a relatively short (stop-the-world) pause, the set of first-level live objects in the old generation are discovered and marked.

2. *Concurrent Marking Phase*: the collector determines, transitively, the remaining live objects using the set of first-level live objects from the previous phase. This phase is executed in parallel to the application (no pause).

3. *Concurrent Pre-Cleaning*: in this phase, the collector attempts to do some of the work from the next step early, concurrently, to decrease total remark time and associated stop-world pause.

4. *Re-Mark Phase*: since the concurrent marking phase works on the heap in parallel to the running application, references may change during its operation, and live objects can be missed. To remedy this, a relatively small stop-the-world pause allows the collector to quickly sweep the generation again for objects it may have missed. Since the bulk of the work was done during the previous, concurrent, phase, this phase results in only a small pause.

5. *Concurrent Sweep Phase*: the generation is swept, and dead objects are reclaimed (their memory locations are marked as free) concurrently while the application is running. No compaction of free space occurs, which can impact object allocation times if the heap gets fragmented.

Note: In the points above, the pauses are shorter relative to the Java SE parallel collector, but they still do exist. You can force the CMS collector to be used with the following Java SE command-line parameter: -XX:+UseConcMarkSweepGC.

Interestingly, while the CMS collector results in smaller pauses and smaller interruption to the running application, it takes longer to do its job (due in large part to the re-mark phase). This is typically the case with low-pause, low-latency collectors. As a result, these collectors will run more often to ensure that enough free memory is produced for the running application. This is true of the CMS collector, as well. In fact, the CMS collector does not wait for the heap to fill up before executing; it starts earlier to avoid that situation. If it determines it cannot keep up with memory allocation demand, the Java VM will default back to a stop-the-world old generation collector.

A larger heap size is usually required when using the CMS collector to ensure enough free memory is available to the running application. This is because the application is allowed to run concurrently with the CMS collector, and will therefore continue to create additional live and dead objects. And although all truly live objects will be marked as such, some objects will become dead references during the concurrent sweep phase. Since the previous phase marked them as live, they will be missed during this collection, and will instead be reclaimed during the next collection. As a result, dead objects can persist in the heap longer before they are collected. These objects are sometimes referred to as *floating garbage*.

To further reduce application pause times, especially on machines with a small number of processors or cores, the CMS collector can break its work up during the concurrent phases (phase 2 and 4 above) into smaller pieces. These smaller pieces of work are scheduled in between application thread executions, and young generation collections, to help ensure all other threads in the system make progress. This option is called incremental mode, and can be turned on via the command-line parameter, -XX:+CMSIncrementalMode.

To save collection time, the CMS collector does not compact the heap in any way, as all of the other collectors do. This leads to fragmentation, and has the unfortunate side effect of increasing memory allocation time. To understand why, let's briefly examine memory allocation with each of the collectors we've discussed so far.

Memory Allocation

The serial, parallel, and parallel-compacting collectors all use a bump-the-pointer algorithm when allocating memory for objects in the old generation. In fact, any sliding compact and copy-based collector will allow bump-the-pointer allocation.

This works by maintaining a pointer to the first free byte immediately after the most recently allocated object. When a new object is created, the size of the memory region required is calculated, the range of bytes from the first free byte to the offset (calculated using the size of the object being allocated) is assigned to the object, and the pointer to the first free byte is "bumped" to the byte immediately after the new object (see Figure 2-13). Note that the apparent space between objects in this figure is only for effect; in reality, there is no free space in between.

The bump-the-pointer technique applies mostly to the old generation, since for the young generation all of the collectors use thread-local allocation buffers (TLAB). Recall that for the young generation, the Eden space is emptied after each collection (live objects are either moved to the survivor space or the old generation, and dead objects are discarded). As a result, when new objects are allocated, the space is non-fragmented and, naturally, the bump-the-pointer algorithm is used. When objects are moved to the old generation, these objects are compacted towards the left side of the space. As objects die, some objects to the right of them are moved to fill in the gap. Therefore the bump-the-pointer algorithm can be used here also.

To further improve the performance of memory allocation, TLAB are used to avoid locking across multiple threads. For instance, when multiple application threads need to allocate from the Eden space, a global lock would be required to

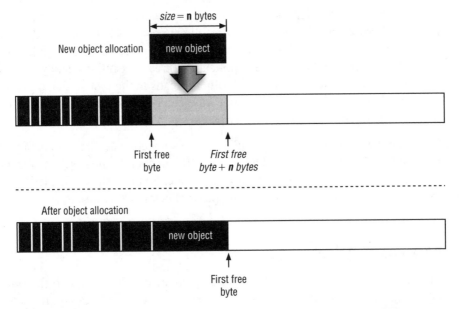

Figure 2-13   Allocating a new object with the "bump-the-pointer" algorithm.

ensure that the first free byte pointer is accessed and modified safely. This would add significant overhead to a commonly executed operation, resulting in a performance penalty. To remedy this, the Java VM creates a TLAB per thread that consists of a small part of the free portion of the heap (see Figure 2-14). Each thread operates within its TLAB privately, without risk of thread contention or the need for locking. When a thread's TLAB fills, it's given a new, empty, TLAB to operate within.

The TLABs are sized, per thread, such that they don't waste too much free memory space. Further, the TLABs are sized according to each thread's allocation rate. The more allocation a thread does, the larger the TLABs will be to avoid the need to create them as often. For threads with slower allocation rates, large TLABs would result in wasted space (as most of the TLAB will remain empty). Therefore, the TLABs for these threads will be sized smaller.

The CMS collector, however, does not use the bump-the-pointer technique. (However, since CMS operates only on the old generation, young generation allocation is not affected, and the bump-the-pointer is indeed used there.) Recall that to avoid pauses, no compaction is done in the old generation. Over time, the result of this is fragmentation of the heap such that only small regions of free memory might exist in between live objects. Since free memory is non-contiguous, a simple bump-the-pointer algorithm cannot be used. Instead, linked lists of free memory regions are maintained and walked to find groups of regions large enough for new object creation requests. Single objects are, therefore, spread across multiple regions of the heap, which requires additional internal accounting.

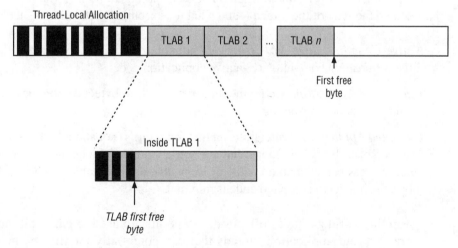

Figure 2-14   TLABs avoid lock contention on concurrent allocations.

To combat fragmentation, the CMS collector assumes future object size demands based on past allocations. It will split or join individual free blocks within the free memory lists to meet those allocation demands. The end result is an overall increase in memory allocation time, at the expense of low-pause garbage collection.

Safepoints

In deep discussions about garbage collection, the term *safepoint* is usually brought up. A safepoint is the means by which the Java VM brings Java code execution to a halt. When a safepoint occurs (more on how in a moment), Java threads are halted and cannot modify the heap or stack, but native threads and Java threads executing native code continue. Safepointing is used within the Java VM for garbage collection, just-in-time (JIT) compilation, code de-optimization and re-optimization, thread interruptions, and the Java VM Tools Interface (JVMTI) for heap dump tools, debuggers, and so on.

Overall, a safepoint equates to a pause in application code, one that occurs voluntarily, ironically enough. Since thread suspension is unreliable or tricky on some platforms, safepoints are implemented via polling at regular intervals. Each Java thread periodically polls a global memory page controlled by the Java VM. When the Java VM deems it necessary, it will activate the safepoint—thereby halting each Java thread not executing native code—by *poisoning* it. It does this by simply placing a lock on an object in the safepoint code that the polling threads synchronize on. When the Java VM-specific operation is complete (i.e., garbage collection), the Java VM unlocks the object within the safepoint code, and all threads resume.

It's important to know how and when threads check for safepoints. Mainly, this is based upon the state of the thread—and what it's executing at the time—such as:

Native Code and Java VM Runtime: safepoint polling is done when these threads transition back into non-native application code.

Interpreted Application Code: the interpreter polls at bytecode boundaries for the thread's code it's running.

Compiled Application Code: polls on method returns (not at method-call time) and loop back-branches (loops that are non-countable). Since most code executes successions of method calls, or loops that are countable (such as a `for` loop), the impact to compiled code is minimal.

For stop-the-world garbage collection, safepoints are used to pause all mutator threads (your application threads that can potentially modify the heap).

For concurrent collectors, safepoints are used to get the heap into a stable state before GC occurs. In the latter case, whether or not the safepoint amounts to a significant pause is dependent upon the GC implementation. For example, the real-time garbage collector (RTGC) within Java RTS uses a type of safepoint, called a *handshake*, which technically doesn't pause application threads, but does require them to execute a small block of code on the RTGC's behalf. When analyzing the thread's runtime behavior, it won't be blocked as seen with stop-world collectors, but instead its execution time will be somewhat extended. This can appear as a pause in processing, as it causes a nominal, but bounded, amount of latency. We'll explore this in more detail in Chapter 10.

The Future: Garbage-First (G1)

Garbage-First is a server-style garbage collector, targeted for multi-processors with large memories, that meets a soft real-time goal with high probability, while achieving high throughput [Detlefs04]. Also known as G1, the garbage-first collector is planned for release with Java SE Version 7, as of this writing.

The G1 collector divides its work into multiple phases, each described below, which operate on a heap broken down into equally sized regions (see Figure 2-15). In the strictest sense, the heap doesn't contain generational areas, although a subset of the regions can be treated as such. This provides flexibility in how garbage collection is performed, which is adjusted on the fly according to the amount of processor time available to the collector.

Regions are further broken down into 512 byte sections called *cards* (see Figure 2-16). Each card has a corresponding one-byte entry in a global card table, which is used to track which cards are modified by mutator threads.

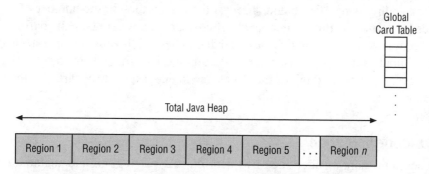

Figure 2-15 With garbage-first, the heap is broken into equally sized regions.

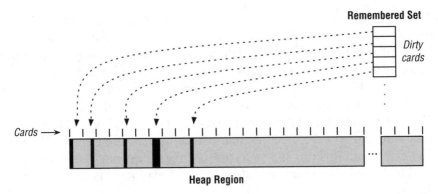

Figure 2-16   Each region has a remembered set of occupied cards.

The G1 collector works in stages. The main stages consist of remembered set (RS) maintenance, concurrent marking, and evacuation pauses. Let's examine these stages now.

RS Maintenance

Each region maintains an associated subset of cards that have recently been written to, called the Remembered Set (RS). Cards are placed in a region's RS via a write barrier, which is an efficient block of code that all mutator threads must execute when modifying an object reference. To be precise, for a particular region (i.e., region *a*), only cards that contain pointers from other regions to an object in region *a* are recorded in region *a*'s RS (see Figure 2-17). A region's internal references, as well as null references, are ignored.

In reality, each region's remembered set is implemented as a group of collections, with the dirty cards distributed amongst them according to the number of references contained within. Three levels of coarseness are maintained: sparse, fine, and coarse. It's broken up this way so that parallel GC threads can operate on one RS without contention, and can target the regions that will yield the most garbage. However, it's best to think of the RS as one logical set of dirty cards, as the diagrams show.

Concurrent Marking

Concurrent marking identifies live data objects per region, and maintains the pointer to the next free byte, called *top*. There are, however, small stop-the-world pauses (described further below) that occur to ensure the correct heap state. A

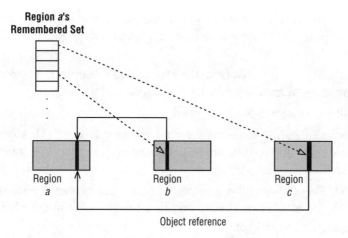

Figure 2-17 A region's RS records live references from outside the region.

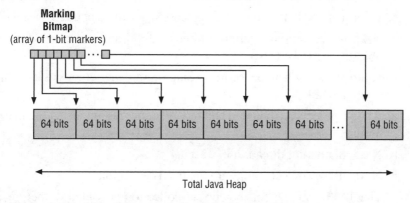

Figure 2-18 Live objects are indicated with a marking bitmap.

marking bitmap is maintained to create a summary view of the live objects within the heap. Each bit in the bitmap corresponds to one word within the heap (an area large enough to contain an object pointer—see Figure 2-18). A bit in the bitmap is set when the object it represents is determined to be a live object. As with the TAMS pointer, there are actually two bitmaps: one for the current collection, and a second for the previously completed collection.

Marking is done in three stages:

1. *Marking Stage*—the heap regions are traversed and live objects are marked:

    a. First, since this is the beginning of a new collection, the current marking bitmap is copied to the previous marking bitmap, and then the current marking bitmap is cleared.

b. Next, all mutator threads are paused while the current TAMS pointer is moved to point to the same byte in the region as the *top* (next free byte) pointer.

c. Next, all objects are traced from their roots, and live objects are marked in the marking bitmap. We now have a snapshot of the heap.

d. Next, all mutator threads are resumed.

e. Next, a write buffer is inserted for all mutator threads. This barrier records all new object allocations that take place after the snapshot into change buffers.

2. *Re-Marking Stage*—when the heap reaches a certain percentage filled, as indicated by the number of allocations since the snapshot in the Marking Stage, the heap is re-marked:

a. As buffers of changed objects fill up, the contained objects are marked in the marking bitmap concurrently.

b. When all filled buffers have been processed, the mutator threads are paused.

c. Next, the remaining (partially filled buffers) are processed, and those objects are marked also.

3. *Cleanup Stage*—when the Re-Mark Stage completes, counts of live objects are maintained:

a. All live objects are counted and recorded, per region, using the marking bitmap.

b. Next, all mutator threads are paused.

c. Next, all live-object counts are finalized per region.

d. The TAMS pointer for the current collection is copied to the previous TAMS pointer (since the current collection is basically complete).

e. The heap regions are sorted for collection priority according to a cost algorithm. As a result, the regions that will yield the highest numbers of reclaimed objects, at the smallest cost in terms of time, will be collected first. This forms what is called a collection set of regions.

f. All mutator threads are resumed.

All of this work is done so that objects that are in the collection set are reclaimed as part of the evacuation process. Let's examine this process now.

Evacuation and Collection

This step is what it's all about—reclaiming dead objects and shaping the heap for efficient object allocation. The collection set of regions (from the Concurrent Marking process defined above) forms a subset of the heap that is used during this process. When evacuation begins, all mutator threads are paused, and objects are moved from their respective regions and compacted (moved together) into other regions. Although other garbage collectors might perform compaction concurrently with mutator threads, it's far more efficient to pause them. Since this operation is only performed on a portion of the heap—it compacts only the collection set of regions—it's a relatively quick operation.

To help limit the total pause time, much of the evacuation is done in parallel with multiple GC threads. The strategy for parallelization involves the following techniques:

GC TLABS: the use of thread local allocation buffers for the GC threads eliminates memory-related contention amongst the GC threads. Forwarding pointers are inserted in the GC TLABs for evacuated live objects.

Work Competition: GC threads compete to perform any of a number of GC-related tasks, such as maintaining remembered sets, root object scanning to determine reachability (dead objects are ignored), and evacuating live objects.

Work Stealing: part of mathematical systems theory, the work done by the GC threads is unsynchronized and executed arbitrarily by all of the threads simultaneously. This chaos-based algorithm equates to a group of threads that race to complete the list of GC-related tasks as quickly as they can without regard to one another. The end result, despite the chaos, is a properly collected group of heap regions.

Note: The CMS and parallel collectors, described earlier, also use work competition and work stealing techniques to achieve greater efficiency.

Garbage-First Tuning

Much of the G1 processing can be controlled by optional command-line parameters, such as indicating how regions are used for young generations, the use of popular object regions, the heuristics for collection set determination, thresholds used for choosing regions to collect, and the timeframes within which the collector should limit its operation, and pauses.

Although the G1 collector is successful at limiting total pause time, it's still only a soft real-time collector. In other words, it cannot guarantee that it will not impact the mutator threads ability to meet its deadlines, all of the time. However, it can operate within a well-defined set of bounds that make it ideal for soft real-time systems that need to maintain high-throughput performance. Let's look now at other GC algorithms that can meet hard real-time requirements.

Real-Time GC Algorithms

Recall that real-time is about determinism and predictability, and knowing that your code will meet its deadlines. As such, a real-time garbage collector is not about fast GC, but is instead about low-latency, predictable GC interruptions (if any), and ensuring that GC activity doesn't cause your system to miss its deadlines. As described above, many low-latency, zero-pause garbage collectors actually take longer to do their work, and start running sooner in the GC cycle. Of course, the specifics vary with the algorithms used, and there are a few approaches. In this section we'll examine the most common real-time garbage collection (RTGC) approaches, how they work, and how they impact a running Java application.

Work-Based GC

The first RTGC algorithm we'll examine is a work-based one. In this approach, each application thread pays part of the GC cost up front, during object allocation. In other words, some collection work is done at the time an application creates a new object. To begin to understand this, let's examine three application threads running in a real-time system with one processor. In this example, shown in Figure 2-19, there is no object allocation, and hence no garbage collection work to be done.

Here we have three threads (T1, T2, and T3) where T3 has the highest priority, T2 the next highest, and T1 the lowest of the three. Even though both T1 and T3 are eligible to run at time 0, T3 executes first and completely because of its priority, and it finishes just before its deadline. This frees T1 to execute at time 1.4, but it's

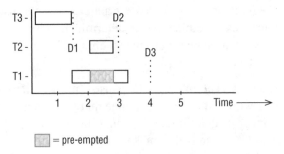

Figure 2-19   Three time-critical threads running on a uniprocessor, real-time system.

soon preempted by T2 because it has a higher priority. T2 finishes before its deadline, and T1 resumes, which finishes its work well before its deadline as well. All threads in this system complete on time.

Let's say that thread T3 is modified, and it allocates an object when it begins. With work-based GC, each thread that creates an object must pay some of the cost of GC work up front. For most work-based GC implementations, this cost is predictable; it doesn't vary much—if any—from allocation to allocation. Because of this, it's relatively easy to implement, and usually there's no issue with the collector keeping up with the demand for free memory. Also, only the threads that allocate memory (and hence create the need for collection to occur) pay the cost of GC. This seems fair, but this can still have a ripple effect throughout a real-time system. We'll examine this in a moment.

First, let's discuss some of drawbacks of this approach. First, the real-time developer must account for GC cost payment with every allocation performed. This is, generally, not something you should burden the Java developer with. Next, the GC cost, while mostly constant, can vary and must be tuned via a configuration parameter to ensure that the collector can keep up. This means that the GC cost isn't entirely predictable. And, as mentioned above, while only threads that allocate memory pay the GC cost, this can affect the entire system. Let's revisit the previous example, where T3 now allocates memory, and hence pays a small GC cost with added execution time (see Figure 2-20).

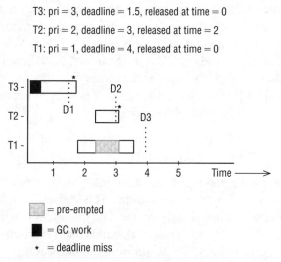

Figure 2-20 Thread T3 now pays part of the GC cost up front. T3 and T2 miss deadlines as a result.

As a result of the GC cost paid by only T3 in this example, both T3 and T2 miss their deadlines. Ironically T1, the thread with the lowest priority, still meets its deadline. Clearly, if the goal is to ensure that garbage collection doesn't cause pauses that interfere with a thread's ability to complete on time, the work-based GC algorithm can fail in some cases. In fact, it's hard to determine all of the cases where it will and will not cause deadline misses, because GC costs may vary, and the interaction amongst threads and memory allocation can change over time. You may determine that an alternative RTGC algorithm be found.

Time-Based GC

Another RTGC algorithm that can be considered is a time-based one. In this case, the garbage collector runs at precise time intervals, for a predetermined length of time. The GC operates at an arbitrary priority with many regular, stop-the-world pauses. In that way, although it may not be running at higher priority than any application threads, it still interrupts them at regular intervals. As a result, you get deterministic garbage collection for the life of the application. Also, since the GC work is spread across each period, the amount of work performed can be made to be small. Therefore, you avoid long pauses and interruptions, and you gain predictability.

So far, the time-based RTGC algorithm sounds very appealing, but there are downsides. For instance, GC work is performed in every period, and affects every application thread regardless of how critical each thread's execution is. Also, there's no guarantee that the collector will be able to keep up with free memory demand. If an event occurs in the system that creates an increased demand for memory over a period of time, the heap may become completely filled. Also, the periodic nature of the high-priority thread the GC runs in limits the deadline magnitudes of application threads, as well as the smallest latencies that the system can achieve. This may not be acceptable if you have a deadline or latency requirement that is smaller in magnitude than the period of the garbage collector.

Looking at our previous example with three real-time threads, adding a periodic GC thread has some sweeping affects (see Figure 2-21).

Here, the GC work is done at the beginning of each time interval. As a result, T3 begins, is interrupted at time 1, and misses its deadline. This causes T1 to start late, only to be interrupted almost immediately by the GC thread. When T1 is about to resume, it's interrupted by T2 (higher priority), which itself is interrupted by the GC thread at time 3. At that point, T2 is almost complete, but misses its deadline. Afterward, T1 resumes, is interrupted again by the GC thread at time 3, and misses its deadline.

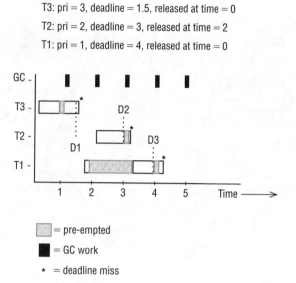

T3: pri = 3, deadline = 1.5, released at time = 0
T2: pri = 2, deadline = 3, released at time = 2
T1: pri = 1, deadline = 4, released at time = 0

= pre-empted

= GC work

* = deadline miss

Figure 2-21   All three threads are affected by the periodic high-priority GC work.

Henriksson's GC

Dr. Roger Henriksson, in his PhD thesis from 1998 [Henriksson98], outlined similar problems with both work-based and time-based garbage collectors in a hard real-time computing environment. His observation was that many real-time systems, including controllers with hard real-time constraints, have a few high-priority threads, but many low-priority threads as well. In effect, these systems act as two in one, a real-time subsystem with a general-purpose subsystem as well. His proposal is for a collector that takes on a dual personality to operate differently in respect to these two subsystems.

What Henriksson proposes is a collector that runs at a lower priority than the higher-priority real-time threads, but at higher-priority than the general-purpose, lower-priority threads that make up the rest of the system. The result is a system where all GC-related work is deferred while the high-priority threads are running. Then, immediately after these threads finish, the GC performs work motivated by their execution. Additionally, while the lower-priority threads are running, the GC acts like a work-based collector. In effect, the collector has two personalities (see Figure 2-22).

There is still only one collector in the system, executing in its own threads. It merely behaves differently when different threads are running, dictated strictly by priority. As seen in Figure 2-23, to the higher-priority threads, the GC appears non-existent: there is no interruption from the GC, nor will GC impose any

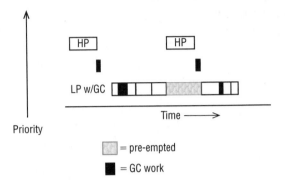

Figure 2-22   High-priority threads are unaffected by GC, while low-priority threads bear the GC burden.

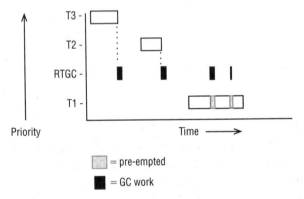

Figure 2-23   The RTGC runs as its own task, but affects threads of differing priorities in different ways.

noticeable latency when a high-priority thread is scheduled to run. To lower-priority threads, however, the GC appears as an incremental, work-based, collector that imposes small, but bounded, pauses. As such, Henriksson describes this approach as a semi-concurrent collector.

Of course, there's more to Henriksson's RTGC than just priority control. The algorithm is based on the work of Rodney Brooks, in his paper that describes a technique to trade memory space for overall system responsiveness [Brooks84]. Let's examine the internals of Henriksson's RTGC now.

Heap Spaces

With this algorithm, the heap is broken into two main sections, the *fromSpace* and the *toSpace*. Similar to other algorithms described earlier in this chapter, objects are allocated in one space (the toSpace) and evacuated from the other (the fromSpace). To avoid contention, objects are evacuated to the left side of the toSpace towards the right, while new objects are allocated from the right side towards the left (see Figure 2-24). The spaces are sized (and grown) such that there is enough free space in between to ensure that neither interferes with the other.

After all objects are evacuated, and the toSpace runs low on free memory, the spaces swap roles and the GC process starts all over again. This is called a *flip*, which is a bounded, atomic operation that involves simply renaming the spaces.

Note that only live objects are evacuated and moved into toSpace. Dead objects are simply abandoned, effectively reclaiming the memory they occupied. Evacuation begins at the roots and proceeds until all live root objects are evacuated. Next, the root objects are recursively traced and all live child objects are evacuated. The scan pointer, which begins with the very first evacuated root object on the left of toSpace, is used to track progress. As each root object is recursively scanned, the scan pointer is bumped to the next root object (to the right).

A tri-color scheme, described earlier in the chapter, is used to track progress: "white" denotes an object that has not yet been checked for liveness (reachability); "grey" denotes an object that is live, but whose children have not yet been scanned; "black" denotes an object that is live, and whose children have all been scanned. When all live objects are marked as "black," and the scan pointer points to the top of the evacuated objects, the evacuation phase is complete.

Read Barrier (Pointer Indirection)

The goal of the Henriksson real-time collector is to work concurrently with other threads, and impose no pauses or latencies on high-priority threads. This means that the GC can be interrupted any time, and it must be careful to not leave the heap in an inconsistent state. This is most critical when evacuating objects, which

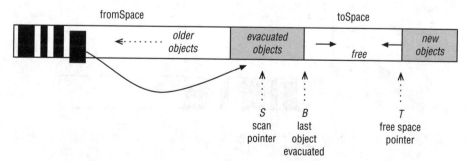

Figure 2-24   Old objects are moved, and new objects are allocated, into toSpace.

effectively moves them (and any referencing pointers) to a different area of the heap. Two strategies are implemented to help with this.

First, objects are copied *completely* to toSpace before any referencing pointers are updated to point to it. Since copying memory is not an atomic operation, a high-priority thread can interrupt it before it's complete. The risk is that a mutator thread may have updated the original copy of the object before the collector can resume the copy from where it left off. To resolve this, a write barrier can be used to mark the object, or track changes to it, but this would result in a slight performance penalty that can add up and cause deadline misses. Instead, in this situation Henriksson chose to abandon an object copy entirely if a context switch occurs in the middle of it. When the collector resumes, it will repeat the object evacuation all over again. This strategy has two positive effects: first, high-priority threads remain unencumbered throughout the evacuation process (i.e., no write barriers); second, each time the GC runs, at most one object evacuation can potentially be abandoned.

The second strategy to help with heap consistency is the use of forwarding pointers. When an object is evacuated, all referring pointers to the object throughout the heap need to be updated. Since this can be an unbounded, time-consuming task (depending upon the number of pointers to update), the problem is alleviated through the use of a forwarding pointer. Throughout the heap, each pointer to an object is actually a pointer to a pointer to the object. There are different ways to implement this strategy; one is to use a global index table of pointers, as shown in Figure 2-25. This requires yet another region of the heap to be maintained and sized accordingly.

Henriksson chose the Brooks forwarding pointer technique because it's more efficient. With this technique, you include a forwarding pointer as part of the object

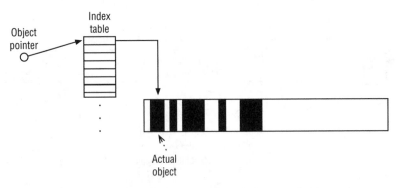

Figure 2-25   An index table stores pointers to the actual objects.

itself (see Figure 2-26). Since each object already contains header information to track its GC status and other information, the forwarding pointer is added here.

When an object is evacuated, the forwarding pointer is changed to point to the new position of the object. In the actual object, the forwarding pointer merely points to itself. The result is that when all pointers to this object throughout the heap are dereferenced, they will yield the actual object's address. A small write barrier (for object updates) is implemented to check for and update the references to the old object in fromSpace to the new copy in toSpace.

Memory Allocation and Reserved Memory

To help the collector determine which portions of the heap are free, and which portions contain live objects, free memory is initialized with a special bit pattern when allocated. This is done to ensure that the collector doesn't confuse free portions of the heap as live objects (whose data may still be contained at the old memory addresses until overwritten). This takes time, and since the goal is to have GC-related activity affect high-priority threads as little as possible, this is not acceptable. To avoid this unbounded, time-consuming initialization task, a certain amount of memory in the free portion of the heap is pre-initialized for high-priority thread memory allocations (labeled as M_{HP} in Figure 2-27).

When high-priority threads create objects, the space is taken from the M_{HP} section. Since the memory is pre-initialized, the only work required is to move the top-of-free-space pointer (the T pointer in Figure 2-27) left by the size of the object being created. The result is a consistently small amount of processing for each new object, regardless of size. However, the position of P is left alone, effectively shrinking the size of M_{HP}. Although there is a risk that subsequent

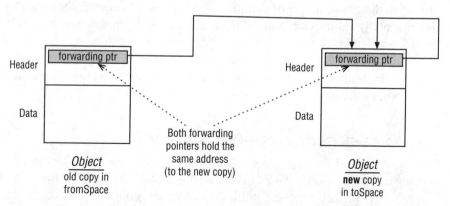

Figure 2-26 Old objects are moved, and new objects are allocated, into toSpace.

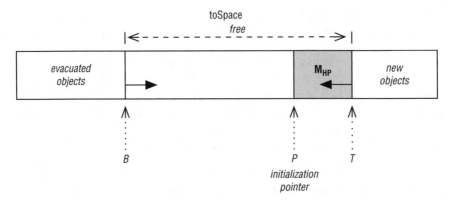

Figure 2-27   A section of free space is pre-initialized and ready for high-priority tasks.

high-priority thread memory allocations can exhaust M_{HP}, effort is made to ensure this section is large enough to avoid this before the GC has chance to run again.

The work required to initialize the M_{HP} section is performed when all high-priority threads are suspended (not running), and when lower-priority threads allocate memory. The goal is to keep the M_{HP} section at a certain size, which is adjusted at runtime by measuring high-priority thread memory allocation heuristics. To achieve this, lower-priority threads are charged with the GC-related activity of pre-initializing an additional part of the free heap for each allocation they make. The amount of memory pre-initialized is always equal to the amount of memory the low-priority threads allocate. In effect, the M_{HP} section is simply shifted to the left for each allocation made by low-priority threads (see Figure 2-28). This work is done via a low-priority thread write barrier at allocation time.

To aid in the pre-initialize of memory after a flip has occurred, the collector will incrementally initialize a portion of the free heap in fromSpace as part of the object evacuation phase. This leaves the fromSpace with an M_{HP} section ready when the next flip occurs. Since this is done as part of the GC work performed when no high-priority threads are running, there is no impact to the real-time portion of the system.

GC Work Deferred by High-Priority Threads

As soon as all high-priority threads are idle, the Henriksson collector enters the high-priority GC phase. At this point, all lower-priority mutator threads are further blocked until this phase is complete. Tasks performed include the pre-initialization of the high-priority thread memory section, M_{HP}, and

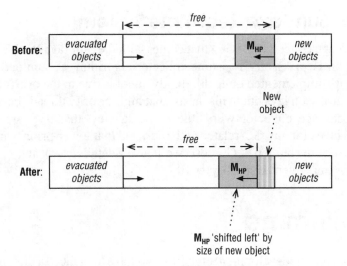

Figure 2-28   Low-priority threads are charged with pre-initializing the M_{HP} section.

the evacuation of remaining objects in fromSpace. When these tasks are complete, the collector will suspend itself and allow lower-priority mutator threads to execute. Of course, at any point during this processing, a high-priority thread may be released and interrupt this GC phase.

GC Work for Low-Priority Threads

GC activity performed for lower-priority threads includes pre-initialization of the M_{HP} section, as described above, as well as the work done through read and write barriers. Some of this processing has already been described. However, for completeness, the low-priority GC-related work performed at these barriers includes:

Allocation: an amount of GC work is performed at allocation time, proportional to the amount of allocation work being requested. You can consider this a GC tax; the more the allocation a thread performs, the more the tax (in terms of GC activity) it's required to pay.

Pointer Assignments: when a pointer is assigned a new value, a check is made to see if the object being pointed to needs to be evacuated. If so, the object is evacuated before the pointer assignment returns.

Pointer Access: when memory is accessed, the forwarding pointer must be dereferenced to arrive at the actual object memory address.

RTGC in the Sun Java Real-Time System

The real-time garbage collector (RTGC) that comes with the Sun Java Real-Time System is based on Henriksson's real-time collector algorithm, as summarized above. Although it's implemented quite differently, it holds true to the overriding principles that Henriksson lays out in his thesis: that high-priority threads be able to interrupt the garbage collector with little or no latency, that they are not interrupted themselves for any GC-related activities, and that lower-priority non-real-time threads bear the burden of GC cost. We'll take a detailed look at how the Java RTS RTGC is implemented in Chapter 10.

The Java Dilemma

For real-time applications, development organizations have long faced a dilemma: use a mainstream programming language such as Java, or some other specialized language (and environment) for real-time development. On the mainstream side, Java is an environment that offers a large development community, lots of resources and tools, and a proven track record. It's also non-deterministic, and introduces an unbounded amount of risk in applications that need time-based guarantees.

On the flip side, specialized real-time environments are often complex, have a smaller development community, fewer resources and tools, and don't integrate well with existing applications. However, they're also deterministic and predictable, ensuring that real-time requirements will be met.

On the surface, it seems like a straightforward decision: use a specialized environment that supports real-time development. However, that environment is typically much more expensive than the mainstream choices. As is often the case, the cost may factor more into the equation than any other variables. So what's the solution?

The ideal solution is an open standards-based platform that formally deals with real-time challenges using a mainstream programming language. You can find one such solution with the Real-Time Specification for Java; namely, the Java Real-Time System from Sun, which implements it. The next chapter will provide an overview of the RTSJ, and prepare for our dive into real-time Java application development.

3

The Real-Time Specification for Java

"Everything happens to everyone sooner or later, if there is time enough."
—George Bernard Shaw

THE Real-Time Specification for Java (RTSJ) defines how Java should behave in a real-time computing context. In fact, the RTSJ was the first Java Specification Request (JSR), and a reason the Java Community Process (JCP) was formed. The specification, led by Greg Bollella, included experts from around the globe, from academia and industry, and is known today as a standard for real-time Java development.

The first published version of the RTSJ was version 0.9, released in 2000. However, this version wasn't meant to be used in the construction of a real-time Java VM, but instead was to be used for further discussion on the specification. As intended, the early specification launched much discussion and work that resulted in the first official version of the RTSJ, version 1.0.1, which was finalized by the Java Community Process in 2005. Version 1.0.2 of the RTSJ was created to clarify some points mainly around threads and events.

To gain access to the latest specification, information about the RTSJ, reference implementations, and other RTSJ-related information, you can visit http://www.rtsj.org. Let's take a look now at the RTSJ, and the issues it addresses, in some more detail.

A Foundation for Real-Time Java

The Real-Time Specification for Java (RTSJ), also known by its Java Specification Request (JSR) number, JSR-001, was formalized in June 2000. The RTSJ approaches the problem of writing real-time code from a different direction than other available software development platforms, such as a typical real-time operating system (RTOS) application-programming interface (API) might. The RTSJ embraces the notion of real-time scheduling theory—introduced in Chapter 1—as a fundamental principle for the development of applications that have temporal correctness requirements. In a sentence, the RTSJ defines how Java should behave in a real-time environment. Its overriding guiding principal is to enhance your ability to write portable, real-time, Java code. However, the RTSJ's complete set of guiding principals include:

Java Environment Agnostic: the RTSJ shall not preclude its implementation in any known Java environment or version of the development kit, such as the Java SE or Java ME platforms. Instead, the goal is for it to allow general-purpose Java implementations for use in server and/or embedded environments.

Predictability: predictable Java application execution shall be the primary concern, with tradeoffs in the area of general purpose computing being made where necessary.

Compatibility: existing Java application code shall run properly on an implementation of the RTSJ.

Java Syntax: there shall be no additions or changes in terms of Java language keywords or syntax.

WORA: the RTSJ respects the importance of the write-once-run-anywhere (WORA) mantra for Java, but shall favor predictability over WORA where necessary.

Consideration for Current and Future Work: although the RTSJ addresses current real-time systems practice, provisions are made to allow it to be extended for future work in this area.

Flexible Implementation: the RTSJ shall allow for flexibility in decisions on implementation. Such decisions include performance/footprint tradeoffs, the choice of scheduling algorithms, and so on.

The National Institute of Standards and Technology (NIST) worked in parallel to the RTSJ expert group (and included many of its members) to outline a list of real-time extensions for Java. The resulting document, *Requirements for Real-Time Extensions for the Java Platform*, outlines the following capabilities that must be supported by the real-time Java extensions [Carnahan99]:

- Support for fixed-priority, round-robin scheduling.
- Mutual exclusion locking with some form of priority inversion avoidance protocol implementation.
- Real-time friendly inter-task synchronization.
- The ability to write interrupt handlers and device drivers in Java.
- The ability to associate a segment of Java code with a hardware interrupt.
- The ability to abort a running task due to a timeout or other condition.

Additionally, to support these capabilities, a list of nine core requirements were defined:

Profile Lookup and Discovery: the ability to define profiles of operation (i.e., low-latency, high-availability, safety-critical, and so on), discover them, and enumerate them at runtime. Note that profiles are not required or specified in the RTSJ, nor are they implemented in any way in Java RTS.

Garbage Collection with Bounded Latency: the inclusion of a real-time-enabled garbage collector, where automatic memory management is required. In cases where automatic memory is not required, or desired, the ability to work without the use of dynamic memory management must be supported. Note that garbage collection is not required nor specified in the RTSJ.

Real-Time Thread Relationships: definition of the relationships amongst real-time threads, and the rest of the system, such as scheduling, dispatch-queue ordering, and priority inversion control.

Synchronization: the ability to support communication and synchronization between Java and non-Java tasks and objects.

Asynchronous Event Handling: the ability to execute Java code in response to external events.

Asynchronous Termination: the ability to terminate a thread safely through some form of communication. The implementation must respect a thread's unwillingness to terminate, the need to maintain data integrity, and the need to ensure that all locks held by a terminating thread are released, where applicable.

Mutual Exclusion with Priority Inversion Avoidance: mutexes should allow real-time threads to control execution, and ensure that a non-real-time thread does not block other high-priority threads from executing.

Real-Time Knowledge: an application should be able to query its thread type to determine if it is real-time, or non-real-time.

Real-Time and Non-Real-Time Relationships: real-time threads and non-real-time threads shall be able to communicate and share data through well-defined means.

Finally, the NIST real-time extensions outline a set of goals that should be addressed by a real-time Java design. In summary, these goals are:

- Flexibility in the degree of real-time support, and associated resource management. For instance, the need to control resource locking to avoid priority inversion, or support for soft real-time versus hard real-time application requirements.
- RTJ support should be possible on any Java Language Specification (JLS)-compliant Java platform. Although the quantities are relative, this includes:
  - Small and large memory constraints, fast and slow processors, single and multiple processor systems, and so on.
  - Systems that are small or large, simple or complex.
  - Standard subsets of implementation to support these requirements.
- Code portability shall be maintained regardless of platform. Portability is defined as having the following qualities:
  - Minimal or no human intervention required for new hardware or software library support.
  - Abstract OS and hardware dependencies.
  - Support standard Java semantics.
  - Should enable the use of existing development tools and libraries.
  - RTJ requirements shall be well defined and guaranteed on all language features.
- Single workloads (applications) must support both real-time and non-real-time tasks.
- Support for separation of concerns at the programming level.
- Support for automated resource requirements analysis either offline or at runtime. This is meant to support both offline (before application execution) and dynamic real-time schedulers.
- Real-time constraints can be specified within application code.

- Support for resource budgets and reservations for CPU time, memory allocation rate, and total memory usage. This should include support for the following:
  - Priority-based scheduling, queuing, and lock contention.
  - Priority inheritance protocols.
  - Dynamic priority changes.
  - Optional deadline-based scheduling.
  - Resource availability queries with asynchronous access.
  - Guaranteed allocation rates.
- Support for components as black boxes. This includes:
  - Dynamic loading of component code.
  - Component-critical section code should be locally analyzable.
  - The ability to enforce space/time limits.
  - Existing Java features and keywords, such as `synchronize`, `wait`, and `notify`, should work as expected.
- A real-time garbage collector must be provided with GC-related statistics made available to the application, such as:
  - GC progress rate must be queryable and configurable.
  - GC overhead must be quantified.
- Support for straightforward integration of external software and hardware components.
- Support usage of RTJ-based components from other languages.
- Support for operating systems that support real-time behavior.

Although this overall list of goals is complete, some of the derived requirements have been left off for brevity. The important information to glean from the NIST requirements and goals is its influence on the RTSJ, which we will continue looking at in detail in the rest of this chapter. Although not all of these requirements are in the RTSJ, we thought it was useful to list them and point out that these requirements did influence the RTSJ design.

Inside the RTSJ

The RTSJ was designed and written by individuals representing both academia and industry, who possess expertise in the areas of real-time scheduling theory, language design, embedded systems design, RTOS development, and other related areas. With the mandate to not change the Java language syntax, the RTSJ outlines seven areas of enhancements for real-time application development with Java. These include the following [Bollella00]:

Thread Scheduling: the specification requires a real-time scheduler implementation, but does not specify the algorithm to be used, and further allows for algorithms to be plugged in at a later time. The required default base scheduler must be priority-based, with at least 28 unique priorities. (Note: an RTSJ-compliant real-time Java VM implementation need not contain its own scheduler, but can rely on the OS scheduler entirely so long as it meets the RTSJ scheduling requirements.)

Memory Management: the RTSJ is independent of any GC algorithm, and does not state any requirements for it. Instead, the specification provides deterministic memory management functions through its definition of new memory areas, and specifies that the collector should not interfere with them.

Resource Sharing: priority inversion control must be implemented via a priority inheritance protocol through the `synchronized` keyword, and a set of wait-free queues.

Asynchronous Event Handling: in order to interact with asynchronous events from the outside world, the RTSJ specifies the need to support the execution of code based on these external events. The execution of this code is scheduled and dispatched by the real-time scheduler.

Asynchronous Transfer of Control: the Java exception handler is to be extended to allow for the immediate shift in execution from location to another in a real-time thread's code.

Asynchronous Thread Termination: again due to external events, a real-time thread may need to terminate, or be terminated, efficiently and quickly. The RTSJ specifies a safe method for thread termination.

Physical Memory Access: allowing byte-level access and object creation in physical memory can help developers in their need to communicate with hardware devices with as little latency as possible.

Note that all RTSJ implementations and extensions shall be within the `javax.realtime` Java package. The rest of this chapter will look at each of these seven areas in more detail, how the package affects Java application development, and existing Java code.

Scheduling

The RTSJ proposes a new system model for the development and deployment of Java applications that have real-time requirements. Understanding this system model is the first step toward understanding the scheduling framework in the RTSJ. The second fundamental construct you need to understand is that the RTSJ abstracts the unit of schedulability beyond the `java.lang.Thread`. In the RTSJ, entities that are scheduled are instances of the Java interface, `Schedulable`, which itself extends `Runnable`.

The RTSJ abstracts the unit of schedulability in this way to allow the application to imbue these schedulable objects with values that characterize their expected behavior and determined requirements with respect to time. But more importantly, this abstraction allows more than just threads to come under the control of the scheduler. For example, event handlers in the RTSJ no longer just execute whenever convenient; they execute under the control of the real-time-enabled scheduler. Thus, in the RTSJ, event handlers are a schedulable entity rather than being, as in a typical RTOS, completely unscheduled. Once an application creates its initial set of `Schedulable` objects with the appropriate characteristics, the application may put those into what we call the *feasibility* set.

All RTSJ implementations must include four class definitions that implement `Schedulable`:`RealtimeThread`(RTT),`NoHeapRealtimeThread`(NHRT), `Async-EventHandler` (AEH), and `BoundAsyncEventHandler` (BAEH)—see Figure 3-1 for the class hierarchy. Instances of these four `Schedulable objects` are visible to and managed by the scheduler. The abstract class, `Scheduler`, represents the real-time scheduler implementation itself. Application logic interacts with the scheduler via methods on one of the concrete subclasses of `Scheduler`.

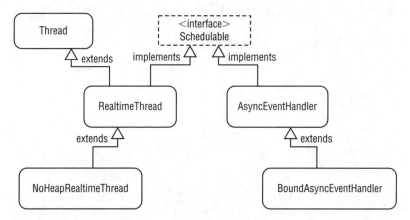

Figure 3-1   The class diagram of `Schedulable` objects.

Memory Management

The RTSJ designers recognized that automatic memory management (garbage collection) is a particularly important feature of the Java programming environment. Therefore, they sought a direction that would allow, as much as possible, for the job of garbage collection to not intrude on the programming task. Additionally, they understood that multiple garbage collection algorithms exist, and therefore chose not to discuss or even require one in particular. We'll examine this in more detail in the section below, *The Heap*.

The RTSJ defines a total of four memory regions: the standard Java heap, scoped memory, immortal memory, and physical memory. These regions are represented by Java classes, each of which extends the `MemoryArea` abstract base class (see Figure 3-2).

The classes, `HeapMemory`, `ScopedMemory`, `ImmortalMemory`, and `ImmortalPhysicalMemory` each represent their respective memory regions, and are described in the next four sections.

The Heap

The heap represents the area of free memory used for the dynamic allocation and automatic reclamation of Java objects, and is referenced by the singleton Java object, `HeapMemory`. In the RTSJ, the heap remains the same as is defined in standard Java. And, for the most part, the same rules apply. For instance, the rules

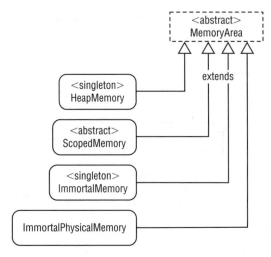

Figure 3-2   The class diagram of `MemoryArea` objects.

governing the lifetimes of objects remain the same, garbage collection still occurs on the heap, and Java applications have very little control over this programmatically.

It's important to realize that the RTSJ does not specify or endorse any garbage collection algorithm, and further, it doesn't even state the need for a garbage collector. However, for implementations that do include a garbage collector, the RTSJ defines the need for a garbage collector that gives developers the ability to reason about its effect on the execution time, preemption, and dispatching of real-time threads. This adds predictability to both the collection and allocation of objects on the heap, above and beyond what's offered in Java SE.

Scoped Memory

The first new concept for memory management that the RTSJ introduces is that of *scoped memory*. This is a region of memory, represented by an object of the ScopedMemory class or one of its subclasses (see Figure 3-3), which you create and size at development time. You can specify parameters, such as the scope's initial size, the maximum size it can grow to, and, optionally, the Runnable object that will execute within that scope.

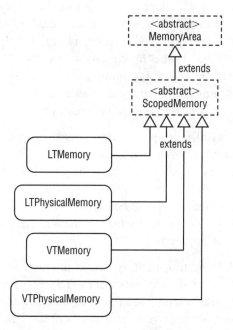

Figure 3-3 The class diagram of ScopedMemory objects.

Each thread has associated with it an allocation context, or simply a region of memory (such as the heap, scoped memory or immortal memory) where object creation takes place. A `Schedulable` will begin executing within a scoped memory region when one of the scope's `enter` methods is called, or when the `Schedulable` is created using the `ScopedMemory` object as a parameter. Once this happens, all memory allocated and objects created (via the keyword `new`) will be from inside this scoped memory region.

Scoped memory differs from the heap in that it's not garbage collected; instead, it uses a form of reference counting to discard the full contents of the scope at once. For instance, the conceptual reference count of the scope is incremented with each call to `enter`, or related methods. In turn, the reference count is decremented with each `Schedulable` that terminates its execution, (or as each call to `enter` returns) and hence exits the scope. At this point, although no garbage collection occurs on the scope, the finalize method for each object within it is called, and the scope is marked for reuse. This operation is concurrent, quick, efficient, and bounded in terms of time.

Immortal Memory

Immortal memory is a special, global region that's created when the real-time Java VM starts up. In the RTSJ, there is only one immortal memory region, and objects created within it live for the life of the Java VM; hence the name immortal. Objects within immortal memory can be referenced from anywhere, and can reference objects that reside anywhere except within a scoped memory region. Likewise, immortal memory is accessible from `java.lang.Threads`, as well as the RTSJ's `Schedulable` objects (such as `RealtimeThread` and `NoHeapRealTimeThread`). The creation and usage of objects in immortal memory are never subject to garbage collection delays, as these objects are never collected or reclaimed.

`Schedulable` objects can enter immortal memory as they do scoped memory regions (via a call to `enter`) since `ImmortalMemory` also extends `MemoryArea`. In this case, the immortal memory region is accessible through the global singleton object, `ImmortalMemory` (and the associated `ImmortalPhysicalMemory` which we will discuss in the next section). `Schedulable` objects can also be created to begin execution in immortal memory via a constructor parameter. This is an important point that we will explore in Chapter 5.

By default, all static data resides in immortal memory, as do interned `String` objects, and static initializers execute there. This is important to remember, since immortal memory is a limited, non-garbage-collected resource that can quickly run out if you declare variables and classes as `static`, and often use static initialization blocks within your code.

Physical Memory

The three classes that allow objects to be created within a specified range of physical memory are LTPhysicalMemory, VTPhysicalMemory, and ImmortalPhysicalMemory. Each of these memory areas takes, as constructors, parameters that specify the base physical memory address of the region, its size, and object type. This object type is a value from the supported set of physical memory object types supported by the RTSJ implementation. However, in many cases, it will be used to denote the region's usage, such as direct memory access (DMA), a shared memory region (with an external application), IO-related objects that need to be aligned in special ways, and so on.

It's anticipated that most real-time Java developers *won't* need physical memory object allocation. However, there are many cases where real-time applications need to communicate with the outside world via specialized hardware, or with low latency. Examples are flight control, industrial automation, robotics, automotive, and so on. In these cases, the RTSJ's support for physical memory access and object creation can be critical. It also allows for the lowest latency possible for network communications, as the RTSJ application can access the actual network interface card (NIC) buffer for incoming and outgoing network packets. With support for physical memory access, the RTSJ allows you to build low-level device drivers in Java.

Resource Sharing

Synchronizing access to resources amongst multiple application threads is a common issue in programming, but becomes more critical in the real-time space. This is because resource locking can affect thread prioritization, and induce unbounded latency in critical operations if not controlled properly. At the base level, the RTSJ specifies the use of wait queues for synchronization blocks that follow these rules:

1. Blocked threads ready to run are given access to synchronized resources in priority order.
2. Priority inversion control must be used for access to all shared resources to avoid unbounded latency. In Java RTS, this is implemented with the priority inheritance protocol.

Priority inheritance in Java RTS is implemented, as required, as a subclass of the RTSJ MonitorControl abstract base class (see Figure 3-4). Resource locking and synchronization go beyond what occurs in Java SE. In the real-time space, priority inversion control and overall latency control are big concerns.

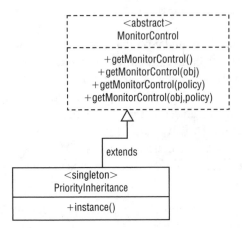

Figure 3-4   The `MonitorControl` class hierarchy for priority inversion control.

To facilitate the exchange of data between no-heap threads, and the rest of a Java application, the RTSJ defines *wait-free queue* classes that support non-blocking, protected access to shared resources. Not only does this allow for safe data transfer, it ensures that code running in a `NoHeapRealtimeThread` won't block on GC-related activity when it synchronizes with an object shared with a standard `Thread`. These wait-free queues, encompassed by the classes `WaitFreeRead-Queue`, and `WaitFreeWriteQueue`, along with priority inversion control will be explored in more detail in Chapter 6.

Asynchronous Event Handling (AEH)

Event processing is a common task executed in many application types, on many platforms, in many programming languages. Similar to the JavaBean event processing classes, the RTSJ's *asynchronous event handler* facility is designed to handle different system and programmer-defined events that real-time applications may need to deal with. Examples include OS-level events (such as POSIX signals), hardware interrupts and related functionality (such as file and network IO), and custom events defined and fired by the application itself. In the RTSJ, two main classes make up the AEH facility (see Figure 3-5):

    `AsyncEvent`—an object of this type represents an application event. As of version 1.0.2 of the RTSJ, the object does not contain related event data.

    `AsyncEventHandler`—an RTSJ `Schedulable` object that is executed by the AEH facility within the real-time Java VM when the related event is fired. This

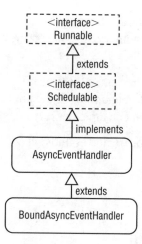

Figure 3-5 Asynchronous event handler code is executed with real-time parameters.

object has associated `ReleaseParameters`, `SchedulingParameters`, and `MemoryParameters` objects, which you populate, to indicate how the event handler is to be scheduled.

The advantage of using the AEH facility is that your code is executed according to the real-time parameters you specify, without the need to explicitly create `RealtimeThread` threads to handle each event. The real-time Java VM handles the real-time threading machinery for you. The only exception is the `BoundAsyncEventHandler`, which allows you to bind the event handler to a dedicated `RealtimeThread` for the life of the event. This ensures some extra timeliness, and removes any jitter associated with assigning a different `RealtimeThread` to the event each time it fires. Although there is some extra overhead involved (since a `RealtimeThread` is dedicated to this event), additional timeliness is obtained.

Asynchronous event handlers can have the following, optional, real-time and other processing-related parameters associated with them:

> **SchedulingParameters**—a priority associated with the event handler (for when the handler is executed in response to the event).

> **ReleaseParameters**—a set of parameters that indicate the estimated cost of event processing, an associated deadline for completing the processing, handlers in case of cost overrun, and deadline miss.

MemoryArea—indicates that the event handler should begin execution in the given memory area, be it the heap, a scoped memory region, or immortal memory.

MemoryParameters—an indication of memory usage and allocation rate, which is used to pace the garbage collector (if applicable), and to limit the amount of heap, scoped, or immortal memory the handler can consume per release.

ProcessingGroupParameters—further indication of, and bounds set on, event processing time.

AEH will be covered in detail in Chapter 6.

Asynchronous Transfer of Control

In the real-time programming space, having the ability to quickly and efficiently transfer control of execution from one body of code to another is sometimes needed. For instance, when executing code that may potentially block, or that has some variability in the time it takes to execute, this transfer may be needed as the deadline looms. The RTSJ defines the ability to perform an *asynchronous transfer of control* (ATC) to satisfy this.

Being essentially an extension to the rules for java.lang.Thread.interrupt(), and operating through Java Exception processing, the ATC operating paradigm should seem familiar to you. In fact, it's via a thrown AsynchronouslyInterruptedException (AIE) exception that the transfer of control is performed. The transfer can be triggered by an asynchronous event (such as a timer expiration), a call to Thread.interrupt(), or a call to AsynchronouslyInterruptedException.fire(). In fact, a special form of the exception is used for timer expiration-based transfer of control to a Schedulable, called Timed (see Figure 3-6).

The details of ATC will be further explained in Chapter 9.

Asynchronous Thread Termination

Real-time systems often model or respond to real-world events that can rapidly change. With this, there may be a need to quickly and efficiently terminate a thread's execution. In many cases, this can make it easier to transition between the many states in which the real-world interface may need to be at any point in time. Often, the use of a meta-thread, or a thread manager, that understands the sub-system state transitions, is the most efficient way to program such a system, where a thread manager tightly controls the lifetime of processing child threads. The details of ATT will be covered along with ATC in Chapter 9.

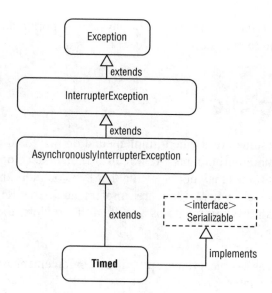

Figure 3-6 A Timed exception is used for timer expirations.

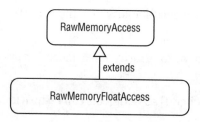

Figure 3-7 The RTSJ allows raw memory access, with restrictions.

Physical Memory Access

Earlier in this chapter, in the section on memory regions, you learned that the RTSJ provides you with the ability to access and create objects within physical memory. A low-level `PhysicalMemoryManager` class is available to the various physical memory accessor classes, such as `VTPhysicalMemory`, `LTPhysicalMemory`, `ImmortalPhysicalMemory`, `RawMemoryAccess`, and `RawMemoryFloatAccess`, to create objects of the correct type that are bound to areas of physical memory with the appropriate characteristics (see Figure 3-7).

Raw memory access, through the last two classes just mentioned, allows physical memory to be used through base and offset values, where the bytes are interpreted as `byte`, `short`, `int`, or `long` values, or arrays of these values. As opposed to physical scoped memory (i.e., VTPhysicalMemory), or physical immortal memory, raw memory cannot contain Java objects.

Optional RTSJ Facilities

The RTSJ offers flexibility in some areas where implementation may be difficult, if not impossible, in some environments. As a real-time Java developer, you need to be aware that these areas may not be available to you on individual RTSJ implementations. However, where they are implemented, the RTSJ requires that they adhere to the requirements as specified. To review, these optional areas are:

Cost Enforcement: Schedulable objects have optional cost enforcement associated for runtime feasibility analysis.

Processing Group Enforcement: Schedulable objects can specify processor usage boundaries.

Deadline < Period: the ability to specify a deadline less than the period for the respective processing group.

Priority Ceiling Emulation: an alternative to priority inheritance for priority inversion avoidance.

Heap Allocation-Rate Enforcement: Schedulable objects can be restricted in terms of their memory allocation rates.

Atomic Raw Memory Access: providing access to fields in raw memory using atomic (non-interruptible) operators.

Raw Memory Float Access: for systems that support floating point, RawMemory-FloatAccess must be implemented; otherwise, it may be left out.

POSIX Signal Handling: the class, POSIXSignalHandler, can be implemented only on systems that support POSIX signal handling. However, for systems that do support it, this is a required class.

The Future of Real-Time Java

Currently, the next revision of the RTSJ is governed by the JCP as JSR 282, which will result in version 1.1 of the RTSJ. To be clear, as of this writing there is no formal or informal draft for RTSJ version 1.1. However, some intended clarifications and enhancements have been listed. In summary, this revision aims to address the following:

Improved Aperiodic `RealtimeThread` *Processing*: add `waitForNextRelease` and release methods to the `RealtimeThread` class to better handle aperiodic processing. This will be in addition to the existing `waitForNextPeriod` method that already exists for periodic `RealtimeThread` objects.

Memory Area Data Transfer: allow the transfer of data across, and references between, otherwise forbidden memory areas through the use of newly defined weak-reference classes. For example, this would make it easier for a `NoHeap-RealtimeThread` to transfer data to a standard `Thread` executing within the heap.

Bi-Directional Reference Rule: relax this rule for parameter objects.

Relative Timers: allow `Timer` objects to be created that support a start time relative to "now," which can be the time they are created, or relative to some other time when they are reset or rescheduled.

Reset Execution Timeouts: enhance the `Timed` class, which is used to timeout the current execution of `Schedulable` objects during ATC processing.

State Queries: add the ability to query the current state of `Timer` and `Realtime-Thread` objects.

CPU Time Queries: add the ability to query elapsed CPU time for `Schedulable` objects.

AEH Memory Area: add the ability for an AEH to automatically enter a specified memory area each time its related event is fired.

Object Reference Counts: consider the ability to count object references, or determine if more than one reference exists to a given object.

Improved Feasibility Analysis: add a blocking factor to the `ReleaseParameters` object for better real-time scheduling feasibility analysis for new real-time tasks.

Resource Limit Events: support the ability to fire asynchronous events in response to exceeding RTSJ resource limits.

Event Data: currently, AEH-related events cannot carry associated data directly. The proposal is to add this ability.

Memory Area Class Loaders: allocate object memory in memory area that contains the associated class loader.

Strings in Immortal Memory: reduce `String` objects' lifetimes when they exist in immortal memory. This will allow for `String` objects, otherwise immutable objects, to be used within IM without exhausting it.

Static Variables in Immortal Memory: consider a facility to allow static initializers to occur in areas other than immortal memory.

Processor Pinning: although some implementations may support this to a limited degree via command-line parameters, an API to allow a specified thread (or thread group) to be pinned to an available CPU or group of CPUs would make this more flexible.

Various RTSJ Clarifications: as with most specification and design documents, some clarification is needed in areas where interpretation may vary.

You can follow JSR 282's progress on the JCP website at:
http://jcp.org/en/jsr/detail?id=282.

The Sun Java Real-Time System

"We must use time as a tool, not as a crutch."
—John F. Kennedy

Aᴿᴹᴇᴅ with a solid understanding of real-time concepts, and the issues that Java has in this context, you're ready to examine the Sun Java Real-Time System. This chapter begins with a discussion on operating system requirements for Java RTS, which currently includes Sun Solaris 10, and some real-time Linux distributions. We'll also describe the act of downloading and installing Java RTS. You'll learn why Solaris 10 and only certain Linux distributions are a requirement for Java RTS through a discussion of some of its built-in support for real-time threads and applications. We'll explore some of the internals of supported platforms as they apply to Java RTS.

Installing and configuring Java RTS in a development environment and a production environment have varying requirements. For production systems, there are security concerns that the Java RTS developers have taken into account, and for which you must provide some additional configuration. For development systems, Java RTS offers a NetBeans plug-in that allows you to create Java RTS projects, generate skeleton real-time code, and debug Java RTS applications at the source level (just as you would any Java application). By the end of the chapter, you will have a working Java RTS development system, and an understanding of what it takes to make your Java RTS applications production-ready.

A Prelude to Java RTS Programming

Java RTS 2.1, the latest as of this writing, is RTSJ version 1.0.2-compliant, and is based on the Sun Java Platform Standard Edition (Java SE) version 5.0, update 16. Although it's based on the Sun HotSpot Java code base, Java RTS is currently a 32-bit client implementation only; a 64-bit version, and the server mode of operation (via the -server option) are soon to be released as of this writing.

Being based on the HotSpot code base, Java RTS is similar to Java SE in many ways. For instance, Java RTS:

- Uses the same unmodified complier, javac.
- Supports many of the same command-line options (although there are some omissions as well as many new ones, discussed later in the chapter).
- Is bytecode-compatible with Java SE, and will run all existing Java .class and .jar files that are Java SE 5-compliant.
- Works with most existing Java SE tools, with some exceptions. We'll examine this in more detail in Chapter 12.

However, being built for real-time systems development, there are significant differences between Java RTS and Java SE. For instance:

- As mentioned above, Java RTS introduces some new command-line options, as well as different default values for some options you may be familiar with. These differences will be discussed in the section *Command-Line Options*, later in this chapter.
- Also mentioned above, some existing Java tools may work differently, or not at all, with Java RTS. We'll examine this in more detail in Chapter 12, *Java RTS Tools*.
- By default, all memory specified by the -Xms and -Xmx command-line options is locked into physical memory at initialization time. This eliminates any jitter associated with paging, and pinning virtual memory to physical memory at runtime.
- Java RTS version 2.1 is a 32-bit-only implementation. This limits it to **less than** 4GB of maximum addressable memory space.
- In Java RTS, Just-in-Time (JIT) compilation occurs incrementally, asynchronously, and parallel to code execution. This removes much of the latency and locking introduced by the compiler, as it exists in Java SE.
- The JIT compiler in the Java RTS VM is the client compiler. The Java SE server compiler is not supported as of version 2.1, as many of the generated code optimizations are incompatible with real-time behavior.

- Java RTS supports initialization time compilation, class initialization, and class preloading (referred to as ITC) when the VM starts, in order to remove jitter associated with the JIT compiler. We'll examine this feature in the section *Java RTS Code Compilation*, later in this chapter.

- The Java Virtual Machine Profiler Interface (JVMPI)—intended for tools vendors to develop profilers that work in conjunction with the Java VM—is not supported in Java RTS.

- As outlined in the RTSJ, all static initializers, interned `Strings`, `Class` data, and variables and objects created with static initializers allocate memory from the Java RTS immortal memory space, and are never garbage collected.

- Because the real-time garbage collector (RTGC) does not compact memory (instead it splits objects across blocks of free memory when necessary), the memory requirements of a typical Java application may increase by about 10 to 30 percent.

The Java RTS virtual machine is a completely separate Java VM implementation, and must be installed in its own unique directory, even on systems that have Java SE already installed. The installations of the two cannot be combined; they must exist in different directory trees within the same computer. Also, Java SE is not required to be installed on the system; Java RTS is a complete, stand-alone implementation of the Java platform. Before we get into the Java RTS installation, let's look at what's required from the base platform.

Operating System Support

As with any real-time software, Java RTS requires real-time support from the operating system (OS) it runs on. This includes Solaris 10, from update 3 onward, and currently two real-time Linux distributions. Here is the complete list of supported operating systems:

Sun Solaris 10: Solaris has had POSIX real-time support built in for many years. Java RTS runs well on an unmodified Solaris 10 installation, on Intel or AMD x86/x64, or Sun SPARC-based systems.

SUSE Linux Enterprise Real-Time 10: otherwise known as SLERT, this x86/x64 Linux distribution from Novel is engineered for low latency, hard real-time application support, with POSIX real-time compliance.

Red Hat Enterprise Messaging/Real-Time/Grid: otherwise known as Red Hat MRG (pronounced *merge*), this is an x86/x64 Linux distribution engineered for low latency hard real-time application support. MRG is also POSIX real-time compliant.

Both Linux distributions are based on the open-source real-time version of the Linux kernel, which is version 2.6.21 or later. This kernel is fully preemptable, and it supports high-resolution timers, priority inheritance, interrupt shielding, and schedulable interrupts. In fact, any Linux with a kernel version equal to or later than 2.6.21 contains the required real-time extensions to run Java RTS. However, only SLERT and MRG are supported as of this writing. Let's begin to take a look at the supported operating systems, and the qualities they have that allow Java RTS to achieve real-time application behavior.

Solaris and Real-Time

Since version 8, Solaris has contained support for real-time applications. This includes partial POSIX real-time compliance. Solaris was designed from the start with real-time capabilities in mind, with features such as bounded dispatch latency, schedulable interrupts, and a fully preemptable kernel. Here is a complete list of the real-time capabilities of Solaris 10:

Processor Sets: Solaris allows processors on a multi-processor machine to be grouped and dedicated to running a particular application. When defined, a processor set can also be shielded from executing interrupts. This removes all jitter related to scheduling interrupt threads, and threads from other applications.

Fully Preemptible Kernel: The Solaris kernel is fully preemptable and does not require manipulation of hardware interrupt levels to protect critical data [McDougal07]. Locks are used to synchronize critical kernel data. As a result, high-priority application threads can freely interrupt lower-priority kernel threads (and other application threads) with bounded, low-latency, dispatch times.

Schedulable Interrupt Handlers: Interrupt handlers are schedulable entities in Solaris, and run at fixed priority levels. This means they are scheduled, and preemptable, as other application threads are. Consequently, thread activity does not need to be suspended during interrupt handling, and interrupt priority levels don't need to be manipulated by the kernel or programmer.

Real-Time Schedulers: Solaris allows custom schedulers to be installed through a plug-in architecture, but also comes with different schedulers by default. Multiple schedulers can actually run concurrently. Solaris comes with a *timeshare scheduler* (TS), an *interactive scheduler* for UI-based systems (IA), and a *real-time fixed priority scheduler* (RT) needed for real-time application support. There are other scheduler variants in Solaris, but the RT scheduler is what applies to this conversation.

Real-Time Thread Class: Threads in Solaris can be in one of six thread classes. They are, in order of increasing base priority, *Interactive (IA), Timeshare (TS), Fixed Priority (FX), Fair Share (FSS), System (SYS)*, and *Realtime (RT)*—see Figure 4-1. Threads of the RT class run at the highest priority in the system (even higher than the kernel's threads which are in the SYS class). Only interrupts run at higher priority, but can be isolated from the processors running RT class threads through the use of Solaris processor sets and interrupt shielding (where a set of processors are excluded from servicing interrupts).

Real-Time Dispatch Queues: RT class threads are handled on a separate dispatch queue than threads in the rest of the system.

Priority Inheritance: Solaris implements its sleep queues and priority scheduling based on an abstraction called the *turnstile* to handle priority inversion control. With this, Solaris implements a priority inheritance protocol whereby a higher-priority thread will allow a lower-priority thread to execute in preference to it when it holds a lock on a shared resource. The previously lower-priority thread will then execute, release the shared lock, and return to its normal priority. The turnstile maintains references to both the reader and writer threads for each shared resource, and ensures priority inversion does not occur for

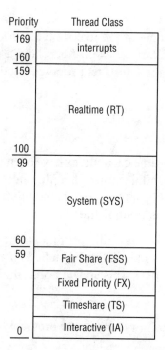

Figure 4-1   The Solaris thread priority classes.

real-time threads. It also ensures that the original, higher-priority, thread will resume execution once the shared object lock is released.

High-Resolution Timers: Internally, the Solaris kernel uses a system facility called `gethrestime()`, which exposes high-resolution timer ticks-at the nano-second level-for real-time interval timers (the bold letters are meant to highlight the abbreviation used for *high resolution*). This facility is made accessible via a kernel driver that is installed along with Java RTS.

Interprocess Communication: Solaris allows data to be shared between processes, with synchronization for safety. This includes facilities such as POSIX message queues, POSIX semaphores, shared memory, memory-mapped files, named pipes, domain sockets, and Solaris Doors.

Asynchronous IO: Solaris 10 provides a facility named the *Event Completion Framework* to allow IO events to be handled asynchronously by an application. With this facility, once the IO request is made, neither the OS nor the application need to interact until the request completes. At that point, an event is fired asynchronously to signal completion of the IO request. No application polling or specialized timers are required. For more information on the Event Completion Framework, see http://developers.sun.com/solaris/articles/event_completion.html.

This section provides only an overview of some of the real-time facilities built into Solaris. These features exist in OpenSolaris as well. Let's take a similar high-level tour of the real-time facilities in the latest, real-time-enabled Linux kernel.

Linux and Real-Time

Since version 2.6.21 of the Linux kernel, real-time capabilities have been built in. In some cases, you need to enable these capabilities through a plug-in or download. For instance, both SLERT and RH MRG contain separate modules that get layered on top of the latest Linux kernel and distribution files.

The *rt-linux* package, available through the `apt-get` utility for the latest Ubuntu and Debian Linux distributions, should be downloaded and installed on all other Linux distributions besides SLERT and RH MRG. This update brings the following real-time capabilities to Linux:

Priority Inheritance: As with Solaris, the priority inheritance protocol is implemented to avoid priority inversion.

High-Resolution Timers: Unlike previous Linux kernels, which supported timers at millisecond granularity, this kernel supports timers at microsecond granularity.

Preemptable Kernel: All threads within the kernel, as well as application threads, are truly preemptable, with low latency for thread preemption and dispatching. Without the preemptable kernel configuration, when a thread makes a system call into the kernel, it cannot be preempted. This can cause unbounded latency if a low-priority application thread makes a system call just before a higher-priority thread is released. With the preemptable Linux kernel, the lower priority thread can be interrupted even while making a system call [Jones08].

Interrupt Binding: Interrupts can be bound to a specific processor or Linux cpuset, leaving other processors free from interrupt-related jitter.

Process Binding: Entire processes, or specific process threads, can be bound to a specific processor, processor list, or Linux cpuset to avoid jitter related to scheduling other application threads on the processor(s).

Memory Pinning: Virtual memory regions can be pinned to physical memory to remove paging-related jitter.

Real-Time Threads: A real-time thread class has been added to allow higher priority application processing to occur within the kernel. These are not to be confused with RTSJ `RealtimeThreads`.

Fine-Grained Prioritization: Support for finer-grained thread prioritization has been added for more control over event processing.

Schedulable Interrupts: Interrupts are now handled by kernel threads, and can be scheduled and preempted as with other threads in the system.

Spin-Lock Removal: All spin locks, which can otherwise introduce latency and priority inversion, have been removed and replaced with a sleep-lock mechanism similar to Solaris' Turnstiles (see the previous section, *Solaris and Real-Time*, for more information).

POSIX IPC and Shared Memory: Real-time POSIX-defined FIFO message queues and shared memory regions for application data sharing and resource locking has been added.

Adaptive Locking: Changes to the underlying Linux lock implementation to reduce OS context switch times, as well as the number of context switches, when resource contention occurs.

As you can see, Linux distributions based on the real-time kernel extensions offer a variety of real-time features that make it quite different from the general-purpose Linux distributions available. Real-time applications, such as Java RTS and its applications, require these capabilities in order to be POSIX real-time compliant. With this basic understanding of OS-related dependencies behind us, let's take a look at the Java RTS installation procedure for both Solaris and Linux.

Installing Java RTS

As mentioned earlier in this chapter, Java RTS includes a separate Java VM implementation, based on HotSpot Java SE version 1.5, update 16. Therefore, even if your Solaris 10 or compliant real-time Linux installation already has Java SE installed, you need to install Java RTS into its own directory; it's not something that can be layered on top of Java SE, nor is it simply a set of new libraries. It's an implementation of the RTSJ that comes with its own customized Java VM binaries, runtimes, JDK libraries, and tools.

Likewise, there are separate installation packages available for install on Solaris 10, SLERT, and RH MRG. You can go to Sun's Java web site to locate the latest evaluation copy of Java RTS for your platform. Fortunately, installing Java RTS on any of these platforms is a straightforward process that we'll examine in detail now.

Solaris Installation

The Java RTS package for Solaris 10 includes two main sets of components:

> *The Java RTS Runtime*: the Java VM binaries and libraries for RTSJ compliance
>
> *Solaris Kernel Modules*: kernel modules to expose OS high-resolution timers

First, you must have Solaris 10 (with either Updates 4, 5, or 6, as of this writing) installed on compatible hardware. It's recommended that your system consist of at least 1GB RAM, and at least two processors (or one processor with two cores). Installing the package in the /opt partition is common and recommended, but not required.

It's important to remember that there are separate Java RTS packages for both SPARC and x86/x64-based systems. Be sure to download and install the correct package that matches your system's architecture.

The Java RTS VM and Kernel Modules

The first step is to expand the archive file that contains the Java RTS VM package. This file, SUNWrtjv.zip, can be expanded in the /tmp directory with the following commands:

```
$ cp SUNWrtjv.zip /tmp
$ cd /tmp
$ /usr/bin/unzip SUNWrtjv.zip
```

Next, install the package with the following command:

```
$ /usr/sbin/pkgadd -d /tmp SUNWrtjv
```

During the package install, you'll be asked for a location to install the files (the default is /opt), and if you would like a rights profile to be created for a local "Java Real-Time System User" user. This is generally a good idea, unless you wish to administer user rights from a central location. If so, you can answer "no" to this question, and later add appropriate rights to the user(s) who will execute Java RTS applications. We'll take a look at these rights and privileges in the next section. If all goes well, the procedure will end with a message that indicates the installation was successful.

On x86/x64 machines, Java RTS uses the high-resolution local Advanced Programmable Interrupt Controller (APIC) timer as the primary time source for timed events. This includes the RTSJ Clock API, timer expirations, periodic thread releases, and deadline monitoring logic. Access to the API is required to ensure that the finest time precision is achieved. If your system doesn't feature a local APIC, or if it's not accessible (as is the case with many laptops), then the Java RTS VM will write the following warning to the standard output on startup:

```
The cyclic driver's backend does not rely on the local APIC timer;
using legacy PIT timer
```

In this case, Java RTS falls back to the legacy Programmable Interrupt Timer (PIT), where the precision of timed events is limited to ten milliseconds by default on modern hardware. This precision can be raised to one millisecond by editing the /etc/system file, setting the hires_tick variable to 1. You'll need to reboot your system after you change the setting.

The Solaris kernel modules are contained in the SUNWrtjc package (within the SUNWrtjc.zip file). However, if the system you're installing Java RTS onto is a *sun4v* machine based on the UltraSPARC T1 or T2 processor, use the SUNWrtjc.v package instead (within the SUNWrtjc.v.zip file). Simply replace the file and package names, in the instructions below, with the name SUNWrtjc.v.

Begin by copying and expanding the SUNWrtjc.zip file in the /tmp directory with the following commands:

```
$ cp SUNWrtjc.zi /tmp
$ cp /tmp
$ /usr/bin/unzip SUNWrtjc.zip
```

Next, install the package with the following command:

```
$ /usr/sbin/pkgadd -d /tmp SUNWrtjc
```

After being asked for installation confirmation, and receiving output as to the progress of the operation, you should receive a message telling you the install was successful. It's important to note that the installation may fail (or at least produce a warning) if the package version does not match the version of Solaris 10 you are installing on. You must be sure to attain the packages for the correct Solaris 10 update that you are installing them on. Unfortunately, there are currently no standard, supported, packages available for OpenSolaris, or any other versions of Solaris, at this time.

Since the installation involves the addition of Solaris kernel-level device drivers to your system, you must reboot after the packages have been successfully installed.

User Access and Privileges

By nature, Solaris 10 is a secure and reliable operating environment. Many features of Java RTS rely on Solaris resources that require a certain level of privilege to execute. You can run a Java RTS application as the *root* user to attain these privileges by default, but this is not recommended for a shared or production deployment, as it's not secure. It's better to execute the Java RTS VM from a user account that has the proper individual privileges to achieve real-time application behavior. Lacking the right privileges can impact the performance and capabilities of your real-time Java applications.

Since Solaris supports role-based access control (RBAC), you can create a user role that contains the required privileges for Java RTS, and assign it to the appropriate user accounts on your Solaris system. In fact, this role was created for you automatically, if you answered "yes" to this question during the installation procedure for Java RTS (as outlined earlier in this chapter).

You can assign this role (named "Java Real-Time System User") to a user via the Solaris Management Console (via the /user/sbin/smc command), or with the `usermod` command. For instance, the following command will assign the role (with all the required Java RTS privileges) to the user `ebruno`:

```
$ /usr/sbin/usermod -P "Java Real-Time System User" ebruno
```

Remember to replace the above sample user, `ebruno`, with the names of actual users on your system.

Alternatively, since this role is only effective for users defined locally on the system in question, you may choose to forego this option, and instead assign the individual privileges required by Java RTS to each user account you desire. This is useful in scenarios where user accounts are managed centrally, via a rights server, and local user accounts are not defined. These privileges are:

`sys_res_config`—allows a user/process to create, delete, configure, and assign processor sets.

`proc_priocntl`—allows a user/process to elevate its priority above its currently assigned priority, and change its scheduling class (this includes the RT thread class).

`proc_loc_memory`—allows a user/process to lock virtual memory pages in physical memory (and eliminate paging).

`proc_clock_highres`—allows a user/process to use high-resolution timers, as exposed from within the Solaris kernel.

To assign privileges to a user, you can either use the Solaris Management Console, or execute the `/usr/sbin/usermod` command. For instance, to assign all of the required Java RTS privileges to a user (ebruno in this case) listed above, execute the following command (make sure you have enough privilege to do so; you may need to ask your system administer to handle this step):

```
$ /usr/sbin/usermod -K defaultpriv=basic,sys_res_config,
[ccc]proc_priocntl,proc_lock_memory,proc_clock_highres ebruno
```

Make sure this command is entered as one line. You should remember to replace the user, ebruno from this example, with the actual username(s) that you wish to assign these privileges. To assign these privileges to a non-local user, make sure you add a line such as the one below to your master `/etc/user_attr` file:

```
<username>:::::type=normal;profiles=Basic Solaris User;
[ccc]defaultpriv=basic,sys_res_config,proc_priocntl,proc_lock_memory,
[ccc]proc_clock_highres
```

Again, this entry must be entered as one complete line within the central `user_attr` file. The following warning messages indicate that you do not have the level of privileges necessary to gain access to the real-time system resources:

```
Warning: Insufficient effective privileges; temporal behavior is
         not predictable
Warning: You don't have the privilege to use high-resolution timers
Warning: Switching to the low resolution (10ms) timers
Warning: Disabling the cyclic driver as the high-resolution
         timers are not used
Warning: unable to lock pages into memory
Warning: Cannot use the real-time scheduling class.
```

If you see any of these messages, you'll need to review the security and privilege settings for the user you use to execute the Java RTS VM. Next, let's look at a similar installation for a compliant real-time Linux-based system.

Linux Installation

Installation of Java RTS on Linux is achieved through what's known as a *tarball* (all of the individual Java RTS files are contained within one .TAR archive file). To install, simply expand the tarball in the base directory you'd like Java RTS to reside. However, this location must be writable by the users who will execute Java RTS applications.

To begin, change to the base directory you'd like Java RTS installed (such as the recommended /opt), and execute the following command:

```
$ tar xvf java_rts-2.1.tgz
```

Of course, this command assumes the Java RTS installation file is `java_rts-2.1.tgz`; replace it with the appropriate filename if it varies from the sample above. It's recommended, for improved determinism and low-latency, that the /tmp directory be set to `tempfs` to be memory resident. Java RTS uses this area to store temporary files while your Java RTS application is running.

Also, recapping from the discussion on Linux requirements earlier in this chapter, Java RTS must be installed on a supported real-time Linux distribution based on a kernel version later than or equal to 2.6.21 with both the `CONFIG_PREEMT` and `PREEMPT_RT` configurations installed and active. Again, as of this writing, this includes the SUSE Linux Enterprise Real-Time (SLERT) and Red Hat Message Realtime Grid (MRG) Linux distributions.

For both RH MRG and SLERT, a `realtime` group is created at OS installation time, and the configuration for this group is done at that time also. Resource limits must be set in the pluggable authentication model (PAM) for the system. To do this, add the following four lines to the system's `/etc/security/limits.conf` file:

```
@realtime       soft    cpu         unlimited
@realtime       -       rtprio      100
@realtime       -       nice        40
@realtime       -       memlock     unlimited
```

This grants the `realtime` processing group access to the resources it needs, such as processor time, the ability to lock memory pages, and access to the real-time thread class. User accounts that need to execute Java RTS applications must be added to this group to achieve deterministic behavior. The following warning messages indicate that you do not have the level of privileges necessary to gain access to the real-time system resources:

```
Warning: unable to lock pages into memory
Warning: Cannot use the real-time scheduling class.
```

If you see either of these messages, you'll need to review the security and privilege settings for the Linux user you use to execute the Java RTS VM.

Guide to Determinism

In Chapter 1, we defined jitter as the detection of irregular variations, or unsteadiness, in some measured quantity. For a real-time application, jitter is used to describe variations in the completion times of a task. This time can be a response to an event such as a network message, or some real-world physical element (such as a sensor) that your application interfaces with. For Java specifically, it can be variations in the worst-case completion time due to garbage collector interference. Java RTS ensures that all sources of jitter can be controlled, or eliminated, through its implementation of the RTSJ requirements.

Determinism is related to jitter—or more accurately, the absence of it. As opposed to Java SE, Java RTS provides your Java applications with deterministic behavior. However, as with any technology, you need to have a strategy to use it to its fullest, and ensure that you enable the Java RTS VM to provide your application with the best deterministic behavior. Although the remainder of this book will step you through the various portions of the Java RTS API sets, and show you how and when to use them properly, this section sets the foundation for that extended discussion. Here, we'll see where the common sources of jitter are, what portions of Java RTS help in those areas, and other parts of Java RTS—besides the API—that you must be aware of to attain deterministic behavior in your Java application.

For instance, in the sections below, we'll take a look at code compilation options, real-time garbage collector tuning, the use of processor sets in various scenarios, tuning critical reserved memory, and of course, the use of the Schedulable interface.

Use Real-Time Threads

Although it would be ideal, you cannot simply take an existing Java SE application, run it on the Java RTS VM, and expect deterministic, real-time behavior. At the very least, you must do three things to begin with:

1. Determine which portions of your code are time-critical. In most real-time applications, only a small portion of the system requires determinism.
2. Run the time-critical portion of code in a Schedulable object, such as RealtimeThread, instead of within a java.lang.Thread. Only Schedulable objects will be prioritized in favor of the garbage collector and other system events.
3. Set the priority of the Schedulable running your time-critical code appropriately. This step requires more thought than it does code, as the priority is simply a parameter provided when the Schedulable object is created.

With that said, recall that it's absolutely acceptable to run a Java SE application alongside a Java RTS application, on the same system. The Java RTS VM is able to schedule the resources such that the critical real-time threads within the real-time application get priority over the standard threads in the Java SE application. However, also remember that the only way to achieve deterministic behavior with Java RTS is to run your time-critical code within a Schedulable object (RTT, NHRT, or an AEH).

As a simple example, let's look at Listing 4-1. Here, a child thread is created within the Java main function. Since there's no deterministic way to set the thread's priority, we won't even attempt to. Of course, we could add a call to Thread.setPriority(), but there's no assurance that this will truly affect the priority, or run the thread in preference to the garbage collector.

Listing 4-1   Creating a child `java.lang.Thread`

```
public class Main {

    public static void main(String[] args) {
        Thread t = new Thread() {
            public void run() {
                // do something here...
            }
        };

        t.start();
        // main thread continues to do other things...
    }
}
```

In this example, the child thread is created inline for brevity. In reality, a better pattern is to create a class that implements `Runnable`, then create a thread to run it within. However, it's clear that any of the processing that occurs within the child thread will be non-deterministic; there's no guaranteed completion time, and external events such as garbage collection will cause unbounded jitter. See Listing 4-2 to see what it takes to real-time-enable the same code with Java RTS (and the RTSJ).

Listing 4-2   Creating a deterministic child `javax.realtime.RealtimeThread`

```
public class Main {

    public static void main(String[] args) {
        PriorityParameters sched =
          new PriorityParameters(
            PriorityScheduler.instance().getMinPriority());

        RealtimeThread rt = new RealtimeThread(sched) {
            public void run() {
                // do something here...
            }
        };

        rt.start();

        // main thread continues to do other things...
    }
}
```

The changes have been placed in bold font to highlight them. A `PriorityParam-eters` object has been created to identify the priority to run the child thread. Next, instead of Thread, a RealtimeThread is created, and the priority parameter object is passed to it in the constructor. That's it. No more changes, but deterministic behavior has been achieved. In reality, the exact processing that occurs within the child thread may affect determinism also, but for the sake of this simple example, and for illustration purposes, we're going to ignore that. The net change is an additional line of code (for the PriorityParameters object), and a class name change from Thread to RealtimeThread.

Also, keep in mind that although we chose to execute this thread at the minimum RTSJ priority, this is still higher than GC threads and standard Java threads. The default base priority for a RealtimeThread is higher than all java.lang.Threads that are running, the JIT compiler, and the real-time garbage collector's starting priority.

Java RTS loosely defines ranges of thread priorities, which we'll examine in detail in Chapter 5. These priorities roughly map to the range shown in Figure 4-2. There are three overall ranges of priorities: non-real-time, soft real-time, and hard real-time. Normal java.lang.Thread instances, the JIT compiler, and other non-critical components within your application and the Java RTS VM run within the non-real-time range.

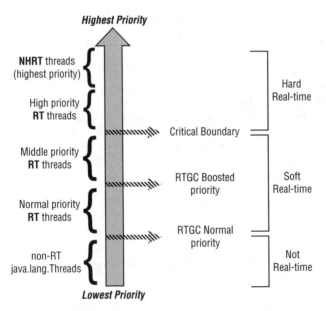

Figure 4-2   The range of thread priorities in Java RTS.

For now, understand that the RTGC works within a sub-range of priorities, starting from its base normal priority, to a boosted priority (obviously higher than its normal priority), and to a maximum, critical boundary. This priority range maps to three different RTGC modes as defined here:

RTGC Normal Mode: when the amount of free memory falls below an initial threshold, called the *startup memory threshold*, the RTGC will run at its normal (base) priority.

RTGC Boosted Mode: when the amount of free memory falls below a secondary threshold, called the *boosted memory threshold*, the RTGC priority is raised to its higher, boosted priority.

Deterministic Mode: when memory reaches a critically low threshold, called the *critical reserved bytes threshold* (more on this later in the chapter), all but critical real-time threads (including low to mid-priority RTTs) will be blocked on allocation until the RTGC completes a GC cycle.

Let's examine these RTGC modes, what happens to your application in each, and how to tune the RTGC to operate as efficiently as possible with the best determinism for your application.

Tuning the Real-Time Garbage Collector

The real-time garbage collector (RTGC) in Sun's Java RTS VM is based on Roger Henriksson's thesis, which we examined in Chapter 3. It avoids the pitfalls associated with both time-based and work-based collectors in that it performs GC work interleaved with non-real-time application threads, it never interrupts critical real-time threads, and it works concurrently and incrementally (hence without stop-world pauses). The only time it interrupts a thread under normal conditions is to look at its stack, where local variables and operands are stored. However, when a thread's stack is scanned, other threads are unaffected, therefore the pause time is small and its effects limited. The end result is that:

- RTGC scales well on multi-processor systems.
- Non-real-time threads that perform a lot of memory allocation will bear more of the GC burden.
- Critical `RealtimeThreads` don't get interrupted.
- `NoHeapRealtimeThreads` benefit from smallest latency (there is *no* garbage collection interference).

Instead of working to guarantee deterministic behavior for *all* threads within an application, the Java RTS RTGC ensures hard real-time behavior for only the critical real-time threads (a subset), and soft real-time behavior for all others. As a result, the overhead associated with RTGC (processing that can adversely affect application throughput) is limited to the analysis of the allocation rate and memory needs of real-time threads within a Java RTS application. This also helps with configuration. For instance, although the RTGC is mainly self-tuning—it modifies its behavior at runtime by analyzing the application's memory needs over time—there are some parameters that can be tuned manually. These are mostly limited to defining memory thresholds, priority levels, and the number of processors the RTGC can execute on. In reality, most of these parameters serve to configure the auto-tuning nature of the RTGC; they do not replace or disable it as a result. Let's begin to examine the ways you can manually tune the RTGC in the sections that follow.

Tuning RTGC Normal Mode

Recall that the RTGC waits to run until free memory falls below an initial threshold. At that time, the RTGC runs at an initial priority, constrained to run on a specific number of processors (all of them, by default, but you can configure this). By default, all real-time threads, even those running at the minimum real-time priority, run at a higher priority than the RTGC does in normal mode. The RTGC constantly measures worst-case allocation rates, and to ensure determinism, will run long enough to produce enough free memory for the application to consume. It's important to ensure that enough free memory is available at all times for your time-critical threads, or they will be blocked at allocation time if there is not enough. There is one setting in particular (called RTGCCriticalReservedBytes) that you can use to adjust the amount of critical reserved memory left available to critical threads. However, we'll examine this later in the chapter. For now, to adjust normal-mode RTGC operation, the following command-line options can be tuned:

RTGCNormalPriority—set to the lowest real-time priority by default, all other higher-priority threads will preempt the RTGC. By default, this includes all RTT and NHRT instances. If the RTGC has trouble keeping up with memory allocation, perhaps as memory usage bursts occur within your application, you can set this priority higher. When you do so, the RealtimeThread instances running at a priority lower than the value you provide here will be preempted when the RTGC runs. Keep this in mind, as it can affect the determinism of those threads.

NormalMinFreeBytes—this value overrides the free-memory threshold value that triggers RTGC to begin. Increasing this value (up to the maximum heap size as specified with the -Xmx switch) causes the RTGC to run sooner, and more often. This can adversely affect application throughput as, overall, the RTGC will consume more processor time. However, if your application goes through allocation bursts that cause free memory to become exhausted, adjusting this value might be necessary to avoid your `RealtimeThreads` from being blocked.

`RTGCNormalWorkers`—this value overrides the number of parallel worker threads that the RTGC will create to perform automatic memory collection. Constraining this value to a small subset of total processors available on your system will leave more processing power available for critical real-time threads, and even the non-critical and non-real-time threads in your application. However, setting this value too low can adversely affect the RTGC's ability to produce enough free memory, forcing it to run in boosted mode (more on this later). You need to set this value after observing the RTGC's behavior without any overridden tuning options by reviewing the RTGC debug output. You can turn this on with the `+PrintGC` and `+RTGCPrintStatistics` switches. We'll explain how to interpret the output later in this chapter.

Let's look at a sample usage of these options. Sun estimates that to ensure determinism, the RTGC will require roughly 25% of the processing power of the system it's running on. Assuming an eight-processor system, the following options will tune the RTGC to run almost continuously on two of the processors, in normal mode:

```
$ /opt/jrts/bin/java –Xms1G –Xmx1G –XX:NormalMinFreeBytes=1G
[ccc]–XX:RTGCNormalWorkers=2 ...
```

Although it's broken up into multiple lines above, this needs to be entered all on one line. Again, by setting the minimum free memory threshold equal to the total heap size, we're instructing the RTGC to run continuously. However, since we've limited it to two of the eight total available processors on this system, there is still the majority of processing power available to all of the threads in the application.

This configuration has some specific advantages for attaining determinism:

- It helps to ensure a near-constant production of free memory. This helps to ensure free memory is never exhausted and threads don't get blocked at allocation time.

- It effectively pins the RTGC worker threads to specific processors (as they rarely suspend) and limits jitter due to context switching. This helps to ensure that the processors executing the RTGC worker threads maintain a warm CPU cache, directly applicable to the work it has been performing over time. If these threads were context switched off their processors, and then made active again on new processors, the code and data within the CPU caches will most likely not be relevant to the RTGC operation.

- With the RTGC threads running continuously, you increase the determinism and predictability in the system overall, as there is not jitter associated with RTGC threads starting unexpectedly in the middle of application processing. Although theoretically this should not affect time-critical threads, OS activity can be a cause of jitter. Also, it helps to maintain a level of determinism for even the non-critical, and non-real-time, threads in your application.

To be accurate, you can't be assured that the RTGC will run continuously, even with this configuration. To understand why, note that the Java RTS RTGC is not generational; it operates on the entire heap during each cycle. Also note that the *default* RTGC configuration allows it to consume all *available* processors if memory requirements dictate. It does so to ensure deterministic behavior for critical real-time threads. Remember that RTTs with higher priority than the RTGC boosted priority will not be interrupted by RTGC activity, thereby preserving real-time behavior for those threads. However, to make sure that it doesn't consume all the processing power of the system continuously—thereby starving all *non-critical* and *non-real-time* threads—the RTGC pauses for a pre-determined amount of time between each cycle, with a cycle being defined as the traversal of the entire heap. You can override the default wait time by setting the `RTGCWait-Duration` command-line option.

The overall goal remains the same: to start the RTGC cycle early enough so it completes its cycle with enough free memory without having to enter boosted mode, since running in boosted mode may result in additional jitter for non-critical real-time threads. Therefore, the entire discussion so far is relative only to the RTGC operating in normal mode. If the RTGC needs to elevate to boosted mode, these tuning options aren't enough. The next section examines boosted mode, and how to tune it with the relevant command-line options.

Tuning RTGC Boosted Mode

If memory continues to fall while the RTGC runs in normal mode, and continues to fall until it passes below a second threshold (the boosted memory threshold), the RTGC will enter boosted mode. In this mode, the RTGC launches more worker threads, and boosts them to a higher priority. To adjust when the RTGC enters boosted mode, and the characteristics of how it runs once there, use the following options:

`RTGCBoostedPriority`—by default, this value is a mid-range priority between the minimum real-time priority and the highest real-time priority. Running at a higher priority than normal means that lower-priority real-time threads (those you deem not as critical) will be subject to interruptions from the RTGC on a single-processor system, or a system with far fewer processors available than application threads. However, running in preference to a subset of real-time threads helps to increase the amount of free memory produced in a given time frame. Keep in mind that this can significantly impact the determinism of your application.

BoostedMinFreeBytes—this value overrides the free-memory threshold value that triggers the RTGC to enter boosted mode (with increased priority). Increasing this value causes the RTGC to enter this mode sooner, and more often. This can adversely affect application throughput *and* determinism, as the RTGC will consume more processor time, and interrupt those real-time threads running at normal real-time priority. However, boosted mode is the last chance the Java RTS VM has to ensure enough free memory is produced before all of your RealtimeThreads are blocked on allocation.

RTGCBoostedWorkers—when the RTGC enters boosted mode, this value defines the total number of worker threads that will be launched to perform the actual collection. Normally, this should be set to a value higher than RTGCNormalWorkers. However, setting it equal to RTGCNormalWorkers will effectively cause the existing number of RTGC worker threads, when in boosted mode, to work at a higher priority than in normal mode.

Taking the sample usage of RTGC options from the previous section, let's now add tuning for boosted mode. Let's assume, for the moment, that your system parameters have changed since we first tuned the RTGC. Based on the changes, and some measurements of system performance, let's say we've determined that it's not in our best interest to have the RTGC run continuously under normal conditions. Instead, we wish for it to run continuously only when free memory reaches the boosted mode threshold. Again assuming an eight-processor system, we have the following options (all on one line):

```
$ /opt/jrts/bin/java –Xms2G –Xmx2G
[ccc]–XX:NormalMinFreeBytes=1G –XX:BoostedMinFreeBytes=512M
[ccc]–XX:RTGCNormalWorkers=1 –XX:RTGCBoostedWorkers=2 ...
```

Here we've instructed the RTGC to operate with one worker thread when in normal mode, which doesn't start until half of the 2-gigabyte heap is consumed. If, even as the RTGC reclaims memory, free memory drops below 512 megabytes—the boosted mode threshold in this example—the RTGC will enter boosted mode. At that point, two worker threads will perform RTGC work at a boosted priority (the default boosted priority, in this case).

Increasing the number of worker threads in both normal and boosted mode increases the ability of the RTGC to keep up with time-critical thread allocation demand, but is more disruptive to non-critical and non-real-time threads. Therefore, it's important to understand your application's memory needs, and to observe the RTGC behavior under various running conditions (normal and stressed) before settling on a final set of command-line values.

Expert-Level RTGC Tuning

For both normal and boosted modes of operation, the RTGC supports more command-line tuning options than we've discussed so far. However, these options require a thorough understanding of the RTGC in Java RTS, as well as your application's memory allocation and usage profiles under all conditions. We'll introduce these options in this subsection, but we suggest you gain a thorough understanding of how they affect your application before setting them on your production systems.

First, let's review that, by default, all real-time threads run at a higher priority than the RTGC in normal mode. You can override the RTGC normal mode priority with the `RTGCNormalPriority` command-line option. Increasing this value results in quicker RTGC cycles, as fewer real-time threads will be able to preempt it. This improves latency and determinism for the higher-priority real-time threads, and can result in an overall increase in system throughput (because the RTGC is running for less time).

RTGC Auto-Tuning Options

Moving on, there are other auto-tuning options that can be adjusted. As discussed earlier, you can set precisely when RTGC will begin in normal and boosted modes via the respective `NormalMinFreeBytes` and `BoostedMinFreeBytes` options. However, you can affect these thresholds without setting them explicitly by adjusting the RTGC's auto-tuning options. Using auto-tuning and related options, you allow the RTGC to adjust the thresholds according to memory usage patterns at runtime. However, by default, the options are set conservatively so that the RTGC does not run too often.

> **Warning:** It's advised that you take great care when working with these options, and avoid adjusting them altogether if you're unsure of their effects.

Auto tuning within the RTGC will modify these threshold values gradually, with each cycle, to achieve the best balance between free memory percentage, determinism, and application throughput. This process is called *sliding*, and a sliding value is used to modify the normal and boosted free memory thresholds with each collection. You can control some factors that go into the sliding value calculation, but first let's describe how it's calculated.

The goal is to spread out the amount of time spent garbage collecting even when allocation bursts take place. To do this, and ensure that the RTGC runs more often when demands call for it, the sliding value is calculated using a method of depreciation. For each cycle, the sliding value is calculated to be the higher of two values:

- The amount of memory allocated during the current GC cycle.
- The previous sliding factor depreciated according to a *slide factor*, plus a second value called the *safety margin*.

As a result, the RTGC will start its next cycle, or be elevated to boosted mode, when free memory falls below this threshold. Below is the calculation for the sliding value; it uses the previous sliding value, the amount of memory allocated in the current cycle (noted as "allocated"), and the slide factor:

$$SlidingValue_{new} = \text{MAX}(\text{allocated}, SlidingValue_{previous} * (100 - SlideFactor) / 100))$$

The resulting sliding value is used to calculate the final threshold for either normal mode or boosted mode with the following calculation:

$$Threshold = \text{MAX}(MinFreeBytes, (SlidingValue * (100 + SafetyMargin) / 100))$$

The end result is the sliding value, which is a prediction of the amount of free memory that will be required during the current RTGC cycle. The slide factor is a value you can override, which is converted to a percentage, and is used to depreciate the sliding value from the previous RTGC cycle. The safety margin is used to ensure that the RTGC starts soon enough to avoid entering boosted mode too often. Since both calculations are used together for both the normal and boosted thresholds, make the following substitutions:

MinFreeBytes: either `NormalMinFreeBytes` or `BoostedMinFreeBytes`

SlideFactor: either `NormalSlideFactor` or `BoostedSlideFactor`

SafetyMargin: either `NormalSafetyMargin` or `BoostedSafetyMargin`

As we've been discussing, you can adjust these six values (since each set of three applies to both normal and boosted mode) via command-line options. When you specify a *MinFreeBytes* value, the sliding values and thresholds for both normal and boosted modes are still calculated. However, the end result of the calculation is compared with the value you specify in *MinFreeBytes*. The larger value of the two (the calculated one, and the one you provided) is the value that is actually used.

In effect, increasing the *SlideFactor* value reduces the effects of memory allocation bursts, and although the RTGC will run longer in these cases, it prevents the RTGC from running *too* long, even when memory allocation suddenly increases. It takes more than one or two complete GC cycles for the RTGC to get through this initial learning and auto-tuning phase, as it grows to understand the allocation needs of your application. Setting the *MinFreeBytes* accordingly helps get through this phase efficiently.

RTGC Deterministic Mode

When free memory continues to decrease, and falls below a third threshold called the *critical reserved bytes threshold*, the RTGC enters what's called *deterministic mode*. When in this mode, the RTGC runs as though it's in boosted mode (at boosted priority, and with additional worker threads as defined by `RTGCBoosted-Workers`), but with one additional characteristic; all non-critical threads are blocked on memory allocation. This has two benefits: first, non-real-time, non-critical threads (all those below the critical boundary priority level) don't receive an `OutOfMemoryException` in response to their requests for memory; and second, a reserved portion of the heap remains available to satisfy allocation requests for your application's critical real-time threads. Although getting into this state isn't ideal, the Java RTS VM provides enough of a cushion to ensure that the real-time portion of your application will continue to run even under low-memory situations.

Continuing to starve the RTGC of processor cycles to free enough memory may result in what's called *saturation*. At this point, the entire heap is exhausted, and all threads will be suspended to allow the RTGC to produce free memory. For now, let's ignore that and focus on deterministic RTGC mode, and how to adjust critical reserved memory.

Critical Reserved Memory

As we just discussed in the previous section, when free memory goes below the critical reserved bytes threshold, the RTGC enters deterministic mode. However, by default, the amount of critical reserved bytes is set to zero, and the RTGC will not enter this mode unless you set it to a value greater than zero. You can do this with the `RTGCCriticalReservedBytes` command-line option. When you set this value, the Java RTS VM sets aside that portion of the heap and marks it as reserved for only the critical real-time threads, which are those threads with a priority higher than the critical boundary setting. You can override this default value with the `RTGCCriticalBoundary` command-line option. As discussed earlier, when free memory drops to the critical reserved bytes threshold, all threads will be blocked on allocation except for the critical real-time threads.

To gain a better understanding, let's look at an example. For instance, assume we have a heap defined to be 2 gigabytes, and we've set the `RTGCCriticalReserverd-Bytes` to 256 megabytes—see Figure 4-3. The critical reserved bytes threshold is now 256 megabytes, and when the amount of free memory drops below this, the RTGC enters deterministic mode.

Keep in mind that the larger you set the `RTGCCriticalReservedBytes` value, the less heap space that's left overall to non-critical threads in your application. However, depending upon the dynamics of your application and its allocation profile, it can help preserve the real-time behavior of your application when the heap becomes full.

It's interesting to note that once in deterministic mode, the RTGC will be free to work concurrently in the portion of the heap up to the critical reserved bytes threshold, while the critical real-time threads work, unencumbered, in the heap region reserved for them—see Figure 4-4.

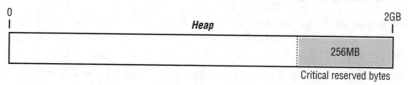

Figure 4-3   The heap and the critical reserved bytes threshold.

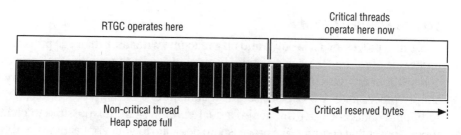

Figure 4-4   Reserving heap space allows for better concurrency.

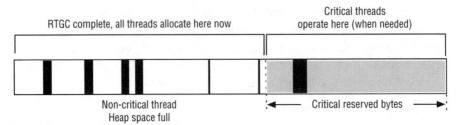

Figure 4-5   Although not generational, the Java RTS heap regions have effectively flipped.

As a result, with a properly configured system, you can achieve an alternating effect, where RTGC and critical threads operate concurrently within separate parts of the heap—see Figure 4-5. This alternating effect between the parts can continue efficiently without preventing the critical real-time threads from making forward progress, or missing deadlines.

The benefit of this is obvious: the real-time behavior of critical threads is preserved even under low memory conditions, and the RTGC can continue to produce free memory. However, in deterministic mode, throughput overall is decreased, perhaps significantly, as non-critical threads are blocked on allocation. Therefore you may need to work with the RTGC output to adjust these options, and balance your application's throughput needs with real-time behavior.

Processor Bindings

Binding `Schedulable` objects to a processor or set of processors can help ensure determinism, and decrease the worst-case execution time in your application. Doing so helps to eliminate some latency related to context switching, and processor cache refreshes. With Solaris, you can create a processor set and shield those processors from handling interrupts, thereby reducing potential jitter even more. With Linux, you can ensure processor affinity, but not all distributions support interrupt shielding. Let's first take a look at Java RTS processor set binding with Solaris.

Solaris Processor Sets

Creating a processor set is only valid on a machine with more than one processor or processor core. For the sake of this discussion, we'll treat individual processor cores within a multi-core processor and single-core processors the same; they are simply processors. A processor set must contain one or more processors. Therefore, on a dual-processor (or, again, a dual-core) system, it's possible to create a processor set that contains one processor to dedicate to your application's real-time `Schedulable` objects.

To create a Solaris processor set, you must follow these steps:

1. Log in as a user with *root* privilege.
2. Execute the /usr/sbin/psrset command with the –c option. This creates the processor set and returns its ID.
3. Add each processor to the processor set one at a time by processor ID; IDs are zero-based. The syntax for the command is:

```
# /usr/sbin/psrset –a <pset id> <cpu id>
```

For example, the following set of commands creates a processor set, and adds four processors (assuming a system with eight total processors, and no other processor sets created at this time):

```
# /usr/sbin/psrset –c
  created processor set 1
# /usr/sbin/psrset –a 1 4
  processor 4: was not assigned, now 1
# /usr/sbin/psrset –a 1 5
  processor 5: was not assigned, now 1
# /usr/sbin/psrset –a 1 6
  processor 6: was not assigned, now 1
# /usr/sbin/psrset –a 1 7
  processor 7: was not assigned, now 1
```

4. Next, you should shield the processors in this set from interrupts with the /usr/sbin/psradm command, executed once per CPU in the set. The syntax for the command is:

```
# /usr/sbin/psradm –i <cpu id>
```

You can create more than one processor set and use them in different ways. For instance, you can choose to start the entire Java RTS VM in the processor set we just created with the following sample command line:

```
# /usr/sbin/psrset –e 1 /opt/jrts/bin/java ...
```

As a result, processor set 1, which we just defined to contain four of the eight processors on this system, will be dedicated to the Java RTS VM. The four processors in this set will execute no other threads except those owned by the Java RTS VM. Since we shielded the set's processors from interrupts, they won't be interrupted by hardware devices. Keep in mind that only the processors in this set (four of the total eight in the system) will be available to execute your application threads. This means that if the remaining four processors are idle, they'll remain idle even if your application is processor bound. However, overall, processor sets help with the determinism required for a real-time application.

Processor sets can be used in a different way with Java RTS, however. For instance, you can bind just RealtimeThread or NoHeapRealtimeThread instances within your application to a processor set. This helps ensure that the same set of processors will be used to execute your real-time code. The result is less context-switching jitter for real-time threads, and warm processor caches (with far fewer cache misses), which can remove a surprisingly large amount of jitter from your application.

To do this for RealtimeThread instances, start by defining a processor set as we did above. Next, use the RTSJBindRTTToProcessorSet command-line option, along with the processor set ID. For NoHeapRealtimeThread instances, use the RTSJBind-NHRTToProcessorSet option the same way. Look at the following two examples:

> *To bind* RealtimeThread *instances to a processor set (on Solaris only):*
> ```
> $ /opt/jrts/bin/java –XX:RTSJBindRTTToProcessorSet=1 ...
> ```

> *To bind* NoHeapRealtimeThread *instances to a processor set (on Solaris only):*
> ```
> $ /opt/jrts/bin/java –XX:RTSJBindNHRTToProcessorSet=1 ...
> ```

In fact, these two command line options can be used together. You can bind both NHRTs and RTTs to a single processor set (by using the same processor set ID), or to different processor sets (with different processor set IDs) to ensure no interference.

All other threads within the Java RTS VM will run on the remaining processors not in the processor set. This includes the RTGC worker threads, the JIT compiler, and so on. Therefore, using these commands helps to isolate the processing of your critical application threads from not only other threads in the system, but within the same Java RTS VM process as well. Let's take a look at how you can do the same thing with Linux.

Linux Processor cpusets

Linux supports the concept similar to Solaris processor sets, called *cpusets*. You can choose to run the entire Java RTS VM in a cpuset (which you define before the VM starts) for added determinism overall. Also, you can assign your application's RTTs and/or NHRTs to cpusets, or simply a comma-separated list of processors, to isolate them and reduce their jitter (as we did with Solaris). To do this, the command-line options are similar, but slightly different. For example:

> *To bind* RealtimeThread *instances to four processors (on Linux only):*
> ```
> $ /opt/jrts/bin/java –XX:RTSJBindRTTToProcessors=4,5,6,7
> ```

To bind `RealtimeThread` *instances to a cpuset named 'rt' (on Linux only):*
`$ /opt/jrts/bin/java –XX:RTSJBindRTTToProcessors=/dev/cpuset/rt`

To bind `NoHeapRealtimeThread` *instances to a cpuset named 'rt' (on Linux only):*
`$ /opt/jrts/bin/java –XX:RTSJBindNHRTTToProcessors=/dev/cpuset/rt`

To bind `NoHeapRealtimeThread` *instances to four processors (on Linux only):*
`$ /opt/jrts/bin/java –XX:RTSJBindNHRTTToProcessors=4,5,6,7`

Java RTS Code Compilation

Jitter is often used to express the variations in completion times that lead to non-deterministic application behavior. So far, we've spoken a lot about jitter and determinism in terms of garbage collection, and processor bindings. Another source of jitter is just in time (JIT) compilation of Java bytecode at runtime. Although the JIT compiler in Java RTS is asynchronous and works incrementally to interfere with application execution as little as possible, significant jitter can still be introduced early in an application's execution.

Another, related, source of jitter is the on-demand resolution of symbols, such as classes, and the methods and data fields within those classes. Symbol resolution occurs the first time code is executed within the VM, and requires additional VM-specific code be executed synchronously. This can lead to significant jitter and deadline misses—clearly unacceptable behavior in a real-time system. To remove jitter from both JIT compilation and symbol resolution, Java RTS supports a new mode called initialization time compilation (ITC). With it, Java RTS allows you to specify classes and methods to be compiled and initialized at VM startup time, thereby eliminating all associated jitter at runtime.

You can control which classes and methods are compiled with ITC, thereby leaving the remaining (non time-critical) code to be JIT compiled. The important thing for you to do is identify the critical code that needs to be compiled before execution of that code begins, and ensure ITC is applied. Fortunately, Java RTS can help you achieve this, simply by running your real-time application and exercising its functionality.

Initialization-Time Compilation

To specify which classes and methods are to be compiled at Java RTS VM initialization, you must supply a file that contains this information in the following format:

```
<class name> <method name> <method signature>
```

All of this information needs to be formatted in a way the VM understands. For instance, class names need to be fully qualified, and method signatures need to be precise, as in this example, taken from the Java RTS documentation:

java/io/PrintStream	println	()V
java/io/PrintStream	println	(Ljava/lang/string;)V
java/io/PrintStream	write	(< BII)V

There are two ways to generate this list. You can either add the applicable classes, methods, and signatures to this file by hand, or you can have Java RTS generate the list for you. To do this, add the -XX:+RTSJBuildCompilationList option to the command-line when you start Java RTS, and then exercise your application's time-critical code paths.

When execution is terminated, you should be left with a file named nhrt.precompile. Although the name leads you to believe it includes only the code executed within NoHeapRealtimeThread instance, this isn't the case. It contains the names of all classes and methods for threads executed whose compilation policy was ITC. This includes all RTSJ Schedulable objects.

Once the file has been generated (either by hand or automatically with the RTSH-BuildCompilationList option), you can provide it as input to the Java RTS VM with the rtsj.precompile option. In fact, you can continue to leave both the options to generate the file, and to use the file, on the command line from this point onward. For example, the following will generate the pre-compile file when the application is first executed, and then use it each time thereafter:

```
$ java -X:+RTSJBuildCompilationList /
-Drtsj.precompile=nhrt.precompile ....
```

The file is generated only when the Java RTS VM is shut down; therefore no file IO jitter will be experienced when generating or updating this file. Every time the application is run with both the options to generate and use the nhrt.precompile file, entries for new methods executed with each run will be added to the file.

Pre-Initialize Classes

The second part of ITC is to pre-initialize the time-critical classes at VM startup. This avoids any jitter that would otherwise be associated with initializing them when they are first executed. Again, you have two ways to accomplish this; you can add the following line as part of your application's startup code for each class you'd like to be pre-initialized:

```
java.lang.Class.forName(<class name>, true, <class loader>);
```

Alternatively, you can have the Java RTS VM create the list, and write it to a file, while your code executes with the `-XX:RTSJBuildClassInitializationList` command-line option. Once created, you can instruct the VM to use it with the `-Drtsj.preinit=nhrt.preinit` option thereafter:

```
$ java -X:+RTSJBuildClassInitializationList /
-Drtsj.preinit=nhrt.preinit ...
```

Note that the classes within the pre-initialization file will be listed in the order of execution.

Preload Classes

The third part of ITC is to preload the time-critical classes at VM startup. If you use pre-initialization, the classes are preloaded by default, and this step is unnecessary. However, in case you chose to preload the classes independently, this section describes the process.

Once again, you have two ways to accomplish this: you can generate a file of fully qualified class names that you wish to be preloaded, or you can have the Java RTS VM generate it for you at execution time. To instruct the VM to both generate the file and use it, use the following command-line:

```
$ java -X:+RTSJBuildPreloadList -Drtsj.preload=nhrt.preload ...
```

From this point onward, the classes within this list will be preloaded, with all references resolved at VM startup. This includes references to static variables, instance variables, virtual methods, static methods, and class data.

Applying Initialization Time Compilation Mode (ITC)

Now we'll discuss the details surrounding the usage of ITC. It's important to understand how ITC works differently based on thread type, and how to apply it to achieve the best determinism and application throughput. For instance, in order to eliminate any potential for deadline misses, NHRTs allow only ITC-based compilation, not JIT. This means if you don't supply the needed ITC command-line options and files, the code executed by NHRTs in your application will be interpreted. Since this isn't a good scenario in terms of latency and responsiveness, it's recommended that you always supply the proper compilation and pre-initialization files with an application that contains NHRTs.

`RealtimeThread` instances offer a hybrid of both determinism and throughput, and therefore will default to JIT compilation when ITC is not specified. One slight drawback to ITC compilation is that code is not subject to re-optimization based on changing runtime characteristics, as with JIT compilation. Therefore, JIT-compiled code has a potential advantage in terms of performance and throughput over time. It's recommended that you measure your application to see if it meets its deadlines even when RTT code is interpreted. If so, you can safely leave it to be JIT compiled, and benefit from continual performance optimizations. However, to ensure the least amount of jitter, or if your application misses deadlines when interpreted, it may be best to use ITC even for your application's `RealtimeThread` instances.

By default, instances of `java.lang.Thread` (JLT) use incremental JIT compilation, asynchronously, also. Without it, there's a danger that a JLT holding a lock on an object shared by an RTT will block that RTT while its code is compiled synchronously. This can introduce unbounded latency to the RTT's execution as it blocks on the locked object. To avoid this, asynchronous incremental JIT compilation is used for JLTs also.

LogJitterProneEvents

To debug ITC-mode compilation, you can use a combination of the `-XX:+Log-JitterProneEvents`, and the `-XX:+PrintCompilation` command-line flags. When the option, `LogJitterProneEvents`, is set, the VM will produce a file named `hs_jitter_pid<pid>`, where `<pid>` is the process id of the Java RTS VM. Within the output, you will see the following events:

Entering Steady Mode: you can define sections of code within your application that represent the application's steady state, or mode. To do this, call the `enter` and `exit` methods on the `SteadMode` class (part of the RTSJ extended package) as your code enters and exits steady mode, respectively.

Interpreted Method <m>: this message indicates that a method, m, was interpreted.

C-Heap Malloc: allocation of a VM internal buffer occurred. The buffer type, the amount of memory allocated, and memory address are also included.

C-Heap Free: an internal VM buffer has been freed.

Oop Allocation Failed for Critical Thread: the VM failed to allocate a contiguous block of memory from the Java heap for a critical thread. The allocation will be retried, split across free blocks.

Split Oop Allocation Failed for Critical Thread: not enough free heap space to satisfy the allocation request. The thread calling thread must wait for RTGC to complete.

Class Initialization Attempt <class>: initialization of <class> begun.

Actual Class Initialization <class>: successful completion of <class> initialization.

Calling Class Static Initializer <class>: static initializer for <class> called.

Field Patching: this indicates that compiled code patching has taken place.

Klass Patching: compiled code patching.

Invokevirtual Patching: compiled code patching.

Invokeinterface Patching: compiled code patching.

Patching Call: compiled code patching.

The output shown below is a sample of some output from `LogJitterProneEvents`, taken from the Java RTS 2.1 documentation:

```
1213625734174692917, 3, 18:
    C-Heap malloc, N/A, 0x0826a060 16 CHeapObj-new
1213625734177445726, 3, 18:
    class initialization attempt, Thread-0,
com.sun.rtsjx.Finalizer
1213625734177482742, 3, 18:
    Actual Class Initialization, Thread-0,
com.sun.rtsjx.Finalizer
1213625734177510434, 3, 18:
    Calling Class Static Initializer, Thread-0,
com.sun.rtsjx.Finalizer
1213625734843048306, 30, 21:
    C-Heap malloc, N/A, 0x0826a2d0 160 CHeapObj-new
1213625734843341384, 30, 21:
    interpreted method, RealtimeServerThread-0,
    virtual void javax.realtime.AsyncEventHandler.run1()
1213625734843631236, 30, 21:
    interpreted method, RealtimeServerThread-0,
    virtual jboolean javax.realtime.AsyncEventHandler.setup-
      ReleaseEnv()
1213625734843796212, 30, 21:
    interpreted method, RealtimeServerThread-0,
    virtual void TCK.AbsoluteTimeTest$1.handleAsyncEvent()
1213625734844012649, 30, 21:
    interpreted method, RealtimeServerThread-0,
    virtual void java.lang.Object.notify()
```

continued

```
1213625734844128823, 30, 21:
   C-Heap malloc, N/A, 0x0826a3a0 12 CHeapObj-new
1213625734844224219, 30, 21:
   interpreted method, RealtimeServerThread-0,
   virtual jboolean javax.realtime.AsyncEventHandler.setup-
     ReleaseEnv()
1213625734845736678, 3, 18: C-Heap malloc, N/A, 0x0826a3e0 12
     CHeapObj-new
```

PrintCompilation

Another useful way to debug ITC compilation, to be sure that all critical methods are compiled at initialization time, and not JIT compiled, is to see exactly what the JIT compiler does while your application runs. To do this, add the -XX: +PrintCompilation command-line option to your application's startup script. The output includes useful information such as the methods that are JIT compiled, and some related status.

The format of the output begins with a compilation number (starting at 1, and increasing with each method that is JIT compiled). Next, a series of up to five symbols are displayed immediately after the number. Table 4-1 explains the symbols.

Table 4-1   Explanation of output from the -XX:+PrintCompilation command-line option

Characterposition	Symbol	Description
1	*Blank*	Normal method JIT compilation.
	%	On-stack replacement. When this number reaches a certain threshold, compilation is triggered.
	*	Compilation of native method call wrapper.
2	*Blank*	Unsynchronized method.
	S	Synchronized method.
3	*Blank*	The method does **not** have exception handlers.
	!	The method **does** have exception handlers.
4	*Blank*	Non-blocking.
	B	Blocking compilation. Calling thread needs to wait until JIT is complete for this method.

Table 4-1   Explanation of output from the -XX:+PrintCompilation command-line option (*continued*)

Characterposition	Symbol	Description
5	*Blank*	Compilation performed for a non-real-time thread (JLT).
	R	Compilation performed for an RTT.
	N	Compilation performed for an NHRT.

Following the five character positions described above, the applicable class and method name are displayed, and the size of the bytecode compiled. Below is part of a sample output for the PrintCompilation command-line option:

```
    1       java.lang.String::hashCode (60 bytes)
date(535601072243)
    2  !    sun.nio.cs.UTF_8$Decoder::decodeArrayLoop (1814 bytes)
date(535611750882)
    3       java.lang.String::charAt (33 bytes)
date(535667500724)
    4       java.lang.String::replace (142 bytes)
date(535672589449)
    5  b    java.util.Properties$LineReader::readLine (383 bytes)
date(535689088883)
    6  !    sun.nio.cs.UTF_8$Encoder::encodeArrayLoop (698 bytes)
date(535702159900)
    7       java.lang.String::indexOf (151 bytes)
date(535733814272)
    8       java.lang.String::lastIndexOf (156 bytes)
date(535747160379)
    9    R  java.lang.String::charAt (33 bytes)
date(549271294006)
10     R  java.lang.String::hashCode (60 bytes)
date(549271754406)
11     R  java.lang.String::equals (89 bytes)
date(549272120420)
12*    R  java.lang.System::arraycopy (0 bytes)
date(550590674255)
13     R  java.nio.Buffer::position (43 bytes)
date(551305550109)
14     R  java.nio.ByteBuffer::arrayOffset (35 bytes)
date(551415803108)
15     R  java.nio.CharBuffer::arrayOffset (35 bytes)
date(551628687107)
```

There are some interesting items to point out in this sample. For instance, item 2 contained an exception handler; item 5 indicates blocking compilation (the calling thread was blocked while JIT occurred); items 9 through 15 occurred for an RTT; and item 12 in particular contained a native call wrapper. Taking a quick look at output such as this can help to find methods that weren't included in the ITC list, such as those compiled when an RTT executed them (indicated with an 'R'). You may decide to change the execution characteristics used to generate the ITC lists, or to manually add them to the lists that are already generated.

Interpreting RTGC Statistics

As with Java SE, you can gather information about garbage collection while the application is running by turning on the proper command-line options. For instance, with Java RTS, you can view basic RTGC information with the -XX:+PrintGC option, such as:

```
[GC 2047K->1925K(2048K, non-fragmented: current 122K / min 1K /
worst 0K, blocked threads: max 1 / still blocked 0 requesting
0 bytes, dark matter: 75K in 177 blocks smaller than 2048 bytes)
<boosted during 62887 microseconds> {CPU load: 1.05 recycling /
0.04 since last GC}, 0.0635765 secs]
```

The first two numbers indicate the amount of used memory at the beginning and the end of the GC cycle; the "->" arrow visually indicates this. The third number, which appears after the open parenthesis, is the total amount of heap memory. Therefore, based on these numbers, RTGC started when memory was nearly exhausted, as expected. To improve determinism in many cases, you may have to start RTGC sooner using the command-line options described throughout this chapter.

Also reported is non-fragmented memory, which is the amount of memory that can be efficiently allocated. In this output, you can see that it reach as low as 1 kilobytes in this cycle, and was down to 0 bytes over all cycles. This is expected since GC starts when memory is nearly exhausted, by default. It also explains why one thread blocked on allocation, in this example. However, by the end of the cycle, no threads were blocked, indicating that enough free memory was produced.

The "dark matter" reported here is fragmented free memory, which is 75 kilobytes in this output. Also, free memory blocks smaller than 2,048 bytes are not immediately recycled, which is why their quantity is pointed out (177 blocks in this case). Since the Java RTS RTGC is *not* a compacting collector, these blocks will become available only if contiguous blocks happen to be freed, or if the RTGC decides to reduce the size of these dark-matter blocks dynamically. This happens only if the RTGC cannot produce enough free memory over time.

The output also shows that RTGC entered boosted mode during this cycle. This boost lasted for 62,887 microseconds, or about 63 milliseconds. The two numbers after "CPU load:" indicate how much processing power was consumed by the RTGC in this cycle, and overall since the last cycle. With this output, 1.00 indicates 100% processor usage; therefore 1.05 indicates it executed threads on up to two processors. Taking into account the amount of time the RTGC remained suspended after the last cycle, and the amount of time it ran during this cycle, the total system processor load since the last cycle was .04 percent. The final number is the total RTGC processing time for this cycle, in seconds.

You can gather more detailed information about each RTGC cycle with the -XX:+RTGCPrintStatistics command-line option. Note that this option needs to be used with the +PrintGC option. Take a look at some sample output from these two options together:

```
[GC 434K->434K(32768K, non fragmented:
current 32333K / min 32333K / worst 31717K,
blocked threads: max 0 / 0 still blocked (for 0 bytes),
dark matter: 259K in 1155 blocks smaller than 2048 bytes)
<completed without boosting> {GCing: 82% CPU, Cycle: 37% CPU}
GC cycle stats:
 RTGC completed in normal mode (1 CPUs at priority 11)
 End free bytes: 33109408 bytes
 Min free bytes: 33374720 bytes
 Next boosted threshold: 0 bytes
 Next normal threshold: 33554432 bytes
 Allocations during the GC:
        in deterministic mode: 0 bytes
                    (worst 0 bytes, average 0 bytes)
       in boosted+deterministic modes: 0 bytes
                    (worst 0 bytes, average 0 bytes)
      in normal+boosted+deterministic modes: 0 bytes
                    (worst 240704 bytes, average 4879 bytes)
Total CPU cost: 8135067 nanoseconds
      Pacing CPU cost: 265783 (3 %)
      Serial CPU cost: 1019191 (12 %)
      Parallel worker_0 CPU cost: 6850093 (84 %)
Bytes allocated by critical threads:
      in deterministic mode: 0 bytes
      total for this cycle: 0 bytes
      grand total: 0 bytes
Minimum RTGCCriticalReservedBytes: 0 bytes, 0.0118796 secs]
```

Once you understand the basic output from +PrintGC, the additional statistics are straightforward. You clearly see how many processors were consumed, the RTGC mode of operation, the priority the RTGC threads executed at, and information about critical reserved bytes usage.

With the data from these command-line options, you're ready to tune RTGC to be as efficient as possible, while providing both the optimal throughput and determinism for your application. In the section *Command-Line Options*, we'll examine all of the command-line options for Java RTS broken out by category. In the RTGC category specifically, we'll take a look at some of the RTGC tuning command-line options, and how to use them.

Using the RTSJ Clock API

The built-in Java `Date` and `Time` APIs used to generate timestamps, and perform other time-related functions, are themselves sources of jitter. This includes `java.util.Date`, and calls to `System.currentTimeMillis()`. Much of the time synchronization that happens automatically can appear as significant jitter in measured worst-case execution times. The solution is to use the RTSJ `Clock` API, designed to provide the same functionality with high resolution, and little to no jitter.

To use the RTSJ `Clock` API to create timestamps or high-resolution timings, begin by gaining a reference to the singleton real-time clock object via the `getRealtimeClock()` method call on the `javax.realtime.Clock` object. To calculate a timestamp with nanosecond resolution (on hardware that supports it), use code like that shown in Listing 4-3.

Listing 4-3   The `java.realtime.Clock` Object

```
javax.realtime.Clock rtClock =
    javax.realtime.Clock.getRealtimeClock();

javax.realtime.AbsoluteTime beginTime;
javax.realtime.AbsoluteTime endTime;

// get start time and convert to nanoseconds
beginTime = rtClock.getTime();
long lBegin = (beginTime.getMilliseconds() * 1000000L) +
    rtWallClockTimeBefore.getNanoseconds();

// do processing here...

// get end time and convert to nanoseconds
endTime = rtClock.getTime();
long lEnd = (beginTime.getMilliseconds() * 1000000L) +
    rtWallClockTimeBefore.getNanoseconds();
```

In addition to the high-resolution timing shown above, the AbsoluteTime and RelativeTime classes in the javax.realtime package, you can also create java.util.Date and java.util.Time objects for all date and time operations. We'll explore the Clock API in more detail in Chapter 5, when we discuss real-time thread programming with Java RTS.

Command-Line Options

In this section, we'll go over all Java RTS command-line options, beginning with the RTGC-related settings. All of the options are broken out roughly by category. Since they're not part of the official Java API, these options can vary from release to release of Java RTS, and they're not applicable to other implementations of the RTSJ. The only exceptions are those that begin with "RTSJ" in their name. Note that their usage is not recommended unless you have a complete understanding of their affects.

Each of the options listed needs to be preceded with "-XX:" and some options—those that are boolean flags—need to be preceded with "+" to be turned on, or "-" to be turned off. For instance, to turn on a boolean flag that is off by default (such as the output of RTGC statistics), use the following option:

```
-XX:+RTGCPrintStatistics
```

To turn off a boolean option that is on by default (such as background JIT compilation), use the following:

```
-XX:-BackgroundCompilation
```

For -XX: options that take values, you must include an equal sign between the option name and the value, without any spaces, such as:

```
-XX:ImmortalSize=128M
```

Let's take a look at the Java RTS options now, and discuss their effects. Note that some options are only available for debugging purposes, and work only with the debug version of the Java RTS VM, java_g. These commands are marked as "debug only."

RTGC-Related Options

The command-line options in Table 4-2 are meant to tune the real-time garbage collector within Java RTS, and are generally outside the scope of the RTSJ. Recall that since they're not part of the official Java API, these options can vary from release to release of Java RTS.

Table 4-2   RTGC Options; precede each with "-XX:"

Option	Default value	Description
PrintGC	0	With this option, only basic informational messages about RTGC activity will be displayed, with minimal details related to each GC cycle as they occur.
RTGCPrint-Statistics	False	With this option, verbose information about RTGC activity will be displayed, containing many details related to each GC cycle as they occur.
UseRTGC	True	Use the real-time garbage collector for automatic memory management. If false, Java RTS will use the non-real-time serial collector from Java SE. Using this is sometimes helpful during application debugging.
RTGCNormal-Priority	11	This defines the priority the RTGC operates at in normal mode.
RTGCBoost-edPriority	RTGCCritical-Boundary	This defines the priority the RTGC operates at in boosted mode.
RTGCCritical-Boundary	OS specific: - 40 on Solaris - 35 on Linux	This defines the base priority for critical real-time threads. Threads at and above this priority are considered critical, and will not be blocked on allocation or RTGC activity. This is by default equal to the following calculation: (RTSJMinPriority + RTSJMaxPriority) / 2. On Solaris, this equals 40; on Linux this equals 35.
RTGCCritical-ReservedBytes	0	This equals the amount of the heap in bytes reserved for critical real-time threads when the heap reaches the critical reserved bytes threshold. This threshold is also set to this option. You must configure this option appropriately to achieve determinism under low memory situations.
RTGCNormal-Workers	0 (unlimited)	The maximum number of worker threads launched by the RTGC when in normal mode. By default it will launch an unlimited number of threads. You should set this value to limit the number the threads.
RTGCBoost-edWorkers	0 (unlimited)	The maximum number of worker threads launched by the RTGC when in boosted mode. By default it will launch an unlimited number of threads. You should set this value to limit the number the threads. Note: RTGCBoostedWorkers and RTGCNormalWorkers are absolute thread counts; they are not additive.

Table 4-2   RTGC Options; precede each with "-XX:" (*continued*)

Option	Default value	Description
NormalMin-FreeBytes	0	The free memory threshold that triggers RTGC work to begin in normal mode. By default, RTGC waits until the heap is basically full before it begins to reclaim dead objects.
BoostedMin-FreeBytes	0	The free memory threshold that triggers RTGC to transition to boosted mode.
NormalSlide-Factor	20 (percent)	The speed at which sudden allocation bursts are ignored while the RTGC is in normal mode. This must be a value between 1 and 100, as it represents a percentage.
BoostedSlide-Factor	10 (percent)	The speed at which sudden allocation bursts are ignored while the RTGC is in boosted mode. This must be a value between 1 and 100, as it represents a percentage.
NormalSafety-Margin	10 (percent)	The variation in allocation rate that is accepted before the normal free memory threshold is increased. This must be a value between 1 and 100, as it represents a percentage.
BoostedSafe-tyMargin	20 (percent)	The variation in allocation rate that is accepted before the boosted free memory threshold is increased. This must be a value between 1 and 100, as it represents a percentage.
RTGCWait-Duration	10 (milliseconds)	The amount of time, in milliseconds, that all RTGC threads are suspended after a GC cycle. In other words, the minimum time delay between successive RTGC cycles. The only exception to this is when the entire heap is exhausted (including critical reserved bytes), or when GC is explicitly requested.

Memory-Related Options

The command-line options in Table 4-3 affect or display information about memory regions and Java stacks with the Java RTS VM.

For development and debugging purposes, you can request the structure of the heap and other memory areas to be output on startup with the

Table 4-3   Java RTS Memory Options; precede each with "-XX:"

Option	Default value	Description
ImmortalSize	32M	The size of the immortal memory region. Note: this is in addition to the heap; it is not taken from the heap.
ScopedSize	16M	The total amount of memory available to scoped memory regions. Note: this is in addition to immortal memory and the heap.
RTSJShowHeapLayout (debug only)	False	This command outputs the size and configuration of the memory regions in the Java RTS VM. Although the output refers to these regions as generations, they simply map to the heap, the region where the VM keeps class and other data (perm gen), and the RTSJ gen, which includes immortal memory and scoped memory regions.
RTSJEnableImmortal AllocationProbe (debug only)	True	On Solaris, DTrace is a tool that outputs almost endless information about what is occurring on a running system, from-application code, through the OS kernel, and even into hardware microcode in many cases. It does this by examining what are referred to as *probe points*. Applications can define their own probe points, and Java RTS is no exception. This flag turns on the DTrace probe point that outputs data whenever an allocation is performed within immortal memory.
RTSJTraceScopeStacks (debug only)	False	Recall from our discussion on the RTSJ in Chapter 3 scopes have rules in terms of stacking. As child real-time threads enter scoped memory regions, and create their own, they affect the overall scope stack. You can view this information with each change to the stack for each scope with this option.

-XX:+RTSJShowHeapLayout option. The resulting output will look similar to the following:

```
RTHeapGen total 65536K, used 0K
[0x43000000, 0x47000000, 0x47000000)
RT heap space 65536K, 0% used [0x43000000, 0x47000000)
```

```
rtsj-mark-sweep perm gen total 65536K, used 0K
[0x47000000, 0x4b000000, 0x4b000000)
 the RTSJPermSpace 65536K, 0% used
[0x47000000, 0x47000000, 0x4b000000)
RTSJ gen total 67584K, used 0K
[0x4b000000, 0x4f200000, 0x4f200000)
ImmortalSpace ImmortalSpace 32768K, 0% used
[ 0x4b000200, 0x4b000000 0x00000000 0x4b000000
0x4d000000, 0x08116d20]
 ImmortalPhysicalReserved 0x4d000000-0x4d100000
 ScopedPhysicalReserved 0x4d100000-0x4d200000
 ScopedFree list start:
  33554432 bytes (32768KB)
0x4d200000-0x4f200000 in chunk 0x8112d60 (p=0x0 n=0x0 cs=2048)
 ScopedFree list end: 32768KB (plus 0 bytes)
```

In summary, what this output tells us is that the total Java RTS heap is 64MB is size, and currently contains no live objects. Also, immortal memory is sized at 32MB, and there are currently no scoped memory regions defined. However, there is 32MB total space available for scoped memory allocations when they occur. As scoped memory regions are created, they will be listed in this output. You can also see data about the permanent generation, and physical memory regions.

Thread-Related Options

The command-line options in Table 4-4 affect or display information about threading within the Java RTS VM.

Table 4-4   Java RTS Memory Options; precede each with "-XX:"

Option	Default value	Description
RTSJTraceThreading (debug only)	False	When enabled, the Java RTS VM will output information about real-time thread scheduling events. This information is quite verbose, and includes thread start, terminate, block, wait, release, and priority modification events.
RTSJTraceThreadBinding	False	When enabled, a message will be output when a thread is assigned a processor.

continued

Table 4-4   Java RTS Memory Options; precede each with "`-XX:`" (*continued*)

Option	Default value	Description
VMStackTrace-AtRTSJException (debug only)	False	When enabled, stack trace information is printed when RTSJ-specific exception occurs, whether it's caught or uncaught.
RTSJForceCyclic (Solaris only)	–	For Solaris, a cyclic driver is included with the Java RTS installation. However, some systems don't expose the correct component (APIC) to achieve high-resolution timers. When this option is left unset, the default is for Java RTS to attempt to use the cyclic driver, and if that fails, it will default to the system's built-in timer support. However, supplying `true` for this option instructs the Java RTS VM to exit if the cyclic driver cannot be used. Supplying `false` for this option tells the VM to use the built-in timer only.
RTSJBindRTTTo-ProcessorSet (Solaris only)	–	When a valid Solaris processor set ID is provided, all `RealtimeThreadSchedulables` are bound to run on processors within that processor set only. Also, the processors in the set will run no other threads except the `RealtimeThreads` in the application. Solaris only!
RTSJBindRTTTo-Processors (Linux only)	–	When a comma-separated list of processor IDs are provided, all `RealtimeThreadSchedulables` are bound to run on those processors. Also, the specified processors will run no other threads except the `RealtimeThreads` in the application. Linux only!
RTSJBindNHRT-ToProcessorSet (Solaris only)	–	When a valid Solaris processor set ID is provided, all `NoHeapRealtimeThreadSchedulables` are bound to run on processors within that processor set only. Also, the processors in the set will run no other threads except the `NoHeapRealtimeThreads` in the application. Solaris only!
RTSJBindNHRT-ToProcessors (Linux only)	–	When a comma-separated list of processor IDs are provided, all `NoHeapRealtimeThreadSchedulables` are bound to run on those processors. Also, the specified processors will run no other threads except the `NoHeapRealtimeThreads` in the application. Linux only!

Asynchrony-Related Options

The command-line options in Table 4-5 affect or display information about asynchronous event handling, transfer of control, and thread termination within the Java RTS VM.

Compiler and Interpreter-Related Options

The command-line options in Table 4-6 affect or display information for the VM interpreter, JIT compiler, and Java RTS ITC.

Table 4-5 Java RTS Asynchrony Options; precede each with "-XX:"

Option	Default value	Description
RTSJSignalThreadPriority	RTSJMaxPriority	The priority of the thread that handles POSIX signals.
RTSJForceHighRes-Timer (Solaris only)	–	By default, with no option specified, the Java RTS VM will use high-resolution timers internally if available, and if the user is permissioned; otherwise it will fall back to the built-in timers. If set to true, the VM will use high-resolution timers, but will exit if it cannot. If set to false, the VM will use the built-in timers.
RTSJHighResTimer-ThreadPriority	RTSJMaxPriority	The priority of the thread that releases timer-based event handlers.
RTSJDeadlineMonitor-ingThreadPriority	RTSJMaxPriority	The priority of the thread that monitors for real-time thread deadline misses.

Table 4-6 Java RTS Compiler and Interpreter Options; precede each with "-XX:"

Option	Default value	Description
RTSJTraceNHRT-Interpreted	False	When set to true, information is output to trace bytecode executed in interpreted mode for NHRTs.

continued

Table 4-6   Java RTS Compiler and Interpreter Options; precede each with "-XX:" (*continued*)

Option	Default value	Description
RTSJTraceInterpreter-Entry	False	When set to true, and used with either the RTSJTraceNHRTInterpreted or Trace-Bytecodes option, tracing is restricted method names only.
ITCJLT	False	When set to true, the ITC policy applies to `java.lang.Thread` instances, where methods within the precompile list are compiled at class initialization. All other methods are JIT compiled incrementally at runtime. When false, `Thread` instances are JIT compiled only.
ITCRT	True	The default is to apply the ITC policy to all `RealtimeThread` instances for methods in the precompile list. All other methods are JIT compiled if the JITRT option (described next) is set to true.
JITRT	True	When set to true, all `RealtimeThread` instance methods that are not in the precompile list (for ITC) are JIT compiled incrementally at runtime.
BackgroundCompilation	True	When set to true, JIT compilation occurs in the background, incrementally and asynchronously with execution, at runtime. When set to false, JIT compilation occurs synchronously with execution, which can cause unbounded pauses. Setting this option to false will affect determinism, and is not recommended when RTGC is used.
RTSJBuildCompilation-List	False	When set to true, the Java RTS VM will generate a file containing the methods that were executed as part of this run for all threads whose ITC policy is set to true.
RTSJBuildPreloadList	False	When set to true, the Java RTS VM will generate a file containing the classes whose methods were compiled at initialization time.

Table 4-6 Java RTS Compiler and Interpreter Options; precede each with "-XX:" (*continued*)

Option	Default value	Description
RTSJBuildClassInitializationList	False	When set to true, the Java RTS VM will generate a file containing the classes whose methods were compiled at initialization time (as with RTSJBuildPreloadList) except with the methods listed in order of initialization.
CompilationList	nhrt.precompile	Use this option to specify the name of the file that the Java RTS VM creates for the results of the RTSJBuildCompilation option.
PreLoadList	itc.preload	Use this option to specify the name of the file that the Java RTS VM creates for the results of the RTSJBuildPreloadList option.
PreInitList	itc.preinit	Use this option to specify the name of the file that the Java RTS VM creates for the results of the RTSJBuildClassInitializationList option.
CompilePreLoaded	False	When set to true, **all** methods for each class referenced in the precompile or preload list are compiled at initialization time. When false (the default) only the methods specifically within the nhrt.precompile file are compiled at initialization.
PrintCompilation	False	When set to true, the Java RTS VM will output the JIT compiled methods at runtime.

Table 4-7 Java RTS Optimization Options; precede each with "-XX:"

Option	Default value	Description
UseInlineCaches	False	When set to true, Java SE's original implementation and use of inline code caches will be used.

continued

Table 4-7   Java RTS Optimization Options; precede each with "-XX:" (*continued*)

Option	Default value	Description
RTSJUseInlineCaches	True	When set to true, a variant of Java SE's inline cache implementation is used that leads to more deterministic application behavior.
UseCHA	False	When set to true, Java SE's original implementation of virtual method inline caching is used. This is turned off by default because it can affect determinism.
RTSJUseGuardedCHA	True	When set to true, a variant of Java SE's virtual method inline cache implementation is used that leads to more deterministic application behavior.

Java RTS Optimization Options

The command-line options in Table 4-7 affect or display information options that trade off determinism for increased throughput and performance. Note that the default values of all four optimization options are negated when the default garbage collector is switched from RTGC to serial GC.

Part II

Inside Java RTS

5

Threads, Scheduling, and New Memory Models

"The only reason for time is so that everything doesn't happen at once."
—Albert Einstein

IN a real-time environment, it's important to ensure the timely and predictable execution of tasks. This implies that the system make conscious decisions about priorities, resource usage profiles, and latency requirements when scheduling individual tasks, or threads. Java RTS works closely with its host operating system to properly schedule threads to achieve the deadlines of *all* running tasks. It begins with a `Schedulable` object, for which there are four types in the Java RTS system, controlled by a real-time scheduler.

This chapter begins with a discussion of thread priorities and the effect that shared resources and objects have on them. The discussion continues with a look at the various kinds of `Schedulable` objects available within Java RTS, and how they are scheduled within the Java RTS VM. In addition, Java RTS defines new threading models, and hence new `Thread` classes, which we'll examine in detail. The chapter concludes with a more detailed look at the various memory areas that Schedulable objects can execute within, along with some usage patterns to illustrate. By the end of this chapter, you should have a thorough understanding of how the new `Thread` classes are scheduled, how to implement them in your application, the different ways to schedule them (i.e. periodic versus aperiodic) and how to effectively use them in various allocation contexts.

Schedulable Objects

The RTSJ proposes a new system model for the development and deployment of Java applications that have real-time requirements. Understanding this system model is one step toward understanding the scheduling framework in the RTSJ. Another fundamental construct you need to understand is that the RTSJ abstracts the unit of schedulability beyond the `java.lang.Thread`. In the RTSJ, and hence within Java RTS, things that are scheduled are instances of the Java interface, `Schedulable`, which itself extends `Runnable`—see Figure 5-1.

This is done to allow the application to imbue these schedulable objects with values that characterize their expected behavior and determined requirements with respect to time. But more importantly, this abstraction allows more than just threads to come under the control of the scheduler. For example, event handlers in the RTSJ no longer just execute whenever convenient, they execute

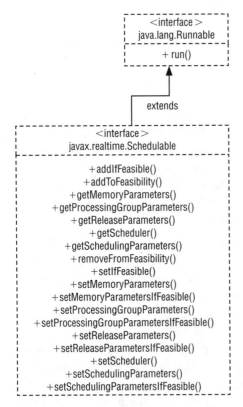

Figure 5-1   The `Schedulable` interface.

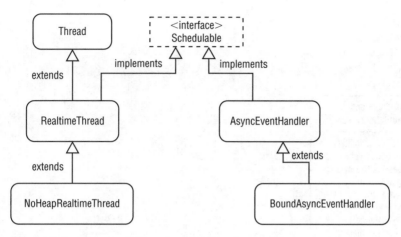

Figure 5-2   The class hierarchy of Schedulable objects.

under the control of the real-time-enabled scheduler. Thus, in Java RTS, event handlers are a schedulable entity rather than being, as in a typical OS, completely unscheduled.

Java RTS includes four class definitions that implement Schedulable: Realtime Thread (RTT), NoHeapRealtimeThread (NHRT), AsyncEventHandler (AEH), and BoundAsyncEventHandler (BAEH)—see Figure 5-2 for the class hierarchy. Instances of these four Schedulable classes are visible to, and managed by, the scheduler. The abstract class, Scheduler, represents the real-time scheduler implementation itself. Application logic interacts with the scheduler via methods on one of the concrete subclasses of Scheduler, such as the PriorityScheduler.

We'll explore the RealtimeThread and NoHeapRealtimeThread classes later in this chapter. The remaining two classes, AsyncEventHandler and BoundAsync EventHandler, will be covered in Chapter 8. For now, let's look at how you define important characteristics of Schedulable objects, such as deadlines, periods, and priorities. We'll begin with a quick discussion of real-time scheduling in Java RTS, and how it complies with the RTSJ.

The Real-Time Scheduler

The priority scheduler (see Figure 5-3) is required in all RTSJ implementations; however, particular applications may include additional schedulers. When the application code creates instances of the four Schedulable classes, they can be given a set of characteristics that both define and mandate certain behavior, such as release characteristics and priority.

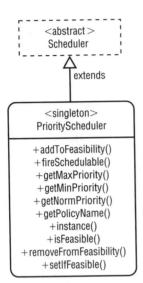

Figure 5-3   The RTSJ base scheduler requirement is priority-based scheduling.

The PriorityScheduler object is a singleton, and a reference to it can be obtained through its static instance method. With it, you can determine the various priority ranges of the given scheduler, the priority of a given thread, and the feasibility of the current set of Schedulable objects. You can also alter the running system by adding new Schedulable objects with a feasibility check; changing an existing Scheduable's parameters with a test for feasibility; and triggering an asynchronous event to fire.

Scheduling Parameters

Traditional priority is the dispatch time metric used by the required priority scheduler in Java RTS. This scheduler, as well as any other scheduling algorithms, may define a subclass of SchedulingParameters abstract class to communicate any additional values necessary for the scheduling algorithm to do its job. The RTSJ defines the PriorityParameters class (see Figure 5-4) for the required priority scheduler that simply holds the priority of the Schedulable.

Java RTS defines two subclasses of SchedulingParameters to provide parameters to be used by the priority scheduler. When creating new Schedulable objects, you will often need to use one or both of these subclasses to properly schedule your new object. Let's take a look at these subclasses now.

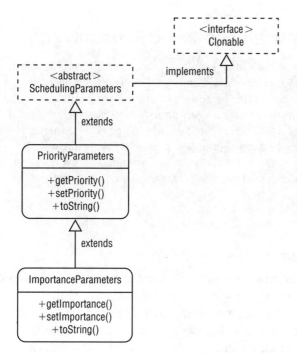

Figure 5-4 The class hierarchy for `SchedulingParameters` and its subclasses.

PriorityParameters

Instances of the `PriorityParameters` class are assigned to `Schedulable` objects whose execution eligibility is determined by their priority. You simply create a new instance or share an existing one, provide an integer value for the priority as the constructor, and assign it to an existing `Schedulable` (see Listing 5-1).

Listing 5-1 Setting the `Schedulable`'s priority

```
RealtimeThread rt = new RealtimeThread();
int maxPri = PriorityScheduler.instance().getMaxPriority();
PriorityParameters p = new PriorityParameters(maxPri);
rt.setSchedulingParameters(p);
// ...
```

First, `Schedulable` object `rt` is created with no scheduling parameters defined. Next, the scheduler's maximum priority is determined, and a `PriorityParameters` object is created with that value. Finally, this object is assigned to the `Schedulable`, which begins executing at this new priority at its next release.

Time-Share Versus Priority-Based Scheduling

Code running within a `Schedulable` object, such as `RealtimeThread`, executes according to a fixed-priority preemptive scheduling policy. Threads scheduled according to this policy are granted the highest range of scheduling priorities on the system, and preempt all threads running at lower priority. However, threads running at a regular Java priority level (JLTs) are scheduled according to a time-sharing policy, which provides fair allocation of processor resources among threads. The intent is to provide good response time to non-time-critical interactive threads, and good throughput to processor-bound threads, but not to provide any temporal guarantee.

ImportanceParameters

In any system, overload conditions (sometimes refered to as *saturation*) can occur when more than one thread is released at the same priority. If the scheduler determines that not all of the threads will be able to meet their deadlines, an additional scheduling metric may be used. In Java RTS, this metric is represented by the `ImportanceParameters` class, and you can use it to communicate which threads of equal priority should be given preference in an overload condition (see Listing 5-2).

Listing 5-2   Using `ImportanceParameters`

```
RealtimeThread rt1 = new RealtimeThread();
int maxPri = PriorityScheduler.instance().getMaxPriority();
ImportanceParameters i1 = new ImportanceParameters(maxPri, 1);
Rt1.setSchedulingParameters(i1);
// ...

RealtimeThread rt2 = new RealtimeThread();
ImportanceParameters i2 = new ImportanceParameters(maxPri, 2);
rt1.setSchedulingParameters(i2);
// ...

// Increase rt1's importance above rt2
i1.setImportance(3);
```

First, `RealtimeThread` rt1 is created. Next, the scheduler's maximum priority is determined. Next, we create an `ImportanceParameters` object, and specify both a priority and an importance value. This object simultaneously sets the thread's priority and importance value in the constructor with the call to `setSchedulingParameters`.

Sometime later in the code, a second `RealtimeThread`, `rt2`, is created. This thread is given an `ImportanceParameters` object whose importance value is one greater than `rt1`'s value. This means `rt2` will be scheduled in preference to `rt1` in overload conditions. However, as the last line of code shows, you can adjust the importance values at a later point in time. In this case, after the call is made, `rt1` will run in preference to `rt2` in overload conditions according to the new importance values.

Release Parameters

Release characteristics, embodied in an instance of the class `ReleaseParameters` (see Figure 5-5), indicate to the runtime system whether the `Schedulable` is to be released periodically, sporadically, or aperiodically (see Chapter 1 for these definitions). Instances of `ReleaseParameters` also include the cost per release, start time, and handlers for missed deadlines or cost overruns. However, it's important to note that cost enforcement and feasibility analysis are not implemented in this version of Java RTS.

Note that all time-based parameters use the RTSJ's high-resolution timer facility, and may therefore be expressed in nanosecond granularity. The actual implemented granularity is implementation-dependent.

A single `ReleaseParameters` object can be provided in the constructor of more than one `Schedulable` object. This is a one-to-many relationship. As a result, changes to a `ReleaseParameters` object, such as a change to the object's deadline, will affect the scheduling of *all* associated `Schedulable` objects (see Listing 5-3).

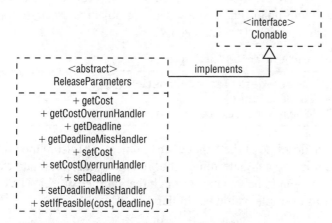

Figure 5-5   The `ReleaseParameters` abstract base class.

Listing 5-3   Seting a Schedulable's release parameters

```
RealtimeThread rt1 = new RealtimeThread();
RealtimeThread rt2 = new RealtimeThread();
RealtimeThread rt3 = new RealtimeThread();
RelativeTime milli = new RelativeTime(1,0);
ReleaseParameters p = new PeriodicParameters(milli);

rt1.setReleaseParameters(p);
rt2.setReleaseParameters(p);
rt3.setReleaseParameters(p);

RelativeTime deadline = milli;

// Set the deadline for all 3 Schedulable objects
p.setDeadline(deadline);

// The following has no affect on scheduling
deadline = new RelativeTime(2,0);
```

When a ReleaseParameters object is provided to a Schedulable object through its constructor, or through the setReleaseParameters method as shown above, the two are considered bound. As a result, changes to the ReleaseParameters object (its cost or deadline) are visible to the Schedulable object and the Java RTS scheduler. However, although setDeadline and other methods take a RelativeTime object as a parameter, changes to the provided RelativeTime object's time value do not propagate to the associated Schedulable objects.

Conversely, you can determine the release characteristics of a given Schedulable object by calling the getReleaseParameters method on it. From there, you can call the appropriate methods on the ReleaseParameters object returned to examine all of its release characteristics (see Listing 5-4).

Listing 5-4   Examining a Schedulable's release parameters

```
ReleaseParameters r = rt1.getReleaseParameters();
RelativeTime d = r.getDeadline();
System.out.println("Deadline set to: " + d.toString());
```

Here, we determine the deadline of the Schedulable object, rt1, from the previous example and print it. We can determine other release parameters, and even modify them by setting them to new values through the returned object. The output from the code in this example would be similar to:

```
Deadline set to: (1 ms, 0 ns)
```

Since the ReleaseParameters class is abstract, you must use one of its subclasses, PeriodicParameters or AperiodicParameters (or its subclass, Sporadic

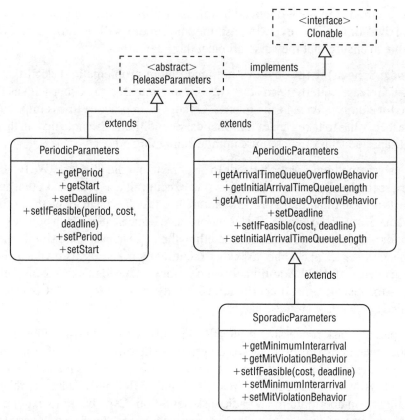

Figure 5-6 The class diagram for `ReleaseParameters`.

`Parameters`) illustrated in Figure 5-6. In fact, we've already alluded to these subclasses in the code samples used so far.

Before we look at these subclasses in detail, let's clarify how Java RTS defines periodic, aperiodic, and sporadic tasks. Periodic tasks are straightforward; they represent code that's executed according to a time-based period. This period is defined by the `ReleaseParameters` subclass, `PeriodicParameters`, which we'll examine shortly. At this point, let's examine how Java RTS accommodates `Schedulable objects` that have a release pattern that is either aperiodic or sporadic.

Sporadic and Aperiodic Tasks

Recall from Chapter 1 that a sporadic release pattern means the interval between releases is given as a minimum. For example, it can be described such that two subsequent releases will never occur closer than *n* time units. These are handled as though they were periodic tasks with the minimum inter-arrival time used as the period. There is some over-provisioning because, by definition, the sporadic Schedulables will not all be released as often as their given minimum inter-arrival times. However, in case they are, there will be processor cycles available to ensure that they also all meet their deadlines.

Aperiodic Schedulable objects are much more problematic. Recall that the aperiodic release pattern means that two or more releases can occur with as little as zero time units between each release. Of course, in practice this is impossible, but the theory has to take care of this boundary condition. Also note that, in theory, a single aperiodic task may require infinite computing power.

Obviously, something practical needs to be done to handle this case. We typically define a special periodic task whose job is to execute all aperiodic tasks that arrive before its release time. In real-time literature this task has been given the unfortunate name of *sporadic server*. This is unfortunate because it can be a point of confusion for people new to real-time scheduling theory discussions. It simply means that this task serves aperiodic tasks by executing them during its own execution for each release of itself. Additionally, since it may not need to execute once every period—for instance, if no aperiodic task needs to be executed—it is properly classified as a sporadic release pattern.

Most aperiodic task processing in Java RTS revolves around responding to asynchronous events driven by real-world systems. Therefore, much of it is geared towards being used in an asynchronous event handler, which is the main topic in Chapter 8. However, you can still create RTT and NHRT objects that are released according to an aperiodic or sporadic task definition. Let's begin to explore this through the use of the ReleaseParameters subclasses, PeriodicParameters, AperiodicParameters, and SporadicParameters.

PeriodicParameters

Using a PeriodicParameters object as the release parameter causes the Schedulable object to be released on a regular time-based period. This object can be supplied to the Schedulable object's constructor, or set later through the setReleaseParameters method, as shown in Listing 5-5, in bold.

Listing 5-5   Setting release parameters while running

```
// Create the Schedulable
RealtimeThread rt = new RealtimeThread();

// Set SchedulingParameters for priority
int normPri = PriorityScheduler.instance().getNormPriority();
PriorityParameters pri = new PriorityParameters(normPri);
rt.setSchedulingParameters(pri);
```

```
// Start the Schedulable
rt.start();
```

```
// Set a one-millisecond period
RelativeTime milli = new RelativeTime(1,0); // 1 milli
RelativeTime delay = new RelativeTime(1000,0); // 1 second
PeriodicParameters per = new PeriodicParameters(delay, milli);
rt.setReleaseParameters(per);
```

In this sample, we create a Schedulable object that simulates a temperature gauge monitor. After it's created, we set it to run at a normal real-time priority by calling setSchedulingParameters with a PriorityParameters object, and then start execution. Next, we create two high-resolution timer objects; the first represents the one millisecond period at which this periodic Schedulable object will be released. The second represents a one-second delay before the Schedulable is released for the first time. This delay is optional, and can be omitted by leaving the period as the only parameter in the constructor.

When you specify a start delay, the Schedulable will not be released (become eligible to execute) until the specified delay expires, after start is called, as shown in the last line of code above. As a result, the Schedulable object's run method will not be entered for the first time until *after* the specified delay (see Figure 5-7).

Being periodic, this Schedulable object will be released precisely at the beginning of each specified time period (each one-millisecond interval in the code sample above). This implies that the object will perform its processing and become suspended within that timeframe in advance of its next scheduled release. For this sample, the processing—or execution cost—is expected to be less than

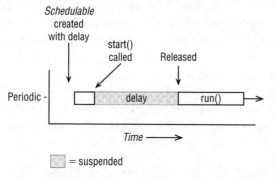

Figure 5-7 A periodic Schedulable object started with a delay.

one millisecond (which is its period). After each release, once processing is completed, the Schedulable suspends itself by calling waitForNextPeriod, which is a member method of the RealtimeThread subclass. We'll examine this method in detail in just a little while.

Java RTS Minimum Period

The Java RTS virtual machine enforces a minimum period of 50 microseconds for periodic real-time threads by default, on both Solaris and Linux implementations. If you request a smaller period, it will be accepted without an exception being thrown. However, quietly, Java RTS will increase the period to equal the minimum. On Solaris, you can change the minimum by setting the cyclic_min_interval variable in the file, /platform/<arch>/kernel/drv/cyclic.conf, to a reasonably smaller value. Setting this value too small can cause erratic behavior or even a system hang.

AperiodicParameters

For real-time tasks that may be released at any time, perhaps due to a system event or message arrival, for instance, an aperiodic Schedulable object can be defined. You use the AperiodicParameters class to specify its release characteristics, such as:

- The execution cost
- The deadline
- Code to handle execution cost overruns
- Code to handle deadline misses
- The arrival time queue

The execution cost is merely a hint for feasibility analysis within Java RTS, and as of this version doesn't do too much. Even if it were implemented in Java RTS, cost would have little meaning for aperiodic threads since there is no equivalent call to waitForNextPeriod, as there is with a periodic thread. As a result, there is no standard way to communicate to the VM when processing is complete, and cost cannot be accurately measured. Likewise, since it's unknown when an aperiodic thread will be released, it's difficult to measure deadline misses; it can really only be measured the first time the Schedulable is started, since that implies its release.

Because of this, we're going to focus on the arrival time queue. Since Java RTS, and even your aperiodic Schedulable object for that matter, has no control over the aperiodic thread's release times, a new release may occur while your object is processing a prior release. To handle this situation, and to ensure your code doesn't miss events to process, Java RTS manages an arrival queue on behalf of your `Schedulable` object. You need to inform the VM of how to size the queue, and how to handle queue overflow situations, via the following `AperiodicParameters` class methods:

`setInitialArrivalTimeQueueLength()`—sets the initial number of elements (releases) the queue can hold before an overflow condition occurs. This is set once when the `Schedulable` object is created; subsequent calls are ignored.

`setArrivalTimeQueueOverflowBehavior()`—defines how to handle the case where the arrival queue overflows (where all empty space in the queue is occupied with queued releases). The acceptable values are:

`arrivalTimeQueueOverflowExcept`—when set to this value, an `ArrivalTime-QueueOverflowException` will be thrown if an arrival occurs when the arrival queue is full.

`arrivalTimeQueueOverflowIgnore`—when set to this value, if an arrival occurs when the arrival queue is full, it will be ignored; it will not be queued, and no `Exception` will be thrown.

`arrivalTimeQueueOverflowReplace`—when set to this value, if an arrival occurs when the arrival queue is full, this arrival replaces the last one put on the queue.

`arrivalTimeQueueOverflowSave`—when set to this value, if an arrival occurs when the arrival queue is full, the queue is lengthened to hold the new arrival without replacing others. This is the default behavior and will be used unless you explicitly set it to one of the other behavior values in this list.

`setInitialArrivalTimeQueueLength(int initial)`—sets the initial size of the arrival queue. What happens when this queue fills and a new arrival occurs is up to the behavior defined by `setArrivalTimeQueueOverflowBehavior`.

Note: Arrival Queue Maximum Length When the SAVE policy is used, the arrival queue can grow unbounded. To prevent this, and the potentially large amounts of resources consumed if this were allowed, Java RTS imposes a maximum queue size of 16384 by default. You can override this default by setting the `Arrival-QueueMaxSize` Java property to a larger or smaller value. For instance, adding `-DarrivalQueueMaxSize=256` to the command line when Java RTS is started will limit the arrival queue to 256 entries.

We'll discuss this class, how to use it properly, and in what situations it's meant to be used, later in this chapter when we discuss `RealtimeThread` objects, and in Chapter 8, on asynchronous event handlers.

SporadicParameters

Like an aperiodic task, a sporadic task is not released on a regular time period. However, unlike an aperiodic task that can be released at any time repeatedly without restriction, a sporadic task defines a minimum time between releases. In other words, the time between one release and a subsequent release must at least be equal to or greater than a defined time value. We call this value the *minimum interarrival time* value (see Figure 5-8).

In this figure, the minimum interarrival time (MIT) value is one millisecond. This means that at least one millisecond must elapse between releases of this sporadic task; it can be greater than or equal to it, but never less. In this example, with the first release at $t=0$, the second release at $t=1$ms, and the third at $t=1.8$ms, clearly the MIT has been violated.

Being a type of aperiodic task, the `SporadicParameters` class inherits from the `AperiodicParameters` class, including the arrival time queue functionality. However, this class adds a set of similar methods to define the minimum inter-arrival time value and what should be done if it's violated. These methods are:

`setMitViolationBehavior()`—defines how to handle the case where the MIT value is violated. The acceptable values are:

> **`mitViolationExcept`**—when set to this value, an `MITViolationException` will be thrown if the time difference between the current release and the previous release is less than the specified minimum interarrival time.

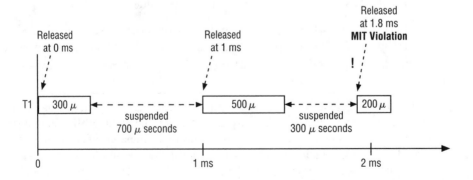

Minimum Interarrival Time = 1ms

Figure 5-8   A MIT violation.

mitViolationIgnore—when set to this value, the current release will be ignored if the time difference between the current release and the previous release is less than the specified minimum interarrival time.

mitViolationReplace—when set to this value, the minimum interarrival time violation is effectively ignored, and if the arrival queue is full, information for this release arrival will replace the last one placed on the queue.

mitViolationSave—when a new arrival occurs and the minimum interarrival time is violated, the arrival queue will be lengthened to store the new arrival without replacing others.

setMinimumInterarrival(RelativeTime min)—sets the minimum interarrival time value. What happens when this setting is violated and a new arrival occurs is up to the behavior defined by setMitViolationBehavior.

Now that we've explored the classes that define periodic, sporadic, and aperiodic Schedulable objects, let's take a look at the most commonly used Schedulable objects within Java RTS: RealtimeThread and NoHeapRealtimeThread.

Real-Time Threads

The RTSJ defines the Schedulable interface for objects that have more precise scheduling parameters than Java SE's java.lang.Thread. The classes that implement the Schedulable interface inherit this behavior, and are subject to priority-based scheduling as defined by Java RTS's scheduling characteristics. In this section, we'll focus on what this means for the two real-time thread classes in Java RTS: RealtimeThread, and NoHeapRealtimeThread. The following is a list of semantics for both thread types:

Priority-Based Dispatching: all Schedulable objects are subject to priority-based dispatching.

Garbage Collection: the collector must not block the execution of real-time threads running at higher priority. The relationship among RTTs and the collector is strictly based on priority dispatching. This means that the collector will be suspended (when safe) when a thread of higher priority is released, and the collector will not interrupt higher-priority threads that are running.

Synchronization: real-time threads are still subject to object locking semantics as they exist in Java SE. However, priority inversion control is implemented to ensure that priority inversion does not occur, and cannot cause unbounded latency.

Periodiodicity: periodic real-time threads can set a period in their constructor, and call `RealtimeThread.waitForNextPeriod()` after the processing for each release. Barring any deadline misses or cost overruns, the thread will be released precisely on the next period's time boundary, regardless of the length of time (or variation in time) of processing for each release. We'll discuss this in detail in the section, Implementing Periodic Threads, later in this chapter.

Interruption: the flow of control and interruption of real-time threads is governed by the asynchronous transfer of control facility in Java RTS (described in Chapter 8).

Both real-time thread types inherit from `java.lang.Thread`, and can take a Runnable class as a parameter when created. Alternatively, you can also create a custom class that extends `RealtimeThread` or `NoHeapRealtimeThread` directly. In the programming sense, real-time threads are nearly identical to standard threads. The only differences are the scheduling-related parameters, such as the priority and release characteristics, the way they're actually scheduled in the system, and certain memory access rules. For example, a `NoHeapRealtimeThread`, as its name implies, cannot access the heap, but a `RealtimeThread` has no such restriction. Let's look at that class in detail first.

Using RealtimeThread

The `RealtimeThread` (RTT) class extends `java.lang.Thread` (referred to as a JLT in this text); it implements the `Schedulable` interface, and is therefore a valid object to execute your time-critical code within. By default, a `RealtimeThread` object executes with the heap as its current memory context, and for the most part behaves similar to a JLT. The difference is that the lowest RTT priority is higher than that of the garbage collector, the just-in-time compiler, and all other JLTs running in the system.

You can specify an RTT's priority, its period (if it's periodic by nature), its memory allocation rate, and an alternative memory context by providing a `SchedulingParameters` object, a `ReleaseParameters` object, and a `MemoryParameters` object in the constructor, respectively. In fact, to offer the most in flexibility, there are four `RealtimeThread` constructors, each taking different combinations of the parameters just mentioned:

`RealtimeThread()`—this constructor takes no parameters, therefore it has no defined release characteristics, and it runs at the base real-time priority with the heap as its memory context. It's important to note that both the release and priority parameters can still be set and/or modified at a later time.

RealtimeThread(SchedulingParameters)—this constructor takes an instance of SchedulingParameters—discussed earlier in the chapter—to specify the thread's priority, but it still has no defined release characteristics, and it uses the heap.

RealtimeThread(SchedulingParameters, ReleaseParameters)—this constructor allows you to specify both the thread's priority and its release parameters.

RealtimeThread(SchedulingParameters, ReleaseParameters, MemoryParameters, MemoryArea, ProcessingGroupParameters, Runnable)—this constructor allows you to provide everything necessary to completely define a RealimeThread's execution behavior. You can leave some of these parameters as null, and provide only the subset that you require. We'll explore this with some code examples below.

As a starting example, Listing 5-6 shows a straightforward way to execute some code in a RealtimeThread object.

Listing 5-6   A simple RealtimeThread

```
import javax.realtime.RealtimeThread;

public class SimpleRT {
    public static void main(String[] args) {
        RealtimeThread rtt = new RealtimeThread() {
            public void run() {
                // execute code in real-time here...
            }
        };

        rtt.start();
        // main thread preempted here if 1 CPU!
        // ...
    }
}
```

Any code in the run method will run within the context of the RealtimeThread, using the heap, at the default real-time priority in preference to code running in a lower-priority JLT. Extending this sample slightly—see Listing 5-7—you can run this RealtimeThread at an even higher priority using the second constructor signature described above and a SchedulingParameter object (new code highlighted in bold).

Listing 5-7   Setting the RTT priority

```
import javax.realtime.RealtimeThread;

public class SimpleRT {
    public static void main(String[] args) {
        PriorityParameters sched =
                new PriorityParameters(
                    PriorityScheduler.instance().getMaxPriority());

        RealtimeThread rtt = new RealtimeThread(sched) {
            public void run() {
                // execute code in real-time here...
            }
        };

        rtt.start();
        // main thread preempted here if 1 CPU!
        // ...
    }
}
```

Starting a real-time task this way is convenient for one-off type processing, but can lead to messy code if you use this pattern extensively. Alternatively, as shown earlier in the chapter, you can define a class that extends `RealtimeThread`, and then set the priority and period through calls to `setSchedulingParameters`, and `setReleaseParameters`. However, you can also do so by invoking a `RealtimeThread` constructor from the derived class via a call to `super` as shown in Listing 5-8.

Real-Time Priority Ranges

Java RTS, being based on the RTSJ, provides a range of real-time priorities dedicated to `Schedulable` objects, above the priorities that JLTs execute. On Solaris, there are 60 new real-time priorities defined by default (from 0 to 59), whereas on Linux there are 49 (from 1 to 49). You can override this default via the RTSJNumRTPrio command-line parameter when the Java RTS VM is started. However, on Linux, setting this value above 49 can interfere with software interrupts that execute at priority 50 and higher, potentially affecting system stability. Set this value higher only if your application requires it and you're aware of the possible side affects it may have. You can also further restrict the maximum real-time priority to a lower value than the default by setting the flag accordingly. This may be required if there are other time-critical applications running on your system outside of the VM.

Listing 5-8   Extending the RealtimeThread class

```java
import javax.realtime.*;

public class ReactorCore {

    // Embedded temperature gauge class
    class TempGauge extends RealtimeThread {
        public TempGauge(SchedulingParameters sched,
                         ReleaseParameters rel)
        {
            super(sched, rel); // call RealtimeThread constructor
        }

        public void run() {
            // Periodically check temperature here ...
        }

        private int getReactorTemp() {
            // ...
        }
    }

    private TempGauge temp = null;

    /////////////////////////////////////////////////////////////

    public ReactorCore() {
        // Run at highest priority
        PriorityParameters sched =
            new PriorityParameters(
                PriorityScheduler.instance().getMaxPriority());

        // 1 millisecond periodic release
        ReleaseParameters rel =
            new PeriodicParameters( new RelativeTime(1,0) );

        temp = new TempGauge(sched, rel);
        temp.start();

        // ...
    }

    public static void main(String[] args) {
        ReactorCore core = new ReactorCore();
    }
}
```

With this, the priority and periodic parameters can be passed in the constructor of the TempGauge class—this is convenient. You can go one step further and embed the creation of the SchedulingParameters and ReleaseParameters objects, and the call to start, to further hide the fact that the TempGauge class runs in a RealtimeThread. As a result, the calling code simply creates the TempGauge class like any other, oblivious to the fact that it's starting a high-priority thread as a side effect (see Listing 5-9).

Listing 5-9   RTT implementation hiding

```
import javax.realtime.*;

public class ReactorCore {

    // Embedded temperature gauge class
    class TempGauge extends RealtimeThread {
        public TempGauge(SchedulingParameters sched,
                          ReleaseParameters rel)

        {
            // Run at highest priority
            PriorityParameters sched =
              new PriorityParameters(
                 PriorityScheduler.instance().getMaxPriority());

            // 1 millisecond periodic release
            ReleaseParameters rel =
              new PeriodicParameters( new RelativeTime(1,0) );

            this.setSchedulingParameters(sched);
            this.setReleaseParameters(rel);
            this.start();
        }
        // ...
    }
    private TempGauge temp = null;

    //////////////////////////////////////////////////////////////

    public ReactorCore() {
        temp = new TempGauge();
        // ...
    }
    // ...
}
```

All of the real-time characteristics of the temperature gauge code are hidden completely within the TempGauge class. Although hiding the implementation details in this example may be considered a good thing to some, there are a few drawbacks in this code. First, the calling code has no knowledge of the fact that a thread is being created, and no control over when that thread is started. The code after the TempGauge object is created may be expected to execute right away but in reality may not execute for quite some time later. Further, this behavior will change depending upon the number of processors available to execute the code. These unexpected side effects can lead to errant application behavior.

Second, consider that the extends keyword is an expression of the "*is a*" relationship in object-oriented programming. Strictly speaking a temperature gauge is not a thread. The fact that the temperature gauge code is set to run in its own thread is an implementation detail that, according to some, should be decided *outside* of the TempGauge class implementation. Therefore, you may prefer to modify the TempGauge class to implement the Runnable interface, and create the thread externally. The Realtime-Thread class takes this into account with its forth constructor (see Listing 5-10).

Listing 5-10   Using RealtimeThread and Runnable

```
public class ReactorCore {
    // Embedded temperature gauge class
    class TempGauge implements Runnable {
        public TempGauge() {
            // ...
        }

        public void run() {
            // Periodically check temperature here ...
        }

        private int getReactorTemp() {
            // ...
        }
    }

    private TempGauge temp = null;

    ////////////////////////////////////////////////////////////////

    public ReactorCore() {
        // Run at highest priority
        PriorityParameters sched =
            new PriorityParameters(
                PriorityScheduler.instance().getMaxPriority());

        // 1 millisecond periodic release
        ReleaseParameters rel =
            new PeriodicParameters( new RelativeTime(1,0) );
```

continued

```
        // Create the temperature gauge business logic class
        temp = new TempGauge();

        // Create the RealtimeThread to execute TempGauge
        RealtimeThread rtt =
            new RealtimeThread(

                sched, rel, null, null, null, temp);

        rtt.start();
        //...
    }
    //...
}
```

In this example, the TempGauge class has no knowledge of the thread it's to execute within. Therefore, the calling code is required to create the RealtimeThread and provide the scheduling and release parameters, as well as the TempGauge Runnable object, in the constructor. The three null values provided in the RealtimeThread constructor are for the MemoryParameters, MemoryArea, and ProcessingGroupParameters parameter objects, respectively. As a result, Java RTS defaults to running the RealtimeThread with the Java heap as the allocation context. (We'll explore the memory-related parameters at the end of this chapter.)

Either implementation (extending RealtimeThread, or implementing Runnable) is correct and works equally well. The pattern you choose to implement throughout your code is a personal choice, and you may even decide to use both in different situations, depending upon the circumstances. To Java RTS, it makes no difference which pattern you decide to use.

Using NoHeapRealtimeThread

A NoHeapRealtimeThread is a type of RTT with additional semantics. First, code running within an NHRT cannot access the heap in any way. Second, there is no synchronization between the NHRT and the garbage collector. As a result, a NoHeapRealtimeThread can safely interrupt the garbage collector at any time, and hence can preempt the collector with no additional latency beyond the system's standard thread preemption/dispatch time. Contrast this to Realtime Thread, which must otherwise wait for the collector to reach a safe preemption point to ensure the heap is in a consistent state.

NoHeapRealtimeThread objects must be created and started in either a scoped memory region, or in immortal memory (described in the section *Memory Models* in this chapter). When started, execution begins within the specified memory area, and the code must never access or reference an object on the heap.

If by chance a `NoHeapRealtimeThread` does attempt to access the heap, a `MemoryAccessError` error will be thrown. This can prove tricky, and can be a frustrating matter for new NHRT programmers to overcome. This chapter introduces a helper class to make it easier to create and start NHRT objects from within any memory region, class, and thread.

Like a `RealtimeThread`, a `NoHeapRealtimeThread` instance accepts references to `SchedulingParameters` and `ReleaseParameters` objects in its constructors. However, unlike `RealtimeThread` constructors, these constructors always require a reference to a valid, non-null memory region as an allocation context. These constructors are:

NoHeapRealtimeThread(SchedulingParameters, MemoryArea)—this constructor takes an instance of `SchedulingParameters`—discussed earlier in the chapter—to specify the thread's priority, and a region of memory as the allocation context (other than the heap).

NoHeapRealtimeThread(SchedulingParameters, ReleaseParameters, Memory Area)—this constructor allows you to specify the thread's priority, its release parameters, and a region of memory as the allocation context (again, not the heap).

NoHeapRealtimeThread(SchedulingParameters, ReleaseParameters, Memory-Parameters, MemoryArea, ProcessingGroupParameters, Runnable)—this constructor allows you to provide everything necessary to completely define a `NoheapRealimeThread`'s execution behavior. You can leave some of these parameters as null, and provide only the subset that you require. However, you must always provide a non-heap region of memory as the allocation context before the thread is started.

The NHRT `start` method implements an additional check to ensure that the thread's execution starts in a non-heap region of memory. Valid memory regions include the Java RTS immortal memory region, or an application-defined scoped memory region. Listing 5-11 shows what may be the simplest way to create and start a `NoHeapRealtimeThread` object.

Listing 5-11 Simple `NoHeapRealtimeThread` creation

```
import javax.realtime.*;

public class MyApp {
    static {
        // Create NHRT (within immortal memory)
        NoHeapRealtimeThread nhrt =
```

continued

```
      new NoHeapRealtimeThread(
        null, ImmortalMemory.instance()))
    {
      public void run() {
          // Execute NHRT code here...
      }
    };
    nhrt.start();
  }

  public static void main(String[] args) {
  }
}
```

Although there's no code in the `main` method, the code within the `static` block executes when the `MyApp` class is instantiated, which occurs when the Java RTS VM starts. And being `static`, all of the objects created inside exist within immortal memory, which satisfies the requirement for a `NoHeapRealtimeThread` (NHRT) object. However, creating and executing NHRTs this way just isn't convenient. Let's look at a more reasonable example that involves first creating a thread that enters immortal memory as its allocation context, and then creates and starts an NHRT. The code in Listing 5-12 takes what we've done so far with the temperature gauge example and modifies it accordingly.

Listing 5-12   Explicit creation of an NHRT

```
import javax.realtime.*;
public class Main {
    class TempGauge implements Runnable {
        public TempGauge() {
        }

        public void run() {
            boolean ok = true;
            while ( ok ) {
                // Check reactor core temp...
                ok = NoHeapRealtimeThread.waitForNextPeriod();
            }
        }

        private int getReactorTemp() {
            // get reactor core temperature ...
        }
    }

    static TempGauge temp = null;

    public Main() {
```

```
RealtimeThread rtt = new RealtimeThread() {
    public void run() {
        ImmortalMemory.instance().enter(
        new Runnable() {
            public void run() {
                // Run at highest priority
                int maxPri =
                    PriorityScheduler.instance()
                        .getMaxPriority()
                PriorityParameters sched =
                    new PriorityParameters(maxPri);

                // 1 millisecond periodic release
                ReleaseParameters rel =
                    new PeriodicParameters(
                    new RelativeTime(1,0) );

                // Create the temperature gauge class
                temp = new TempGauge();

                // Create NHRT to execute TempGauge
                NoHeapRealtimeThread nhrt =
                    new NoHeapRealtimeThread(
                        sched, rel,
                        null, ImmortalMemory.instance(),
                        null, temp);

                nhrt.start();
            }
        });
    }
};

rtt.start();
}

public static void main(String[] args) {
    Main main = new Main();
}
}
```

The code in bold type represents the areas of change from the RealtimeThread version of this example. First, the TempGauge class instance is declared as static to ensure it resides in immortal memory. Next, immortal memory is set as the allocation context via the call to enter on the ImmortalMemory singleton object. However, this method requires a Runnable object to begin execution from within the region, therefore one is created as an anonymous inner class. As a result, this code is immediately executed within immortal memory, where all of the required objects are allocated.

However, it's important to note something first. In a way, we have a chicken-and-egg problem: we want to create a `NoHeapRealtimeThread` (whose reference cannot exist on the heap), but we cannot do this from a `Thread` because it cannot enter a scope immortal memory. Only a `Schedulable` object (i.e. a `RealtimeThread`, a `NoHeapRealtimeThread`, or an `AsynchEventHandler`) can do this. Therefore, we create a `RealtimeThread` first that acts as an intermediary to do this for us. From here, immortal memory is safely accessed.

> **Note: JLTs and Immortal Memory**   To be clear, although a JLT cannot enter immortal memory via the `MemoryArea.enter` method, it can through `executeIn-Area`. However, it must provide an instance of a Runnable object to execute within immortal memory.

The RTT is not the only intermediary, though. This code sample illustrates a common pattern where an anonymous inner `Runnable` class is provided to execute in a memory region other than the heap. When the RTT, which is started on the heap, attempts to enter immortal memory, it creates a `Runnable` object to pass to the call to `ImmortalMemory.enter`. This on its own isn't a problem, but since it's created in immortal memory, it's never reclaimed. Doing this for each `NoHeapReal timeThread` that's created and/or started results in what can be considered a memory leak. The immortal memory that each of the enclosed `Runnable` objects consumes is effectively wasted.

This problem can be eliminated by simply calling `ImmortalMemory.enter` without the `Runnable` from the RTT, as shown in Listing 5-13. Note that this is a simplified version of Listing 5-12, therefore much of the code has been omitted.

Listing 5-13   Eliminating memory leaks when creating NHRTs

```
// ...
public Main() {
    RealtimeThread rtt = new RealtimeThread() {
        public void run() {
            ImmortalMemory.instance().enter();

            // Create release and scheduling params,
            // TempGauge, and NHRT objects below...

            // ...

            nhrt.start();
        }
    };
}
// ...
```

We wanted to explore both forms of the enter method to illustrate the different patterns available to you to enter non-heap memory areas. However, to make it even more convenient to work with NHRTs, we've created a factory object that makes it easier to create and start code to execute within an NHRT. The class, called NoHeapHelper, requires you to implement your application code in a class that extends Runnable—which is a reasonable requirement. Next, you pass in a reference to the Class itself (not an object instantiated from your class), to one of the NoHeapHelper constructors using *<YourClass>*.class method. You can optionally pass in a memory area, but it's not required. By default, the helper class will instantiate and execute the Runnable in immortal memory unless you provide a scoped memory region to use. Creating and starting your code within an NHRT is now as simple as writing code similar to Listing 5-14.

Listing 5-14   Using NoHeapHelper

```
import javax.realtime.*;
import noheaphelper.*;

public class Main {
    public static void main(String[] args) throws Exception
    {
        NoHeapHelper nhrtHelper =
                new NoHeapHelper(TempGauge.class);

        nhrtHelper.start(); // an NHRT is now running
    }
}
```

In this small example, we've seemingly created and started an NHRT from a standard JLT. The NoHeapHelper class (see Listing 5-15) performs all of the steps in the previous sample code, except that it's all encapsulated, hidden, and reusable. To use it, simply provide a reference to the class object for your class that implements the Runnable interface. This class is instantiated in either immortal memory, or an optional scoped memory object that you can provide in the NoHeapHelper constructor.

Listing 5-15   The NoHeapHelper Class

```
import javax.realtime.*;
public class NoHeapHelper extends RealtimeThread
{
    private Class runnable = null;
    private SchedulingParameters sched = null;
    private ReleaseParameters rel = null;
    private MemoryArea mem = null;
```

continued

```java
private MemoryParameters memP = null;
private ProcessingGroupParameters pgP = null;

public NoHeapHelper() {
    this.mem = ImmortalMemory.instance();
}

public NoHeapHelper(Class runnable) {
    this();
    this.runnable = runnable;
}

public NoHeapHelper(MemoryArea mem)
  throws Exception {
    this.mem = mem;
    if ( mem instanceof HeapMemory )
      throw new Exception (
        "MemoryArea must be ImmortalMemory or ScopedMemory");
    if (MemoryArea.getMemoryArea(mem) instanceof HeapMemory)
      throw new Exception ("MemoryArea created on the heap");
}

public NoHeapHelper(MemoryArea mem, Class runnable)
  throws Exception {
    this(mem);
    this.runnable = runnable;
}

public NoHeapHelper(
    SchedulingParameters sched, ReleaseParameters rel,
    MemoryParameters mp, MemoryArea mem, Class runnable)
  throws Exception {
    this(mem, runnable);
    this.sched = sched;
    this.rel = rel;
    this.memP = mp;
}

public void setRunnable(Class runnable) {
    this.runnable = runnable;
}

public void setSchedulingParams(SchedulingParameters sched){
    this.sched = sched;
}

public void setReleaseParams(ReleaseParameters rel) {
    this.rel = rel;
}
```

```
public void setMemParams(MemoryParameters memP) {
    this.memP = memP;
}

public void setProcessingGroupParams(
  ProcessingGroupParameters p) {
    this.pgP = p;
}

static NHRTStarter starter = new NHRTStarter(); // see below

public void run() {
    try {
      synchronized( starter ) {
        starter.runnable = this.runnable;
        starter.rel = this.rel;
        starter.sched = this.sched;
        starter.mem = mem;
        starter.memP = this.memP;
        starter.pgP = this.pgP;
        mem.enter(starter);
      }
    }
    catch ( Exception e ) {
        e.printStackTrace();
    }
}

//////////////////////////////////////////////////////////////
// Embedded class NHRTStarter

static class NHRTStarter implements Runnable {
    public Class runnable = null;
    public SchedulingParameters sched = null;
    public ReleaseParameters rel = null;
    public MemoryArea mem = null;
    public MemoryParameters memP = null;
    public ProcessingGroupParameters pgP = null;

    NHRTStarter() { }

    public void run() {
        try {
            // Create the runnable and the NHRT and start it
            Runnable r = (Runnable)runnable.newInstance();

            // Clone any NHRT constructor parameters
            // in the current non-heap memory context.
```

continued

```
            // This includes SchedulingParameters,
            // ReleaseParameters, and Memoryparameters.
            // ProcessingGroupParameters is not yet
            // implemented by Java RTS
            PriorityParameters sp = null;
            ReleaseParameters rp = null;
            MemoryParameters mp = null;
            ProcessingGroupParameters pgp = null;
            if ( sched != null )
                sp = (PriorityParameters)sched.clone();

            if ( rel != null ) {
                if ( rel instanceof PeriodicParameters )
                    rp = (PeriodicParameters)rel.clone();
                else if ( rel instanceof AperiodicParameters)
                    rp = (AperiodicParameters)rel.clone();
                else
                    rp = (SporadicParameters)rel.clone();
            }

            if ( memP != null )
                mp = (MemoryParameters)memP.clone();

            if ( pgP != null )
                pgp = (ProcessingGroupParameters)pgP.clone();

            NoHeapRealtimeThread nhrt =
                new NoHeapRealtimeThread(
                    sp, rp,
                    mp, getCurrentMemoryArea(),
                    null, r);

            nhrt.start();

        }
        catch ( Exception e ) {
            e.printStackTrace();;
        }
    }
  }
}
```

The NoHeapHelper class has four constructors:

NoHeapHelper()—this constructor takes no parameters. The memory region defaults to immortal memory, although this can be changed prior to starting the NHRT.

NoHeapHelper(Class runnable)—here, you provide your `Runnable Class`'s object reference. As in the first constructor, the memory region defaults to immortal memory but can be changed later.

NoHeapHelper(MemoryArea mem)—this constructor allows you to provide a memory region to execute the NHRT within. You will need to provide your code's `Runnable Class` object before it's started, however.

NoHeapHelper(SchedulingParameters s, ReleaseParameters r, Memory-Parameters mp, MemoryArea mem, Class runnable)—this constructor allows you to provide scheduling parameters, release parameters, the parameters related to allocation, the memory area to start the NHRT within, and the `Runnable Class`, all at once.

Regardless of the constructor used, you can always provide the other parameters via the various `setX` methods available, such as `setReleaseParameters`. Once all of the parameters have been provided, you can call the `NoHeapHelper.start` method to start the NHRT with your provided `Runnable` code.

Since `NoHeapHelper` itself extends `RealtimeThread`, calling `start` begins its execution within an RTT, and its `run` method, which performs two main functions:

- All provided objects—i.e. the `Runnable Class`, memory area, release parameters, and so on—are copied over to the single `static` instance of another class, called `NHRTStarter` (more on this below). Being `static`, this object lives in immortal memory, and there is only one instance of it shared across all instances of `NoHeapHelper`, which is why access to it is synchronized. Using one static instance ensures no non-heap memory is wasted.

- The single instance of the `NHRTStarter` object, which implements `Runnable`, is provided to the call to enter the specified memory area. Recall that if no memory area was provided, this defaults to immortal memory.

At this point, the `NHRTStarter` code is executed within the appropriate memory region, and its own `run` method is called. Note that the following steps are performed within the `NoHeapHelper` object instance's thread (which is the enclosing `NoHeapHelper` RTT):

1. The provided `Runnable` is created using Java Reflection. The reason it's created this way, and not simply provided in the constructor instead of the `Class` object, is to ensure that it's created within the proper non-heap memory area. This allows `NoHeapHelper` to be used from a `java.lang.Thread` object, and also saves the calling thread the complication of entering the appropriate memory region to create the `Runnable`.

2. Each of the other objects, such as ReleaseParameters, Schedulable-
Parameters, and so on, is copied into the current non-heap memory context
via calls to clone. This method provides an exact copy of the object in the
current memory region.

3. Next, the NoHeapRealtimeThread itself is created with all of the required
parameters. Some of these parameters may be null, such as the SchedulingParameters, in which case the default will be used as defined by the
NoHeapRealtimeThread constructor. Note that a call to getCurrentMemo-
ryArea() is used to provide the appropriate memory allocation context.

4. Finally, the NHRT is started, and the provided Runnable code begins to
execute within it, with the proper memory allocation context.

While the internals of this class may take some review to absorb, it's an easy class
to use. You saw a simple example, earlier, where it was used to execute an NHRT
within immortal memory. The code in Listing 5-16 shows how easy it is to create
and provide a scoped memory area with NoHeapHelper.

Listing 5-16   Using NoHeapHelper with ScopedMemory

```
import javax.realtime.*;
public class Main {
    static ScopedMemory sm = new LTMemory(8192000);

    public static void main(String[] args) throws Exception {
        NoHeapHelper nhrtHelper =
                new NoHeapHelper(sm, TempGauge.class);

        nhrtHelper.start();
    }
}
```

We'll examine the creation and usage of scoped memory in detail later. The point
of this code sample is to show how easy it is to start an NHRT running within a
scoped memory region. Going further, the code in Listing 5-17 defines release
characteristics and a specific priority at which to run the NHRT.

Listing 5-17   Setting scheduling and release parameters with NoHeapHelper

```
import javax.realtime.*;
public class Main {
    static ScopedMemory sm = new LTMemory(8192000);

    public static void main(String[] args) throws Exception {
        NoHeapHelper nhrtHelper =
                new NoHeapHelper(sm, TempGauge.class);
```

```
PriorityParameters pri =
    new PriorityParameters(
        PriorityScheduler.instance().getMaxPriority() );

PeriodicParameters per =
    new PeriodicParameters(
        new RelativeTime(1,0) );

nhrtHelper.setSchedulingParams(pri);
nhrtHelper.setReleaseParams(per);

nhrtHelper.start();
  }
}
```

This code shows two additional calls to the NoHeapHelper class to set the scheduling and release parameters before start is called. Again, we've provided a scoped memory region as the allocation context, but immortal memory could have been used here also.

Although we've touched upon Schedulable object release parameters throughout our discussion so far, it's time to discuss it in more detail. In the next section, we'll examine how to define periodic, aperiodic, and sporadic real-time threads in Java RTS.

Implementing Periodic Threads

We've already covered the PeriodicParameters class, and the RealtimeThread class, in previous sections. Here, we'll discuss using both of them to create periodic real-time threads, and how to handle deadline misses if they occur. Continuing with the temperature gauge example, if the time-critical requirement is to check the temperature of a physical device every millisecond, we need to create a real-time thread with a one-millisecond period. In this case, the deadline is also considered to be one millisecond, as the processing of the temperature must complete before the thread's next release (or, once per millisecond).

The sleep function of a JLT won't suffice in this case; that function merely suspends the thread for *about* the amount of time you request. It doesn't take into account the thread's processing time, nor does it use the system's high-resolution timer. For a real-time guarantee, the first step is to run the task in a RealtimeThread. Second, you need to call RealtimeThread.waitForNextPeriod in place of Thread.sleep. This method works with the Java RTS scheduler, and the release characteristics of the specific RTT, to ensure that your task is released precisely at

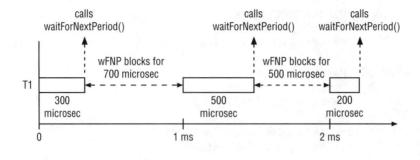

wFNP = waitForNextPeriod()

Figure 5-9   `waitForNextPeriod()` releases on precise time boundaries for periodic real-time threads.

the time boundary requested, no matter how busy the system is. It also takes into account your task's processing time between each release, and the corresponding call to `waitForNextPeriod` (see Figure 5-9)

Here, the thread has a one-millisecond period, and is released on each one-millisecond time boundary regardless of its processing time per release. The call to `waitForNextPeriod` ensures this by working with the priority scheduler within Java RTS. You can set up this scenario yourself with code similar to Listing 5-18.

Listing 5-18   Using `waitForNextPeriod`

```
import javax.realtime.*;

public class ReactorCore {

    // Embedded temperature gauge class
    class TempGauge extends RealtimeThread {
        public TempGauge(SchedulingParameters sched,
                         ReleaseParameters rel) {
            super(sched, rel); // call RTT constructor
        }

        public void run() {
            while ( true ) {
                // Check reactor temp here...

                boolean ok = waitForNextPeriod();
                if ( ! ok ) {
                    // Handle deadline miss here...
                }
            }
        }
    }
```

```
        private TempGauge temp = null;

        //////////////////////////////////////////////////////////////

        public ReactorCore() {
            // 1 millisecond periodic release
            ReleaseParameters rel =
                new PeriodicParameters( new RelativeTime(1,0) );

            temp = new TempGauge(null, rel);
            temp.start();
            // ...
        }

        public static void main(String[] args) {
            ReactorCore core = new ReactorCore();
        }
    }
```

This code creates the scenario shown in Figure 5-9. The RTT is guaranteed to be released on every one-millisecond boundary as requested. However, there is a caveat we need to cover; there's a potential to miss the deadline in two cases:

- System overload: if the system is overloaded with too many high-priority tasks, and becomes processor-bound, there's a chance your RTT may miss its deadline. This will only happen in Java RTS if there are other, higher-priority, tasks executing. As a result, if an RTT misses its deadline, the call to waitForNextPeriod will return a false value (as opposed to true when the deadline is met).

- Execution cost overrun: if your code's execution time exceeds the release time or otherwise causes your periodic thread to miss its deadline (again, the period in this case), the result is a deadline miss. This will cause the wait-ForNextPeriod call to return a false value indicating the deadline miss.

You can simply check for a false return value and handle deadline misses that way. However, you can also provide a separate object to be called when a deadline miss occurs. This allows you to define a common set of code to handle deadline misses that may occur in different parts of your code. Let's explore this pattern now.

Deadline Miss Handler

Throughout this chapter, you may have noticed how difficult it is to study one part of the RTSJ without touching upon other parts simultaneously. For example, when we looked at ReleaseParameters and SchedulingParameters, we discussed them in the context of the RealtimeThread class even though we didn't cover that class in detail yet. Likewise, although we won't cover asynchronous event handlers in detail until Chapter 8, we need to preview it here, as the RTT deadline miss handler class is implemented as one. Therefore, bear with us as we introduce only some of it here; we'll go into detail in a later chapter.

In Listing 5-19, a simple RTT class named MyTask is defined as a one-millisecond periodic time-critical task. The deadline handler is implemented in class DeadlineMissHandler, which extends AsynchEventHandler as discussed. In the constructor, the priority is set to a value higher than the periodic RTT it's associated with to help ensure it gets processing time when a deadline miss occurs.

Listing 5-19   Using deadline miss handlers

```
import javax.realtime.*;
public class Main {
    class MyTask extends RealtimeThread {
        public MyTask() {
        }

        public void run() {
            while ( true ) {
                boolean ok = waitForNextPeriod();
            }
        }
        // ...
    }

    class DeadlineMissHandler extends AsyncEventHandler {
        private Schedulable sched = null;
        public DeadlineMissHandler(Schedulable sched) {
            super(new PriorityParameters(
                PriorityScheduler.instance().getMaxPriority()),
                null, null, null, null, null);
            this.sched = sched;
        }

        public void handleAsyncEvent() {
            // Handle the deadline miss here. i.e. change period
            PeriodicParameters release =
                new PeriodicParameters(
                    new RelativeTime(5,0) ); // 5ms
            setReleaseParameters(release);

            // Need to reschedule the periodic thread here
            if ( sched instanceof RealtimeThread)
                ((RealtimeThread)sched).schedulePeriodic();
```

```
        }
    }

    public Main() {
        // Create the Schedulable
        MyTask task = new MyTask();

        // Create this task's deadline handler
        DeadlineMissHandler dmh = new DeadlineMissHandler(task);

        // Set a one-millisecond period and deadline
        RelativeTime period = new RelativeTime(1,0); // 1 milli
        PeriodicParameters release =
            new PeriodicParameters( null, period,
                                    null, null,
                                    null, dmh);

        task.setReleaseParameters(release);

        task.start();
    }

    public static void main(String[] args) {
        Main m = new Main();
    }
}
```

The RTT is created first, then the deadline handler, which is given a reference to the RTT it's to be associated with. Next, the release parameters are defined, providing the period (one millisecond), and the deadline handler object reference. The result is an instance of the `PeriodicParemeters` class, where the period and deadline handler are provided—the remaining parameters are left as `null`. This means that the RTT will start immediately without delay, and the deadline (otherwise specified as the fourth parameter in the constructor) will be equal to the RTT's period by default. You can provide a `RelativeTime` object in this parameter to specifically set the deadline, but it can only be a value equal to or less than the period. You cannot create a periodic `RealtimeThread` object with a deadline greater than the period.

Since feasibility analysis is not implemented in Java RTS (as it's optional in the RTSJ) we won't bother to specify a cost (the third parameter in the constructor), which would otherwise give an indication of the expected execution time of the real-time task.

Once the `PeriodicParameters` object is created with applicable parameters set, it's provided to the RTT via the call to `setReleaseParameters` on object `task`. Finally, the RTT is started, and real-time periodic processing begins. You can further modify this sample to set a specific priority for the RTT, or a tighter deadline. Before we move along to explore the implementation of aperiodic threads, keep in mind that all of the concepts discussed in this section related to `RealtimeThread` apply to `NoHeapRealtimeThread` code as well.

Implementing Aperiodic Threads

An aperiodic thread is one where there is no defined minimum or maximum time between releases. The RTSJ doesn't define any facilities for an aperiodic `RealtimeThread` object besides one that is used either for one-time use, or one that waits (and blocks) on a resource repeatedly. This resource can be a shared object, or some sort of IO operation. There is no equivalent to `RealtimeThread.waitForNextPeriod`, such as a `waitForNextRelease` method, which is planned in the next version of the RTSJ via JSR 282. For now, however, you'll need to define your own aperiodic release semantics. We'll explore some sample uses of an aperiodic `RealtimeThread` in this section.

One-Time Use

The fundamental use case for an aperiodic RTT is for one-time processing of a task at a real-time priority. Further, this processing can take place within immortal memory or scoped memory to achieve the best determinism. One such example is the response to a pilot's request to turn off autopilot on a commercial airliner. Although this is not a periodic task, it's a task that must complete within a bounded time frame to allow the pilot to gain control over the aircraft deterministically. Listing 5-20 illustrates a basic implementation (minus the actual autopilot code).

Listing 5-20   A simple aperiodic `RealtimeThread`

```
import javax.realtime.*;
public class FlightControl {
    SchedulingParameters sched = null;
    AperiodicParameters rel = null;

    public FlightControl() {
        this.sched = new PriorityParameters(
            PriorityScheduler.instance().getMaxPriority() );

        this.rel = new AperiodicParameters();

        rel.setArrivalTimeQueueOverflowBehavior(
            AperiodicParameters.arrivalTimeQueueOverflowSave);
    }
```

```
    public boolean disableAutopilot() {
        RealtimeThread rt =
            new RealtimeThread( sched, rel ) {
                public void run() {
                    // execute critical code here
                    // ...
                }
            };

        rt.start();
        return true;
    }

    // ...

    public static void main(String[] args) {
        FlightControl fc = new FlightControl();
        // ...
        fc.disableAutopilot();
    }
}
```

In this example, it's clear that the `RealtimeThread` is created for one-time use only. The `SchedulingParameters` and `ReleaseParameters` objects are created ahead of time to limit the amount of processing required when the call to disable autopilot is made. Let's take a look at an example of an aperiodic `RealtimeThread` that blocks on an object.

Object Blocking

In Listing 5-21, we create two threads of operation: the first is a thread that listens for new requests from a client. The second is an aperiodic `RealtimeThread` implemented similar to the example above, but with the logic contained within a `Runnable` class. Only portions of the code are shown, since much of it is repeated from other samples. Below, we see the implementation of the `Runnable` class that is executed within the `RealtimeThread`. This thread, and the thread that accepts new requests, share a static queue.

Listing 5-21 Aperiodic RTT lock signaling

```
public class RequestProcessor implements Runnable {
    private static List<Socket> queue = new LinkedList<Socket>();
    public RequestProcessor() {
    }
```

continued

```java
public void run() {
    while ( true ) {
        try {
            Socket conn;
            synchronized ( queue ) {
                while ( queue.isEmpty() ) {
                    try {
                        queue.wait();
                    }
                    catch ( InterruptedException e ) { }
                }

                // Grab the request off the top of the queue
                conn = queue.remove(0);
            }

            // Handle this request and send a response
            sendResponse( conn );
        }
        catch ( Exception e ) {
            e.printStackTrace();
        }
    }
}

private void sendResponse(Socket conn) {
    // ...
}

public static void processRequest(Socket request) {
    synchronized ( queue ) {
        queue.add( request );
        queue.notifyAll();
    }
}
}
```

Here, the code blocks on the queue that holds the requests. Access to this object is synchronized since other threads can add to this queue by calling the static method RequestProcessor.processRequest. When a new request is added to the queue via a call to processRequest, all waiting threads are notified, which causes the call to queue.wait to return within the aperiodic RealtimeThread's run loop. As a result, the request is processed and a response is sent.

IO Blocking

Although an aperiodic RTT can be used to block on IO, such as network or file-based IO, an asynchronous event handler is a better implementation for this. Since this is the topic of Chapter 8, we won't explore this in any more detail now. However, if you did decide to use an RTT or NHRT for this, the code would be similar to the previous example. The only difference would be the object to block on. In this case, it would most likely be an implementation based on the `java.io.*` library.

Memory Models

We've already touched upon the new memory models available in Java RTS, both in this chapter and in Chapter 3 where we discussed the RTSJ. As a review, there are three types of memory available in Java RTS: the standard Java heap, scoped memory regions, and an immortal memory region. These regions are represented by Java classes, each of which extends the `MemoryArea` abstract base class (see Figure 5-10).

If we look at the `MemoryArea` class in detail, we find a set of methods that allow you to execute code within that area directly, determine the overall size of the region and the amount of free space remaining, and allocate objects within it (without necessarily entering it)—see Figure 5-11.

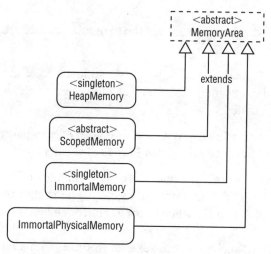

Figure 5-10   The class diagram of `MemoryArea` objects.

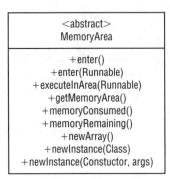

Figure 5-11   The MemoryArea abstract class.

Note: Default Memory Area Size Constraints   By default, Java RTS constrains immortal memory to a maximum of 32MB, and each scoped memory area to 16MB. You can override these values for immortal and scoped memory with the –XX:ImmortalSize and –XX:ScopedSize command-line parameters, respectively. Note, however, that the VM will round these numbers perhaps up or down when started. Therefore, to be sure what the actual sizes are, also include the –XX:+RTSJShowHeapLayout flag on the command line.

The constructors for this class have been left off the diagram so they could be described here in detail:

MemoryArea(long size)—create an instance of the particular memory region of the specified size in bytes.

MemoryArea(long size, Runnable logic)—create an instance of the particular memory region of the specified size, and execute the given Runnable when MemoryArea.enter is called.

MemoryArea(SizeEstimator size)—create an instance of the particular memory region of the size indicated by the given SizeEstimator object.

MemoryArea(SizeEstimator size, Runnable logic)—create an instance of the particular memory region of the size indicated by the given SizeEstimator object, and execute the given Runnable when MemoryArea.enter is called.

When creating a memory region, such as a ScopedMemory object, with a Runnable provided in the constructor, a subsequent call to enter starts that Runnable within the current thread of execution, with the new memory region as the allocation context (see Listing 5-22).

Listing 5-22 Using ScopedMemory

```
import javax.realtime.*;
public class MyApp extends RealtimeThread {

    class MyLogic implements Runnable {
        public MyLogic() {
            // ...
        }

        public void run() {
            // ...
        }
    }

    static ScopedMemory sm = null;

    public MyApp() { }

    public void run() {
        // execute MyLogic in scoped memory in current RTT
        int memSize = 4096000; // ~4MB in size
        sm = new LTMemory( memSize, new MyLogic() );
        sm.enter();
    }

    public static void main(String[] args) {
        MyApp app = new MyApp();
        app.start();
    }
}
```

Otherwise, if you create a memory region without giving a Runnable in the constructor, you need to provide the Runnable object in the call to enter, as shown in Listing 5-23.

Listing 5-23 Using ScopedMemory and a Runnable

```
import javax.realtime.*;
public class MyApp extends RealtimeThread {

    class MyLogic implements Runnable {
        public MyLogic() {
            // ...
        }

        public void run() {
            // ...
```

continued

```
        }
    }

    static ScopedMemory sm = null;

    public MyApp() { }

    public void run() {
        // execute MyLogic in scoped memory in current RTT
        int memSize = 4096000; // ~4MB in size
        sm = new LTMemory( memSize );
        sm.enter( new MyLogic() );
    }

    public static void main(String[] args) {
        MyApp app = new MyApp();
        app.start();
    }
}
```

If you fail to provide the Runnable in the call to enter in the above example, you will receive the following exception:

`java.lang.IllegalArgumentException: MemoryArea did not have a Run-nable attached.`

However, if you wish to execute only a small piece of code in immortal memory or scoped memory without creating a separate Runnable class, you can use an anonymous inner class as shown in Listing 5-24 (and as seen in other examples in this chapter).

Listing 5-24   ScopedMemory and inner classes

```
import javax.realtime.*;
public class MyApp extends RealtimeThread {
    public void run() {
        System.out.println(
            "Current memory area = " + getMemoryArea());

        ImmortalMemory.instance().executeInArea(
            new Runnable() {
                public void run() {
                    Object obj = new Object();
                    System.out.println(
                        "'obj' allocated in memory area = " +
                        MemoryArea.getMemoryArea(obj));
```

```
                }
            }
        );
    }

    public static void main(String[] args) {
        MyApp myApp = new MyApp();
        myApp.start();
    }
}
```

The output from this class (below) shows that the RTT is executing on the heap, but that obj is allocated from within immortal memory:

```
Current memory area = javax.realtime.HeapMemory
'obj' allocated in memory area = javax.realtime.ImmortalMemory
```

Regardless, when either enter or executeInArea is called, the associated Runnable is entered anew. This can cause a StackOverflowException if you call MemoryArea.enter from within a Runnable object's run method, as seen in Listing 5-25.

Listing 5-25   A memory region error

```
import javax.realtime.*;
public class Main extends RealtimeThread {

    public void run() {
        System.out.println("in Main run()");
        ImmortalMemory.instance().enter(this);

        // Intend to do stuff in immortal memory...

        // ERROR: STACK OVER FLOW!!!!!
    }

    public static void main(String[] args) throws Exception {
        Main app = new Main();
        app.start();
    }
}
```

In the remainder of this chapter, we'll focus on some patterns of usage around immortal memory and scoped memory that haven't already been discussed. First, let's take a look at the memory access rules that are important to understand.

Memory Access Rules

There are certain restrictions on references to objects, mainly regarding those within a ScopedMemory region. This restriction applies to some scope-to-scope object references as well. Figure 5-12 illustrates these restrictions.

As shown in Figure 5-12, objects within a scope can reference objects within the same scope, and objects on the heap. Objects on the heap cannot reference objects in a scope, and objects in one scope cannot reference objects in a different scope, unless that scope is an outer scope. Table 5-1 contains a complete list of allowed and restricted references between memory regions.

The real-time Java VM must check that these assignment rules are not violated for every object assignment at runtime. This can impact application performance and throughput to some degree, but it is a bounded, measurable operation.

Recall that Java is a safe language with automatic memory management. As a result, you're assured that dangling pointers (pointers to objects no longer considered live) will never occur. Each Java reference must always be to a valid live object, or null. Therefore, references to an object in a scoped memory region must never exist from the heap or immortal memory, because the objects within

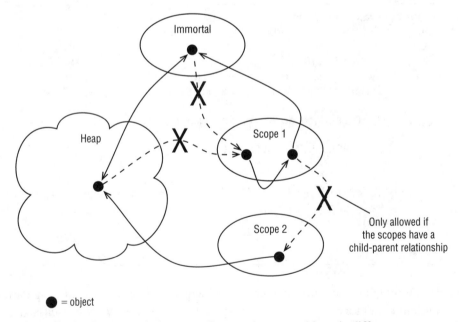

Figure 5-12   Some restrictions on references between objects in different memory regions.

Table 5-1   Assignment rules to/from different memory regions

An Object in:	Can Reference Heap	Can Reference Immortal	Can Reference Scoped
Heap	Yes	Yes	No
Immortal	Yes	Yes	No
Scoped	Yes	Yes	Yes, if in the same scope, or in an outer scope. Otherwise, no.
Local Variable	Yes	Yes	Yes

the scope can be reclaimed at any time. They are not under the control of the code holding the reference, or by the garbage collector within the Java VM.

The same restriction applies to inter-scope references as well, with one exception. Since scopes can be stacked in terms of being a `Schedulable` object's current allocation context, an object from one scope can refer to objects in an outer (longer living) scope in the parent-child relationship that scopes have. We'll discuss the stacking of scopes and parenting rules later, but for now understand that references are allowed from inner scopes to more outer scopes, but not the other way. Let's take a look at some usage patterns for scoped memory areas now.

Scoped Memory

Recall from Chapter 3 that a scoped memory area is really a `ScopedMemory` class instance (see Figure 5-13), which you create and size at development time. You can specify the scope's initial size, the maximum size it can grow to, and a `Runnable` object that will execute within that scope.

Because garbage collection does not occur within a scope, objects within it live for the entire lifetime of the scope before the reference count drops back to zero. Therefore, once an object is created within it, its associated memory is consumed for that cycle. As a result, uncontrolled object creation can result in the consumption of all free space within the scope, and an out-of-memory condition on subsequent allocations. Hence you should take care when creating objects, especially immutable objects such as `String`, and ensure the scoped memory region is sized appropriately. As seen in Figure 5-13 there are four types of scoped memory regions:

LTMemory—a scoped region of memory that is guaranteed to have linear time object allocation when the used space within the scope is less than the initial size. Recall that when a scoped memory region is created, it has an initial size, all of which is free memory. As objects are allocated, the amount of free memory obviously decreases, until the entire scope is filled, at which point it will be expanded (see Figure 5-14). Allocation time is guaranteed as long as the scoped memory area doesn't need to grow to accommodate the allocation.

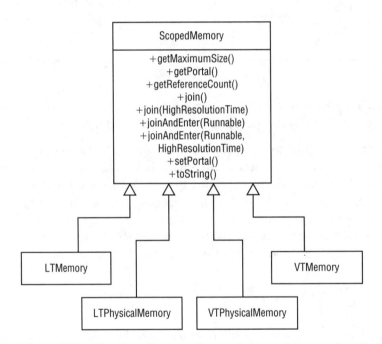

Figure 5-13   The class diagram of ScopedMemory objects and methods.

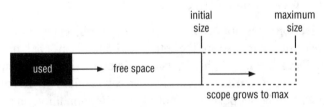

Figure 5-14   An LTScopedMemory region will grow from its initial size to a specified maximum.

LTPhysicalMemory—a region with the same performance guarantees and restrictions as LTMemory, which allows objects to be allocated in physical memory.

VTMemory—a scoped region with no allocation time guarantees (variable time).

VTPhysicalMemory—a region that allows objects to be allocated in physical memory, but with no allocation time guarantees.

Scoped memory is created within a Java RTS application by instantiating one of these four scoped memory classes. Any Schedulable object (which therefore excludes java.lang.Thread) can execute within a scope, and scopes can be nested with restrictions. These restrictions involve both the Schedulable object's nesting of ScopedMemory areas, and the fact that each ScopedMemory area has a parent scope. In general, scopes are nested as with a stack, and are subject to what is called the *single parent rule*.

For all Schedulable objects, the initial allocation context used for its first release is the context designated at the time of its creation. At that point, all allocation performed via the keyword new is done in the current allocation context, unless a specific memory area is specified and the newInstance or newArray keyword is used (see Listing 5-1).

Otherwise, Schedulable objects behave as if they held their memory area context in a structure called the *scope stack*. This structure is manipulated by both the creation of new Schedulable objects, and calling the methods enter, joinAndEnter, executeInArea, and newInstance. The scope stack is accessible through via the following methods on the RealtimeThread class:

getCurrentMemoryArea()—static method that returns the current allocation context.

getInitialMemoryAreaIndex()—static method that returns the position of the object's initial allocation context (given when the Schedulable was created) in the memory area stack.

getMemoryArea()—non-static method that returns the memory area used when the Schedulable was created.

getMemoryAreaStackDepth()—static method that returns the number of memory areas on the stack that the calling Schedulable has access to.

getOuterMemoryArea(index)—static method that returns a reference to the memory area at the stack at index given. Stack access is zero-based; therefore the memory area that is currently in context has an index equal to (getMemoryAreaStackDepth()-1).

Memory areas on a scope stack may be referred to as *inner* or *outer* relative to other entries in that scope stack. An *outer scope* is further from the current allocation context on the current scope stack and has a lower index (closer to the root of the hierarchy tree). When invoked on an instance of ScopedMemory, the methods executeInArea, newInstance and newArray require the associated memory area to be an outer scope on the calling Schedulable's scope stack.

The Single Parent Rule

The RTSJ *single parent rule* states that each ScopedMemory object has a single parent. When first created, the scope's parent is undefined. Once it has been assigned a parent, it cannot be given another parent value besides "no parent."

When a Schedulable enters it, the scope's parent becomes either the thread's scope, or what is called the *primordial scope* if no scope is in context at the current time. The primordial scope is not an actual memory region, but is instead a marker for all outermost memory areas. All first-level ScopedMemory objects, the heap, and immortal memory have the primordial scope as their parent. Also note that only Schedulable objects have scope stacks; this means that java.lang.Thread objects can only be created on and executed within the heap, or immortal memory.

Effectively, the single parent rule prevents the application from creating cycles in the scope tree. While a Schedulable and its child Schedulable objects can all execute in a single scope, an unrelated Schedulable object cannot execute within that scope. While we won't go into great detail on the single parent rule here, as that be found in the RTSJ, it will come into play in some of the patterns we discuss, and we will provide both visual and come examples.

First, assume that we have created four scoped memory areas, *a*, *b*, *c*, and *d*, as shown in Figure 5-15. Also shown are the heap and immortal memory areas, which are considered to be part of the primordial scope.

Let's assume that RealtimeThread R1, created on the heap, begins to execute within scope *a*. The result is a scope stack for R1 that looks like that in Figure 5-16. The active scope stack for R1 would consist of only scope *a*. Scope *a*'s parent is the primordial scope.

Figure 5-15   The memory regions at the start of our example.

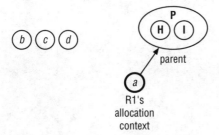

Figure 5-16 The scope stack for R1 after it starts in scope a.

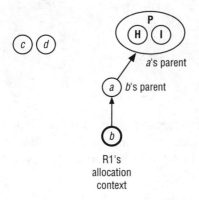

Figure 5-17 The scope stack for R1 after it enters scope b.

Next, if R1 were to enter scope *b* via a call to enter, the new allocation context would now be scope *b*, whose parent scope is scope *a*, as shown in Figure 5-17. Note that R1's active scope stack would be equal to the current scope stack, which is P←*a*←*b*.

The *active* scope stack (as viewed by a particular Schedulable object) can differ from the scope stack when the Schedulable calls executeInArea. When this method is called, the scope stack is unwound to the scope that is the allocation context. For instance, if R1 were to call executeInArea with scope *c*, the result would be as shown in Figure 5-18.

As a result, although the scope stack is P←*a*←*b*←*c*, the active scope stack for the Schedulable contains only scope *c*. Going further, if R1 then called enter for scope d, the scope stack would be P←*a*←*b*←*c*←d, and the active scope stack would be c←d.

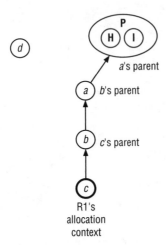

Figure 5-18   R1 calls executeInArea for scope c.

Scoped Memory Usage Patterns

We've already shown one example of scoped memory usage, albeit a simple one, with the NoHeapHelper class earlier in this chapter. In one sample, we simply created a ScopedMemory object within which the NHRT was started. However, there are a few more patterns we'd like to explore here.

Scoped Run-Loop Pattern

A common usage pattern is to create a scoped memory region for a Schedulable object to repeatedly enter and perform periodic processing within. This way, the time-critical processing that takes place isn't subject to potential garbage collection latencies, no matter how small they may be, but the memory consumed during the periodic processing is still reclaimed at the end of each period. This is called the *scoped run-loop pattern*, as presented in [Pizlo04], and is shown in Listing 5-26.

Listing 5-26   The scoped run-loop pattern

```
import javax.realtime.*;
public class MyApp extends RealtimeThread {
    public MyApp() {
        ReleaseParameters rel =
            new PeriodicParameters(
                new RelativeTime(1,0 )); // 1 millisecond

        this.setReleaseParameters(rel);
    }
```

```
class MyLogic implements Runnable {
    public void run() {
        // execute code within a scope...
    }
}

static ScopedMemory smArea = new LTMemory(4096000); // ~4MB

public void run() {
    MyLogic logic = new MyLogic();

    while ( true ) {
        smArea.enter(logic);
        waitForNextPeriod();
    }
}

public static void main(String[] args) {
    MyApp app = new MyApp();
    app.start();
}
}
```

In this code, the inner class, MyLogic, implements the actual business logic that's driven by the periodic RealtimeThread object, MyApp. However, with each periodic iteration through MyApp's run loop, enter is called on a ScopedMemory object with MyLogic as the Runnable to execute within it. This means, for each iteration through the loop, our business logic is executed within the scoped memory region, with all new objects created within it. Additionally, all of these objects are reclaimed when processing is complete. The scoped memory area is effectively reset and made completely available again for the next periodic iteration.

Multi-Scoped Object Pattern

It's sometimes necessary for an object reference to span more than one scope, either to share or preserve state across a scope's lifetime. The multi-scope object pattern safely defines a way to share an object between different scoped memory areas. In the example below, we revisit the temperature gauge sample, but this time there are some significant changes. First, the application runs in a Realtime-Thread within a scoped memory region represented by the ScopedMemory object smMain. This thread is created and immediately started. The MyApp constructor passes the scoped memory region (smMain) to the superclass constructor, and then defines its period. Soon after, the code in the run method—highlighted in bold in Listing 5-27—begins to execute.

Listing 5-27   Multi-scoped object pattern

```java
import java.util.*;
import javax.realtime.*;
public class MyApp extends RealtimeThread {
    public MyApp(MemoryArea mem) {
        super(null, null, null, mem, null, null);

        ReleaseParameters rel =
          new PeriodicParameters(
            new RelativeTime(1,0 )); // 1 milli

        this.setReleaseParameters(rel);
    }

    class TemperatureData {
        private Vector data = new Vector();
        public Vector getData() {
            return data;
        }
        class SafeAdd implements Runnable {
            String val;
            SafeAdd( String v) {
                val = new String(v);
            }

            public void run() {
                data.addElement( cloneString(val) );
            }

            private String cloneString(String s) {
                try {
                  String r =
                    (String)getMemoryArea().
                        newInstance(String.class);
                  r = r.copyValueOf( s.toCharArray() );
                  return r;
                }
                catch ( Exception e ) { }
                return null;
            }
        }
        void update(String val) {
            MemoryArea mem = MemoryArea.getMemoryArea(this);
            mem.executeInArea( new SafeAdd(val) );
        }
    }
}
```

```
class TempGauge implements Runnable {
    public TemperatureData history;
    public void run() {
        String v = "Temperature=" + getCurrentTemp();
        history.update(v);
    }
    private long getCurrentTemp { /*...*/ }
}

static ScopedMemory smMain = new LTMemory(4096000); // ~4MB
static ScopedMemory smGauge = new LTMemory(4096000); // ~4MB

public void run() {
    TemperatureData temp = new TemperatureData();
    TempGauge gauge = new TempGauge();
    gauge.history = temp;

    int times = 0;
    while ( times++ < 10 ) {
        smGauge.enter(gauge);
        waitForNextPeriod();
    }
    // ...
}

public static void main(String[] args) {
    MyApp app = new MyApp(smMain);
    app.start();
}
}
```

The TemperatureData class is the object that's shared across scopes. It's created within the scope smMain, as well as the TempGauge class instance, which implements Runnable. With each iteration of the periodic loop, the second scoped memory area, represented by the ScopedMemory object smGauge, is entered with the TempGauge instance as the logic to execute. Within its run method, a String object is created that contains the current temperature, and this is provided to the TemperatureData object named history. The issue here is that the history object resides in the smMain scope, while the temperature String resides in the smGauge scope. Therefore the data needs to be safely copied into the proper scope and stored as part of the history of temperature data to be read from later.

The logic to accomplish this is contained within TemperatureData's embedded class SafeAdd, which gets created when the client calls TemperatureData. update. When update is called, the TemperatureData object's memory area (smMain) is retrieved, and a SafeAdd class (which implements Runnable) instance is provided in the call to executeInArea. At this point, the allocation context switches from smGauge (since the call was made from the TempGauge class) to smMain, the data given is safely copied into the smMain memory scope, and it's added to the Vector of temperature data.

As a result, the logic to interface with the physical world and read the current temperature is executed within its own scope, free from garbage collection latency. With each call, the objects allocated within it are reclaimed, and the scope is ready to be used again. In the end, the history of temperature data resides in a separate scope, not governed by the lifetime of the stateless temperature class or its own scoped memory area.

The Portal Object

Each ScopedMemory object may contain what's called a *portal object*. This object is set via the setPortal method, and calling getPortal retrieves it. The portal provides a safe way for multiple threads to share an object within a scope. The portal object can be any object allocated with the scope itself, or an outer scope. It can be an object of any class available to your application even an array of references to objects. However, keep in mind that when the scope's reference count goes to zero, the scope is reclaimed and the portal object is cleared.

The following example creates three threads whose actions are governed by the contents of the portal object. The first thread to run will set the portal object, while the others will read from it and, in this example, take different action (see Listing 5-28).

Listing 5-28   Using the ScopedMemory portal object

```
import javax.realtime.*;
public class MyApp extends RealtimeThread {
    static ScopedMemory sm = new LTMemory(4096000);//~4MB
    public MyApp(MemoryArea mem) {
        super(null, null, null, mem, null, null);
    }

    class Worker implements Runnable {
        public void run() {
            synchronized (sm) {
                long id =
                    RealtimeThread.currentRealtimeThread().getId();
                String msg = (String)sm.getPortal();
                if ( msg == null ){
```

```
                msg = "Thread " + id +
                        " is the portal controller";
                sm.setPortal(msg);
                System.out.println(
                  "Thread " + id + ": I am controller");
            }
            else {
                System.out.println(
                  "Thread " + id + ": " + msg);
            }
        }
    }
}


    public void run () {
        for ( int i = 0; i < 3; i++ ) {
            Worker w = new Worker();
            RealtimeThread r =
              new RealtimeThread(null, null, null, sm, null, w);
            r.start();
        }
    }

    public static void main(String[] args) {
        MyApp app = new MyApp(sm);
        app.start();
    }
}
```

When the application is started, the main thread, itself an RTT, executes within the ScopedMemory object sm. Next, three additional RTTs are created, each given a unique instance of the same Runnable class (Worker). The first thread to execute attempts to get the portal object, but finds that it's not set yet. Therefore it sets it and, in this example, takes action as the "controller" of the portal. Of course, your code can take any action that's appropriate. The remaining threads, when they execute, attempt to get the portal object, find that it's been set, and process the contents of the object. Since the portal object is not inherently safe, access to it is synchronized through the one object they all have in common: the ScopedMemory object itself. When executed, the output from this example is:

```
Thread 10: I am controller
Thread 11: Thread 10 is the portal controller
Thread 12: Thread 10 is the portal controller
```

Physical Memory

The three classes that allow objects to be created within a specified range of physical memory include `LTPhysicalMemory`, `VTPhysicalMemory`, and `Immortal-PhysicalMemory`. Each of these memory areas takes, as constructors, parameters that specify the base physical memory address of the region, its size, and object type. This object type is a value from the supported set of physical memory object types supported by the RTSJ implementation. However, in many cases, it will be used to denote the region's usage, such as direct memory access (DMA), a shared memory region, IO-related memory, memory that needs to be aligned in special ways, and so on.

It's anticipated that most real-time Java developers *won't* need physical memory object allocation. However, there are many cases where real-time applications need to communicate with the outside world via specialized hardware, or with low latency. Examples are flight control, industrial automation, robotics, automotive, and so on. In these cases, the RTSJ's support for physical memory access and object creation can be critical. It also allows for the lowest latency possible for network communications, as the RTSJ application can access the actual network interface card (NIC) buffer for incoming and outgoing network packets. With support for physical memory access, the RTSJ allows you to build low-level device drivers in Java.

6

Synchronization

"Time is like the wind; it lifts the light and leaves the heavy."

—Doménico Cieri Estrada

IN order to meet the requirements of the RTSJ, and achieve real-time behavior, Java RTS has a modified implementation of the `synchronized` keyword. This change is part of the overall set of changes made to thread scheduling and resource sharing that affects how threads interact in Java RTS. This chapter will dive into the internals of these changes, and will explain how potential problems, such as priority inversion, have been solved without violating the principals of the Java language. Later in the chapter, we'll examine new classes that control how both real-time and non-real-time threads can share resources and communicate safely using wait-free queues.

Resource Sharing

Synchronizing access to resources amongst multiple application threads is a common issue in programming, but becomes more critical in the real-time space. This is because resource locking can affect thread prioritization and induce unbounded latency in critical operations if not controlled properly. At the base level, the RTSJ specifies the use of wait queues for synchronization blocks that follow these rules:

1. Blocked threads ready to run are given access to synchronized resources in priority order.
2. Priority inversion control must be used for access to all shared resources to avoid unbounded latency. In Java RTS, this is implemented with the priority inheritance protocol.

Priority inheritance in Java RTS is implemented, as required, as a subclass of the RTSJ MonitorControl abstract base class (see Figure 6-1).

The RTSJ defines this base class so that implementers can extend it and build their own priority inversion control protocols. Besides priority inheritance, which is what Java RTS has implemented, another common choice is the priority ceiling emulation protocol (PCEP). We won't go into detail about PCEP, as it's not implemented in Java RTS. However, let's review the methods of the MonitorControl class:

getMonitorControl()—this method returns a reference to the MonitorControl object that implements the priority inversion policy currently in effect.

getMonitorControl(obj)—this methods returns a reference to the Monitor-Control object that implements the priority inversion policy of the given object.

setMonitorControl(policy)—this method allows you to set the default monitor control policy to the one provided. This policy will be used for all subsequently allocated objects.

setMonitorControl(policy, obj)—this method allows you to set the monitor control policy to the one provided for the given object only. The calling code must already own a lock on obj when this method is called.

In general, resource locking and synchronization goes beyond what occurs in Java SE. In the real-time space, priority inversion control and overall latency control are big concerns. Let's take a look at these issues now.

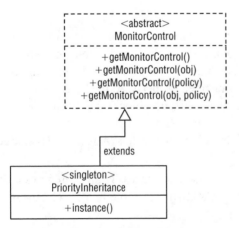

Figure 6-1   The MonitorControl class hierarchy for priority inversion control.

Priority Inversion Control

Priority inversion is a problem outlined in Chapter 1, where, due to object locking, a lower-priority thread can run in preference to a higher-priority, unbounded thread. This is clearly a problem for a real-time application where event processing needs to be strictly prioritized. The RTSJ addresses this problem and requires that each RTSJ implementation enhance its support for synchronized methods and statements to implement a protocol of its choosing, represented by the MonitorControl base class, for all threads. This ensures that there will be no unbounded priority inversions.

As an example, look at the code in Listing 6-1. There are three classes that extend RealtimeThread: HighPriority, MedPriority, and LowPriority. As their names imply, each RTT runs at a high priority, medium priority, and low priority, respectively. There is also the main application thread, also an RTT, which runs at the highest priority (higher than the other three threads).

Listing 6-1   Priority inversion control in action

```java
import javax.realtime.*;
public class MyApp extends RealtimeThread {
    static public Object lock = new Object();
    class HighPriority extends RealtimeThread {
        public HighPriority() {
            // set priority to high
            int pri =
                PriorityScheduler.instance().getMaxPriority()-1;
            PriorityParameters sched =
                new PriorityParameters(pri);
            this.setSchedulingParameters(sched);
        }
        public void run() {
            System.out.println("H\t\t\tGetting Lock");
            synchronized ( lock ) {
                for ( int i = 0; i < 100; i++ ) {
                    System.out.println("H\t\t\t*");
                }
                System.out.println("H\t\t\tReleasing Lock");
            }
            System.out.println("H\t\t\tTERM");
        }
    }

    class MedPriority extends RealtimeThread {
        public MedPriority() {
```

continued

```
        // set priority to mid-point
        int hi =
          PriorityScheduler.instance().getMaxPriority();
        int lo =
          PriorityScheduler.instance().getMinPriority();
        PriorityParameters sched =
            new PriorityParameters((hi-lo)/2);
        this.setSchedulingParameters(sched);
    }
    public void run() {
        for ( int i = 0; i < 100; i++ ) {
            System.out.println("M\t\t*");
        }
        System.out.println("M\t\tTERM");
    }
}

class LowPriority extends RealtimeThread {
    public LowPriority() {
        // set priority to lowest
        int pri =
          PriorityScheduler.instance().getMinPriority();
        PriorityParameters sched =
            new PriorityParameters(pri);
        this.setSchedulingParameters(sched);
    }
    public void run() {
        System.out.println("L\tGetting Lock");
        synchronized ( lock ) {
            for ( int i = 0; i < 100; i++ ) {
                System.out.println("L\t*");
            }
            System.out.println("L\tReleasing Lock");
        }
        System.out.println("L\tTERM");
    }
}

public MyApp() {
    // set priority to highest
    int pri =
      PriorityScheduler.instance().getMaxPriority();
    PriorityParameters sched =
        new PriorityParameters(pri);
    this.setSchedulingParameters(sched);
}
```

```
public void run() {
    LowPriority low = new LowPriority();
    MedPriority med = new MedPriority();
    HighPriority high = new HighPriority();

    low.start();
    System.out.println("Main: LowPriority STARTED");

    System.out.println(
      "Main: Yielding for .5 milliseconds");
    RelativeTime abs = new RelativeTime(0,500000);
    try {this.sleep(abs);} catch( Exception e ) { }

    med.start();
    System.out.println("Main: MedPriority STARTED");

    high.start();
    System.out.println("Main: HighPriority STARTED");
}

public static void main(String[] args) {
    MyApp app = new MyApp();
    app.start();
}
}
```

The classes HighPriority and LowPriority both share access to a synchronized resource, named lock. However, if all three threads were created and started at the same time, the high-priority thread would begin running first, and the priority inversion wouldn't occur. Therefore, for the sake of this example, the low-priority thread is created first in the main application run method (shown in bold), and the application yields for 0.5 milliseconds before starting the medium-and high-priority threads. When run on a single-processor server, this gives the low-priority thread a chance to execute long enough to acquire a lock on the shared object and execute for a short time.

Next, when the remaining threads are started, the high-priority thread attempts to lock the shared object and is blocked. At this point in time, the priority inheritance protocol in Java RTS takes affect, and raises the low-priority thread's priority to be equal to the high-priority thread. If the VM didn't do this, both the high-priority thread and the low-priority thread would have to wait for the medium-priority thread to run before further progress is made. Instead, with priority inheritance, this doesn't happen. The result is that the low-priority thread gets to release its lock on the shared object sooner, allowing the high-priority thread to run, and then the medium-priority thread.

Priority Inheritance in Action

The output below demonstrates this code in action. Here, you can see the output for each thread preceded by a letter that represents its name; L for the low-priority thread, M for the medium-priority thread, and H for the high-priority thread. For simplicity, from this point onward in this example, we'll refer to all three threads by these initials. An asterisk is printed with each iteration through each thread's run loop, and each thread's output is tabbed differently to help it line up appropriately. Additionally, H and L print a message when they attempt to acquire, and then release, a lock on the shared object. Finally, each thread outputs the message, "TERM" when it terminates (which happens after 100 iterations).

```
Main: LowPriority STARTED
Main: Yielding for .5 milliseconds
L    Getting Lock
L       *
L       *
L       *
L       *
L       *
L       *
L       *
L       *
Main: MedPriority STARTED
Main: HighPriority STARTED
H               Getting Lock
L       *
L       *
L       *
L       *
  ...
L       *
L    Releasing Lock
H               *
H               *
H               *
H               *
  ...
H               *
H               Releasing Lock
H               TERM
M       *
M       *
M       *
M       *
  ...
```

```
M       *
M       TERM
L   TERM
```

Note: In the output above, some lines have been omitted (indicated by an ellipsis) to reduce the length.

The first thing you'll notice is that L acquires a lock on the shared object immediately after the main thread yields, and it executes a few times through its loop. Soon after, the main thread is re-released and starts both M and H. When H runs, it first tries to get a lock on the shared object (shown as the first bold line above), but it cannot, since L owns it. Therefore, Java RTS elevates L's priority, and it begins to run at H's priority (shown as the second bold line above). L continues to run to completion (some of the output has been truncated to save space), and then releases its lock. This is seen as the third bold line above. Immediately afterward, H is unblocked, and runs to completion. Finally, after H terminates, M runs to completion, and M and L both terminate in that order due to priority.

Wait-Free Thread Communication

The use of `NoHeapRealtimeThreads` provides the best determinism and latency possible for a real-time Java application. However, the fact that code executing in these threads cannot access the heap can pose some limitations, such as when data needs to be exchanged with `RealtimeThreads` or standard `Threads`. To facilitate the exchange of data between no-heap threads, and the rest of a Java application, the RTSJ defines *wait-free queue* classes that support non-blocking, protected access to shared resources. Not only does this allow for safe data transfer, it ensures that code running in a `NoHeapRealtimeThread` won't block on GC-related activity when it synchronizes with an object shared with a standard `Thread`. These wait-free queues, encompassed by the classes `WaitFreeReadQueue`, and `WaitFreeWriteQueue`, will be explored in this chapter. The class, `WaitFreeDequeue`, which is essentially an aggregation of the first two, has been deprecated as of version 1.0.1 of the RTSJ, and will not be looked at further.

Keep in mind that the intended use of these classes is for the exchange of data between objects with hard real-time requirements, and those with non-real-time requirements. This includes any combination of use between NHRTs, RTTs, and JLTs.

Using WaitFreeWriteQueue

The `WaitFreeWriteQueue` is intended for use by RTTs that must never block when adding objects to the queue. It supports a `write` method for one non-blocking producer, and multiple consumers that may potentially block when dequeuing objects via the `read` method. The queue `write` method always returns in bounded time, and the producer is not subject to any jitter caused by the queue consumer. If you intend to have more than one `Schedulable` object write to the queue, you must explicitly synchronize access to the queue yourself. The following are the class constructors:

`WaitFreeWriteQueue(capacity)`—constructs a queue with the specified maximum capacity.

`WaitFreeWriteQueue(capacity, memory)`—constructs a queue with the specified maximum capacity, and allocates internal queue elements within the given memory area.

`WaitFreeWriteQueue(writer, reader, capacity, memory)`—constructs a queue with the specified maximum capacity, and allocates internal queue elements within the given memory area. Further, the provided queue writer and reader `Runnable` objects are checked for compatibility with the given memory area.

The class diagram in Figure 6-2 shows the rest of the methods within the `Wait-FreeWriteQueue` class. We'll discuss how to use this class through an example soon.

While producers never block, there is the potential that the consumers will. Therefore, if the consumers cannot keep up with the rate of messages being added to the queue, there's the potential for it to grow infinitely. The issue is, of course, that computers don't have infinite storage. To handle this scenario, when you

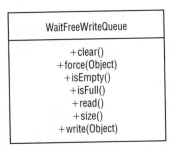

Figure 6-2   The `WaitFreeWriteQueue` class methods.

create a wait-free queue of either type, you must specify its maximum capacity. As a result, when the non-blocking producer attempts to `write` to a queue that has reached its capacity, the call will simply return `false`, and the object will not be inserted.

Alternatively, if a particularly important event occurs that requires an object to be placed on the queue regardless of whether it has reached its capacity, you can call the method `force`. This method performs an unconditional write to the queue either into a vacant position, or by overwriting the most recently inserted object if the queue is full. In this case, a `false` return value indicates that the insert occurred *without* overwriting a previously inserted object. Let's look at a code example to demonstrate both calls in action, in Listing 6-2, below.

Listing 6-2   The `WaitFreeWriteQueue` class in action

```
import javax.realtime.*;
public class MyApp extends RealtimeThread {
    public static WaitFreeWriteQueue queue =
            new WaitFreeWriteQueue(5);

    class QProducer implements Runnable {
        public void run() {
            int times = 0;
            while ( times++ < 100 ) {
                String s = "This is msg# " + times;
                queue.write(s);
                RealtimeThread.waitForNextPeriod();
            }
            queue.force("term");
        }
    }

    class QConsumer implements Runnable {
        public void run() {
            try {
                boolean loop = true;
                while ( loop == true ) {
                    String msg = (String)queue.read();
                    System.out.println("QConsumer recvd: "+msg);
                    if ( msg.equalsIgnoreCase("term") )
                        loop = false;
                }
            }
            catch ( Exception e ) {
                e.printStackTrace();
            }
```

continued

```
            }
        }

    public MyApp() { }

    public void run() {
        startConsumer();
        startProducer();
    }

    private void startConsumer() {
        new Thread( new QConsumer() ).start();

        // Yield to give the consumer a chance to start
        try { RealtimeThread.sleep(1); } catch ( Exception e ){}
    }

    private void startProducer() {
        ImmortalMemory.instance().enter(
            new Runnable() {
                public void run() {
                    PeriodicParameters rel =
                        new PeriodicParameters(
                            new RelativeTime(1,0));
                    PriorityParameters sched = ...
                    new NoHeapRealtimeThread(
                        sched, rel, null,
                        ImmortalMemory.instance(),
                        null, new QProducer() ).start();
                }
            });
    }

    public static void main(String[] args) {
        new MyApp().start();
    }
}
```

In this simple application, the main thread—itself an RTT—starts the queue producer as an NHRT with immortal memory as its allocation context, and the queue consumer as a JLT. The queue is a WaitFreeWriteQueue instance declared as static; hence it resides in immortal memory. This makes it safely accessible to both the producer and consumer threads. Note that the main thread starts the consumer, and then yields to ensure it's ready and waiting for queued messages by the time the producer is started.

The queue is defined to hold a maximum of five messages before new calls to write are ignored. If the consumer cannot keep up, up to five messages will be enqueued before newer messages get lost. To help demonstrate this, the producer creates String objects, each with a sequential message number, and calls write. When the consumer receives a message, it displays its text and, hence, the message number. If any messages are lost due to the queue overflowing, you will see gaps in the sequence numbers, as displayed in the output below:

```
QConsumer received: This is msg# 1
QConsumer received: This is msg# 2
QConsumer received: This is msg# 3
QConsumer received: This is msg# 4
QConsumer received: This is msg# 5
QConsumer received: This is msg# 7
QConsumer received: This is msg# 8
QConsumer received: This is msg# 11
QConsumer received: This is msg# 12
QConsumer received: This is msg# 13
QConsumer received: This is msg# 14
QConsumer received: This is msg# 15
QConsumer received: This is msg# 16
QConsumer received: This is msg# 17
QConsumer received: This is msg# 18
QConsumer received: This is msg# 19
QConsumer received: This is msg# 20
QConsumer received: This is msg# 21
QConsumer received: This is msg# 36
...
QConsumer received: This is msg# TERM
```

Scanning the output, you can see several instances of lost messages, such as message number 6, 9, 10, 22, and so on. However, the consumer waits for a special queued message to know when to terminate. This message contains the text "TERM," which indicates it should terminate. Since this message is deemed important to the application, the producer writes it to the queue via a call to force to ensure it gets sent.

If you run this example, you can adjust the amount of time the producer waits between messages by adjusting its period from 1 to 100 milliseconds. At that period, the consumer should be able to keep up with the message rate, and there should be no skips in the message numbers. Alternatively, you can adjust the queue capacity to change the behavior also. Regardless, this example clearly demonstrates how straightforward it is to use this class. The same is true for the Wait-FreeReadQueue class, which ensures deterministic behavior for the queue consumer thread. Let's take a closer look at that class now.

Using WaitFreeReadQueue

The `WaitFreeReadQueue` class is designed for use by a queue consumer implemented to run within a `NoHeapRealtimeThread`. Although the intent is to free the real-time consumer thread from any GC-related jitter otherwise imposed by the producer thread, you can use this class from any thread(s). The class constructors are:

> `WaitFreeReadQueue(capacity, notify)`—constructs a queue with the specified maximum capacity. If the notify flag is set, the consumer will be notified when blocking on a read.

> `WaitFreeReadQueue(capacity, memory, notify)`—constructs a queue with the specified maximum capacity, and allocates internal queue elements within the given memory area. If the notify flag is set, the consumer will be notified when blocking on a read.

> `WaitFreeReadQueue(writer, reader, capacity, memory, notify)`—constructs a queue with the specified maximum capacity, and allocates internal queue elements within the given memory area. Further, the provided queue writer and reader `Runnable` objects are checked for compatibility with the given memory area. If the notify flag is set, the consumer will be notified when blocking on a read.

The class diagram in Figure 6-3 shows the rest of the methods within the `Wait-FreeReadQueue` class. We'll discuss how to use this class through an example below.

A call by the consumer to the `read` method is non-blocking, and will return either `null` (if the queue is empty) or the next queued message if one is waiting. The call always returns in bounded time, and the reader is not subject to any jitter caused by the queue producer.

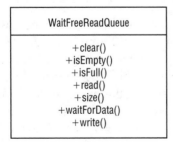

Figure 6-3   The `WaitFreeReadQueue` class methods.

Additionally, the producer will block on a write `call` if the corresponding queue is full, and multiple reader threads must be synchronized explicitly by your own application code. However, writer threads are automatically synchronized by the queue. Let's take a look at a simple example in Listing 6-3, and then analyze its behavior.

Listing 6-3 This code demonstrates the `WaitFreeReadQueue`

```
import javax.realtime.*;
public class MyApp extends RealtimeThread {
    public static WaitFreeReadQueue queue =
        new WaitFreeReadQueue(5, false);

    class QProducer implements Runnable {
        public void run() {
            int count = 0;
            while ( count++ < 100 ) {
                System.out.println("QProducer writing message");
                safeWrite(count);
            }
            safeWrite(-1);
        }

        private void safeWrite(final int count) {
            ImmortalMemory.instance().executeInArea(
              new Runnable() {
                public void run() {
                    try {
                      if ( queue.isFull() )
                        System.out.println("QProducer blocking");
                      if ( count == -1 )
                        queue.write("TERM");
                      else
                        queue.write("Msg #" + count);
                    }
                    catch ( Exception e ) { }
                }
            });
        }
    }

    class QConsumer implements Runnable {
        public void run() {
            while ( true ) {
                while ( ! queue.isEmpty() ) {
                    String msg = (String)queue.read();
                    System.out.println(
                      "NHRT QConsumer received: " + msg);
```

continued

```
            if ( msg.equalsIgnoreCase("TERM") )
                return;
        }
        RealtimeThread.waitForNextPeriod();
    }
  }
}

public void run() {
    startProducer();
    startConsumer();
}

private void startProducer() {
    new Thread( new QProducer() ).start();
}

private void startConsumer() {
    ImmortalMemory.instance().enter(
        new Runnable() {
            public void run() {
                PeriodicParameters rel =
                    new PeriodicParameters(
                        new RelativeTime(250,0));
                int pri = ...
                PriorityParameters sched =
                    new PriorityParameters(pri);
                new NoHeapRealtimeThread(
                    sched, rel,
                    null, ImmortalMemory.instance(),
                    null, new QConsumer() ).start();
            }
        });
}

public static void main(String[] args) {
    new MyApp().start();
}
}
```

The queue is declared as static; therefore, it resides within immortal memory, and is safe to access from both the NHRT consumer and JLT producer code. However, this means that each message placed on the queue must be allocated from within immortal memory also. To accomplish this, the JLT (QProducer) calls the private safeWrite method, which calls executeInArea to create the appropriate String object in immortal memory and place it on the queue. If the queue is full—determined via the call to `queue.isFull`—we know that the subsequent `write` call should block, so this is printed.

The producer thread simply tries to write 100 unique messages to the queue, but will be blocked if the queue is full. Since the queue is declared with a capacity of five, it should fill the queue very quickly. The consumer thread, `QConsumer`, executes within an NHRT with a period of 250 milliseconds. This gives plenty of time for the producer to fill up the queue before the consumer can drain messages from it. When `QConsumer` does execute, it checks that messages are available by calling `queue.isEmpty`. In fact, it calls this method in a loop to effectively drain all available messages from the queue each period. On a uniprocessor, the producer thread will be able to write messages to the queue only when the NHRT consumer is finished reading them, and calls `waitForNextPeriod`. On a multi-processor, the producer will most likely execute in parallel, and begin writing to the queue even as the consumer if reading from it—so long as the queue is not at capacity.

The output below is from a uniprocessor server. Notice that when the producer executes, it writes messages, fills the queue, and then blocks (as shown in bold):

```
QProducer writing message
QProducer writing message
QProducer writing message
QProducer writing message
QProducer writing message
QProducer writing message
QProducer blocking
NHRT QConsumer received: Msg #1
NHRT QConsumer received: Msg #2
NHRT QConsumer received: Msg #3
NHRT QConsumer received: Msg #4
NHRT QConsumer received: Msg #5
QProducer writing message
QProducer writing message
QProducer writing message
QProducer writing message
QProducer writing message
QProducer blocking
NHRT QConsumer received: Msg #6
NHRT QConsumer received: Msg #7
NHRT QConsumer received: Msg #8
NHRT QConsumer received: Msg #9
NHRT QConsumer received: Msg #10
...
QProducer writing message
QProducer writing message
```

continued

```
QProducer writing message
QProducer writing message
QProducer writing message
QProducer blocking
NHRT QConsumer received: Msg #96
NHRT QConsumer received: Msg #97
NHRT QConsumer received: Msg #98
NHRT QConsumer received: Msg #99
NHRT QConsumer received: Msg #100
NHRT QConsumer received: TERM
```

Next, when the NHRT is released, it reads all available messages (five in each case), prints them, and then calls waitForNextPeriod. The producer is then unblocked, and the cycle repeats. When the producer has finished sending the last message, it sends a special message to inform the consumer to terminate.

Let's take a look at an example where the consumer blocks until a message is placed on a WaitFreeReadQueue. This support was added for the case where your NHRT isn't a periodic real-time task, but is instead driven by data placed on a queue aperiodically. The blocking in this case is done through an object internal to the queue; one that the producer and the consumer do not have in common. This preserves the functionality of the wait-free queue, still freeing the real-time consumer from any GC-related jitter incurred by the non-real-time producer.

The following code takes the previous sample, and modifies the consumer NHRT thread to be aperiodic. Instead of operating on a period, it implements a loop that simply waits for a message on a wait-free queue. Once this message arrives, the retrieval and processing of this message is deterministic and free from any producer-related GC jitter. The changes have been highlighted in bold type.

The producer has been modified slightly also. Instead of writing messages to the queue in a tight loop, it now sleeps for a time interval in between. The rate of message processing in the NHRT is now driven by the rate of messages placed on the queue, free from any GC-related interference. Let's look at the changes in Listing 6-4.

Listing 6-4   This code demonstrates the use of waitForData

```
import javax.realtime.*;
public class MyApp extends RealtimeThread {
    public static WaitFreeReadQueue queue =
            new WaitFreeReadQueue(5, true);

    class QProducer implements Runnable {
        public void run() {
            int count = 0;
```

```
            while ( count++ < 100 ) {
                System.out.println("QProducer writing message");
                safeWrite(count);
                try { Thread.sleep(250); } catch (Exception e){}
            }
            safeWrite(-1);
        }

        private void safeWrite(final int count) {
            ImmortalMemory.instance().executeInArea(
              new Runnable() {
                public void run() {
                    try {
                      if ( queue.isFull() )
                        System.out.println("QProducer blocking");
                      if ( count == -1 )
                        queue.write("TERM");
                      else
                        queue.write("Msg #" + count);
                    }
                    catch ( Exception e ) { }
                }
            });
        }
    }

    class QConsumer implements Runnable {
        public void run() {
            try {
                while ( true ) {
                    System.out.println("NHRT QConsumer waiting");
                    queue.waitForData();
                    String msg = (String)queue.read();
                    System.out.println(
                      "   NHRT QConsumer received: " + msg);
                    if ( msg.equalsIgnoreCase("TERM") )
                        return;
                }
            }
            catch ( Exception e ) {
                e.printStackTrace();
            }
        }
    }
    public void run() {
        startProducer();
        startConsumer();
    }
```

continued

```
    private void startProducer() {
        new Thread( new QProducer() ).start();
    }

    private void startConsumer() {
        ImmortalMemory.instance().enter(
            new Runnable() {
                public void run() {
                    int pri = ...
                    PriorityParameters sched =
                        new PriorityParameters(pri);
                    new NoHeapRealtimeThread(
                        sched, null,
                        null, ImmortalMemory.instance(),
                        null, new QConsumer() ).start();
                }
            });
    }

    public static void main(String[] args) {
        new MyApp().start();
    }
}
```

Notice that the non-real-time thread calls `Thread.sleep` between messages—this is to simulate a semi-periodic production of messages. The sleep duration of around 250 milliseconds was chosen so you can witness the consumer thread pausing and waiting for messages to arrive. Next, notice that the consumer NHRT is now aperiodic, and doesn't call `waitForNextPeriod`. Instead, it calls `queue.waitForData`, and `queue.read` immediately after. This is safe as the `read` is guaranteed to return a valid object after `waitForData` returns (unblocks), as long as there is only one consumer thread.

Since the consumer NHRT runs at a higher priority than the producer JLT, it's released first and begins waiting for a message. It's effectively blocked on the queue. As soon as the producer writes a message to the queue, the consumer will unblock, retrieve the message from the queue, and display its contents. If the message contains the `String` "TERM," the NHRT consumer will terminate, as will the application. The output, truncated for space, is below:

```
NHRT QConsumer waiting
QProducer writing message
 NHRT QConsumer received: Msg #1
NHRT QConsumer waiting
QProducer writing message
 NHRT QConsumer received: Msg #2
```

```
NHRT QConsumer waiting
QProducer writing message
 NHRT QConsumer received: Msg #3
NHRT QConsumer waiting
QProducer writing message
 NHRT QConsumer received: Msg #4
NHRT QConsumer waiting
QProducer writing message
 NHRT QConsumer received: Msg #5
NHRT QConsumer waiting
QProducer writing message
 NHRT QConsumer received: Msg #6
NHRT QConsumer waiting
QProducer writing message
 NHRT QConsumer received: Msg #7
NHRT QConsumer waiting
QProducer writing message
 NHRT QConsumer received: Msg #8
...
NHRT QConsumer waiting
 NHRT QConsumer received: TERM
```

The wait-free queues, from the point of producing and/or consuming messages from real-time threads, are meant to be as straightforward as these examples hopefully illustrate. The hard work is done internally within the Java RTS VM; priority inheritance and the absence of shared locks between the real-time and non-real-time threads eliminates jitter and allows deterministic queue processing from within an NHRT.

The Real-Time Clock API

"All my possessions for a moment of time."
—Elizabeth I

THIS chapter explores the implementation of the RTSJ definition of clocks and timers within Java RTS. The classes explored in detail provide jitter-free time operations, and access to a high-resolution clock for timer objects for different types of timers. For instance, you can create timer objects that cause time-related events to fire either periodically, or for one-time use.

The Clock API

Java RTS implements the RTSJ Clock API, which defines real-time clock and timer facilities. These classes should be used in place of calls to System.currentTimeMillis, System.nanoTime, and the java.util.Date class. They represent points in time with the best possible accuracy and precision the underlying hardware can support, and distinguish between absolute points in time, and those relative to a starting point. Additionally, these classes allow the creation of timers that fire either periodically, or for one time only, deterministically. Finally, the Java RTS implementation of these classes satisfies the POSIX real-time requirement of providing access to high-resolution timers. For instance, the code in Listing 7-1 checks and displays the resolution of the real-time clock the system it's executed on.

Listing 7-1   Output the RT clock accuracy

```
import javax.realtime.*;
public class Main {
    public static void main(String[] args) {
        RelativeTime t =
          Clock.getRealtimeClock().getResolution();
      System.out.println(
          "Real-time clock resolution = " + t.toString());
    }
}
```

Since timer resolution is hardware-dependent, you're likely to get different results on different systems you run Java RTS on. When the code in Listing 7-1 is executed on SunFire v240, the accuracy output is: a

```
Real-time clock resolution = (0 ms, 200 ns)
```

Clearly, the timer resolution for Java RTS applications on this machine is 200 nanoseconds. Keep in mind that the system you run Java RTS on must provide access to high-resolution timers, and the user account you execute your application with must have privilege to access the high-resolution timer implementation.

To use the RTSJ Clock API (see Figure 7-1) to create timestamps or high-resolution timings, begin by gaining a reference to the singleton real-time clock object via the getRealtimeClock() method call on the javax.realtime.Clock object, as seen in the previous example. To calculate a timestamp with nanosecond resolution (on hardware that supports it), use code similar to that in Listing 7-2.

Listing 7-2   Real-time clock timestamp code

```
javax.realtime.Clock rtClock =
    javax.realtime.Clock.getRealtimeClock();

javax.realtime.AbsoluteTime beginTime;
javax.realtime.AbsoluteTime endTime;

// get start time and convert to nanoseconds
beginTime = rtClock.getTime();
long lBegin = (beginTime.getMilliseconds() * 1000000L) +
    rtWallClockTimeBefore.getNanoseconds();

// do processing here...

// get end time and convert to nanoseconds
endTime = rtClock.getTime();
long lEnd = (beginTime.getMilliseconds() * 1000000L) +
    rtWallClockTimeBefore.getNanoseconds();
```

In addition to the high-resolution timing shown in Listing 7-2, through a combination of the `Clock` and `AbsoluteTime` classes, you can perform date and time operations. This includes gaining access to `java.util.Date` objects. The complete class diagram for the RTSJ time operations is shown in Figure 7-2.

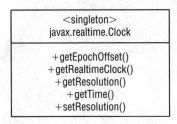

Figure 7-1   The Java RTS `Clock` class.

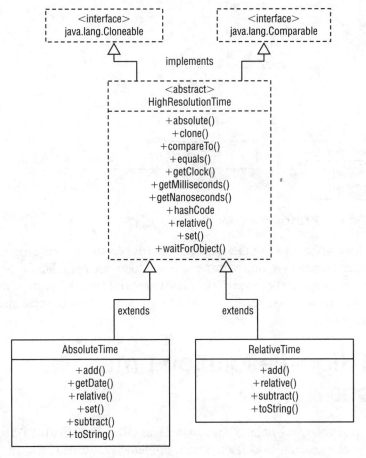

Figure 7-2   The Java RTS time operations.

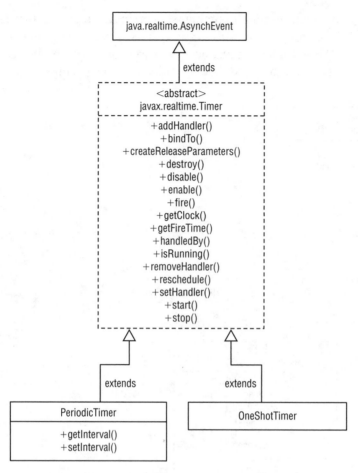

Figure 7-3   The Java RTS timer operations.

We'll take a look at how to use these classes shortly. As mentioned earlier, the Clock API provides access to timers that can be set to expire periodically, or one time only. These classes are PeriodicTimer and OneShotTimer, respectively (see Figure 7-3). Since these classes extend AsynchEvent, we'll examine these classes in detail in Chapter 8.

Java RTS High-Resolution Time Operations

In Java RTS, real-time *time* objects are instances of either the AbsoluteTime or RelativeTime classes, and associated with a singleton real-time clock. In fact, we've already seen these classes used with setting the release parameters for periodic `RealtimeThread` objects in Chapter 5. However, there are more details to these classes that need to be examined.

The `AbsoluteTime` class represents a specific point in time. It's specified and measured in a combination of milliseconds and nanoseconds. Here are the `AbsoluteTime` class constructors:

`AbsoluteTime()`—creates a new object representing a time of 0 milliseconds and nanoseconds.

`AbsoluteTime(AbsoluteTime)`—creates a new object with the same starting time as the given object.

`AbsoluteTime(Clock)`—creates a new object associated with the given RTSJ `Clock` object.

`AbsoluteTime(AbsoluteTime, Clock)`—creates a new object with the same starting time as the given object, and associated with the given RTSJ `Clock` object.

`AbsoluteTime(Date)`—creates a new object with a starting time of `Date.getTime`.

`AbsoluteTime(Date, Clock)`—creates a new object with a starting time of `Date.getTime`, and associated with the given RTSJ `Clock` object.

`AbsoluteTime(long millis, int nanos)`—creates a new object with a starting time represented by the given millisecond and nanosecond components.

`AbsoluteTime(long millis, int nanos, Clock)`—creates a new object with a starting time represented by the given millisecond and nanosecond components, and associated with the given RTSJ `Clock` object.

The `RelativeTime` class represents a time interval, such as a period of time relative to the current time. It's frequently used when specifying a periodic real-time thread's period, a parameter to a `RealtimeThread.sleep` call, or a call to a form of the `wait` method when synchronizing on shared objects. The constructors for the `RelativeTime` class are:

`RelativeTime(long millis, int nanos)`—creates a new object that represents the interval based on the provided milliseconds parameter, plus the provided nanosecond parameter. In this case, the real-time clock is used by default.

`RelativeTime(long millis, int nanos, Clock)`—creates a new object that represents the interval based on the provided milliseconds parameter, plus the provided nanosecond parameter. In this case, the provided clock is used; if null, then the real-time clock is used by default.

RelativeTime()—creates a new object with zeros for both the milliseconds and nanoseconds parameter. The real-time clock is used by default.

RelativeTime(Clock)—creates a new object with zeros for both the milliseconds and nanoseconds parameter. In this case, the provided clock is used; if null, then the real-time clock is used by default.

RelativeTime(RelativeTime)—creates a new object from the one provided.

RelativeTime(RelativeTime, Clock)—creates a new object from the one provided, using the clock provided.

Both HighResolutionTime classes allow you to perform time arithmetic, where you can add and subtract different time objects to derive new time objects. For instance, the code in Listing 7-3 is a very easy way to determine the amount of time a particular operation takes to execute.

Listing 7-3   Timing a real-time operation

```
import javax.realtime.*;
public class Main {
    public static void main(String[] args) {
        // Create the objects beforehand; eliminates jitter
        AbsoluteTime before;
        AbsoluteTime after;
        RelativeTime elapsed;

        before = Clock.getRealtimeClock().getTime();
        // perform operation here...
        after = Clock.getRealtimeClock().getTime();

        elapsed = after.subtract(before);
        System.out.println("Elapsed time: " + elapsed);
    }
}
```

As the comment at the beginning of the code says, we declare the time objects before the timed operation so that the object creating time doesn't get factored into the measurement. Since Clock operations are bounded and deterministic in Java RTS, the calls to getTime are efficient, and consistent, in terms of execution time. In fact, due to inherent jitter in the java.util.Date class, you should use Clock.getRealtimeClock().getTime and the AbsoluteTime it returns for all time-stamping operations, such as that shown in Listing 7-4.

Listing 7-4   Jitter-free Date code

```
AbsoluteTime current = Clock.getRealtimeClock().getTime();
Date time = current.getDate();
System.out.println("Current date/time: " + time);
```

Let's take a look at more involved example of how to use both the `AbsoluteTime` and `RelativeTime` classes.

A Conflated Stock Data Feed Example

Let's examine a situation where we want to send conflated stock price data to client applications. The requirement is to gather all updates for a particular stock ticker as they occur in real-time, but send them no less than ten milliseconds apart. This means that for all updates that occur within each ten-millisecond period, the updates must be added together to form one overall update that is sent to the clients (see Figure 7-4). However, if more than ten milliseconds elapses between single updates, the update data gets transmitted immediately (there's no need to delay any longer).

In the examples shown in this figure, the stock price starts at a value of 10.00. Before the first ten-millisecond conflation period (where an update to clients will be sent) four individual price updates are received from the external data feed for the stock being watched. Each price update is applied to the stock price, but the result is not sent until the conflation period expires. At that time, the stock price is 9.48, which is the value sent in the update to the client applications.

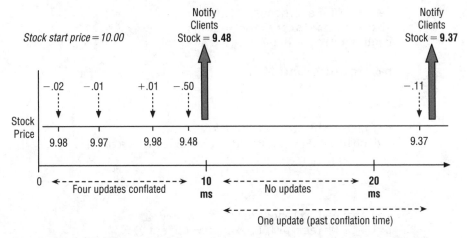

Figure 7-4   Conflated stock ticker updates.

However, during the next conflation period (another ten milliseconds) no price updates are received. Therefore, no conflated price update needs to be sent since the value hasn't changed. However, as soon as the next price update does occur, the resulting price will be sent out immediately (which is 9.37 in this example). At this point, the conflation timer is reset, and updates will be conflated for the next ten milliseconds.

The description and diagram above lay the groundwork for our sample application. There's no need to create a periodic RTT; we'll simply use a starting time (an AbsoluteTime object) and wait on an object that will be signaled when an update occurs. However, we'll use the HighResolutionTime.waitForObject method, which allows us to provide a maximum amount of time to wait. Therefore, with each update, the code will check the time elapsed, and if it's still within the conflation time period, the code will again wait but for the time remaining in the period. Implementing it this way allows us to demonstrate the use of AbsoluteTime and RelativeTime objects, as well as HighResolutionTime arithmetic in one meaningful example. In Chapter 8, we'll modify this application to use a Timer object instead. For now, let's begin looking at Listing 7-5.

Listing 7-5   The conflated stock update application

```
import javax.realtime.*;
public class MyApp {
    Object lock = new Object();
    double update = 0.00;
    final RelativeTime PERIOD = new RelativeTime(10,0); // 10ms

    class Conflater extends RealtimeThread {
        boolean updateOccured = false;
        RelativeTime timeout = PERIOD;
        AbsoluteTime startTime = null;
        double price = 0.00;

        public void run() {
            // ...
        }

        private void updateClients(
          double newPrice, RelativeTime lastUpdate) {
            // ...
        }
    }

    class DataFeed extends RealtimeThread {
        private Object privLock = new Object();
        public void run() {
```

```
        // ...
    }
    private void send(int interval, double change) {
        // ...
    }
}

public MyApp() {
    Conflater conflater = new Conflater();
    DataFeed datafeed = new DataFeed();

    conflater.start();
    datafeed.start();
}

public static void main(String[] args) {
    MyApp app = new MyApp();
}
}
```

From this code, you can see that there are two `RealtimeThread` classes: Conflater, and DataFeed. The `Conflater` class object listens for updates from the `DataFeed` class object, and sends conflated updates to its clients at least every `PERIOD` amount of time. Both RTTs share the object `lock`, and each change to the stock is communicated through update.

The Conflater Class

Let's take a look at class `Conflater` in more detail—see Listing 7-6—as that's where the interesting code is.

Listing 7-6   The Conflater class

```
class Conflater extends RealtimeThread {
    boolean updateOccured = false;
    RelativeTime timeout = PERIOD;
    AbsoluteTime startTime = null;
    double price = 0.00;
    Clock rtClock = Clock.getRealtimeClock();

    public void run() {
        try {
            // Wait to receive start price, and begin conflation
            synchronized ( lock ) {
                lock.wait();
            }
```

continued

```
        // The first update is the starting price
        price = update;
        startTime = rtClock.getTime();
        System.out.println(
          "Conflater received starting price");

        // Now wait for updates, apply them, and send
        // updated price to clients after conflated period
        while ( true ) {
            synchronized ( lock ) {
              // wait for update or period to expire
              update = 0.00
              HighResolutionTime.waitForObject(lock,timeout);

              AbsoluteTime current =
                  rtClock.getTime();
              RelativeTime elapsed =
                  current.subtract(startTime);

              // Check for update or timeout
              if ( update != 0.00 ) {
                // Apply update, and check time
                updateOccured = true;
                price += update;
                System.out.println(
                  "Conflater: update " + update +
                  ", Elapsed=" + elapsed);
                timeout = PERIOD.subtract( elapsed );

                // First update since previous period
                if ( elapsed.getMilliseconds() >
                     PERIOD.getMilliseconds() )
                {
                  // Send update, start new conflation period
                  updateClients(price, elapsed);
                  startTime = rtClock.getTime();
                }
              }
              else {
                // Conflation period expired
                if ( updateOccured )
                {
                  // Send update, start new conflation period
                  updateClients(price, elapsed);
                  startTime = rtClock.getTime();
                }
              }
```

```
                }
            }
        }
        catch ( Exception e ) {
            e.printStackTrace();
        }
    }

    private void updateClients( double newPrice,
                          RelativeTime lastUpdate) {
        System.out.println("Conflater: Updating clients:");
        System.out.println("Conflater:    price=" + newPrice);
        System.out.println("Conflater:    Time since last:" +
                lastUpdate);

        // Send update
        // ...

        // Reset some values
        timeout = PERIOD;
        updateOccured = false;
    }
}
```

The first update received is the starting price. From that point on, the thread enters an infinite loop waiting for an update, or the period to expire—whichever comes first. In the while loop, waitForObject is called with a timeout value, which is initially set to the full ten-millisecond period. Therefore, one of two things can occur: an update arrives, which results in the wait call returning when the lock object is signaled, or the timeout period expires.

When execution continues after waitForObject, the elapsed time since the start of the conflation period is determined, and a check is made to see if a data feed update has arrived. This is simple—if the update price is non-zero, an update occurred. Otherwise the timeout value has expired. In the case of a price update, a flag is set (to be checked later, when the period expires), the price is adjusted accordingly, and the timeout value is set to the time remaining in the current period. However, if the elapsed time since the beginning of the period is greater than the period itself, then we know that a data feed update hasn't been received in the current period and this update needs to be sent to clients right away. The updateClients method is called to perform this.

In the case of a period timeout, a check is made to see if any data feed updates have occurred in the current period. If not, then nothing special is done, and the code again calls waitForObject. If an update has occurred, then a call is made to updateClients, where all clients are given the new conflated stock price. Also, the period start time is reset to the current time in preparation of the new conflation period. The updateClients method also resets the timeout to be equal to the full period, and resets the flag that indicates a data feed update has occurred. The code is now ready to call waitForObject again.

The DataFeed Class

The DataFeed class is simple, but since it uses RelativeTime to create pauses between updates (to simulate updates arriving aperiodically) let's explore it now (see Listing 7-7).

Listing 7-7   The DataFeed class

```
class DataFeed extends RealtimeThread {
    private Object privLock = new Object();

    public void run() {
        // begin first period
        send(0, 10.00); // starting price
        send(2, -.02);
        send(1, -.01);
        send(1, +.01);
        send(2, -.50);
        send(4, 0.00); // just sleep for 4ms

        // begin second period
        send(12, -.11); // update well after period
    }

    private void send(int interval, double change) {
        if ( interval > 0 ) {
            // Wait for elapsed time
            try {
                RelativeTime elapsed =
                    new RelativeTime(interval,0);
                synchronized ( privLock ) {
                    HighResolutionTime.waitForObject(
                        privLock, elapsed);
                }
            }
            catch ( Exception e ) { }
        }

        if ( change != 0.00 ) {
            update = change;
```

```
        synchronized ( lock ) {
           lock.notify();
        }
     }
  }
}
```

This contrived code simulates sending the updates, per period, as shown in Figure 7-4. The first parameter in the send method is the amount of time in milliseconds the code waits before sending the update. The second parameter is the amount the stock price has moved, up or down (a delta value). If the update value passed is zero, the method effectively acts as a high-resolution call to sleep. If the interval is set to zero, the price update is sent immediately.

Sending a price update is a simple operation; the global update delta value is set, and the shared lock object is signaled (informing the Conflater class that the update is available). The succession of calls to send is meant to simulate a random pattern of updates with varying amounts of time between them, such that they recreate the scenario in Figure 7-4.

Application Output

When executed with Java RTS on a uniprocessor, the following output will be observed:

```
Conflater started...
Conflater received starting price
Conflater: update -0.02, Elapsed=(2 ms, 2484 ns)
Conflater: update -0.01, Elapsed=(3 ms, 5276 ns)
Conflater: update 0.01, Elapsed=(5 ms, 3099 ns)
Conflater: update -0.5, Elapsed=(7 ms, 3104 ns)
Conflater: Updating clients:
Conflater:     price=9.48
Conflater:     Time since last update:(10 ms, 0 ns)
Conflater: update -0.11, Elapsed=(13 ms, 5331 ns)
Conflater: update after period
Conflater: Updating clients:
Conflater:     price=9.37
Conflater:     Time since last update:(13 ms, 5331 ns)
```

At the very beginning ($t = 0$), the stock start price is received and the waitForObject loop begins. You can see in the output above that four data feed updates are conflated into the first price update sent out to the simulated clients. The time elapsed when each update is received is relative to the start of the current period (not to each individual update). Therefore, the first update to clients is triggered by the period timeout at $t + 10$ milliseconds.

However, during the second ten-millisecond period, no data feed updates occur. Therefore, when the period expires, nothing is done. When an update finally does arrive 13 milliseconds after the beginning of the second period ($t + 23$ milliseconds), the new price is sent to clients immediately, and the cycle repeats.

Asynchronous Events

"Defer no time, delays have dangerous ends."
—William Shakespeare

ALTHOUGH Java RTS has ample support for periodic, scheduled, real-time tasks, the world doesn't always work that way. Many real-world events are asynchronous in nature; it's simply unknown when these events will occur. Java RTS allows you to bind the execution of your code to events both within the JVM, and outside of it (also called "happenings"). In this chapter, we'll examine what it takes to create an asynchronous event handler with Java RTS.

We'll examine the various kinds of asynchronous events that Java RTS has support for, and how to create custom event handlers. Also, we'll look at timer-based events that fire either once or repeatedly according to a predefined period.

Asynchronous Event Processing

Event processing is a common task executed in many application types, on many platforms, in many programming languages. Similar to the JavaBean event processing classes, the RTSJ's *asynchronous event handler* (AEH) facility is designed to handle different system and programmer-defined events that real-time applications may need to deal with. Events that are external to the real-time Java VM are often referred to as *happenings*. Examples include OS-level events (such as POSIX signals), hardware interrupts and related functionality (such as file and network IO), and custom events defined and fired by the application itself.

In the RTSJ, two main classes make up the AEH facility (see Figure 8-1):

AsyncEvent—an object of this type represents the event itself. As of the RTSJ, the object does not contain related event data. This needs to be delivered through other means.

AsyncEventHandler—an RTSJ Schedulable object that is executed by the AEH facility within the real-time Java VM when the related event is fired. This object has associated ReleaseParameters, SchedulingParameters, and MemoryParameters objects, which you populate to indicate how the event handler is to be scheduled.

The advantage of using the AEH facility is that your code is executed according to the real-time parameters you specify, without the need to explicitly create RealtimeThread threads to handle each event. The real-time Java VM handles the real-time threading machinery for you. With the BoundAsyncEventHandler class, you can bind the event handler to a dedicated RealtimeThread for the life of the event. We'll discuss these classes and their differences in the next section.

The center of the AEH facility is the event itself, which is represented by the AsyncEvent class (see Figure 8-2). This class is used to handle internal, application-defined events, events external to the Java VM, and timer-based events.

Specifically, Java RTS supports one-shot timers that fire at specific times with a class appropriately named OneShotTimer, and periodic timers with a class named PeriodicTimer (see Figure 8-3). A PeriodicTimer fires precisely at each time interval, after firing initially at a specified time.

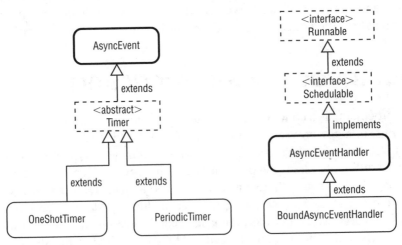

Figure 8-1   Asynchronous event handler code is executed with real-time parameters.

The RTSJ requires that a high-resolution, OS-level, precision timer be made available to the real-time Java VM. This allows periodic real-time threads, as well as RTSJ `Timer` objects, to fire at their precise times and intervals, when appropriate. For instance, a 500-microsecond timer or periodic `RealtimeThread` object should fire precisely at each 500-microsecond boundary. In both of these cases, there are no calls to `Thread.sleep`; the real-time VM handles the guarantee of time for you.

```
                    AsyncEvent
          +addHandler()
          +bindTo()
          +createReleaseParameters()
          +fire()
          +handledBy()
          +removeHandler()
          +setHandler()
          +unbindTo()
```

Figure 8-2 `AsyncEvent` represents an abstract event.

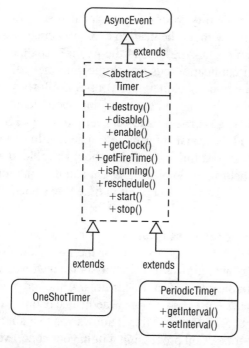

Figure 8-3 Java RTS supports two types of timer-based events.

To support this, and other real-time timer-based code in your application, the Java RTS implements the Clock API—discussed in Chapter 7—which supports high-resolution, low-latency, time-related calls. The high-resolution clock is used for periodic RealtimeThread and Timer objects. For timer-related events, your handler code is released for execution within a bounded, measurable, time.

It all starts by defining an event with the AsyncEvent class. You can either instantiate an object of this class directly, or extend it with your own class if you need to add additional behavior or state. You can set release parameters to, say, have the event fire periodically; you can bind the object to an event external to the VM; or you can call the event's fire method directly based on some internal condition in your application. In all of these cases, the event handlers—those objects that extend AsyncEventHandler and add themselves as a handler for this event—are notified that the event has been fired. Let's take a look at how to implement asynchronous event handlers now.

Building an Asynchronous Event Handler

As mentioned above, with the AEH facility, your code is executed according to the real-time parameters you specify, without the need to explicitly create RealtimeThread objects to handle each event. You extend the AsyncEventHandler class (see Figure 8-4) to focus on application business logic, and the real-time Java VM handles the real-time threading machinery for you. This allows you to create numerous event handlers in your code without worrying about dedicating all of the resources associated with a RealtimeThread per event. In Java RTS, the AEH facility is designed to handle this scenario far more efficiently. In fact, the RTSJ specifies that the real-time Java VM implementation should be able to handle up to tens of thousands of asynchronous, real-time, event handlers (although the actual number of active, firing, handlers at any point in time is expected to be much lower).

However, the BoundAsyncEventHandler class is an exception. It allows you to bind the event handler to a dedicated RealtimeThread for the life of the event. This ensures some extra timeliness, and removes any jitter associated with assigning a different RealtimeThread to the event each time it fires. Although there is some extra overhead involved (since a RealtimeThread is dedicated to this event), additional timeliness is obtained. The advantage is that it allows you to maintain a consistent implementation of real-time event processing within your code, even if a subset of them requires dedicated processing resources.

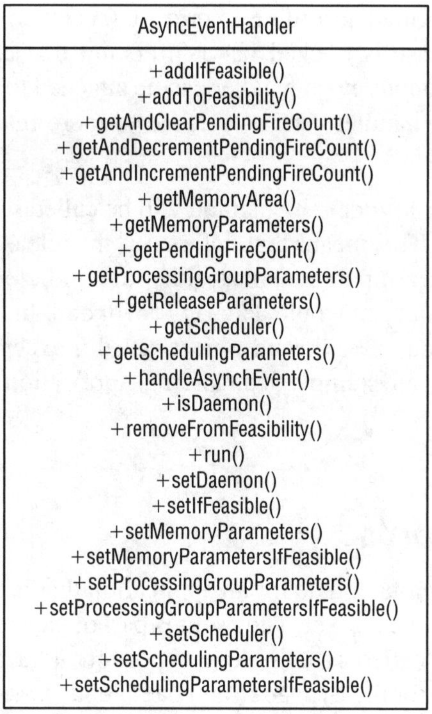

```
+-------------------------------------------+
|            AsyncEventHandler              |
+-------------------------------------------+
|           +addIfFeasible()                |
|           +addToFeasibility()             |
|       +getAndClearPendingFireCount()      |
|    +getAndDecrementPendingFireCount()     |
|    +getAndIncrementPendingFireCount()     |
|           +getMemoryArea()                |
|           +getMemoryParameters()          |
|           +getPendingFireCount()          |
|       +getProcessingGroupParameters()     |
|           +getReleaseParameters()         |
|             +getScheduler()               |
|         +getSchedulingParameters()        |
|           +handleAsynchEvent()            |
|              +isDaemon()                  |
|           +removeFromFeasibility()        |
|                 +run()                    |
|              +setDaemon()                 |
|             +setIfFeasible()              |
|           +setMemoryParameters()          |
|       +setMemoryParametersIfFeasible()    |
|       +setProcessingGroupParameters()     |
|   +setProcessingGroupParametersIfFeasible()|
|              +setScheduler()              |
|          +setSchedulingParameters()       |
|      +setSchedulingParametersIfFeasible() |
+-------------------------------------------+
```

Figure 8-4   The AsyncEventHandler class diagram.

Asynchronous event handlers can have the following optional, real-time and other processing-related parameters associated with them:

SchedulingParameters—a priority associated with the event handler (for when the handler is executed in response to the event).

ReleaseParameters—a set of parameters that indicate the estimated cost of event processing, an associated deadline for completing the processing, and handlers in case of cost overrun, and deadline miss.

MemoryArea—indicates that the event handler should execute in the given memory area, be it the heap, a scoped memory region, or immortal memory.

MemoryParameters—an indication of memory usage and allocation rate, which is used to pace the garbage collector (if applicable), and to limit the amount of heap, scoped, or immortal memory the handler can consume per release.

ProcessingGroupParameters—further indication of, and bounds set on, event processing time.

The release of event handlers is performed according to priority (specified when each AEH is created), and each release is tracked via a fire count that can be queried. Also, more than one asynchronous event handler can be attached to a single asynchronous event, and a single handler can be attached to more than one event.

The handler is released and its handleAsyncEvent method will be called serially each time its associated event is fired. This means that, internally, the releases are queued. You can set the handler's release parameters as either aperiodic or sporadic to control interarrival times just as you would a RealtimeThread. In fact, a handler can do almost anything a RealtimeThread object can do, except call waitForNextPeriod. Let's begin with an example of an internal application event and handler.

Internal Application Events

In this example, the event is a stock quote update for an application that is tracking the movement of some equities in the market. The event is part of each Stock class object, simply stored in an array called stocks. A good portion of the application code is in Listing 8-1; the code for the Listener and DataFeed classes and some methods of the main class MyApp are missing but will be filled in during the discussion below.

Listing 8-1   The data feed asynchronous event sample application

```
import java.util.*;
import javax.realtime.*;
public class MyApp {
    class Stock {
        public Stock (String s, double v) {
            symbol = s;
            value = v;
            event = new AsyncEvent();
        }
        public String symbol;
        public double value;
        public AsyncEvent event;
    }
    static Stock[] stocks = null;

    class Listener extends AsyncEventHandler {
        // ...
    }
```

```java
class DataFeed implements Runnable {
    // ...
}

public Main() {
    // Create the Stock objects with event objects
    stocks = new Stock[5];
    stocks[0] = new Stock("JAVA", 3.99);
    stocks[1] = new Stock("YHOO", 12.82);
    stocks[2] = new Stock("MOT", 4.52);
    stocks[3] = new Stock("MSFT", 20.37);
    stocks[4] = new Stock("AAPL", 94.50);

    // Create the listeners for these stocks
    for ( int s = 0; s < stocks.length; s++ ) {
        Listener l = new Listener(stocks[s].symbol);
        addListener(stocks[s].symbol, l);
    }

    // Start the DataFeed thread to generate updates
    PeriodicParameters rel =
            new PeriodicParameters(new RelativeTime(500,0));
    RealtimeThread datafeedRTT =
            new RealtimeThread(
                null, rel, null,
                null, null, new DataFeed() );
    datafeedRTT.start();
}

public double addListener(
  String symbol, AsyncEventHandler aeh) {
    // ...
}

public double getValue(String symbol) {
    // ...
}

public static void main(String[] args) {
    MyApp app = new MyApp();
}
}
```

When the application starts, the code in the MyApp main class constructor first creates five Stock objects. Each stock's symbol and initial value are provided in the constructor, where these values are stored, and the stock's AsyncEvent object is created. Next, objects of the Listener class are created for each stock in the application. Java RTS supports more than one asynchronous event handler object for each event, but to keep this example simple for now, there is only one listener per stock. The Listener class constructor takes the stock symbol String—for which it's listening to updates for—as its parameter.

The call to addListener associates the given Listener object to the specified stock symbol. The code locates the Stock object in the array by symbol, and calls AsyncEvent.addHandler, providing the Listener as the parameter. The method setHandler isn't used as it would effectively replace the current event handlers that were set prior to the call. In effect, it acts to remove all other handlers currently set for a particular event, and sets the given object as the one and only handler. The call to addHandler, as opposed to setHandler, supports the addition of more than one handler per event. You can see the complete method implementation in Listing 8-2.

Listing 8-2   Adding listeners

```
public double addListener(String symbol,

                          AsyncEventHandler aeh) {
    for ( int s = 0; s < stocks.length; s++ ) {
        if ( stocks[s].symbol.equalsIgnoreCase(symbol)) {
            stocks[s].event.addHandler(aeh);
            return stocks[s].value;
        }
    }
    return -1; // symbol not found
}
```

The Listener class itself extends AsyncEventHandler, and it overrides the handleAsyncEvent method implementation. This method is called each time the associated event object is fired. This is where the business logic to retrieve and display the new stock quote is implemented, as shown in Listing 8-3.

Listing 8-3   Handling events

```
class Listener extends AsyncEventHandler {
    String symbol;
    public Listener(String symbol) {
        this.symbol = symbol;
    }

    public void handleAsyncEvent() {
        double value = getValue(symbol);
        System.out.println(
```

```
          "Listener(" + symbol + "):\tUpdate for " +
          symbol + "=" + value + " on thread: " +
          RealtimeThread.currentThread().getName());
    }
}
```

The implementation outputs the new stock value, as well as the thread name within which it's executed. The code to fire the event is part of the DataFeed class, which is shown in Listing 8-4.

Listing 8-4   The DataFeed class

```
class DataFeed implements Runnable {
    Random random = new Random(System.currentTimeMillis());

    public void run() {
        while ( true ) {
            // Pick a stock at random
            int stock = random.nextInt(stocks.length);

            // Move up or down?
            boolean up = random.nextBoolean();

            // How much?
            int factor = random.nextInt(4) + 1;

            // Apply change
            double change = .01 * factor;
            if ( ! up )
                change *= -1;
            stocks[stock].value += change;

            // Notify handler(s)
            stocks[stock].event.fire();

            RealtimeThread.waitForNextPeriod();
        }
    }
}
```

The DataFeed object runs within a periodic RTT, where it randomly picks a stock symbol, modifies the price, and fires the stock's specific AsyncEvent object by calling the fire method. It's at that point that Java RTS releases the event's associated listener object(s). When the handler executes, its handleAsyncEvent method is invoked, executing the code we examined just prior. This completes the application processing for a stock price update.

Running the application produces two updates per second (which is the DataFeed object's RTT period) but this can be adjusted. Each update picks a Stock object at random, determines its movement at random (up or down), and then generates the price change—also at random. When a Listener object receives the event, it prints out the stock symbol, the new price, and the thread name it's currently executing within (see Listing 8-5).

Listing 8-5   Sample application output

```
Listener(AAPL): Update for AAPL=94.52 on RealtimeServerThread-4
Listener(JAVA): Update for JAVA=3.97 on RealtimeServerThread-0
Listener(YHOO): Update for YHOO=12.79 on RealtimeServerThread-1
Listener(MOT):  Update for MOT=4.51 on RealtimeServerThread-2
Listener(MSFT): Update for MSFT=20.34 on RealtimeServerThread-3
Listener(AAPL): Update for AAPL=94.5 on RealtimeServerThread-4
Listener(MOT):  Update for MOT=4.50 on RealtimeServerThread-2
Listener(AAPL): Update for AAPL=94.52 on RealtimeServerThread-4
Listener(AAPL): Update for AAPL=94.53 on RealtimeServerThread-4
Listener(MOT):  Update for MOT=4.52 on RealtimeServerThread-2
Listener(MOT):  Update for MOT=4.47 on RealtimeServerThread-2
Listener(MSFT): Update for MSFT=20.31 on RealtimeServerThread-3
Listener(AAPL): Update for AAPL=94.49 on RealtimeServerThread-4
Listener(YHOO): Update for YHOO=12.81 on RealtimeServerThread-1
Listener(AAPL): Update for AAPL=94.53 on RealtimeServerThread-4
```

You can see that although RTTs aren't explicitly created for each Listener, Java RTS does provide one when the event is fired. Although it appears that there's a thread per handler, this is not the case! Each AEH object is given a uniquely identified thread name, but there are only a very small number of native threads running to execute them. In our case, when we ran this test with up to 1000 simulated Stock objects, and hence 1000 AEH objects, only two native threads were used to execute the code. You can see this in the Java RTS Thread Scheduling Visualizer (TSV) tool, which will be explored in more detail in Chapter 12. A portion of the display is shown in Figure 8-5.

Figure 8-5   The native threads in the AEH example.

The top row of dashed lines is the `RealtimeThread` that executes the `DataFeed` periodic task. Each vertical line in that row indicates when it was executing, which matches its 500-microsecond period. The two rows of dashed lines at the bottom of the picture represent the two native threads that executed the handler code for each stock update. You can see by this output that the AEH work was divided up between these two threads.

Using a Runnable as a Handler

In the example we just examined, the `Listener` class extended the `AsyncEvent-Class`, and therefore when an event was fired, its `handleAsyncEvent` was called directly. This doesn't have to be the case. Alternatively, you can implement the event listener business logic within a `Runnable` class, as you would if you were going to run it within a `RealtimeThread` directly. However, when it's associated with an asynchronous event object instead, its `run` method will be executed each time the event is fired. The code in Listing 8-6 is a modified version of the `Listener` class from the previous example.

Listing 8-6   The modified `Listener` class

```
class Listener implements Runnable {
    String symbol;
    public Listener(String symbol) {
        this.symbol = symbol;
    }

    public void run() {
        double value = getValue(symbol);
        System.out.println(
            "Listener(" + symbol + "):\tUpdate for " +
            symbol + "=" + value + " on thread: ");
    }
}
```

The `Listener` class now implements `Runnable`, and does *not* extend `AsyncEvent-Handler` as it did before. Due to this change, the code that was in the `handle-AsyncEvent` method is now placed in the `run` method. To have this `Runnable` invoked when the event is fired, we must change some code in the application's `Main` method, as shown in Listing 8-7.

Listing 8-7   The modified `Main` method

```
public Main() {
    // Create the Stock objects with event objects
    stocks = new Stock[5];
    stocks[0] = new Stock("JAVA", 3.99);
```

```
stocks[1] = new Stock("YHOO", 12.82);
stocks[2] = new Stock("MOT", 4.52);
stocks[3] = new Stock("MSFT", 20.37);
stocks[4] = new Stock("AAPL", 94.50);

// Create the listeners for these stocks
for ( int s = 0; s < stocks.length; s++ ) {
    Listener listener = new Listener(stocks[s].symbol);

    AsyncEventHandler handler =
        new AsyncEventHandler(listener);

    addListener(stocks[s].symbol, handler);
}

// ...
}
```

The Listener object is now provided as a parameter in the AsyncEventHandler constructor, which in turn is provided in the call to event.addHandler. The default implementation of the AsyncEventHandler class is to call the run method of the given Runnable (when one is provided), executing it within a RealtimeThread.

Although the end result is that the application runs the same whether you implement it this way, or by having Listener extend AsyncEventHandler, it offers you consistency in how you write your real-time code. Whether you decide to execute your business logic in a RealtimeThread directly, or through the AEH facility of Java RTS, you still place your business logic in a Runnable object either way. This consistency makes it easier to change that decision later, if the dynamics or requirements of your application changes.

We can go further, and have the handler execute within a dedicated Realtime-Thread while still using the AEH facility if required by your application. Let's take a look at how to do that now.

Bound Asynchronous Event Handlers

If it becomes desirable or necessary to eliminate the potential jitter associated with creating and/or assigning an RTT to a handler when each event is fired, your code can instead extend BoundAsyncEventHandler to achieve this. With this class, your handler is permanently bound to a dedicated RealtimeThread. Revisiting the example application in Listing 8-1, a simple change to the Listener class to extend BoundAsyncEventHandler will illustrate this.

When you execute the code, a casual observation shows no difference in behavior. However, again analyzing the application's execution with the TSV tool tells a different story. Although we can't show it here, scrolling through the TSV displays shows all of the native threads created and running; one for each `Bound-AsyncEventHandler` object in the system.

Working with Event Fire Count

Recall that Java RTS guarantees to queue releases (due to an event object being fired) and call your handler back for each event. To do this serially, your handler will be released repeatedly, once for each event fired. Each time your handler is released, however, it gets placed on a priority queue within the real-time scheduler and must wait to start execution. This is fine, and it enables events processing to be prioritized with other events and tasks running in the system.

However, Java RTS gives you a chance to check if there are other event releases pending for your handler by checking the event's fire count. Knowing this value allows you to handle all of the event releases within one call to the handler's `handleAsyncEvent` or `run` method. This saves your code, and the rest of the system, from having the handler repeatedly released and rescheduled within the OS. Checking the fire count, and processing each queued release in your handler is straightforward, and can be done with the modifications to the `Listener` class's `handleAsyncEvent` method from the previous example, as shown in Listing 8-8.

Listing 8-8   Modified event handler

```
public void handleAsyncEvent() {
    if ( getPendingFireCount() > 1 )
        System.out.println("** Updates Queued! ***");

    do {
        double value = getValue(symbol);
        System.out.println(
                "Listener(" + symbol + "):\tUpdate for "+
                symbol + "=" + value + " on thread: "+
                RealtimeThread.currentThread().getName());
    } while ( getAndDecrementPendingFireCount() > 0 );
}
```

For informational purposes only, a line of code has been inserted to indicate when the pending fire count is greater than 1. It should always be at least equal to 1 when the `handleAsyncEvent` method is called; a value greater than that indicates that releases are queued. Note: this line can safely be removed without affecting event processing or the pending fire count value.

Next, the existing method's business logic is wrapped in a do...while loop, where a call is made to the getAndDecrementPendingFireCount. As its name implies, each call to this method returns the fire count, and then subtracts 1 from it. There are two related calls that may be more applicable in certain cases:

getAndIncrementPendingFireCount()—This method increments the event's fire count after its current value is returned. Scenarios where this may be needed include cases where the handler release is being processed, but due to an error or a failed transaction, for example, you need to roll back the processing of the event. Doing so will ensure that the handler is released at least one more time, giving your code a chance to process it again (with better results, hopefully).

getAndClearPendingFireCount()—this method returns the current fire count, and then clears it, effectively removing all currently queued releases for this event.

In fact, in the case of the stock update example, the method getAndClearPendingFireCount is ideal. Since each stock's value is updated with each release, handling queued updates will only return the latest result of those updates. In other words, if a particular stock were updated repeatedly, *n* times, too quickly for the event handler to be released and executed even once, the intermittent values of the stock would be overwritten. Looping through the pending fire count in the handler will only return the latest stock price each time. Therefore, this method would be more efficiently implemented to use the getAndClearPendingFireCount method.

External Events—Happenings

The AsyncEvent class contains a method called bindTo that allows you to bind that event to a happening. To illustrate, let's use the autopilot example we used in Chapter 5. In this case, let's assume there's a happening defined for an interface to a physical autopilot button. When it's pressed, it toggles the autopilot system on or off, depending upon its state at the time the button is pressed. Listing 8-9 is a simplified example of what this code might look like.

Listing 8-9 Autopilot implementation

```
import javax.realtime.*;
public class MyApp {
    AutopilotButton button = new AutopilotButton();
    AutopilotHandler handler = new AutopilotHandler(button);

    class AutopilotButton extends AsyncEvent {
        private boolean on = false;
```

```
    public AutopilotButton() {
        this.bindTo("autopilot");
    }

    public boolean isOn() {
        return on;
    }

    public void fire() {
        on = !on;
        super.fire();
    }
}

class AutopilotHandler extends AsyncEventHandler {
    AutopilotButton button = null;

    public AutopilotHandler(AutopilotButton button) {
        this.button = button;
        this.button.addHandler(this);
    }

    public void handleAsyncEvent() {
        boolean state = button.isOn();
        if ( state == true )
            System.out.println("Autopilot turned on");
        else
            System.out.println("Autopilot turned off");

        // ...
    }
}

public MyApp() {
    button = new AutopilotButton();
    handler = new AutopilotHandler(button);
    // ...
}

public static void main(String[] args) {
    MyApp app = new MyApp();
}
}
```

In this code, the AutopilotButton class extends AsyncEvent, and keeps its on/off state. The fire method is overridden to toggle the state of the autopilot flag each time the button is pressed. When the event is fired, the AutopilotHandler object, which extends AsyncEventHandler, is notified. Since it was given a reference to the AutopilotButton object as part of its constructor (with which it add itself as a handler), it can query the button for its state each time it's notified that it has changed. With this implementation, we've encapsulated the autopilot happening and button state within one class, and the processing needed to handle the state change in another class.

Because Java RTS uses a RealtimeThread to execute the event and event handler code, you can be guaranteed of deterministic behavior when the autopilot happening/event occurs. Further, to prioritize this event properly in the system (considering there may be other real-time and non-real-time events that might occur), and because AsyncEventHandler is a Schedulable object, you can set the handler's priority via the setSchedulingParameters call (Listing 8-10).

Listing 8-10   Autopilot event handler

```
class AutopilotHandler extends AsyncEventHandler {
    AutopilotButton button = null;

    public AutopilotHandler(AutopilotButton button) {
        this.button = button;
        setSchedulingParameters(
          new PriorityParameters(
            PriorityScheduler.instance().getMaxPriority() ));
        this.button.addHandler(this);
    }

    public void handleAsyncEvent() {
        // ...
    }
}
```

Note: Happenings in Java RTS 2.1   As of the latest version of Java RTS at the time of this writing, there are no happenings defined besides two specifically created for testing. The RTSJ is vague on the requirements of happenings, and specifies them as being implementation-specific. It's difficult to forecast what types of external happenings developers will need, and the RTSJ doesn't define a way for happenings to be defined at runtime. Perhaps in a future version of the RTSJ and/or Java RTS, this will be addressed.

Another set of system events that can be handled similarly includes the POSIX signals for UNIX systems. Let's take a look at this now.

Handling POSIX Events

You can write a simple event handler to listen for and be notified of POSIX system events for those implemented on your platform. The javax.realtime. POSIXSignalHandler class, combined with an AsyncEventHandler class that you write, will achieve this. Listing 8-11 is an example that shows how straightforward this is.

Listing 8-11 POSIX signal handler

```
import javax.realtime.*;
public class MyApp {
    SigintHandler handler = null;
    final int RTSJ_MAX_PRI =
        PriorityScheduler.instance().getMaxPriority();

    class SigintHandler extends AsyncEventHandler {
        public SigintHandler() {
            setSchedulingParameters(
                new PriorityParameters(RTSJ_MAX_PRI));
        }

        public void handleAsynchEvent() {
            System.out.println("SIGINT occurred");
        }
    }

    public MyApp() {
        handler = new SigintHandler();
        POSIXSignalHandler.addHandler(
            POSIXSignalHandler.SIGINT, handler);
    }

    public static void main(String[] args) {
        MyApp app = new MyApp();
        // ...
    }
}
```

In this example, the SigintHandler class (the first bold line) extends AsyncEvent-Handler, and sets itself to run at the highest real-time priority when created.

POSIX Signals Handler

Java RTS spawns an internal thread to handle POSIX signals, and notify your application when one you're interested in fires. By default, this thread runs at the RTSJMaxPriority value. If you require, you can set this value lower (anywhere within the range of minimum and maximum real-time priorities) via the command-line parameter RTSJSignalThreadPriority. Keep in mind that setting this value too low may impact the VM's ability to notify your application threads of POSIX events in a timely manner.

It's simply provided in the call to POSIXSignalHandler.addHandler (the second bold line). You must specify one of the available and implemented POSIX signals, or application-defined signal, to receive notification. In this case, we have requested notification of interrupts.

Specifying a Memory Area

Five of the seven available constructors for the AsyncEventHandler class take a boolean flag named noheap. When set to true, the handler object will be run with the characteristics of a NoHeapRealtimeThread. As such, it cannot reside within, or access memory allocated within, the heap. It can only work in and with immortal memory, or a scoped memory area. When noheap is set to false, which is the default, the handler runs with the characteristics of a RealtimeThread. This allows it to reside in and access memory allocated within any memory area; the heap, immortal memory, or scoped memory. The code in Listing 8-12 illustrates the use of the noheap flag, and the restrictions associated when you set it to true.

Listing 8-12   The noheap flag

```
import javax.realtime.*;
public class Main extends RealtimeThread {
    class MyLogic implements Runnable {
        AsyncEvent event;
        public MyLogic(AsyncEvent event){
            this.event = event;
        }
        class SomeEventHandler extends AsyncEventHandler {
            public SomeEventHandler(boolean noheap) {
                super(noheap);
            }

            public void handleAsyncEvent() {
                System.out.println("MyEvent received in area "+
                    RealtimeThread.getCurrentMemoryArea());
                try {
                    // ERROR!
                    String s =
                        (String)HeapMemory.instance().
                            newInstance(String.class);
                }
                catch ( Exception e ) {
                    e.printStackTrace();
                }
            }
        }
    }
```

```
    public void run() {
        SomeEventHandler handler =
            new SomeEventHandler(true);
        event.addHandler(handler);
    }
}

public void run() {
    AsyncEvent event = new AsyncEvent();
    MyLogic logic = new MyLogic(event);
    ImmortalMemory.instance().executeInArea(logic);
    event.fire();
}

public static void main(String[] args) {
    Main app = new Main();
    app.start();
}
}
```

When the application starts, the main application `RealtimeThread` object is started. When its `run` method executes, the following occur:

1. The event object is created on the heap, which is allowed. The Java RTS asynchronous event-handling infrastructure takes care of calling each handler within the proper execution context.

2. The `Runnable` class `MyLogic`—which implements the business logic—is instantiated and the event object is provided in the constructor.

3. Immortal memory is entered with the `MyLogic` object by calling `execute-InArea`. We'll take a look at this class in a moment.

4. Finally, with the event and its handler created, the code fires the event.

In step 3, when the `executeInArea` is called, the `MyLogic` code is executed within the calling thread (the application's main `RealtimeThread`) and the following steps take place:

1. The `SomeEventHandler` class, which extends `AsyncEventHandler` class, is created with the `noheap` flag set to `true`.

2. The handler is added to the event's list of handlers via the `addHandler` call.

Running this application successfully delivers the event to the handler, which prints out a message as a result. However, for illustration purposes, the second part of `handleAsyncEvent` attempts to allocate memory on the heap. Since this handler was created with the noheap flag set to true, this is an illegal operation. The following is the output that this sample application produces:

```
MyEvent received in area javax.realtime.ImmortalMemory
javax.realtime.MemoryAccessError
   at javax.realtime.MemoryArea.newInstance0
   at javax.realtime.MemoryArea.newInstance_internal
   at javax.realtime.MemoryArea.newInstance
   at scopedaeh.Main$MyLogic$SomeEventHandler.handleAsyncEvent
   at javax.realtime.AsyncEventHandler.run1(AsyncEventHandler.
   java:879)
```

From the output, you can see that the event was delivered and the handleAsync-Event method was called, but a MemoryAccessError was thrown when the attempt was made to allocate an object on the heap. If you were to change the noheap flag to false, this allocation would succeed, as the handler would run as though it were a RealtimeThread.

You can combine the NoHeapHelper class introduced in Chapter 5 with the use of asynchronous event handling to make it easier to use it from code running within an NHRT. Let's take a look at a simple example. The code in Listing 8-13 shows a Runnable class to be executed from within an NHRT.

Listing 8-13   Provide a Runnable

```
import javax.realtime.*;
public class MyLogic implements Runnable {
   class SomeEventHandler extends AsyncEventHandler {
      public SomeEventHandler(boolean noheap) {
         super(noheap);
      }

      public void handleAsyncEvent() {
         System.out.println("Event received in area " +
            RealtimeThread.getCurrentMemoryArea() );
      }
   }

   AsyncEvent event = null;
   SomeEventHandler handler = null;

   public MyLogic() {
      event = new AsyncEvent();
      handler = new SomeEventHandler(true);
      event.addHandler(handler);
   }
```

```
    public void run() {
        event.fire();
    }
}
```

The difference with this class from the one before is that the event object and handler are both maintained within the Runnable class, MyLogic. With NoHeapHelper, it's very easy to run this code within an NHRT in either immortal memory, or even scoped memory, as shown in Listing 8-14.

Listing 8-14   Using NoHeapHelper

```
import javax.realtime.*;
public class Main {
    public static void main(String[] args) throws Exception {
        NoHeapHelper nhrtHelper =
                new NoHeapHelper(MyLogic.class);
        nhrtHelper.start();
    }
}
```

As it stands, this code will execute MyLogic, the event, and the event handler all within immortal memory. If you'd like to use a scoped memory area, simply provide a ScopedMemory object as the first parameter in the NoHeapHelper constructor, as shown in Listing 8-15.

Listing 8-15   Using scoped memory

```
import javax.realtime.*;
public class Main {
    static ScopedMemory sm = new LTMemory(4096000); //~4MB
    public static void main(String[] args) throws Exception {
        NoHeapHelper nhrtHelper =
                new NoHeapHelper(sm, MyLogic.class);
        nhrtHelper.start();
    }
}
```

When running in scoped memory, the handler inherits the scope stack of its creator, and the single parent rule applies just as it does for RTTs and NHRTs. The code in Listing 8-16 illustrates how to execute an event and handler within a scoped memory area, with or without specifying noheap as true.

Listing 8-16   Scoped memory AEH

```
import javax.realtime.*;
public class Main extends RealtimeThread {
    static ScopedMemory sm = new LTMemory(4096000); //~4MB;
```

continued

```
class MyLogic implements Runnable {
    class SomeEventHandler extends AsyncEventHandler {
        public void handleAsyncEvent() {
            System.out.println("MyEvent received in area "+
                RealtimeThread.getCurrentMemoryArea());
        }
    }

    public void run() {
        AsyncEvent event = new AsyncEvent();
        SomeEventHandler handler = new SomeEventHandler();
        event.addHandler(handler);
        event.fire();
    }
}

public void run() {
    sm.enter(new MyLogic());
}

public static void main(String[] args) {
    Main app = new Main();
    app.start();
}
}
```

The difference with this code from previous examples is that the MyLogic class object, event object, and handler object all reside and operate within a scoped memory region, in what is effectively a RealtimeThread each time the event is fired.

Time-Based Events

So far, the discussion has focused on processing events that are either application-specific, or external (i.e., POSIX signals of happenings). However, Java RTS allows you to the use the AEH facility to handle time-based events also. This helps simple cases where your real-time code must query the state of physical devices on a regular basis, or where your code must perform some action for only a limited amount of time once triggered. We'll explore both of these cases in this section.

Note that within Java RTS, there is only one internal thread created to handle timer expiration events. Therefore, timer events are serialized, which can affect the behavior of timer events handlers when more than one timer fires at the same time. If this happens, the release of the first timer's event handler(s) can delay the release of the second timer's handler(s), regardless of priority. However, once the handlers are all released, they will execute according to priority. Therefore, the only time this may be noticeable is when a timer with a large number of handlers associated with it gets handled first by the internal timer thread.

One-Shot Timers

Often, the need arises to perform an operation once after a certain amount of time passes, or for a certain duration of time only. For instance, when an elevator reaches a desired floor, this signals the doors to open. After a predetermined amount of time, the doors will automatically attempt to close. This is an excellent use of a one-shot timer in a real-time application. The OneShotTimer class in Java RTS (see Figure 8-6) is designed to provide this behavior, essentially as an asynchronous event that gets fired once, when its time-out period expires.

The OneShotTimer class constructors are:

OneShotTimer(HighResolutionTime, AsyncEventHandler)—this defines a one-shot timer that fires at a specified time (if an AbsoluteTime object is provided) or after a specified amount of time from when start is called (if a RelativeTime object is provided). If null is provided, the timer expires immediately. Regardless, when the timer expires, the given AsyncEventHandler object is called to handle the event. The default Clock is the Java RTS high-resolution real-time clock.

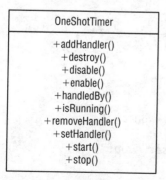

Figure 8-6   The Java RTS OneShotTimer class methods.

OneShotTimer(HighResolutionTime, Clock, AsyncEventHandler)—this defines a one-shot timer that fires at a specified time (if an `AbsoluteTime` object is provided) or after a specified amount of time from when `start` is called (if a `RelativeTime` object is provided). If `null` is provided, the timer expires immediately. Regardless, when the timer expires, the given `AsyncEventHandler` object is called to handle the event. The given `Clock` object is what this timer is based on.

High-Resolution Timer Handler

As with POSIX signal handling, Java RTS spawns an internal thread to handle timer events. By default, this thread also runs at the `RTSJMaxPriority` value. If you require, you can set this value lower (anywhere within the range of minimum and maximum real-time priorities) via the command-line parameter `RTSJHighRes-TimerThreadPriority`. Keep in mind that setting this value too low may impact the VM's ability to notify your application threads of timer expiration events in a timely manner—pun intended ☺.

Once created, the timer is both disabled, and not started. The timer needs to be both enabled and started in order to receive notification that it has expired. For instance, if the timer is started (via a call to `start`) it will expire but not notify your handler. You must also call `enable` to ensure that your code gets notified once the timer expires. Let's examine a sample implementation of an elevator control application that uses both a custom asynchronous event, and a one-shot timer, to perform the door open and close tasks respectively. Examine the code in Listing 8-17.

Listing 8-17   The elevator doors controller application

```
import javax.realtime.*;
public class MyApp {
    final static int TEN_SECONDS = 10000;
    Clock rtClock = Clock.getRealtimeClock();

    class FloorSensor extends AsyncEventHandler {
        public void handleAsyncEvent() {
            System.out.println("FloorSensor event");
            stopElevator();
            openDoors();
        }
    }
}
```

```
class DoorTimer extends AsyncEventHandler {
    public void handleAsyncEvent() {
        // Time has expired - close doors
        System.out.println("DoorTimer expired");
        closeDoors();
    }
}

public void stopElevator() {
    System.out.println("\tStopping elevator");
    // ...
}

public void openDoors() {
    System.out.println(
            "\tOpening doors at time=" +
            rtClock.getTime().getDate());
    // ...

    // start time to close doors
    OneShotTimer doorTimer =
        new OneShotTimer(
          new RelativeTime( TEN_SECONDS, 0 ),
          new DoorTimer() );
    doorTimer.enable();
    doorTimer.start();
}

public void closeDoors() {
    System.out.println(
            "\tClosing doors at time=" +
            rtClock.getTime().getDate());
    // ...
}

public MyApp() {
    FloorSensor handler = new FloorSensor();
    AsyncEvent floorEvent = new AsyncEvent();
    floorEvent.setHandler(handler);
    System.out.println("Elevator moving...");

    // wait some time to simulate elevator motion
    // and then fire floor event
    try { RealtimeThread.sleep(1000,0); }
        catch (Exception e) { }
    floorEvent.fire();
    try { RealtimeThread.sleep(30000,0); }
        catch (Exception e) { }
}
```

continued

```
    public static void main(String[] args) {
        MyApp app = new MyApp();
    }
}
```

In this application, the `FloorSensor` class is an event handler that waits to hear that a requested floor has been reached. When it has, it stops the elevator, and opens the door. This triggers the door-close timer, which is a `OneShotTimer` whose handler is the `DoorTimer` class. When it fires, the `closeDoors` method is called after waiting ten seconds, and presumably the elevator would begin moving again. Running this simulation, we get the following output:

```
Elevator moving...
FloorSensor event
    Stopping elevator
    Opening doors at time=Mon Jan 12 22:01:05 EST 2009
DoorTimer expired
    Closing doors at time=Mon Jan 12 22:01:15 EST 2009
```

By following the output, we see that when the floor sensor event fires, the elevator is stopped and its doors are opened at 22:01:05. Precisely ten seconds later—at 22:01:15—the door timer fires, and the doors are closed. Being a one-shot timer, the door timer will not fire again unless we explicitly call its `enable` and `start` methods again. If you need a timer that repeatedly fires events periodically without intervention, you need to use the `PeriodicTimer` class. Let's take a look at this now.

Periodic Timers

The concept of a periodic timer should be obvious at this point. Java RTS supports the concept of a periodic timer via the `PeriodicTimer` class (see Figure 8-7). When enabled and active, this timer calls your event handler back on the precise time interval you define.

To create a periodic timer, define a class that extends `AsyncEventHandler`, and set it as a handler of a `PeriodicTmer` object. You can set the timer interval and handler (for when it fires) by calling `setInterval` and `setHandler` respectively, or through one of the `PeriodicTimer` class constructors:

PeriodicTimer(start, interval, handler)—this constructor takes a start time (either relative to the current time, or an absolute time in the future), the periodic interval of the timer, and a handler to receive notification each time the event fires. The timer defaults to use the real-time clock.

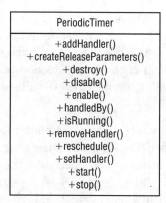

Figure 8-7 The Java RTS `PeriodicTimer` class methods.

`PeriodicTimer(start, interval, Clock, handler)`—this constructor takes a start time (either relative to the current time, or an absolute time in the future), the periodic interval of the timer, a clock to use for the timer, and a handler to receive notification each time the event fires.

Note: Minimum Periodic Timer Interval   Java RTS defines a minimum value for periodic timer firings to protect the system from being overwhelmed by timer-related event handling. By default, this value is 500 nanoseconds, and any attempt to create a periodic timer with a value smaller (other than zero) will result in an `IllegalArgumentException`. The default value can be changed via the Java property, `TimerMinInterval`, where you specify a new value in nanoseconds.

For example, to do this, add `-DTimerMinInterval=800` to the command-line when the Java RTS VM is started. Regardless of the minimum, zero is still a legal value as it causes it to behave like a one-shot timer.

You can add additional timer handlers by calling the `addHandler` method with each handler object. When the timer expires and fires, all of the handlers will be notified. Note that if a start time of 0 or null is given, the timer will fire immediately after it's started, and then after each time interval thereafter. If a valid start time is specified, the timer's first expiration will not occur until that time. It will then fire periodically according to the interval specified thereafter. Let's take a look at an example to illustrate.

Recall the conflated stock update application from Chapter 7 (described in Figure 7-4, and implemented in Listing 7-5). You can refer to Chapter 7 for the complete description, although we'll summarize the concept here. The idea is to insulate clients from every stock update received from a high-frequency market data feed. The individual updates for the stocks we're interested in are conflated over time (applied to a stored price) and sent out to clients at less-frequent time intervals. In our example, the conflation period was 10 milliseconds. Each individual update received from the data feed within each 10-millisecond period was applied to the stock price, but not sent to the client until the 10-millisecond period expired.

Because a periodic timer was not used, the code was relatively complicated, as it had to compute the delta time to the end of the period with each update received. Further, if an update were not received during a full period, then the very next update would need to be sent to clients immediately. In Listing 8-18, we implement this application with a `PeriodicTimer` and an `AsyncEventHandler` to simplify the logic.

Listing 8-18   The simplified conflated stock update application

```
import javax.realtime.*;
public class MyApp {
    double update = 0.00;
    Object lock = new Object();

    class Conflater implements Runnable {
        double price = 0.00;
        Boolean updated = false;
        Boolean sendNextUpdate = false;

        class Listener extends RealtimeThread {
            Conflater conflater;
            public Listener(Conflater conflater) {
                this.conflater = conflater;
            }
            public void run() {
                try {
                    while ( true ) {
                        synchronized ( lock ) {
                            lock.wait();
                        }

                        synchronized ( updated ) {
                            System.out.println(
                                "Listener: update " + update);
                            price += update;
                            updated = true;
                            if ( sendNextUpdate )
                                conflater.run();
                        }
```

```
                }
              }
            catch ( Exception e ) { }
        }
    }

    public Conflater() {
        System.out.println("Conflater started...");
        Listener listener = new Listener(this);
        listener.start();
    }

    public void run() {
        synchronized ( updated ) {
            if ( updated ) {
                updateClients(price);
                updated = false;
                sendNextUpdate = false;
            }
            else {
                sendNextUpdate = true;
            }
        }
    }

    private void updateClients(double newPrice) {
        System.out.println("Conflater: Updating clients:");
        System.out.println("Conflater:    price="+newPrice);

        // Send update
        // ...
    }
}

class DataFeed extends RealtimeThread {
    // ...
}

public MyApp() {
    // Create the conflater handler
    Conflater conflater = new Conflater();
    AsyncEventHandler handler =
        new AsyncEventHandler(conflater);

    // Create the conflation timer
    RelativeTime period =
        new RelativeTime(10,0); // 10ms
```

continued

```
        PeriodicTimer conflateTimer =
                new PeriodicTimer(period, period, handler);
        conflateTimer.enable();

        // Create the data feed
        DataFeed datafeed = new DataFeed();

        conflateTimer.start();
        datafeed.start();
    }

    public static void main(String[] args) {
        MyApp app = new MyApp();
    }
}
```

The DataFeed class is identical to the version in Chapter 7, so it's not shown here. In the MyApp constructor, the Conflater class is given as the Runnable parameter in the AsyncEventHandler constructor. That handler, along with the ten-millisecond periodic interval and start time, is provided in the PeriodicTimer constructor. This means that the Conflater class's run method will be released every ten milliseconds, starting ten milliseconds from the time the timer is started.

As a result, the logic is much simpler. A separate inner class, Listener, is used to receive updates from the Datafeed class. It does this by waiting on a shared lock. When the Datafeed class has a new price update, it signals the lock, at which point the Listener applies the update and sets a flag. When the Conflater timer is fired, the flag is checked. If it's determined that at least one update occurred during that conflation period, the update is broadcast to client applications and the flag is cleared. If no updates occurred, there's nothing else to do.

The resulting application behavior, and hence the output, is the same as in Chapter 7 (minus the timestamp information) with much simpler logic. Here is the output from this modified application:

```
Conflater started...
Listener: update 10.0
Listener: update -0.02
Listener: update -0.01
Listener: update 0.01
Listener: update -0.5
Conflater:  Updating clients:
Conflater:      price=9.48
Listener: update=-0.11
Conflater:  Updating clients:
Conflater:      price=9.37
```

In this chapter, we've examined how asynchronous events can be used in applications, which are fired either by expired timers, or manually through application-defined event objects. In the next chapter, we'll examine how thread execution can be controlled asynchronously through what's called *asynchronous transfer of control*, which is implemented as an extension of the Java `Exception` facility.

Asynchronous Transfer of Control and Thread Termination

"There is a time for departure even when there is no certain place to go."
—Tennessee Williams

IN many types of real-time systems, and in the real-world environments they work in, situations may change quickly and drastically. Java RTS provides support to Java developers to quickly and efficiently transfer processing control from one execution context to another. This is done through an extension to Java's `Exception` facility, and requires that your real-time threads be written with such transfers of control in mind. This chapter discusses the situations where transfer of control may be needed, and what you need to do to your code to enable it and prepare for it. Additionally, we'll look at how `Schedulable` objects can be terminated quickly, yet safely, when certain conditions arise in your application.

Asynchronous Transfer of Control

In the real-time programming space, having the ability to quickly and efficiently transfer control of execution from one section of code to another within a running thread is often desired. For instance, when executing code in a system that can change state suddenly, or that has some variability in the time it takes to execute, this transfer may be needed as a deadline looms. Java RTS implements *asynchronous transfer of control* (ATC) to satisfy this.

Being essentially an extension to the rules for java.lang.Thread.interrupt(), and operating through Java Exception processing, the ATC operating paradigm should seem familiar to you. In fact, it's via a thrown AsynchronouslyInterruptedException (AIE) exception, and the implementation of the Interruptible interface, that the transfer of control is performed. The transfer can be triggered by an asynchronous event (such as a timer expiration), a call to Thread.interrupt(), or a call to AsynchronouslyInterruptedException.fire(). A special form of the exception is used for timer expiration-based transfer of control to a Schedulable, called Timed. Figure 9-1 shows these classes, their relationships, and methods.

Note that with this facility, the execution of code within one Schedulable object can be altered from one method to another via the actions of another Schedulable

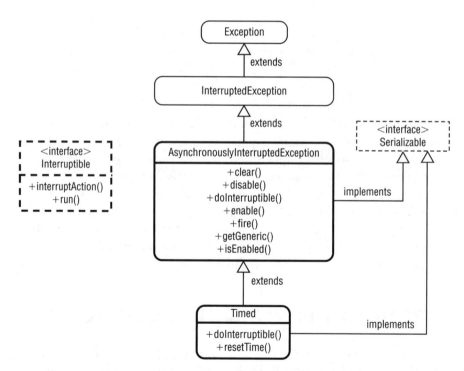

Figure 9-1   The main classes in the Java RTS ATC implementation.

object. To avoid thread-related issues such as deadlock, there are rules that govern how ATC operates, such as:

- ATC will be deferred while the source or target code is executing a synchronized method or block of code, or in the middle of a static initializer.
- There is no resumptive guarantee; execution will not resume from the point where the transfer was initiated. For cases where this is desired, or required, it's necessary to use another mechanism, like an asynchronous event handler, instead of ATC.
- Although the ATC mechanism works similar to exception processing, there must be an intended receiver. This is as opposed to a general-purpose, "catch-all" Exception block often used in exception-processing code. The target must have an explicit catch clause for the AIE exception.
- The AIE exception must be explicitly acknowledged by the target that catches it, either by handling it through a call to AsynchronouslyInterruptedException.doInterruptible(), or by explicitly clearing it via a call to AsynchronouslyInterruptedException.clear().

Additionally, ATCs can be nested, and the target classes must be able to handle the nesting properly. For instance, while processing an AIE, another one can occur. The code must be prepared for this, as well as the fact that the target RealtimeThread threads may be aborted. Later in this chapter we'll explore some sample implementations that simulate both of these scenarios.

Implementing Interruptible Code

Code that can be safely interrupted must exist within a method that declares AsynchronouslyInterruptedException within its throws clause. The class should also implement the Interruptible interface, so that it can be passed as a parameter to the doInterruptible method. The complete process is as follows:

- Create an AsynchronouslyInterruptedException object.
- Call the AIE object's doInterruptible method with a reference to the class that extends Interruptible.
- The Interruptible class's run method will be called.
- The run method, and any other method it calls, may be further marked as interruptible by declaring AsynchronouslyInterruptedException in its throws clause. If they are not, the interruption will be deferred.

The best way to illustrate this further is with a sample application. Let's examine a simulated landing sequence for an aircraft autopilot control system. In this simulation, while automatically landing the aircraft, the application must control many factors in the aircraft's flight. Specifically, it must maintain the heading, the angle of attack, the rate of descent, aircraft speed, and level flight.

However, as soon as the landing gear touches down (detected by a sensor), the characteristics must abruptly change. For instance, the nose gear must be touched down (performed by changing the angle of attack); the speed must be reduced dramatically; and the aircraft must be stopped through a combination of reverse thrusters, wheel brakes, and spoilers. The transition from the landing sequence while in the air to the touch-down sequence can be handled well by the asynchronous transfer of control facility in Java RTS.

In the application, each critical control factor is implemented in its own periodic RealtimeThread where the current conditions are measured, and reacted to. For instance, every ten milliseconds, level flight is checked, whereas the aircraft speed is checked every second. Let's begin with the code in Listing 9-1.

Listing 9-1   The automated landing sequence using ATC

```
import javax.realtime.*;
import java.util.*;
public class Main extends RealtimeThread {
    private int Mode;
    static public final int LANDING_MODE = 1;
    static public final int TOUCHDOWN_MODE = 2;

    static public final int NORM_PRI =
        PriorityScheduler.instance().getMinPriority();

    class LevelFlight extends InterruptibleLandingTask {
        public LevelFlight(
          AsynchronouslyInterruptedException aie) {
          //...
        }

        public void run(AsynchronouslyInterruptedException aie)
          throws AsynchronouslyInterruptedException {
          checkAndLevelWings(); // not interruptible
        }

        private void checkAndLevelWings() {
            //...
        }

        public void interruptAction(
          AsynchronouslyInterruptedException aie) {
```

```
            super.interruptAction(aie);
        }
}

class Airspeed extends InterruptibleLandingTask {
    //...
}

class Altitude extends InterruptibleLandingTask {
    //...
}

class AngleOfAttack extends InterruptibleLandingTask {
    //...
}

class LandingGearSensor extends AsyncEventHandler {
    //...
}

public Main() {
    PriorityParameters priority =
      new PriorityParameters(
            PriorityScheduler.instance().getMaxPriority());
    setSchedulingParameters(priority);
    this.start();
}

public int getMode() { return Mode; }

public void run() {
    try {
        // Start the system flying, but in landing mode
        System.out.println("Beginning landing sequence");
        InterruptibleLandingTask.setMode(LANDING_MODE);

        AsynchronouslyInterruptedException aie =
            new AsynchronouslyInterruptedException();
        Airspeed speed = new Airspeed(aie);
        Altitude alt = new Altitude(aie);
        LevelFlight level = new LevelFlight(aie);
        AngleOfAttack attack = new AngleOfAttack(aie);

        // Create the landing gear event
        LandingGearSensor sensor =
                new LandingGearSensor(aie);
```

continued

```
        AsyncEvent landingGear = new AsyncEvent();
        landingGear.setHandler(sensor);

        // Wait some time and transition to touchdown mode
        RealtimeThread.sleep(5000, 0);
        landingGear.fire();
    }
    catch ( Exception e ) {
        e.printStackTrace();
    }
}

public static void main(String[] args) {
    Main app = new Main();
}
}
```

There are four classes that extend the class InterruptibleLandingTask (see Listing 9-2):

LevelFlight—this class ensures that the wings are level on final approach. Given the criticality of the task, it runs in a periodic RTT with a ten-millisecond period.

Airspeed—this class ensures that airspeed is maintained. It will throttle up and down to maintain a safe landing speed. This task runs in a periodic RTT with a one-second period.

Altitude—this class tracks altitude and measures the rate of descent. In a real implementation, it would modify airspeed and the aircraft's angle of attack to ensure the proper glide slope is maintained. This task runs in a periodic RTT with a one-second period.

AngleOfAtack—this class monitors and maintains the proper angle of attack during landing. For instance, the nose should slightly up, allowing the rear landing gear to touch down first, then the nose gear. Given the need to monitor this flight characteristic (to avoid aerodynamic stall, for instance) this task runs in a periodic RTT with a one-millisecond period.

Each class is interruptible, except LevelFlight; it's important to maintain level wings even as the aircraft touches down, since it's possible that the landing gear on one side of the aircraft can touch down before the other. To accomplish this, the checkAndLevelWings method, called from within run, does not declare AsynchronouslyInterruptedException in its throws clause. Any method that does declare this exception is interruptible. As a result, if AsynchronouslyInterrupted

Exception is fired while executing checkAndLevelWings, the interruption will be deferred until the method exits. We check to see if the interruption was deferred with a call to the method clear. This method will return true, and clear the pending status, if it was indeed interrupted; otherwise it returns false.

Listing 9-2   The InterruptibleLandingTask class

```
import javax.realtime.*;
public class InterruptibleLandingTask
        extends RealtimeThread
        implements Interruptible
{
    static int Mode = -1;
    static public final int LANDING_MODE = 1;
    static public final int TOUCHDOWN_MODE = 2;

    String taskName;
    AsynchronouslyInterruptedException aie;
    boolean interrupted = false;

    public InterruptibleLandingTask(
            String taskName,
            AsynchronouslyInterruptedException aie,
            RelativeTime period,
            int priority) {
        this.aie = aie;
        this.taskName = taskName;
        PeriodicParameters rel =
            new PeriodicParameters(period);
        PriorityParameters pri =
            new PriorityParameters(priority);
        setReleaseParameters(rel);
        setSchedulingParameters(pri);
    }

    public void run() {
        System.out.println("\t"+taskName+" monitor started");
        while ( Mode == LANDING_MODE ) {
            if ( ! aie.doInterruptible(this) )
                RealtimeThread.yield();
            else if ( ! isInterrupted() )
                waitForNextPeriod();

            // For tasks that execute code with deferred
            // interruption, check it here
```

continued

```
            if ( aie.clear() )
                interrupted = true;
        }
        System.out.println("\t"+taskName+" task terminating");
    }

    // Shoud be called via super
    public void interruptAction(
      AsynchronouslyInterruptedException aie) {
        interrupted = true;
        System.out.println(
          "\t"+taskName+" task interrupted *****");
    }

    public boolean isInterrupted() {
        return interrupted;
    }

    // Must be overriden
    public void run(AsynchronouslyInterruptedException aie)
      throws AsynchronouslyInterruptedException {
    }

    public static void setMode(int mode) {
        Mode = mode;
    }
}
```

The InterruptibleLandingTask base class implements the common function-ality for each landing task, as its name implies. The constructor takes an Asyn-chronouslyInterruptedException object, a period, and priority. Since the class extends RealtimeThread, and implements Interruptible, there are two run methods:

RealtimeThread.run—this method gets called when the thread is started. It's here that the task's main loop is implemented, checking the status of the land-ing and calling waitForNextPeriod with each pass. When the landing mode changes to indicate the plane has touched down on the runway, the default action is to exit the loop and terminate the task.

Interruptible.run—this method is invoked when doInterruptible is called on the AsynchronouslyInterruptedException object that was provided in the constructor. Each individual subclass must override and implement this method to perform its own unique landing task business logic.

By default, the base class `interruptAction` method sets a flag when invoked that indicates the task was interrupted. Individual landing tasks must override it but still call the base class—via `super`—to get the specific behavior it requires. For instance, the `Airspeed` and `AngleOfAttack` classes invoke the engine's reverse thrusters and point the nose down respectively when interrupted by the landing mode change.

The `LevelFlight` class, however, does not allow its periodic processing to be interrupted. This is accomplished by calling the method `checkAndLevelWings`, which does not declare `AsynchronouslyInterruptedException` in its throws clause, from `Interupptible.run`. Throwing this exception is how you indicate that the current method can be interrupted when the associated `Asynchronously-InterruptedException` object is fired.

To see an example of a class whose implementation can be interrupted, let's examine `Altitude` (see Listing 9-3). Once the landing gear touches down on the runway, there's no reason to maintain a rate of descent, therefore this task is no longer required. Whatever processing is occurring when the landing mode changes can be safely interrupted, and the RTT can terminate as a result.

Listing 9-3   The `Interruptible` class, `Altitude`

```
class Altitude extends InterruptibleLandingTask {
    public Altitude(AsynchronouslyInterruptedException aie) {
        super( "Altitude",
                aie,
                new RelativeTime(1000,0),
                PriorityScheduler.instance().getMinPriority() );
        start();
    }
    // Interruptible.run
    public void run(AsynchronouslyInterruptedException aie)
      throws AsynchronouslyInterruptedException {
        System.out.println("\tChecking altitude");

        // Simulate a busy task to force an interruption
        RelativeTime slow = new RelativeTime(250,0);
        try { RealtimeThread.sleep(slow); }
            catch ( Exception e ) { }
    }
}
```

Thanks to the base class, the `Altitude` class implementation is straightforward. Like the other landing task implementations in this example, a task name, an `AsynchronouslyInterruptedException` object, a period, and task priority are provided to the base class constructor. Next, the RTT is started, which invokes the `RealtimeThread.run` loop. When `doInterruptible` is called each period, the `Interruptible.run` method (shown in Listing 9-3) is invoked. In this sample, the task sleeps for about 250 milliseconds (a quarter of its period) to simulate it being busy. The result is that when the landing mode changes, this task will more than likely be busy, and will be interrupted. You'll see this in the application output, which we'll explore shortly.

When the application begins, the landing mode is set, an `AsynchronouslyInterruptedException` object is created, and each landing task's class is created and given a reference to this object. Since each class is given the same object, calling its fire method will interrupt whichever one is executing at that time. It also implies that no more than one of them can execute at the same time, as `doInterruptible` will return a `false` value immediately if it's currently executing another `Interruptible` class. In fact, the base class handles this by checking the return value and repeatedly calling it again until it succeeds. Realistically, this isn't the ideal implementation, which would otherwise require an `AsynchronouslyInterruptedException` object for each task. Alternatively, since each task runs in its own `RealtimeThread`, a call to `interrupt` for each thread would achieve the same result. However, for the sake of illustration, this sample implementation has been kept simple.

The application is allowed to run for five seconds before the touchdown sequence is initiated through an asynchronous event handler. To trigger this, the landing gear event object's fire method is called. This causes the event handler (implemented by the `LandingGearSensor` class in Listing 9-4) to be invoked.

Listing 9-4   The `LandingGear` class

```
class LandingGearSensor extends AsyncEventHandler {
   AsynchronouslyInterruptedException aie;
     public LandingGearSensor(
             AsynchronouslyInterruptedException aie) {
        this.aie = aie;
     }

   public void handleAsyncEvent() {
      System.out.println("Landing gear sensor: " +
                         "beginning touchdown sequence...");
      InterruptibleLandingTask.setMode(TOUCHDOWN_MODE);
      aie.fire();
   }
}
```

Once the event is fired, the `LandingGearSensor` handler class method, `handleAsyncEvent`, is invoked. Here, the landing mode is set to indicate that the plane has touched down, and the shared `AsynchronouslyInterrupted-Exception` object is fired. Any landing task that's executing at the time will be interrupted, and all landing tasks will terminate at their next period. The output of this application (shown in Listing 9-5) prints the operation of each landing task during the simulated landing sequence. Note that much of the output has been omitted to save space.

Listing 9-5 The sample landing application output

```
Beginning landing sequence...
   Airspeed monitor started
   Checking airspeed
   Altitude monitor started
   LevelFlight monitor started
   AngleOfAttack monitor started
   Adjusting angle of attack --Horizontal stabilizer up
   Checking altitude
   Adjusting angle of attack --Horizontal stabilizer down
   Adjusting angle of attack --Horizontal stabilizer down
   Adjusting angle of attack --Horizontal stabilizer down
   Adjusting angle of attack --Horizontal stabilizer down
   Wings not level--Right aileron up
   Adjusting angle of attack --Horizontal stabilizer up
   Wings not level--Left aileron up
   .
   .
   .
   Wings not level--Right aileron up
   Adjusting angle of attack --Horizontal stabilizer up
   Checking airspeed
Landing gear sensor: beginning touchdown sequence...
   Altitude task terminating
   LevelFlight task terminating
   AngleOfAttack task terminating
   AngleOfAttack: nose down full
   Airspeed task interrupted *****
   Airspeed: reverse thrust
   Airspeed task terminating
```

When the landing sequence mode changes (shown as the line of output in bold), you'll notice tasks terminating. However, due to the simulated heavy workload of the `Airspeed` class, it gets interrupted while executing (shown as the second line of output in bold). Also note that both `AngleOfAttack` and `Airspeed` perform secondary actions when interrupted or terminated, as part of the touchdown sequence processing.

Overall, this application should serve as an example of how ATC can be used to abruptly alter the state of execution of specific Schedulable classes in a Java RTS application. You are given fine control over which parts of the code can be interrupted, and which cannot, to ensure the safety of your application's implementation.

Implementing Timed Operations

Whether you're building a real-time application or not, there is often a need to implement code that needs to operate for a specified amount of time, or be limited to a maximum amount of execution time. Java RTS supports this paradigm through the asynchronous transfer of control subclass, Timed, shown in Figure 9-2. With this class, code that executes within a Schedulable object can be interrupted when a preset timer expires.

To use the Timed class, create a class that extends the Interruptible interface, and invoke it with code similar to Listing 9-6. The implementation pattern is similar to the ATC pattern we've examined, except that the code is interrupted when a timer expires (as opposed to when some application-specific event occurs).

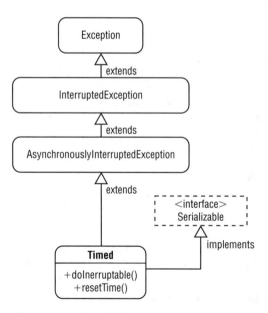

Figure 9-2   The RTSJ Timed class.

Listing 9-6   Invoking an `Interruptible` object with a `Timed` object

```
RelativeTime interval = new RelativeTime(...);
Interruptible interruptible = new MyInterruptible();
Timed t = new Timed(interval);
t.doInterruptible(interruptible);
```

This simple facility can drive time-critical operations, such as a spacecraft's calculated engine burn, or the pulsing of an automobile's anti-lock brake system. Java RTS ensures that when the timer expires, the resulting `Asynchronously-InterruptedException` is generated within a bounded amount of time. It also ensures that no additional memory is consumed by the `Timed` object after its first invocation, making it safe to use repeatedly with `Schedulable` objects that run within `ScopedMemory` regions.

In Listing 9-7, we've implemented a simple application that attempts to execute a critical operation within a specified timeframe. This is done, of course, with a `Timed` object and a class that implements `Interruptible`. Note that there is a slim chance that both SUCCESS and FAILED can be output if the timer fires after SUCCESS is output, but before the method returns. However, for the sake of this simple example, we'll ignore this.

Listing 9-7   The `CriticalOperation` class

```
import javax.realtime.*;
public class MyApp extends RealtimeThread {

    class CriticalOperation implements Interruptible {
        public void run(AsynchronouslyInterruptedException aie)
            throws AsynchronouslyInterruptedException {
            // Execute a processor-intensive operation
            System.out.print("Trying critical operation...");

            // ...

            System.out.println(" SUCCESS");
    }

        public void interruptAction(
            AsynchronouslyInterruptedException aie) {
            System.out.println(" FAILED");
    }
    }
```

continued

```
public void run() {
    RelativeTime interval =
            new RelativeTime(5000,0); // 5-second interval

    Timed timed = new Timed(interval);

    CriticalOperation interuptible =
            new CriticalOperation();

    timed.doInterruptible(interuptible);
}

public static void main(String[] args) {
    System.out.println("Starting up");
    MyApp app = new MyApp();
    app.start();
}
}
```

Note that the Timed operation must occur from within the context of a Realtime-Thread or an AsynchronousEventHandler. In this example, the main class MyApp extends RealtimeThread, and the processing occurs within its run method. When the thread starts, a Timed object is created with a five-second interval. Next, this object is used to execute the CriticalOperation object via a call to doInterruptible. If the operation completes within the five-second interval, it's considered successful. Otherwise, if the operation is interrupted due to timer expiration, its interruptAction method will be invoked and the operation is considered to have failed.

Although this usage pattern is simple, you may prefer to encapsulate the use of the Timed object to hide it from the caller. In Listing 9-8, we've implemented an application that attempts to execute a critical operation. If the task doesn't finish successfully within a given time frame, it's retried the specified number of times. In this example, the CriticalOperation class uses the Timed class to execute an operation, but times out after a specified amount of time passes. The class will retry this operation for the specified number of times. The caller simply creates and starts the operation without bothering with the retry logic.

Listing 9-8   The modified CriticalOperation class

```
import javax.realtime.*;
public class MyApp {
    class CriticalOperation
        extends RealtimeThread
        implements Interruptible {
      RelativeTime interval;
```

```java
      int retries;
      Timed timed;
      boolean expired;

      public CriticalOperation(RelativeTime interval,
                               int retries) {
          this.interval = interval;
          this.retries = retries;
          this.timed = new Timed(interval);
      }

   public void run() {
       expired = false;

       // Attempt the operation - retry if needed
       for ( int repeat = 0; repeat < retries; repeat++ ){
           System.out.print("Trying critical operation");
           timed.doInterruptible(this);
           if ( ! expired ) {
               System.out.println("  SUCCEEDED");
               return;
           }
           timed.resetTime(interval);
       }
   }

   public void run(AsynchronouslyInterruptedException aie)
       throws AsynchronouslyInterruptedException {
       // ...
   }

   public void interruptAction(
          AsynchronouslyInterruptedException aie) {
       System.out.println("  FAILED");
       expired = true;
   }
}

public MyApp() {
    RelativeTime interval =
            new RelativeTime(5000,0); // 5-second wait
    int retries = 3;

    CriticalOperation interuptible =
            new CriticalOperation(interval, retries);

    interuptible.start();
}
```

continued

```
    public static void main(String[] args) {
        MyApp app = new MyApp();
    }
}
```

The `CriticalOperation` class both extends `RealtimeThread`, and implements `Interruptible`; therefore, there are two `run` methods. However, you can easily tell the two apart, as `Interruptible.run` declares an `AsyncronouslyInterruptedException` object as a parameter and within its `throws` clause. When the thread starts, the following steps are taken:

1. The `expired` flag is cleared.
2. `doInterruptible` is called within a loop. If the operation is interrupted due to timer expiration, the `expired` flag is set to indicate this.
3. When `doInterruptible` returns, the expired flag is checked. The following possible actions can take place:
   a. If the operation completed without expiring, this indicates success, and the thread terminates; we are done.
   b. If the operation expired before completing, the `Timed` object's timer is reset, and the loop continues.
4. If the code has retried the operation the number of times specified, the thread terminates, otherwise it loops back to step 2.

With the parameters shown in Listing 9-8, the simulated critical operation is attempted up to three times, with an expiration of five seconds on each attempt. If the operation were to fail on each attempt, the output will be as shown here:

```
Trying critical operation...  FAILED
Trying critical operation...  FAILED
Trying critical operation...  FAILED
```

Of course, if the operation were to succeed, the word "SUCCEEDED" would replace "FAILED," and the loop would terminate with no additional retries.

Asynchronous Thread Termination

In many real-time systems that model or respond to real-world events that rapidly change, there may be a desire to quickly and efficiently terminate a thread's execution in response. In many cases, this can make it easier to transition between the many states the real-world interface may need to be in at any point in time. Often, the use of a meta-thread, or a thread manager, that understands the sub-system state transitions, is the most efficient way to program such a system, where a thread manager tightly controls the lifetime of processing child threads.

Earlier versions of the Java language supplied mechanisms to achieve this, in particular the methods `stop` and `destroy` in class `Thread`. However, since `stop` could leave shared objects in an inconsistent state, it has been deprecated. Likewise, the use of `destroy` can lead to deadlock if a `Thread` is destroyed while it's holding a lock. A goal of the RTSJ was to meet the requirements of asynchronous thread termination without the dangers associated with the deprecated `stop` or `destroy` methods.

This goal has been met through what is known as *asynchronous thread termination* (ATT), and is built upon the asynchronous transfer of control facility. All targeted and effected `RealtimeThreads` transition to their AIE exception processing code and, as a result, abort their normal processing and exit their run methods. Implementing it this way allows shared locks to be released, while allowing the code to exit safely and predictably.

As an example, consider the code in Listing 9-9. This application creates two `Schedulable` objects represented by the classes `Worker1` and `Worker2`. Both classes extend `RealtimeThread`, but also implement `Interruptible`. Both threads contain the same implementation; therefore, only `Worker1`'s code is shown here.

Listing 9-9   Safely terminating `Schedulable` objects

```
import javax.realtime.*;
public class Main {
    class Worker1 extends RealtimeThread
                    implements Interruptible {
        AsynchronouslyInterruptedException aie;

        public Worker1() {
            this.aie= new AsynchronouslyInterruptedException();
            RelativeTime period =
                    new RelativeTime(1000,0);
            ReleaseParameters rel =
                    new PeriodicParameters(period);
            this.setReleaseParameters(rel);
        }

        public void run(AsynchronouslyInterruptedException aie)
          throws AsynchronouslyInterruptedException {
            while ( true ) {
                System.out.println("Worker1 doing work...");
                waitForNextPeriod();
            }
        }
    }
```

continued

```
    public void interruptAction(
            AsynchronouslyInterruptedException aie) {
        System.out.println("Worker1 interrupted");
    }

    public void run() {
        aie.doInterruptible(this);
    }
}

class Worker2 extends RealtimeThread implements Interruptible {
    // ...
}

public Main() {
    Worker1 w1 = new Worker1();
    Worker2 w2 = new Worker2();

    w1.start();
    w2.start();

    try {
        RelativeTime interval = new RelativeTime(3000,0);
        RealtimeThread.sleep(interval);
    }
    catch ( Exception e ) { }

    w1.interrupt();
    w2.interrupt();

    System.out.println("Application terminating");
}

public static void main(String[] args) {
    Main app = new Main();
}
}
```

When the application starts, both worker threads are created and started. Some-time later (three seconds in this case), both worker threads are interrupted by calls to RealtimeThread.interrupt. This action causes both Schedulable objects to safely terminate execution, and the application terminates immediately after. For simplicity, this example simply sleeps three seconds after starting the worker threads. In reality, this action may be triggered by an asynchronous event that is acted upon by a handler in your application, or an expired, timed, operation. The output from this sample application is:

```
Worker1 doing work...
Worker2 doing work...
Worker1 doing work...
Worker2 doing work...
Worker1 doing work...
Worker2 doing work...
Application terminating
```

However it's triggered in your code—an asynchronous event, an error condition that's detected, or timer expiration—Java RTS makes Schedulable object termination safe, reliable, and efficient.

10

Inside the Real-Time Garbage Collector

"Much may be done in those little shreds and patches
of time which every day produces..."
—Charles Caleb Colton

THE real-time garbage collector (RTGC) that comes as part of Sun's Java Real-Time System is a non-blocking, non-generational, fully concurrent mark and sweep collector with no stop-world pauses. It's also an extremely low-latency collector that operates in bounded time for all operations, and operates within a set range of priorities to help achieve predictable behavior. Not only does it work concurrently with mutator (application) threads during all GC phases, it performs its work using parallel collector threads. This classifies it as a fully concurrent, non-blocking, non-moving parallel mark and sweep real-time collector. This is not an easy accomplishment, and in this chapter we'll outline the specific algorithms involved in its implementation.

Being based on Roger Henriksson's thesis on real-time dynamic memory management, the Java RTS RTGC runs at lower priority than `Schedulable` objects. Due to the priority-based scheduling in Java RTS, RTTs are always dispatched in preference to the RTGC threads. Further, because NHRTs cannot access the heap, they experience no interference from the RTGC at all.

It's also important to note that the RTGC, as we'll refer to it in the remainder of this chapter, is extremely flexible in its runtime characteristics. Its tuning options allow you to control many facets of its operation. Although it's based very much on the Henriksson real-time GC algorithm discussed in Chapter 2, through tuning you can alter its behavior to best suit your application's requirements. We'll refer to these alterations as "policies," and we'll describe some sample policies at the end of this chapter.

RTGC Theory of Operation

To achieve the most deterministic behavior, Java RTS attempts to keep the entire Java heap in physical memory. This eliminates any potential jitter from page faults in the heap. This means that the RTGC doesn't need to consider the affects of virtual memory as it operates. Here is a list of characteristics of the Java RTS RTGC:

- It's a mark and sweep collector.
- It's fully concurrent with mutator threads.
- It's a parallel collector, meaning it will perform its work in multiple threads, when applicable. Therefore, it automatically scales according to the number of processors available to it.
- It's non-generational; there is only one main heap region.
- It's a non-moving, non-compacting collector. This fits with the fact that there are no generations, or separate heap regions such as *toSpace* and *fromSpace* (see Chapter 2 for an explanation of these regions). Objects are not moved, and the heap is not compacted in the traditional sense. Although this can lead to fragmentation, strategies are implemented to address it. We'll examine this later in the chapter.
- Concurrent marking uses a snapshot-at-the-beginning (SATB) approach. This will be examined in detail in the next section of this chapter.
- It uses a tri-color marking scheme (white, grey, and black—see sidebar).
- It imposes a write barrier, only activated when the GC is running. In between GC cycles—when the GC threads are idle—this write barrier is removed.
- Because it's a non-moving collector, there is no read barrier.
- It uses fixed-sized memory blocks for object allocation, and will split large objects across memory blocks when required.
- GC threads run at a low real-time priority, above non-real-time java.lang. Threads (JLTs), but lower than application RealtimeThreads (RTTs) when running in normal mode. As discussed in Chapter 4, the RTGC may run with boosted priority if free heap space drops below a specified threshold, but this is meant to be an exceptional case.
- It implements ergonomics, and self-tunes according to mutator allocation rates and overall application behavior.
- It implements occasional handshaking with running mutator threads, which acts like GC safepoints, but *without* stop-world pauses.

Like most collectors, the RTGC operates in phases. There is a mark phase, a sweep phase that follows, and a third phase called *zeroing*. In summary, this phase prepares key global structures for the next GC cycle by emptying values within GC and per-mutator-thread data structures. Let's begin with a detailed look at the marking phase now.

Tri-Color Object Marking

The colors white, grey, and black have slightly different meanings in the different phases, and newly allocated objects are assigned a color dependent on the GC phase. The following outlines how these colors are used:

- *White*: this generally indicates an untraced object. During the sweep phase, all "white" objects are considered dead, and are collected. Newly allocated objects are marked as white in between GC cycles, and during the zeroing phase of a GC cycle.

- *Grey*: this indicates a live object whose child objects (those it refers to) have not yet been completely traced. New objects are allocated and marked "grey" during the mark phase of the GC cycle, but only when the write barrier is being activated. Since this is not an atomic operation (each mutator thread must acknowledge the activation through a handshake), it can take a little time. After the write barrier (described later) is activated, new objects are marked as "black" during the marking phase. Once sweeping is complete, a handshake is performed once again, and new objects are marked as white.

- *Black*: this indicates a live object whose child objects have all been scanned and marked. New objects are allocated and marked black during the sweep phase of the GC cycle.

This color scheme is used with the real-time garbage collector in Java RTS.

Concurrent Marking

The RTGC doesn't begin a garbage collection cycle until the amount of free memory goes below the initial threshold, called the startup memory threshold (discussed in Chapter 4). By default, this occurs when there is almost no free memory left. When it does begin, the marking phase runs concurrently with mutator threads with no stop-world pauses, and virtually no interference with mutator thread progress. With the RTGC, this applies to `RealtimeThread` objects, of course, but there is an attempt to limit the impact on the lower-priority `Thread` objects as well. Since `NoHeapRealtimeThreads` don't use the heap, and are hence subject to no GC-related jitter, we'll omit them from this discussion.

Marking involves the following steps and activities on each mutator thread's stack:

1. Mark all *white* (unmarked) objects as *grey*. This indicates that the object is reachable, but objects it references are not yet marked as reachable.

2. Mark *white* objects that were missed because the mutator thread changed an object reference while in the marking phase. We'll examine this more closely later.

3. Recursively walk object reference graphs and mark all reachable objects (also known as *blackening*). When a *grey* root object and all of its referenced objects are marked, they are considered *black*. When all objects are either *white* (a dead object) or *black* (a live object), the marking phase is complete.

4. Invoke a write barrier to place newly created objects on a special list. We'll examine this later, as well.

Parallel GC threads, called the RTGC *gang worker threads*, perform most of the marking. The mutator threads perform some of the marking themselves during steps 1, 2, and 3 above, if they happen to be running while a GC cycle is in progress. Step 3 is performed solely by RTGC worker threads without any synchronization with mutator threads. To be thorough, the following three conditions must be accounted for during the marking phase, for each mutator thread:

- When a GC cycle begins, some (if not all) of the mutator threads may be suspended. For each mutator thread that is suspended, one of the GC gang worker threads performs the marking of its live objects. In this case, the marking can be performed without any potential latency, and without the mutator thread ever knowing it happened. The only exception is if the mutator thread wakes up during the operation.

- When a GC cycle begins, one or more of the mutator threads may be running. If this is the case, the mutator thread itself performs the marking operation by scanning its own live objects. This is done through a handshake, where the RTGC main thread inserts calls to the marking code into the mutator's stack. The latency (due to the extra processing of marking) involved with the handshake is bounded, and very small.

- For a mutator thread that is released (become eligible for execution) while a GC thread is actively scanning its stack for live objects, there is a small amount of latency incurred while the GC worker thread finishes stack scanning that mutator thread's stack. The mutator will be blocked until this operation is complete.

By default, the number of gang worker threads started by the RTGC is equal to the number of processors/cores available on the server. However, this may be overridden by a command-line parameter setting, or constrained by the number of processors in a processor set assigned to execute the Java RTS VM process.

To accommodate changes for the RTGC in Java RTS, the base Java SE object data structure is extended by two 32-bit words; the first word is the marking chain pointer, used as part of a linked list of marked objects; the second word is used for object splitting on allocation (discussed later in this chapter)—see Figure 10-1. The marking word is the `next` pointer itself (part of the header), and by nature of it holding a non-`null` value, the object is considered marked.

Marking is performed on a single list of global objects (for global variables) as well as on a list per mutator thread used to store marked objects for the associated thread (see Figure 10-2). As the roots are traced for each thread via stack scanning, objects marked as live are placed on the applicable thread's *marked list*. Because these lists are maintained per thread, there is no need to synchronize access, as there would be if a single list were used. Additionally, atomic compare-and-swap (CAS) operations are performed where possible to avoid locking that

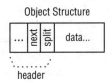

Figure 10-1   The two new header fields for a Java RTS `Object`.

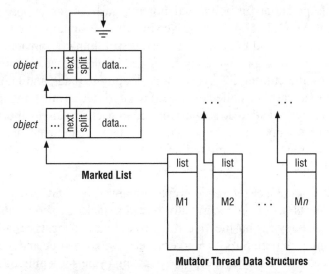

Figure 10-2   Per-mutator lists of marked objects are maintained.

would otherwise be required when testing and updating pointer values. We'll discuss CAS operations as appropriate in this discussion.

As mentioned above, a non-null value in the next header field indicates the object is marked. The next field for the last object in the list is set to a special *end-of-list* value (not null). Note that since this value is non-null, the object is appropriately considered marked.

Snapshot at the Beginning

The RTGC uses a snapshot at the beginning (SATB) technique, as opposed to continuous update marking, for its concurrent marking phase. With SATB, only objects that are unreachable at the beginning of the cycle are collected; objects that become free during a cycle will not. This is done to eliminate much of the rescanning performed when an object reference is updated during a cycle.

Note: RTGC Bounded Operations   Although it's based on the Henriksson real-time collection algorithm, the Java RTS RTGC goes one step further. It tries to limit its disruption of standard threads, as well as real-time threads. Therefore, theoretically, non-real-time threads will benefit from the design and operation of the RTGC. But for true real-time behavior guarantees, your code must execute within a RealtimeThread object.

With SATB, there is potential for additional floating garbage (as opposed to continuous update marking), but on the positive side, there is an upper bound to both the total marking time, and the latency involved with mutator thread stack scanning. Remember, floating garbage consists of dead objects that are missed (and not collected) by the current GC cycle. Both floating garbage and latency issues are important to a real-time collector, as you want to free as much memory as possible at each GC cycle, and to do so with limited impact on running mutator threads. With a continuous-update marking algorithm, stack scanning needs to be repeated to ensure references aren't missed, and live objects aren't mistakenly collected. To explain this, let's look at an example.

Figure 10-3 illustrates an object reference graph as viewed by a GC's marking thread. Here, root objects (i.e., from the mutator thread's stack) are shown above the dotted line. All of the objects that the roots refer to are live, and must be marked as such. Starting from each root, the GC marker thread walks the tree and marks each referenced object as live. At the end of the marking cycle, sweeping begins and all unmarked objects are considered garbage and reclaimed.

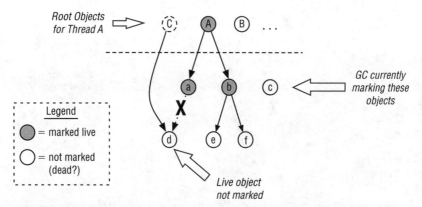

Figure 10-3 With concurrent marking, the mutator thread can change the live object set during marking.

In this example, roots *A* and *B* (and possibly more) existed when marking began, but not *C*. Remember, with the Java RTS RTGC, marking will occur concurrently with mutator threads, so changes to the object graph may occur while the GC marker thread is scanning it. Here, after the marker thread has scanned root *A* and some of its first level references (*a* and *b*), the following occurs:

1. Root *A*, and child objects *a* and *b*, are marked as live by the GC marker thread.

2. Concurrently, the mutator thread does the following:

   a. Creates a new root object, *C*

   b. Creates a reference from *C* to *d*

   c. Breaks a reference from *a* to *d*

The RTGC worker thread will continue graying, and will mark objects *e,* and *f* as live. However, because the reference from *a* to *d* has been broken, the marker thread doesn't find object *d*, and leaves it unmarked. If nothing else were to happen, the marker thread might finish without ever marking *d*, and the sweep phase would collect it as garbage, which is clearly incorrect.

One solution, called *continuous update marking*, is to activate a write barrier when marking begins that sets a flag when updates occur to a thread's root object set. At the end of the marking cycle, the marker thread would check this flag and restart the marking phase if it's set. The result is positive, in that it avoids the error of collecting a live object, but negative in that it requires an entire marking phase to occur again. What's worse, if mutator activity continues to change the root object set, marking may be repeated again, and again, without limit. This delays

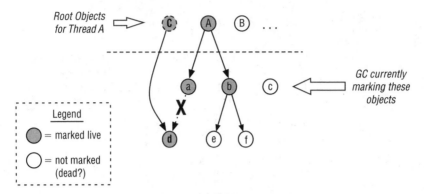

Figure 10-4   A write barrier marks new objects, and old object references to avoid rescanning.

the sweep phase, which makes free memory available to the running mutator threads. As a result, mutator threads—even critical real-time threads—may experience failure or delay due to a low-memory condition.

The goal is to ensure that the delay of the sweeping phase is bounded. However, since an equally important goal is to have no stop-world pauses, the mutator thread must not be blocked in any way. The SATB marking algorithm accomplishes this by activating a write barrier that automatically marks object references on updates, for both the new and old object references. In this case, for example, object *d* would be marked when the reference to it is broken, and root object *C* would be marked upon creation. The result, shown in Figure 10-4, is that objects *C* and *d* are marked as live even though the marker thread never scanned them. Note that this write-barrier is only needed (and hence only activated) when the RTGC is currently in the marking phase.

This approach has one drawback: there exists a potential to mark objects as live when they truly are garbage, thus creating floating garbage. For example, given the previous scenario, if the reference from object *a* to object *d* were broken, but root object *C* was never created with a reference to it, object *d* would have still been marked as live even though there are no references to it—see Figure 10-5.

Floating garbage objects end up getting collected in the next GC cycle. However, in low-memory conditions, this delay can negatively impact the application. This is a tradeoff that the Java RTS design team deemed necessary in a real-time application, as the unbounded delay of the sweep cycle could have the same, if not a more widespread, result.

Objects are added to the head of the marked list. Because of this, there is no walking of the list required, and object insertion is performed in a small, bounded,

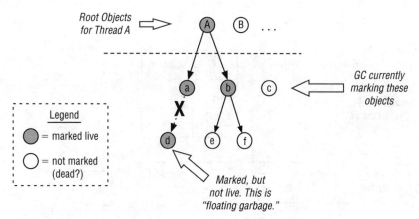

Figure 10-5   SATB-based marking can result in dead objects marked as live.

amount of time. Additionally, by using a CAS operation, this requires no locking of the list. The new marked object has its *next* pointer set to the head of the thread's marked list, and then the thread's marked list pointer is set to this new object (see Figure 10-6).

When marking is complete (all root objects have been scanned, and their references recursively scanned as well), all live objects are marked as black and the marking phase is terminated for this mutator thread. To do this, another handshake is invoked, where the mutator thread copies the head of its marked list to another mutator field, and sets the marked list pointer to a special end-of-list value.

Parallel Marking

GC work during the marking phase per mutator thread is naturally parallelized; it's either performed by the individual mutator threads themselves (if running), or available gang worker threads inside the RTGC for mutator threads that are suspended during this phase. Root graying, the recursive blackening of live object graphs, and additional marking due to mutator changes to the object graph, all occur in parallel and currently to mutator threads. For global data (which includes application global data, static and class data, and internal VM data), the gang workers need to divide the work to help the Java RTS VM scale on multiprocessor servers.

The RTGC uses a row-and-column, grid-based, structure to help parallelize the RTGC marking work on global data. This is structured as an *n*-by-*n* grid of rows and columns, where *n* is equal to the number of GC worker threads. By default,

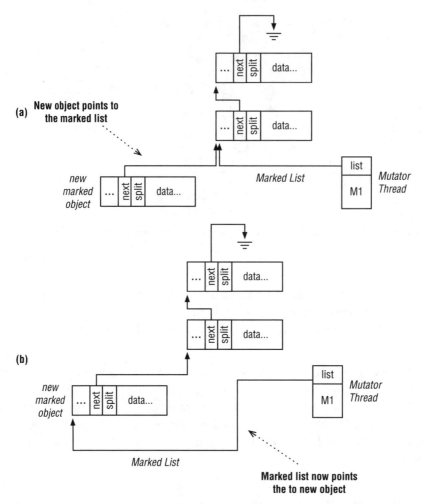

Figure 10-6   In (a), the new object's next field points to the marked list.
In (b), the thread's marked list points to the new object; the insert is complete.

this number is equal to the number of processors/cores available to the Java RTS
VM process, unless changed via command-line arguments. Each row is serviced
by only one RTGC thread, and is implemented as a circular linked-list—the last
entry (column) points back to the first. Each cell in each row points to a linked-list
of objects to be recursively marked, hence creating a three-dimensional data structure (see Figure 10-7).

In this grid, the columns are also connected as lists, but they're not circular in this
case. As with rows, each column is serviced by only one RTGC worker thread.

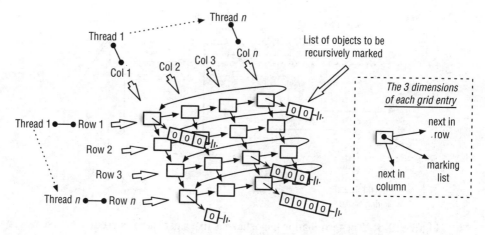

Figure 10-7   Each row is serviced by one thread, making work available to other threads (per column).

The list of objects in each cell contains a *head* pointer (points to first item in the list) and a *last-scanned* pointer, which points to the last object in the list that was recursively scanned and marked. New objects to be scanned are inserted at the head of the list, and the last-scanned pointer works from the end towards the head of the list.

Because one assigned thread feeds each row, and one assigned thread services each column, this arrangement helps to limit synchronization issues. However, there is potential that some threads will remain idle (because their respective column is empty) while others are busy servicing their assigned columns. To help balance the load, when a thread discovers it has no work left on its column, it will attempt to steal work from another column, or from another mutator's marking list.

The RTGC knows that there is no more marking to be done when all the objects in the grid have been recursively marked, and all of the per-mutator marking lists are empty. The lists are retrieved via a handshake. This indicates that there are no additional objects left to mark. At this point, the thread enters the termination protocol—see Figure 10-8.

Once the handshake is complete, with no more marking work left on the grid or any mutator lists, this is the indication that the marking phase can terminate, as there is no marking left to do. If the handshake reveals more marking work is to be done, the RTGC will exit the termination protocol safely and re-enter later. Otherwise, this signals the end of the marking phase, and the beginning of the RTGC *sweep* phase.

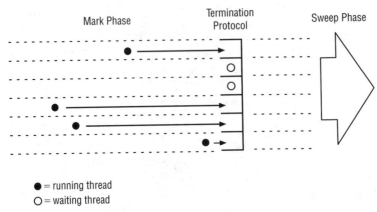

● = running thread
○ = waiting thread

Figure 10-8   The termination handshake is like a gate at the start of the horse race, and gathers threads for the next phase.

Concurrent Sweeping

The point of the sweep phase is to collect all objects in the heap not marked as live during the mark phase. The memory space occupied by these objects is then made available for the allocation of new objects. Put another way, the RTGC threads produce free memory for the mutator threads to consume. Since the RTGC is a non-generational, non-compacting collector, the objects are considered *free in place*, leading to potential gaps of free space of varying size in the heap. This is an issue that must be addressed during allocation, which we'll examine later in this chapter.

Parallelism during the sweep phase (performed by the RTGC gang worker threads only) is accomplished by dividing the heap into equally sized pages, where each page is processed by a single thread. The only exception is when a single object is larger than one page. Note that the page size is set such that the likelihood of this occurring is small. However, if it does occur, the large object is aligned on the page boundary, and all of the pages the object occupies are given to a single worker thread to process as a unit (see Figure 10-9).

Although this figure shows three or more RTGC threads working in parallel, the rules that dictate how many actual RTGC threads operate in the sweep phase are the same as in the mark phase. In fact, the number of gang worker threads available for all phases of garbage collection is equal (ignoring the differences between normal and boosted mode). The same threads simply perform different work based on the phase the collector is in. As a review, by default the actual number of RTGC threads running depends on the number of processor cores available to the Java RTS VM, unless changed via command-line arguments.

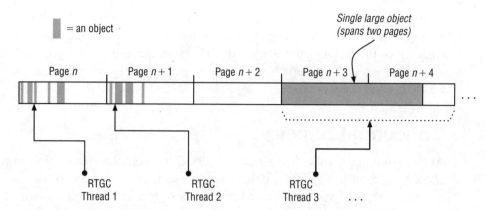

Figure 10-9 Parallel RTGC threads sweep the heap in pages to avoid synchronization issues.

Additionally, there is no hard-coded assignment of pages to RTGC threads. Instead, the threads use a concept called *work stealing* to determine which page, if any, they should sweep next. Again, a CAS operation is used by each thread to claim a page to avoid expensive locking. If the CAS operation succeeds, the thread sweeps the page; if the CAS fails, it means another thread has claimed that page. The thread will repeatedly attempt to claim another page, unless there are no more pages to claim (and sweep).

During the sweep phase, each dead (unmarked) object's data is cleared, but its header values are untouched. As a result, each object remains within its respective list (i.e., the global list, or a mutator thread's marked list). The header portion of each dead object is cleared during the next and last collection phase. The only objects whose data is not cleared, and temporarily not made available for future allocation, are those that are deemed too small. This is what the RTGC calls *dark matter*.

By tracking dark matter within the heap and not making it available for immediate allocation, the RTGC can better fight against fragmentation. This is an important strategy, as the RTGC does not move objects or compact memory in any way. Instead, the RTGC tracks dark matter and waits for adjacent objects to also become free, at which point their blocks will be coalesced into a single, larger, block. To be precise, to fight against memory fragmentation, the RTGC will do the following:

- Combine two groups of contiguous dark matter blocks into one usable block
- Combine a dark matter block with a free block adjacent to it
- For a new dead object that is adjacent (between) two blocks of dark matter (too small to be placed on the free list), combine all three blocks into one

When a thread finishes sweeping its page, it attempts to claim another. If repeated attempts fail, the thread will enter the termination protocol for the sweep phase. Once all of the RTGC gang worker threads enter the termination protocol, this signals the end of the sweep phase, and the beginning of the *zeroing phase*, which we'll examine in detail now.

Concurrent Zeroing

At this point in the collection cycle, the RTGC has completed both the marking and sweeping phases. All live objects have been marked and preserved, and all unmarked objects have been cleared and placed on the free list or considered dark matter. However, the live marked objects still reside within the grid, the global black list, or a mutator "new object" list (the per-mutator marking lists are all empty at this point). These objects must have their marked indicators cleared in preparation for the next cycle. Since each object's *next* field is used for marking and placing it within a list, clearing this value simultaneously un-marks it, and un-links it from a list.

As with marking, zeroing is performed by entering a handshake, which stops mutator threads from chaining newly created objects. At this point, the RTGC gang worker threads parse all of the lists without concern of interference from mutator threads. For global data (not on a mutator list), the n-by-n grid described earlier is used. Parallelism is accomplished in a similar manner, where assigned threads zero the objects within each list, per row. As they traverse the rows and columns, and walk the lists, clearing each object's *next* field effectively prepares them for the next GC cycle and removes them from the list, all in one efficient operation.

Once all mutator lists and the global grid are empty (containing nothing but the special end-of-list marker), the GC cycle is complete and the RTGC will suspend all gang worker threads. This constitutes the end of the GC cycle, and the RTGC will remain suspended for a set period of time, even if free memory is still at or below the threshold to begin GC again. This is to ensure that even low-priority, non-real-time threads can execute. The minimum time period between GC cycles can be configured through a command-line parameter, as described in Chapter 4.

RTGC Memory Allocation

Although a garbage collector's main goal is to produce enough free memory for running applications, its secondary goal is to support the application's consumption of that memory. The RTGC manages the entire Java heap, and sets appropriate values within each new object's header fields. Namely, each object's marking field—the *next* pointer we discussed throughout this chapter—is set differently according to the active GC phase. To accurately track new objects during these phases, the tri-color marking scheme described earlier is used.

As discussed earlier, a write barrier is activated during a GC cycle to properly set an object's header fields accordingly. However, in between cycles, this write barrier is removed, and allocation occurs more quickly. Although it's unfortunate that the allocating mutator threads must pay this penalty, it's a relatively small price to pay for concurrent garbage collection. The alternative, implemented by many non-real-time collectors, is to stop all mutator threads during a GC cycle. Let's examine the heap layout in general, and the strategies implemented to make object allocation as efficient as possible.

Heap Layout

The heap in Java RTS is one large space composed of an array of lists that contain free objects, with no separate *to* or *from* spaces, or generations. (See the discussion of GC algorithms in Chapter 2 for more details on spaces and generations.) The free lists are composed of individual blocks of free memory sized increasingly large, by powers of two. For instance, there are lists of blocks sized at 512 bytes, at 1024 bytes, and so on. The maximum size of blocks kept on the lists is dependent upon the total size the heap is set to at VM startup.

As with the marking and sweeping phases of the GC cycle, objects are inserted into and removed from the free lists via atomic, lock-free, compare-and-swap (CAS) operations. This removes the need for expensive locking and synchronization amongst the GC and mutator threads.

Thread-Local Allocation Buffers

Java RTS makes use of thread-local allocation buffers (TLABs), per mutator thread, to avoid contention between mutator threads when new objects are created. To review from Chapter 2, a TLAB is a portion of the free heap that's reserved for one thread to allocate from (see Figure 10-10). This figure is slightly different from when it was first presented in Chapter 2, as the Java RTS heap does not contain a global *first-free-byte* pointer; since it doesn't move live objects and compact the heap, it cannot.

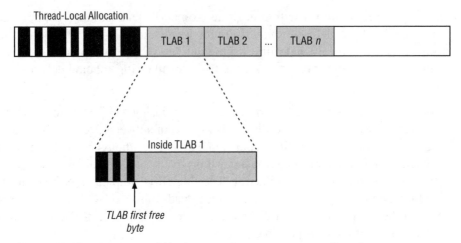

Figure 10-10   TLABs avoid lock contention on concurrent allocations.

All TLABs are 4K bytes in size by default. However, if the heap becomes frag-mented, the VM will return TLABs of smaller size, as needed. When a mutator thread creates a new object, the memory is taken from the thread's active TLAB. If the object is smaller than the free space within the active TLAB, the allocation is very fast and efficient. In fact, the allocation code is inlined with the thread's compiled Java code, producing the fastest possible allocation performance. The only exceptions are when the current TLAB becomes filled, or the object is too large to fit into even an empty TLAB.

In the first case, the VM will request a new TLAB from the RTGC. This is a more expensive, but bounded, scenario. In the second case, where the object size is rela-tively large, the RTGC may decide to place the object outside of the mutator's TLAB. This operation is less expensive than allocating a new TLAB, as it uses atomic operations and hence requires no locking. Although the RTGC is not gen-erational, this is analogous to Java SE's immediate promotion of large objects to the heap's *old generation*.

Object Splitting

As mentioned above, TLAB sizes may fall below the normal 4K if the heap becomes fragmented. This isn't necessarily a problem, unless the size of any one free block is too small to accommodate the next new object to be created. If con-tiguous free blocks cannot be located to fit it, the object will be split across free blocks outside of a TLAB (see Figure 10-11).

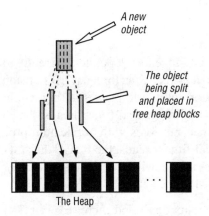

Figure 10-11 New objects may be split across multiple (smaller) free heap blocks.

Although this isn't something exposed to you (as a Java developer), it does require extra accounting and processing within the VM when the object is accessed. As a result, this can affect latency, performance, and throughput overall. Therefore, all effort is made to avoid splitting entirely, but when it does occur, objects are split using the largest free blocks available. In practice, for most objects split across the heap versus those that are placed within one free block, the access time difference is minimal. For arrays, however, performance quickly becomes a concern, but Java RTS has considered this case.

Array Splitting and Caching

Arrays tend to be the largest objects in the heap, and are therefore more than likely to be split across non-contiguous free blocks. Therefore, array access is optimized through the use of an internal index. The best performance is achieved when the array index is contained within a single block. However, through the use of an internal VM array index cache, performance is still good even when the array is split. In the case of a cache miss (an array index that's not in the cache), Java RTS uses a tree structure to locate the array block, within a bounded time frame. Therefore, in the worst-case, the time is $O(\log(n))$ for array access on a block cache miss; however, this is relatively rare.

In the end, the important fact to remember regarding array object splitting, is that all effort is made to ensure bounded, relatively quick access to array indexes even when the array spans non-contiguous heap regions.

RTGC Policies

With its default settings, the Java RTS RTGC appears to operate differently to different application threads. For instance, to non-real-time threads (JLTs), it appears as a partially concurrent collector with stop-the-world pauses during its phases, where each phase runs to completion. To mid-range real-time threads, the RTGC appears as a fully concurrent collector that interferes with application progress very little during its phases. To critical real-time threads, the RTGC doesn't even appear to exist. In fact, `NoHeapRealtimeThreads` will experience no delays from the RTGC regardless of the state of the VM or the heap.

This alone is an achievement, but its benefits don't end there. Every effort has been made to build as much flexibility into the RTGC as possible. Through a multitude of command-line parameters (examined in Chapter 4), the behavior of the RTGC can be tuned, and its behavior modified, to best fit your application's requirements. We'll refer to the resulting modes of operation that can be attained through tuning as *policies*, and we'll explore four sample policies now.

Full-Time RTGC Policy

By setting the proper command-line parameter values, you can configure the Java RTS RTGC to run almost continuously. This may not be something you wish to do on a uniprocessor server, as all lower-priority threads may suffer near-complete starvation. However, on a server with multiple processors and/or cores, this may be an ideal configuration, especially if your application has a high memory allocation rate.

By default, the RTGC will not start until free memory is nearly exhausted. For the most part, this is safe for two reasons:

- Once the RTGC does start, free memory will be produced concurrently without pausing application threads.
- A portion of the heap is reserved for critical real-time threads to further ensure there is free memory available to them.

However, in extreme cases, such as allocation bursts, or bursts of activity, even high-priority real-time threads may be blocked on allocation if the collector cannot keep up. Therefore, you may need to instruct the RTGC to begin each GC cycle sooner—before free memory is exhausted. Remember, though, that this may cause the RTGC to run more often, and hence will reduce application throughput. There's no magic here; with more processor time dedicated to GC, less processor time is available to application threads. However, on a server with enough processor cores, there may be enough processing time available to both your application and RTGC to run together all the time. The configuration for this policy involves setting one additional command-line parameter: `NormalMinFreeBytes`.

The following example Java RTS command-line sets the total heap size to 1GB, and instructs the RTGC to begin a cycle when the amount of free memory drops below 1GB:

```
$ /opt/jrts/bin/java -Xms1GB -Xmx1GB -XX:NormalMinFreeBytes=1G...
```

This command virtually guarantees that there will always be a need to start collecting. However, to further ensure that the RTGC runs continuously, you need to reduce the minimum amount of time it waits to start a new cycle when the previous one ends. You can do this by adding `-XX:RTGCWaitDuration=0` to the above command.

Of course, any of these numbers can be configured differently. You can choose to start a GC cycle when 50% of the heap is exhausted, or 75%, and so on. Also, you can modify the pause time between cycles to be larger than zero, but smaller than the default of ten milliseconds. Finally, you may decide you want to run the RTGC continuously, but only on a subset of available processor cores. You can do this by combining the settings above with the segregated RTGC policy, defined in the next section.

Segregated RTGC Policy

Again, with only the proper command-line parameters, you can configure Java RTS to run only within a subset of available processors/cores (from this point onward, we will simply refer to both as *cores*). By default, the Java RTS RTGC will scale up its parallel processing according to the total number of cores available on the host server. With the *segregated RTGC policy*, you can't bind RTGC threads to particular cores, but you can limit the number of threads it will run in parallel. This leaves other cores available to execute application threads.

To achieve this, recall the discussion on tuning the RTGC from Chapter 4. The RTGC will run in one of three modes: normal mode, boosted mode, and critical mode. The collector starts in normal mode (where RTGC threads run at lower priority), and progresses to boosted mode (where RTGC threads run at higher priority) if it cannot keep up with the application's allocation rate. The RTGC will potentially enter critical mode (where all RTTs are blocked on allocation) if multiple cycles fail to free enough memory for the running application. Java RTS command-line parameters allow you to set the maximum number of worker threads that the RTGC will create while in normal and boosted modes.

A careful review of the GC logs (see Chapter 4 for details) will inform you of the amount of processor time (and hence cores) that the RTGC requires to produce enough free memory for your application. You should be able to determine the requirements for both normal mode, and boosted mode, if the RTGC had the need to run in that mode. Using this, you can safely confine the RTGC to a subset of cores accordingly, via the -XX:RTGCNormalWorkers and -XX:RTGCBoosted- Workers command-line settings. For example, the following command-line sets the maximum number of RTGC threads to two during normal mode, and four during boosted mode (assuming this is run on a server with at least four cores):

```
$ /opt/jrts/bin/java
-XX:RTGCNormalWorkers=2 -XX:RTGCBoostedWorkers=4 ...
```

You can combine this policy with the full-time RTGC policy to instruct the RTGC to run continuously, but only on a subset of server cores. This combines the benefits of both policies, while ensuring that a predetermined number of cores are always available to your application (outside of other system activity). The combined command will look similar to the following example:

```
$ /opt/jrts/bin/java -Xms1GB -Xmx1GB -XX:NormalMinFreeBytes=1G
-XX:RTGCNormalWorkers=2 -XX:RTGCBoostedWorkers=4
```

These numbers are for illustration only. You need to work with your application's allocation needs, the target server capabilities, and the RTGC's activity logs to determine what's best for your specific deployment.

Note that you're not restricted to command-line parameters only to alter the RTGC characteristics. Sun's Java RTS provides an extension API, as part of the com.sun.rtsjx package, to allow you to monitor and alter the RTGC operation at runtime, through Java code within your application. As an example of how to use this API, let's examine the time-based RTGC policy implementation now.

Time-Based RTGC Policy

Again, the Java RTS RTGC is based on the Henriksson-Lund real-time collection algorithm discussed in Chapter 2. However, if you prefer, you can make the RTGC behave as a time-based collector, similar to IBM's Metronome GC [Stoodley07]. With this policy, the RTGC will run at very high priority, at predictable points in time, and for a set amount of time. Of course, with this policy, even your real-time threads will be interrupted at regular intervals, but at least the interruptions are deterministic. Let's explore how this is achieved.

Unlike the previous two policies, which were achieved via command-line settings, this one requires working with the RTGC in Java code. The code in Listing 10-1 contains a controller class, named `TimeBasedRTGC`, which manipulates the RTGC to run according to a specified schedule.

Listing 10-1 The `TimeBasedRTGC` controller class

```
import javax.realtime.*;
import com.sun.rtsjx.*;

public class TimeBasedRTGC implements Runnable {
    final int RTSJ_MAX_PRI =
        PriorityScheduler.instance().getMaxPriority();

    class PriorityHandler extends AsyncEventHandler {
        public PriorityHandler() {
            setSchedulingParameters(
                new PriorityParameters(RTSJ_MAX_PRI));
        }
        public void handleAsyncEvent() {
            int prio =
                FullyConcurrentGarbageCollector
                        .getCurrentPriority();
            System.out.println("RTGC priority="+prio);
        }
    }

    RealtimeThread rtt = null;
    volatile FullyConcurrentGarbageCollector rtgc;
    int start_millis, duration_millis;
    int normalPri, boostedPri;

    // This controller class accepts as input two millisecond
    // values. The first, start_millis, indicates how often the
    // RTGC should start. The second, duration_millis,
    // indicates how long the RTGC should run at high priority.
    // The duration must be less than the period (start).
    public TimeBasedRTGC(int start_millis, int duration_millis)
            throws Exception {
        System.out.println("In TimeBasedRTGC constructor");
        if ( duration_millis >= start_millis)
            throw new Exception(
                "duration must be less than GC period");

        // Make sure the RTGC is running, not Serial GC
        GarbageCollector gc = RealtimeSystem.currentGC();
        if (! (gc instanceof FullyConcurrentGarbageCollector)){
            System.out.println("Must run with RTGC");
            System.exit(1);
        }
        rtgc = (FullyConcurrentGarbageCollector)gc;
```

continued

```java
        this.start_millis = start_millis;
        this.duration_millis = duration_millis;
        normalPri =
          FullyConcurrentGarbageCollector.getNormalPriority();
        boostedPri =
          FullyConcurrentGarbageCollector.getCriticalBoundary();

        PriorityParameters priority =
            new PriorityParameters(RTSJ_MAX_PRI);
        PeriodicParameters period  =
            new PeriodicParameters(
                new RelativeTime(start_millis,0));

        // add a trace to see GC priority changes
        PriorityHandler ph = new PriorityHandler();
        FullyConcurrentGarbageCollector.addPriorityHandler(ph);

        // Create an RTT with the right priority and schedule
        System.out.println("Starting realtime thread");
        rtt = new RealtimeThread(
                    priority, period, null, null, null, this );
        rtt.start();
    }

    private void boostRTGC() {
        FullyConcurrentGarbageCollector.set(
            "NormalPriority", boostedPri);
    }

    private void unBoostRTGC() {
        FullyConcurrentGarbageCollector.set(
            "NormalPriority", normalPri);
    }

    public void run() {
        synchronized ( this ) {
            while (true) {
                // Start a new RTGC cycle
                FullyConcurrentGarbageCollector
                    .startAsyncGC(normalPri);

                // Boost the RTGC priority
                boostRTGC();

                // Start a timer for the specified duration
                try {
                    RelativeTime duration =
                        new RelativeTime(duration_millis, 0);
```

```
            HighResolutionTime
                .waitForObject(this, duration);
        } catch (InterruptedException e) { }

        // Set the RTGC priority back to normal
        unBoostRTGC();

        // Wait for the next start time
        RealtimeThread.waitForNextPeriod();
        }
    }
  }
}
```

The `TimeBasedRTGC` class constructor takes a period and duration as parameters. The period indicates how often you want the RTGC start, such as every ten milliseconds. The duration indicates how long you want it to run at high priority, such as for one millisecond. This means that the duration value must be smaller than the period. In this implementation, all values are in milliseconds, with the smallest period or duration being one millisecond.

Using the Java RTS `com.sun.rtsjx` package, you can gain access to the garbage collector within the VM and monitor its activity, or control portions of its operation. Within the constructor, one of the very first checks is to make sure the Java RTS VM was started with the real-time collector, as opposed to the serial collector. Next, the current settings for the RTGC's normal mode priority, and its critical mode priority, are stored. The code will explicitly boost the RTGC to the critical mode priority for the specified duration. These values are platform-dependent, and are configurable via the command line; therefore there was no reason to hard-code them in this class.

Next, a simple listener class, `PriorityHandler`, is added to receive and log GC priority change events. This class is actually an RTSJ Asynchronous Event Handler (AEH) class, and is provided through the call to `FullyConcurrent-GarbageCollector.addPriorityHandler`. There are other GC-related events that can be received via an AEH, such as GC start and end events, if your application is interested in this information. The `PriorityHandler` AEH is included simply for demonstration purposes, and can be removed from the actual implementation.

Finally, a periodic `RealtimeThread` is created, at high priority, to control the RTGC operation according to the supplied period and duration. The period of the RTT is set to the period value supplied in the `TimeBasedRTGC` class constructor. All of the controller code is contained in the run method, within a `while` loop.

Each time the periodic RTT wakes up, it starts the RTGC, boosts its priority immediately, and then waits for the duration specified using the `HighResolutionTime` class. This ensures that the RTGC will run at boosted priority for precisely the duration given. When the timer expires, the RTT sets the RTGC back to its normal priority, and waits for the next period.

As an example of how simple it is to activate the time-based RTGC policy with this code, simply instantiate the `TimeBasedRTGC` class with the period and run duration, as shown in Listing 10-2, and continue with your application processing.

Listing 10-2   Using the `TimeBasedRTGC` class

```
class MyApp {
    static TimeBasedRTGC gcController = null;
    //. . .

    public MyApp() throws Exception {
        // Run the RTGC for 1 millisecond of every 10
        Main.gcController = new TimeBasedRTGC(10,1);
        //. . .
    }

    public static void main(String[] args) throws Exception{
        MyApp app = new MyApp();
        //. . .
    }
}
```

Of course, there is no guarantee that the RTGC will run for the full duration given, as there may not be enough work for it to perform. However, you will be guaranteed that the RTGC won't run at boosted priority for any length of time *greater* than the duration you specify. Also, most importantly, it's assumed that most people will not want to run the RTGC in this way, as any time-based collector has the following risks:

- The duration is not long enough to produce enough free memory.
- The duration represents the minimum latency that the application can guarantee.

This code serves as an exercise in understanding how you can monitor and manipulate the RTGC from your application, if needed. However, let's examine an RTGC policy that we find works well in many cases, which you can configure for your real-time applications as well. It's called the *isolated RTGC policy*.

Isolated RTGC Policy

One approach to RTGC tuning that we find applicable to many Java RTS applications is called the *isolated RTGC policy*. In this case, RTGC threads are isolated from the application's time-critical real-time threads by binding RTTs and/or NHRTs to processor sets. As also covered in Chapter 4, defining processor sets in both Solaris and Linux is straightforward.

This policy may seem identical to the segregated RTGC policy discussed previously. However, while both effectively limit the RTGC to a subset of processors, the isolated policy dedicates the same subset of cores to your critical threads. This has an advantage in that it removes potential context switching and CPU cache-related issues from the latency equation. It also allows the RTGC to self-tune and run on all of the remaining processors not in the processor set.

However, the disadvantage is that while the application time-critical threads (RTTs and/or NHRTs) are otherwise idle, the processors in the processor set to which they're bound are unavailable to execute any other code in the system. As a result, even when idle, those processors are unavailable to execute RTGC threads or any other non-real-time threads within the Java RTS VM. As with any tuning exercise, the benefits of this policy are best quantified through testing with your particular application. With careful analysis and planning, however, this configuration can help to yield the smallest latency and greatest determinism for a Java RTS application.

To configure it, you need to create a processor set (see Chapter 4 for details), and use one of the related command-line options, as in this example:

```
$ /opt/jrts/bin/java -XX:RTSJBindRTTToProcessorSet=1
```

There are four total command-line options related to processor binding of threads within the Java RTS VM. There are two sets of two—one for Linux, and the other for Solaris—where each set contains an option for RTTs, and the other for NHRTs. See Chapter 4 for a complete explanation and set of examples to illustrate.

Part III

Using Java RTS

11

An Equities Trading System

"Time is a fixed income"
—Margaret B. Johnstone

THIS chapter explores a realistic demonstration application that uses Java RTS. In this case, we've built a simulated equities trading system that operates with both Java SE and Java RTS to directly show the differences between both virtual machines. Namely, with Java SE, the application misses deadlines and important time-critical events that cause it to behave unpredictably. This results in unmitigated risk in the trading system, with a potential loss of money as a result. When updated to run with Java RTS, you'll clearly see this risk disappear as deadlines are met, and trading opportunities are always seized.

We'll explore a total of three versions of the trading system: the first uses Java SE; the second uses `RealtimeThreads` and the RTGC within Java RTS; and the third uses `NoHeapRealtimeThreads`, also with Java RTS, for the best determinism. Besides seeing first-hand the benefits of Java RTS, you'll learn what it takes to convert a standard Java SE application to run on Java RTS with `RealtimeThreads` and `NoHeapRealtimeThreads`.

The Equities Market

The equities market, known as the stock market to most, is generally a public exchange used to buy and sell stock in corporations, or derivatives of stock, at public prices. These prices are often volatile in their movement. Examples of such equities (also known as securities) exchanges in the United States include the New York Stock Exchange (NYSE), the National Association of Securities Dealers Automated Quotations (NASDAQ), and the American Stock Exchange (AMEX). There are others, although these three are very well known.

When you buy stock in a publicly traded corporation, you're investing in the company's future growth, and hence banking on the stock's value to grow along with it. Most people are familiar with the process of contacting a broker to purchase or sell a company's stock (if already owned) at current market value; also known as a *market order*. However, there are other types of equities trading that take place. For example, there are *limit orders* and *stop orders*, which we'll explain now.

Limit Orders

For customers that own a considerable amount of stock, or options to buy stock, in a corporation, brokers support the notion of a limit order to protect them from fluctuations or rapid changes in a stock's price. For instance, a broker can only execute a *buy limit order* at the limit price you specify. This allows you to get into the market on a stock if it rises quickly, without having to watch it continuously. Of course, this only makes sense if you have a strong feeling that the stock is undervalued at the limit price, and will go up in the near future.

Conversely, a *sell limit order* can only be sold at the limit price you specify. For instance, if you own a large quantity of stock that you bought at, say, $15, which is currently trading at $30, you may want to protect yourself from losses if the stock price sinks rapidly. A sell limit order of $21 will instruct the broker to sell your shares if the price hits, or goes below, $21.

With a limit order, the broker guarantees the price with you. Therefore, if the market continues to move, you're assured to buy or sell at the limit price you've set with your broker. Because of this guarantee, you might pay more for a limit order when compared to a market order, but it limits your risk as a result.

Stop Orders

Stop orders are similar to limit orders, but they allow a little more flexibility from a broker's point of view. A *sell stop order* is a broker instruction to sell at the best available price after the price goes below the stop price. This can limit your losses (if the stop price is at or below the purchase price) or lock in at least some of your profits. A *buy stop order* is typically used to limit a loss or protect an existing gain. A buy stop price is always above the current market price.

As with limit orders, you don't have to actively monitor a stock's performance. However, because the order is triggered automatically when the stop price is reached, the stop price could be activated by a short-term fluctuation in a security's price. Once the stop price is reached, the stop order becomes a market order. In a fast-moving market, the price at which the trade is executed may be much different from the stop price.

The use of stop orders is much more frequent for stocks, and futures, that trade on an exchange than in the over-the-counter (OTC) market. Pricing for stop orders will generally be different than for limit orders, due to their added flexibility. Both orders are exposed to market fluctuations, and are therefore dependent on the timely delivery of stock trade data, and the ability to trade on the changing prices in a timely manner. Hence, trading limit and stop orders is a real-time problem.

The Trading System Implementation

Building a broker system to automatically trade limit and stop orders is relatively straightforward in terms of trade execution. In a nutshell, the system needs to monitor a data feed for stock updates on relevant equities (those that customers have placed limit and stop orders on). The trading system engine we'll build in this chapter accepts stop and limit orders on a variable number of equities. The actual number of orders is preset within the system but is configurable to ensure reasonable operation on systems of varying amounts of CPU power and other resources. A scripted set of price updates for these securities will be played through the system, over time, to simulate the natural fluctuations in price. The rate of update will also be configurable to ensure reasonable operation.

The goal is to show that the Java code that is written to respond to prices as they hit and/or pass the thresholds for the stop and limit orders will operate under real-time constraints when running with the Java RTS VM. When running with the standard Java VM price updates may be missed due to Java SE's non-deterministic behavior. As a result, order limits will be missed and stop orders will trade beyond their stop prices, effectively losing money for the parties involved.

The System Architecture

The trading system is made of three main components:

- The simulated data feed—this application, named `Datafeed`, reads prepared stock update data from a file, and streams it over a JMS connection at a periodic rate.

- The trading engine—this application, named TradingSystem, listens for price updates from the data feed application via a JMS connection, and compares the latest prices against the order prices periodically. If there is a delay in this processing, price updates will be missed, the market will continue to move, and the window for trading will be missed as well.

- The graph—this application displays the trading results, which are published as MBeans from the trading engine. With this component, you can clearly see if all trades occur as expected, or if not, when trades occur past their stop order prices, and when limit order prices are missed.

The basic architecture for the system is shown in Figure 11-1. We'll dive into more detail for each component as we go along. If you use an application server, such as Sun's Glassfish, you can use its built-in JMS and JMX facilities. In fact, this is how we configure and run the application. An additional advantage is that Glassfish is open-source, and easily accessible, making it quick and easy to get the application running.

You can use any JMS provider you wish, and you can change the application to use JMS instead of MBeans. The important part of the simulation is what happens inside the trading engine itself, which we'll examine in more detail now.

The Trading Engine

The trading engine is where all the action occurs. It listens for price updates via a JMS consumer, and updates its cache of market prices for each stock it's tracking. The MarketManager class performs this processing. It also maintains an order book, which is filled on startup by reading a file. The OrderManager class

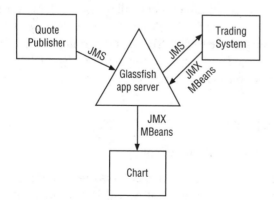

Figure 11-1   The main components in the trading system simulation.

performs this processing, which also periodically compares each limit and stop order price to the latest market price for each stock. If a particular stock's market price has changed to meet an order's criteria for a trade, it will execute a simulated trade.

The order book is maintained as a `HashMap` of stock symbols being tracked, where each entry contains the order sub-book for the applicable stock (see Figure 11-2) as an object of the `SubBook` class. This class maintains two linked lists: one for buy orders stored in ascending order and another for sell orders stored in descending order.

To be precise, the order book is a `java.util.HashMap` of `SubBook` objects, with the key being the stock symbol. The `SubBook` class contains two `java.util.` `LinkedList` objects to hold buy and sell orders. The orders themselves are represented as objects of the `OrderEntry` class, which holds the order price, quantity, and a timestamp.

When a trade does occur, the original order price and the trade execution price are recorded. If the system is able to keep up with each price update, the trade price will always equal the order price. However, if some event delays the `OrderManager` object's processing, it may miss market ticks, and opportunities to trade. In the case of limit orders, the trade price will be different than the order price, and this results in lost money for the broker who has to honor the original price with the order holder.

For instance, let's examine a simple scenario where a limit order of quantity 100 is placed in the system for $10. Let's assume the stock is trading at $11, then

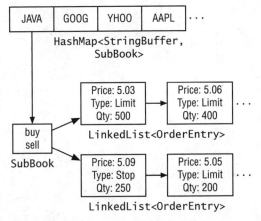

Figure 11-2   The order book maintains lists of buy and sell orders per stock.

suddenly starts dropping in value to $10, $9, and so on. The MarketManager object will receive each price update, and update the stock's value in its cache to $10, then $9, and so on accordingly. However, if the OrderManager were delayed, missed its period and the $10 update, and then discovered that the stock moved to $9, it would execute the $10 trade at $9, for a loss of $1 per unit of stock. Multiplied by the order quantity of 100, this amounts to a $100 loss for the broker. In real life, the trade volumes are typically higher, and the number of orders this can happen with is greater. Therefore these losses add up quickly.

The Java SE Version

The trading engine design is basically the same regardless of whether it runs on Java SE or Java RTS. The Java SE version (shown in Figure 11-3) maintains the cache of recent market prices, as well as the order book, in the Java heap. The MarketManager and OrderManager objects each run within their own java.lang.Threads (JLTs). Periodically, the OrderManager compares the order book prices to the cache of recent market prices, per stock. And, to review, the MarketManager implements a JMS consumer to receive stock price updates via JMS.

Here, everything exists in the heap: the threads, the market data, and the order data. In Listing 11-1, you can see the main class that creates the OrderManager and MarketManager Runnable objects, and then starts the threads.

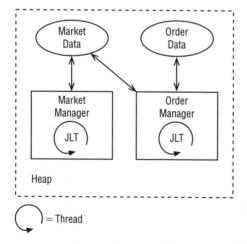

Figure 11-3   The trading engine design for Java SE.

Listing 11-1 Trading Engine main class for Java SE

```java
import com.trader.tradingengine.*;
import com.trader.data.*;
public class Main {
    public static void main( String[] args ) {
        try {
            // Create the Runnable worker classes
            MarketManager marketMgr = new MarketManager();
            OrderManager orderMgr = new OrderManager(marketMgr);

            orderMgr.displayOrderBook();

            // Create and start Threads
            Thread marketThread = new Thread(marketMgr);
            Thread orderThread = new Thread(orderMgr);
            marketThread.start();
            orderThread.start();

            // Need to force GC to occur
            while ( true ) {
                System.gc();
                Thread.sleep(1000);
            }
        }
        catch ( Exception e ) {
            e.printStackTrace();
        }
    }
}
```

The OrderManager object is given a reference to MarketManager in order to gain access to its market data cache. Upon creation, OrderManager loads in the list of limit and stop order prices from a file. Next, two java.lang.Thread objects are created (for OrderManager and MarketManager) and then started. Finally, a loop is started on the main thread to call System.gc (suggesting that garbage collection should occur) every second. This is done to ensure that some GC events occur, and intentionally cause jitter to occur, while trading activity is taking place. (Note that this jitter would occur anyway, this just ensures that it shows up while the application is trading.) The rest of the activity takes place within the two worker threads just created.

The MarketManager Class

The MarketManager implementation is mostly the same in all versions of the application, with some minor changes in the no-heap real-time version. Listing 11-2 contains most of the code for this class, which is a JMS listener. The JMS code will not be covered here since it's not the focus of discussion, but the full class implementation is available online for you to review and try.

Listing 11-2   The MarketManager class

```
package com.trader.tradingengine;
import java.util.*;
import javax.jms.*;
import javax.naming.*;
public class MarketManager implements Runnable, MessageListener
{
    // JMS specific
    private Connection connection = null;
    private Session session = null;
    private Destination destination = null;
    private MessageConsumer consumer = null;
    // ...

    // The Market Book
    HashMap<String,StringBuffer> marketBook =
        new HashMap<String,StringBuffer>(111);

    public MarketManager() {
    }

    public void run() {
        try {
          setupJMS("jms/QuoteUpdates");
        }
        catch ( Exception e ) {
          e.printStackTrace();
        }
    }

    private void setupJMS(String destinationName)
      throws Exception {
        // Create JMS connection ...
    }

    private void close() {
        // Close JMS connection ...
    }

    public void displayMarketBook() {
        // ...
    }

    public double getLastTradePrice(String symbol) {
        // Get the order book for this symbol if it exists
```

```
        try {
            return Double.parseDouble(
                        marketBook.get(symbol).toString() );
        }
        catch ( Exception e ) { }
        return 0;
    }

    // Market updates arrive as JMS Topic messages
    public void onMessage(Message msg) {
        try {
            TextMessage update = (TextMessage)msg;

            // Parse update ...

            onUpdate(symbol, price );
        }
        catch ( Exception e ) {
            e.printStackTrace();
        }
    }

    private void onUpdate(String symbol, String price) {
        StringBuffer sbPrice = marketBook.get(symbol);
        if ( sbPrice == null ) {
            sbPrice = new StringBuffer(15);
            marketBook.put(symbol, sbPrice);
        }

        sbPrice.replace(0, price.length(), price);
    }
}
```

The only public methods in this class are the JMS onMessage callback, displayMarketBook (for debug purposes), and getLastTradePrice—which is called periodically by the OrderManager object for each stock on which an order exists. The JMS updates arrive in the form of an XML string (see Listing 11-3).

Listing 11-3 Market update XML

```
<updates>
   <update>
      <symbol>JAVA</symbol>
      <datetime>2009-04-28T13:59:25.993-04:00</datetime>
      <price>9.1700</price>
   </update>
</updates>
```

When an update arrives via an asynchronous JMS message, onMessage is called, and the XML is parsed. Next, the onUpdate method is called with the stock symbol, and the new market last-traded price. If this is the first update for the given stock, its symbol and price are inserted into the market cache, which is a HashMap. If it's not the first update for this stock, the existing entry is looked up by symbol (a String), and the previous price StringBuffer is replaced with the new price StringBuffer. This ensures that new objects and memory are not allocated with each subsequent update per stock symbol.

The getLastTradePrice method returns the latest market price for a given stock symbol. It locates the stock's entry in the market cache HashMap, and converts the price StringBuffer to a double value, which it returns.

The OrderManager Class

Order prices are compared with the latest market prices every two milliseconds. Since updates are not sent out less than five milliseconds apart, this ensures there is plenty of time to catch every market update unless there is unforeseen latency. Listing 11-4 contains the important parts of the OrderManager class, which we'll explore in detail now.

Listing 11-4   The OrderManager class

```
package com.trader.tradingengine;
import ...;

public class OrderManager implements Runnable
{
    //...
    private StringBuffer tradeXML =
      new StringBuffer(512);
    private MarketManager marketMgr = null;
    private TradeManagement tradeMgr = null;
    private OnMessage onMessage =
      new OnMessage("OrderManager");
    private MissedTrade missedTrade =
      new MissedTrade("OrderManager");

    // The order book
    class SubBook {
      LinkedList<OrderEntry> buy = new LinkedList<OrderEntry>();
      LinkedList<OrderEntry> sell = new LinkedList<OrderEntry>();
    }
    HashMap<StringBuffer,SubBook> orderBook =
        new HashMap<StringBuffer,SubBook>(111);

    public OrderManager(MarketManager marketMgr)
      throws Exception {
```

```java
    this.marketMgr = marketMgr;
    this.tradeMgr = new TradeManagement("LimitStopTrades");

    // Read the local file "orders.csv" and add the orders
    //...
}

public void enterOrder( double price, int quantity,
                        StringBuffer symbol, int type) {
    OrderEntry newEntry =
        new OrderEntry(symbol, price, quantity, type);

    // Get the order book for this symbol if it exists
    SubBook sb = orderBook.get(symbol);
    if ( sb == null ) {
        sb = new SubBook(); // create new subbook
        orderBook.put(symbol, sb);
    }

    // Get the right sub book (but or sell orders)
    LinkedList<OrderEntry> orders = null;
    if ( newEntry.isBuyOrder() )
        orders = sb.buy;
    else
        orders = sb.sell;

    // Find the correct location for this order
    for ( int i = 0; i < orders.size(); i++ ) {
        OrderEntry entry = orders.get(i);
        if ( newEntry.comesBefore(entry.getPrice()) ) {
            orders.add( i, newEntry );
            return;
        }
    }
    orders.addLast(newEntry); // at end of list
}

public void displayOrderBook() {
    //...
}

private StringBuffer[] getOrderBookKeys() {
    //...
}

public void run() {
    //...
}
```

continued

```
private boolean checkForTrade(
  OrderEntry entry, double marketPrice) {
    //...
}

private StringBuffer generateTradeXML(
  OrderEntry entry, double tradePrice) {
    // Generate Trade XML
    //...

    // Send the XML using an MBean
    tradeMgr.notifyTrade( tradeXML.toString() );
    return tradeXML;
}
}
```

The OrderManager contains the order book, which again is a HashMap of buy and sell orders per stock symbol. The OrderEntry class represents orders (Listing 11-5), which holds the order's stock, price, quantity, and order type. When a new order is entered, the enterOrder method is called. Here, the order book entry for the applicable stock is located (order added if this is the first order for the stock), and the proper sub-book is located (buy or sell). Finally, the order is entered into the list in the proper place.

Listing 11-5   The OrderEntry class

```
package com.trader.data;
public class OrderEntry {
    private boolean active;
    private double price;
    private long quantity;
    private StringBuffer symbol;
    private int type;

    // ...
}
```

Once all the orders are entered, and the OrderManager thread is started, the run method (Listing 11-6) is where all the order matching takes place. Here is a step-by-step summary of the logic:

1. The current time in nanoseconds is stored. This is used to measure the time between invocations, and to sleep for the proper time period.

2. The order book is traversed, one stock at a time. The following occurs per stock:

   a. The sell orders are retrieved, and each order price is compared with the stock's current market price to see if a sell trade should occur.

b. The buy orders are retrieved, and each order price is compared with the stock's current market price to see if a buy trade should occur.

3. The time between invocations of the periodic loop is calculated and stored. This data will be graphed to visually inspect for latency and jitter.

4. Knowing that the loop should iterate precisely every two milliseconds, and also knowing how long the processing of the current iteration has taken, the amount of time to sleep in order to wake up on the next two-millisecond boundary is calculated. If for some reason this calculation is out of range (i.e. the current processing took two milliseconds), the code defaults to a two-millisecond sleep time.

Listing 11-6   The `OrderManager.run` method

```
public void run() {
   long starttime = onMessage.startCall();
   while ( true ) {
      getOrderBookKeys();

      // Loop to compare market to order prices
      for ( int i = 0; i < orderBookKeys.length; i++ ) {
         StringBuffer symbol = orderBookKeys[i];
         StringBuffer sPrice =
            marketMgr.marketBook.get(symbol.toString());
         if ( sPrice == null )
            continue;
         double marketPrice =
            Double.parseDouble( sPrice.toString() );

         // Get the sub book for this symbol
         SubBook sb = orderBook.get(symbol);
         if ( sb.sell != null ) {
            for ( int x = 0; x < sb.sell.size(); x++ ) {
               OrderEntry entry = sb.sell.get(x);
               if ( checkForTrade( entry, marketPrice ) )
                  break; // trade occurred
            }
         }

         if ( sb.buy != null ) {
            for ( int x = 0; x < sb.buy.size(); x++ ) {
               OrderEntry entry = sb.buy.get(x);
               if ( checkForTrade( entry, marketPrice ) )
                  break; // trade occurred
            }
         }
      }
```

continued

```
        long waitTime = System.nanoTime() - starttime;
        onMessage.endCall(starttime);
        starttime = onMessage.startCall();
        if ( waitTime > 0 && waitTime < 2000000 )
            Thread.sleep(
                waitTime/1000000, ((int)waitTime)%1000000);
        else
            Thread.sleep(2);
    }
}
```

The logic to check for and execute a trade is contained in the `checkForTrade` method (Listing 11-7), and varies depending upon the type of order: buy or sell, and limit or stop order. The code switches on the order type, and determines that a trade should occur in the following situations:

Stop-Loss Sell Order: If the latest market price for the applicable stock has moved at or lower than the order price, execute a trade.

Limit Sell Order: If the latest market price is equal to the order price, execute a trade. If the market price has slipped below the order price, send a missed trade warning notification.

Stop-Loss Buy Order: If the latest market price for the applicable stock has moved at or above than the order price, execute a trade.

Limit Buy Order: If the latest market price is equal to the order price, execute a trade. If the market price has move above the order price, send a missed trade warning notification.

Listing 11-7   The `checkForTrade` method

```
private boolean checkForTrade(OrderEntry entry,
                                double marketPrice) {
    if ( ! entry.isActive() )
        return false;

    switch ( entry.getType() )
    {
    case OrderType.STOP_SELL:
        if ( marketPrice <= entry.getPrice() ) {
            generateTradeXML(entry, marketPrice);
            entry.setActive(false);
            return true;
        }
        break;
```

```
            case OrderType.LIMIT_SELL:
                if ( marketPrice == entry.getPrice()  ){
                    generateTradeXML(entry, marketPrice);
                    entry.setActive(false);
                    return true;
                }
                else if ( marketPrice < entry.getPrice() ) {
                    missedTrade.sendMissedTrade(
                            entry.getType(), entry.getPrice(),
                            marketPrice, entry.getSymbol());
                }
                break;

            case OrderType.STOP_BUY:
                if ( marketPrice >= entry.getPrice() ) {
                    generateTradeXML(entry, marketPrice);
                    entry.setActive(false);
                    return true;
                }
                break;

            case OrderType.LIMIT_BUY:
                if ( marketPrice == entry.getPrice()  ) {
                    generateTradeXML(entry, marketPrice);
                    entry.setActive(false);
                    return true;
                }
                else if ( marketPrice > entry.getPrice() ) {
                    missedTrade.sendMissedTrade(
                            entry.getType(), entry.getPrice(),
                            marketPrice, entry.getSymbol());
                }
                break;
        }
        return false;
    }
}
```

When a trade is to be executed, the generateTradeXML method is called to create the trade notification message. In reality, an actual trade would be executed, but in this example, the trade is simulated and the notification is sent as an MBean via JMX. The notification contains an XML string (see Listing 11-8) that contains the trade type, the associated stock symbol, a timestamp, the original order price, the actual traded price, and the volume. This data is used by the charting application to determine if a loss had occurred due to a missed trade opportunity, which is determined by the difference between the order and trade prices multiplied by the volume.

Listing 11-8   The trade notification XML

```
<trades>
    <trade>
        <type>Buy</type>
        <symbol>JAVA</Symbol>
        <datetime>2009-04-28T13:59:25.993-04:00</datetime>
        <tradeprice>9.1700</tradeprice>
        <limitprice>9.1700</limitprice>
        <volume>1000</volume>
    </trade>
</trades>
```

When this version of the application is run with Java SE, several unfortunate events occur (see Figure 11-4). In the chart, many things are displayed. The vertical lines that run from top to bottom on the graph indicate garbage collection (GC) events. You'll also notice a line graph that starts at the bottom of the chart and spikes quite often. This line (the scale is on the left Y-axis) measures that actual time from one invocation of the trading loop to the next. It should be two milliseconds apart, but often spikes much higher. In many cases, these spikes are correlated to GC events.

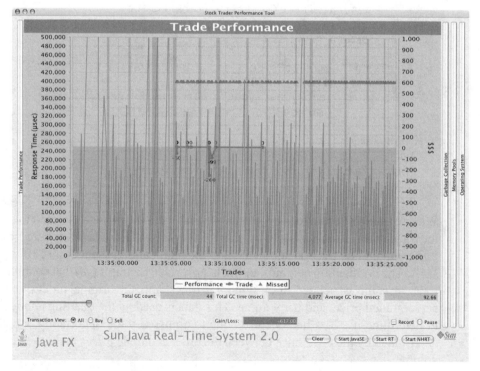

Figure 11-4   Trading results on Java SE.

Right away this is a bad indication, and it shows that real-time behavior is not occurring in this application. When trades do occur—indicated by the dark line graph in the center of the chart, you'll see that it dips below zero according to the scale on the right-hand Y-axis. This indicates that trades occurred at prices beyond their stop order prices. The numerous dark triangles along the top of the chart indicate trades that couldn't take place because the market moved beyond the associated limit order price before a trade could be executed.

Clearly, Java SE is not the proper execution environment for this trading application. Let's take a look at the changes needed to real-time enable the code, and the results when it's run on Java RTS.

The Java RTS Version

In the first real-time version of the trading system, we'll simply convert the application's time-critical code to run within a `RealtimeThread`. To make things fair, both the `MarketManager` and the `OrderManager` `Runnable` objects will be run within `RealtimeThreads` (see Figure 11-5).

Nothing else will be changed; all of the code and data will still reside and operate within the heap, subject to the real-time garbage collector (see Listing 11-9). Remember from previous chapters that RTT objects by default run at higher priority than the RTGC, which was not the case for the JLTs in the previous example. Also, by setting the RTTs to a high priority, other events in the system, both inside and outside the VM, shouldn't interrupt our time-critical processing.

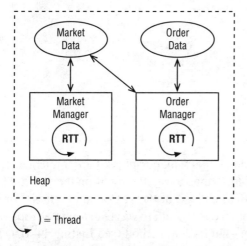

Figure 11-5 The trading engine with `RealtimeThreads`.

Listing 11-9   The trading system main class for Java RTS

```
import com.trader.tradingengine.*;
import com.trader.data.*;
import javax.realtime.*;
public class Main {
    public static void main( String[] args )
        try {
            // Create the Runnable worker classes
            MarketManager marketMgr = new MarketManager();
            OrderManager orderMgr = new OrderManager(marketMgr);

            orderMgr.displayOrderBook();

            // Create and start RealtimeThreads
            PriorityParameters pri =
              new PriorityParameters(
                PriorityScheduler.instance().getMaxPriority());
            PeriodicParameters period =
              new PeriodicParameters( new RelativeTime(2,0) );
            RealtimeThread orderThread =
              new RealtimeThread( pri, period,
                                  null,null,null,orderMgr);

            RealtimeThread marketThread =
              new RealtimeThread( null, null,
                                  null, null, null, marketMgr);

            marketThread.start();
            orderThread.start();

            while ( true ) {
                System.gc();
                Thread.sleep(1000);
            }
        }
        catch ( Exception e ) {
            e.printStackTrace();
        }
    }
}
```

Because both the MarketManager and OrderManager classes are implemented as Runnable objects, not much needs to change to run them within their own RTTs. In fact, not one line of code needs to change in MarketManager class. For the OrderManager class, the only difference is the call to waitForNextPeriod—and the removal of the sleep calculation—in its run method (see Listing 11-10). The remainder of the code is the same, and has been omitted.

Listing 11-10   The real-time `OrderManager.run` method

```
public void run() {
   long starttime = onMessage.startCall();
   while ( true ) {
      // ...

      onMessage.endCall(starttime);
      starttime = onMessage.startCall();
      RealtimeThread.waitForNextPeriod();
   }
}
```

Note that the time between invocations of the loop in the `run` method is still tracked as it was in the non-real-time version. This is reported and graphed in the same chart application used with the Java SE version. When the updated code is run on Java RTS with the same data feed, the results are as shown in Figure 11-6.

Here, you'll notice many differences when compared with Figure 11-4. First, notice that GC events still occur often as indicated by the long vertical bars.

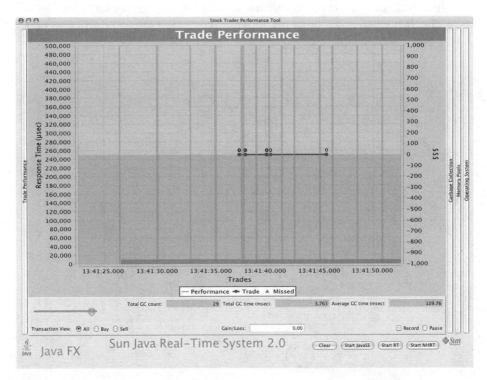

Figure 11-6   Trading results on Java RTS.

However, the first key difference is that the timing through the time time-critical loop is always a consistent two milliseconds, as shown by the flat line graph along the very bottom of the chart. Next, when trades occur, they each execute when the market price matches the order price precisely; there are no missed market events. Hence there is no loss of money. It's important to note that GC events do occur while trading occurred; they simply don't interrupt the time-critical trade execution code. Instead, the RTGC executes in the intervals between the executions of periodic thread's trading logic, as governed by the call to waitForNextPeriod.

Although this application yields the desired outcome (no missed trades), let's examine what it takes to run the trading logic within a NHRT, with the data in ImmortalMemory.

The Java RTS No-Heap Version

In the no-heap version of the trading system, the code is quite different. For starters, the time-critical trade execution code—within OrderManager—now runs within a NoHeapRealtimeThread. As a result, the market cache, the order book, and the OrderManager class all reside within immortal memory (see Figure 11-7). The MarketManager, however, remains mostly the same and still executes within a RealtimeThread.

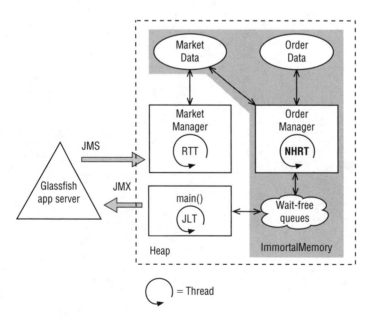

Figure 11-7   The trading engine with NoHeapRealtimeThreads and ImmortalMemory.

The main reason for this is that both the JMS and JMX infrastructures require access to the heap. Further, because of this, transferring trade-related data requires the use of the Java RTS wait-free read and write queues (see Chapter 6). The reason is that the time-critical `OrderManager` code executing in the NHRT needs to transfer this data to a JLT running in the heap. The wait-free queues ensure that the NHRT is not subject to jitter from the JLT.

As a result, the wait-free queues, the market data cache, the order book, and other data are stored as static members in the static class `IMArea` (see Listing 11-11). Being created by static initializers, these objects reside in immortal memory by default.

Listing 11-11   The static `IMArea` class

```java
public class IMArea {
    public static WaitFreeReadQueue freePerfStatsPool;
    public static WaitFreeWriteQueue queuedPerfStatsPool;
    public static WaitFreeReadQueue freeTradeStatsPool;
    public static WaitFreeWriteQueue queuedTradeStatsPool;

    // Market prices cache
    public static HashMap<String,MarketPrice> marketBook =
        new HashMap<String,MarketPrice>(111);

    // The order book
    public static HashMap<String,SubBook> orderBook =
        new HashMap<String,SubBook>(111);

    //...
}
```

The next change is the addition of a static initialization block of code within the application's main class to be executed immediately on startup (see Listing 11-12). The code within the block is executed within a `RealtimeThread` created in place, as NHRTs cannot be created by JLTs. It's here that both the `MarketManager` and `Order-Manager` objects are created. We'll discuss the changes to these two classes later.

Listing 11-12   The application static initializer code block

```java
import javax.realtime.*;
...
public class Main {
    static RealtimeThread rt;
    static int MAX_PRI =
        PriorityScheduler.instance().getMaxPriority();

    static {
        rt =
```

continued

```
    new RealtimeThread(new PriorityParameters( MAX_PRI ),
            null, null, ImmortalMemory.instance(),
            null, null ) {
  public void run() {
      try {
          Main main = new Main();

          // Create performance and trade notifier
          IMArea.onMessage =
              new OnMessage("OrderManager");
          IMArea.tradeNotifier =
              new TradeManagement("LimitStopTrades");

          // Create the Order Manager
          PriorityParameters pri =
            new PriorityParameters( MAX_PRI );
          PeriodicParameters period  =
            new PeriodicParameters(
            new RelativeTime(2,0) );
          IMArea.orderMgr =
              new OrderManager(
                  sched, period,
                  ImmortalMemory.instance() );

          // Create the Market Manager
          MarketManager marketMgr =
              new MarketManager(
                  pri, HeapMemory.instance());

          // Read order data and enter the orders
          main.readFileAndEnterOrders();
          IMArea.orderMgr.displayOrderBook();

          // Start threads
          IMArea.orderMgr.start();
          marketMgr.start();
      }
      catch ( Throwable e ) {
          e.printStackTrace();
      }
  };
};

//...

public static void main(String[] args) {
    //...
}
}
```

The main application JLT executes a loop in the `main` method, where it continuously checks for new trade notification objects to report as MBeans (see Listing 11-13). Each time through the loop, two wait-free queues are checked: one for trade notifications, and one for performance statistics. This data is sent via JMX to the listeners.

Listing 11-13   The main application loop for trade notifications

```java
public static void main(String[] args) {
    Main.rt.start();
    StatsData stats = null;
    try {
        while ( true ) {
            try {
                // Pull a trade message off the queue
                stats =
                 (StatsData)IMArea.queuedTradeStatsPool.read();
                if ( stats != null ) {
                    // Send the trade data via JMX
                    String td = generateTradeXML(stats);
                    IMArea.tradeNotifier.notifyTrade( td );

                    // Place trade obj back on the free queue
                    IMArea.freeTradeStatsPool.write(stats);
                }

                // Pull a stats message off the queue
                stats =
                 (StatsData)IMArea.queuedPerfStatsPool.read();
                if ( stats != null ){
                    IMArea.onMessage.recordCall(
                        stats.startTime, stats.endTime);

                    // Place stats obj back on the free queue
                    IMArea.freePerfStatsPool.write(stats);
                }
            }
            catch ( Exception e ) {
                e.printStackTrace();
            }

            Thread.sleep(1);
        }
    }
    catch ( Exception e ) {
      e.printStackTrace();
    }
}
```

As you can see in Listing 11-13, there are actually four queues: two for trade notifications, and two for performance statistics. As an object is pulled from one queue, the data is extracted, and the object is placed onto the other, associated, queue. Objects are recycled this way to ensure that new objects aren't created, which would otherwise continually consume immortal memory since they never get collected. The queue breakdown is:

queuedTradeStatsPool: implemented as a WaitFreeWriteQueue since the time-critical NHRT code writes new trade notifications to it. Messages are read by the main JLT.

freeTradeStatsPool: the main JLT places empty (recycled) trade notification messages here. It's implemented as a WaitFreeReadQueue since the time-critical NHRT takes empty objects from this queue to populate with new trade data.

queuedPerfStatsPool: implemented as a WaitFreeWriteQueue since the time-critical NHRT code writes new performance statistics data to it. Messages are read by the main JLT.

freePerfStatsPool: the main JLT places empty (recycled) performance statistics messages here. It's implemented as a WaitFreeReadQueue since the time-critical NHRT takes empty objects from this queue to populate with new trade data.

The OrderManager Class

The OrderManager class (see Listing 11-14) has been modified to directly extend the NoHeapRealtimeThread class. In the constructor, code has been added to set the base NHRT class priority and period, as well as the memory area to work within. You can provide a reference to immortal memory, or to a scoped memory region.

Listing 11-14   The no-heap OrderManager class

```
import javax.realtime.*;
...
public class OrderManager extends NoHeapRealtimeThread {
    MemoryArea memArea;
    public OrderManager(PriorityParameters priority,
                        PeriodicParameters period,
                        MemoryArea area) throws Exception {
        super(priority, period, null, area, null, null);
        this.memArea = area;
        IMArea.freeTradeStatsPool =
          new WaitFreeReadQueue(100, true);
```

```
    IMArea.queuedTradeStatsPool =
        new WaitFreeWriteQueue(100);
    IMArea.freePerfStatsPool =
        new WaitFreeReadQueue(100, true);
    IMArea.queuedPerfStatsPool =
        new WaitFreeWriteQueue(100);
}

public void enterOrder( double price, int quantity,
                        String symbol, int typeman tar)
                            throws Exception {
    try {
        OrderEntry newEntry =
            (OrderEntry)memArea.newInstance(OrderEntry.class);
        newEntry.price = price;
        newEntry.quantity = quantity;
        newEntry.type = type;
        newEntry.symbol = symbol;
        newEntry.setActive(true);

        // Get the order book for this symbol if it exists
        SubBook sb = IMArea.orderBook.get(newEntry.symbol);
        if ( sb == null ) {
            // Create a new order book for this symbol
            sb = (SubBook)memArea.newInstance(SubBook.class);
            IMArea.orderBook.put(newEntry.symbol, sb);
        }

        // Get the right sub book (buy or sell orders)
        LinkedList<OrderEntry> orders = null;
        if ( newEntry.isBuyOrder() )
            orders = sb.buy;
        else
            orders = sb.sell;

        // Find the correct location for this order
        for ( int i = 0; i < orders.size(); i++ ) {
            OrderEntry entry = orders.get(i);
            if ( newEntry.comesBefore(entry.getPrice()) ) {
                orders.add( i, newEntry );
                return;
            }
        }
        // Just add the order to the end of the list
        orders.addLast(newEntry);
    }
    catch ( Throwable e ) {
        e.printStackTrace();
```

continued

```
        }
    }

    public void run() {
        // ...
    }

    private boolean checkForTrade(
      OrderEntry entry, double marketPrice) {
        // ...
    }

    private synchronized void createTradeObj(
        // ...
    }

    // ...
}
```

Also in the constructor, the wait-free queues are created. When orders are entered via calls to enterOrder, care is taken to ensure that objects are allocated from the memory area provided in the constructor. Although the OrderManager itself operates within the proper memory region, the enterOrder method can be called from threads operating in other memory regions; therefore this explicit memory region allocation is required.

When the OrderManager NHRT is started, execution begins in its run method (see Listing 11-15). Although the logic is the same as with the previous versions of OrderManager we've examined in this chapter, the first key difference is the use of the immortal objects (shown in bold). The second difference is the use of the wait-free queues for transferring the performance statistics to the main JLT.

Listing 11-15   The NHRT OrderManager run method

```
public void run() {
    try {
        Clock clock = Clock.getRealtimeClock();

        int counter = 0;
        loopStartTime = clock.getTime().getNanoseconds();

        // Loop to compare market to order prices
        while ( true ) {
            int count = IMArea.orderBookKeys.length;
            for ( int i = 0; i < count; i++ ) {
                MarketPrice mktPrice =
                  IMArea.marketBook.get(IMArea.orderBookKeys[i]);
```

```
        if ( mktPrice == null )
            continue;
        double marketPrice = mktPrice.getPrice();
        SubBook sb =
          IMArea.orderBook.get(IMArea.orderBookKeys[i]);

        // Walk the list of sell orders
        for ( int x = 0; x < sb.sell.size(); x++ ) {
            OrderEntry entry = sb.sell.get(x);
            if (checkForTrade(entry,marketPrice)==true)
                break;
        }

        // Walk the list of buy orders
        for ( int x = 0; x < sb.buy.size(); x++ ) {
            OrderEntry entry = sb.buy.get(x);
            if (checkForTrade(entry,marketPrice)==true)
                break;
        }
    }

    long loopEndTime = System.nanoTime();

    counter = 0;
    StatsData perf =
      (StatsData)IMArea.freePerfStatsPool.read();
    if ( perf != null ) {
        perf.messageType = StatsData.MESSAGE_TYPE.PERF;
        perf.startTime = loopStartTime;
        perf.endTime = clock.getTime().getNanoseconds();
        IMArea.queuedPerfStatsPool.write(perf);
    }

    loopStartTime = clock.getTime().getNanoseconds();
    waitForNextPeriod();
    }
  }
  catch ( Exception e ) {
      e.printStackTrace();
  }
}
```

As in the previous versions, the logic that checks for and executes trades is done in the checkForTrade method. This method is the same as with previous versions; however, the way trade notifications are created has changed. In this version, the createTradeObj method (see Listing 11-16) uses the second set of wait-free queues to transfer the trade notifications messages to the main JLT.

Listing 11-16 The `createTradeObject` method.

```
private synchronized void createTradeObj(
  OrderEntry entry, double tradePrice) {
    // Use WaitFreeReadQueue
    StatsData trade =
     (StatsData)IMArea.freeTradeStatsPool.read();
    trade.startTime = loopStartTime;
    trade.messageType = StatsData.MESSAGE_TYPE.TRADE;
    trade.symbol = entry.getSymbol();

    if ( entry.isBuyOrder() )
        trade.tradeType = StatsData.STATS_TYPE.BUY;
    else
        trade.tradeType = StatsData.STATS_TYPE.SELL;

    trade.tradePrice = tradePrice;
    trade.tradeQty = entry.getQuantity();
    trade.entryPrice = entry.getPrice();
    trade.endTime = System.nanoTime();

    // Use WaitFreeWriteQueue
    IMArea.queuedTradeStatsPool.write(trade);
}
```

Now that we've reviewed the changes to the `OrderManager` class, which mainly involve the usage of a non-heap memory area, let's examine some of the changes to the `MarketManager` class for this version of the application.

The MarketManager Class

The `MarketManager` class has been modified to directly extend the `RealtimeThread` class. This is not a requirement, as its implementation is virtually the same as in the previous real-time example we saw earlier in this chapter. We do this solely to be consistent with the `OrderManager` class, which extends NHRT. The only other changes involve the use of the `IMArea` static class to access the cache of the latest market prices. This includes the use of a `Runnable` as a parameter in the call to `MemoryArea.enter()`, to ensure that updates are processed from within the proper memory area (see Listing 11-17).

Listing 11-17 The `MarketManager` for the NHRT application

```
public class MarketManager
  extends RealtimeThread implements MessageListener {
    MemoryArea memArea;
    // ...
```

```
    public MarketManager(PriorityParameters pri,
                         MemoryArea area) {
        super(pri, null, null, area, null, null);
        memArea = area;
    }

    class MarketUpdater implements Runnable {
        public void run() {
            mktPriceObj = IMArea.marketBook.get(symbol);
            if ( mktPriceObj == null ) {
                mktPriceObj =
                  new MarketPrice(null, price, 0, null);
                IMArea.marketBook.put(
                  new String(symbol), mktPriceObj);
            }
            else {
                // Replace the existing contents of the price
                // StringBuffer to avoid allocating more memory
                mktPriceObj.setPrice(price);
            }
        }
    }

    private void onUpdate(String s, String p){
        try {
            synchronized ( IMArea.marketBook ) {
                price = new Double(p).doubleValue();
                symbol = s;
                area.enter( new MarketUpdater() );
            }
        }
        catch ( Throwable e ) {
            e.printStackTrace();
        }
    }

    // ...
}
```

The parent MarketManager class's member variables, price and symbol, are used to transfer the data to the MarketUpdater Runnable. Therefore, access to these variables is synchronized. This is done mainly as a precaution, as the Runnable will execute from within the same RTT as MarketManager the code is written. However, if the code were changed to run the update logic in a separate thread, leaving out the synchronized block would lead to a nasty bug.

Note that in the `MarketUpdater.run` method, care is taken to overwrite the contents of existing `StringBuffer` price values to ensure that memory is not allocated and wasted within the non-heap memory area. The end result is safe market update logic regardless of which memory region this class is executed from within the heap, immortal memory, or a scoped memory region.

Application Configuration

Configuring the application to run requires an application server with JMS and JMX capabilities. In this section, we'll discuss what it takes to get the application running in your environment. Both the Datafeed and the TradingSystem application looks for the following JNDI objects for JMS messaging:

> jms/ConnectionFactory—the JNDI name of the JMS connection factory

> jms/QuoteUpdates—the JNDI name of the JMS publish/subscribe `Topic` that quotes are published on

You'll need to pre-configure these JMS resources and start the JMS provider ahead of time for the application to work. You can use any JMS provider you feel comfortable with, but we used Sun's Glassfish server as it's easily obtainable, available as open source, and provides JMX functionality for the application's MBeans as well. You can download Glassfish at `http://glassfish.dev.java.net/`, and install it in the recommended folder (which is `/opt/SDK` on UNIX). As for the remainder of the applications, it's recommended that you place them in the following directories:

- Data feed: `/opt/RTDemo/Datafeed`
- Trading System: `/opt/RTDemo/TradingSystem`
- RTT Trading System: `/opt/RTDemo.RTTradingSystem`
- NHRT Trading System: `/opt/RTDemo/NHRTTradingSystem`
- Chart GUI: `/opt/RTDemo/RTGUI`

Each application has its own startup script named "run" in its subdirectory. The order you execute the applications is important, starting with the chart GUI application; next, run the TradingSystem application; and finally, run the Datafeed application. In place of the TradingSystem application, you can try RTTradingSystem, or the NHRTTradingSystem. You'll need to restart the Datafeed application each time.

12

Java RTS Tools

"They say that time changes things, but you actually have to change them yourself."

—Andy Warhol

DEVELOPING Java RTS applications is very similar to developing Java SE applications. Because the language is unchanged, Java RTS can and will execute an unmodified Java SE class or JAR file without issue. As such, you should develop a Java RTS application as you would any Java application. In fact, you have every right to rely upon the Java RTS VM to take care of all issues related to time for you. Simply create `RealtimeThreads` to execute your time-critical code, set their priorities accordingly, and let the VM do all the work.

However, there are times, as with any real-time application, that you'll need help building and debugging your application. Java RTS has DTrace probe points, and JMX support, to allow you to explore the details of your application's execution. Also, Sun has made available the Thread Scheduler Visualizer (TSV) tool to give you insight, graphically, as to how your application behaves in its production environment, and how its tasks are scheduled. In this chapter, we'll discuss how to use the NetBeans and Eclipse IDEs to develop a Java RTS application, and how to use DTrace and the TSV tool to debug it.

Java RTS Development

This section will touch on how to configure a development environment for Java RTS application development. We'll explore both the NetBeans and Eclipse IDEs, however we won't go into too much detail as both applications employ rapid release cycles. This book would be hopelessly out of date before it hits the shelves otherwise. Instead, we'll take a cursory look at how to set up the classpath for both IDEs to support Java RTS projects.

Keep in mind that although you can code and compile on common desktop environments such as Windows, Mac OS X, and non-real-time Linux distributions, you won't be able to run your application in those environments. However, a Net-Beans plugin for Java RTS development is available that allows you to deploy and debug these applications on remote Solaris 10 or real-time Linux environments. As we write this, the NetBeans plugin is undergoing major changes, so again, we won't cover it in too much detail. Instead, check the book's web site for the timely information related to the latest plugins and development tools available.

Remote Debugging with the NetBeans Plugin

Once you install the Java RTS NetBeans plugin modules, you'll be able to easily start Java RTS projects, which will be listed as a project type when you create a new project. Additionally, the Java Platform Manager wizard has been updated to allow cross development from a local environment to your Java RTS deployment environment.

The wizard provides a "Real Time Java" folder in the platform panel, where you specify the deployment execution process parameters through the profile. Multiple profiles can be created and used at any time (i.e., for different deployment servers). The deployment and execution protocols use the UNIX *rcp* and *rsh* utilities, respectively. Here are the parameters you need to specify:

Host Name: the name or IP address of the remote machine on which Java RTS is installed.

User Name: the user login name on the target host.

Remote JDK Location: the location of the Java RTS installation on the remote target.

Remote JAR Location: The location on the remote target where the aba RTS application JAR file is to be copied.

JVM Arguments: the JVM arguments to be used at runtime.

Once all these parameters have been specified, click the *Close* button at the bottom right of the wizard. The Java Platform Manager wizard also supports the notion of profiles, which record sets of deployment and execution parameters. You can use the *Profile* drop-down list, and the Add, Remove, Import, Export buttons to save and manage various deployment and execution profiles.

You're now ready to code, deploy, and debug your Java RTS application in your local environment, while it actually executes on a supported Java RTS host. Let's take a look at alternative means for doing Java RTS development.

Alternative Development Environments

You can use any version of NetBeans or Eclipse within your favorite desktop environment to develop Java RTS applications, even without a special plugin. You simply need to reference the two Java RTS-specific JAR files from within the Java RTS distribution. In particular, you will need to add references to both the rt.jar and rt2.jar files, which exist within the jre/lib path within your Java RTS installation (i.e. /opt/SUNWrtjv/jre/lib). Let's take a look at the easiest ways to do this for both IDEs now.

Create a NetBeans JRTS Platform

Within NetBeans, which is at version 6.5 as we write this, you can add a new Java platform by selecting the *Java Plaforms* menu option from the *Tools* top-level menu. When the Java Platform Manager window opens, click on the Add Platform button to add the new JRTS platform (see Figure 12-1).

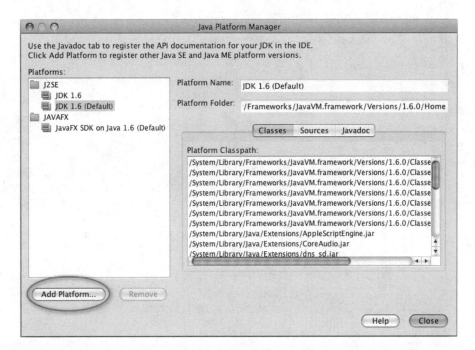

Figure 12-1   Adding a Java platform to NetBeans.

When you do this, browse your local Java RTS installation (you can simply copy the directory structure to your local desktop), and select *Next*. In the next window (see Figure 12-2), name the platform and hit *Finish*. You've created a Java RTS platform that you can use with new Java RTS projects, even on your local development desktop environment.

When you create a new project, right-click on the project name and choose *Properties* from the pop-up menu to display the *Project Properties* window. Select the *Libraries* entry in the *Categories* display on the left side of the window, and click on the *Java Platform* drop-down box (see Figure 12-3).

Select the Java RTS platform you created previously, click OK, and you're ready to begin Java RTS application development.

Alternatively, you don't have to create a new Java platform at all. Instead, you can simply add the two Java RTS JAR files, described earlier, to your project within the same Project Properties window (see Figure 12-4).

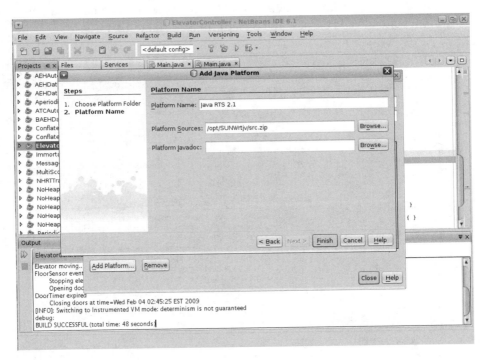

Figure 12-2   Adding a Java platform to NetBeans.

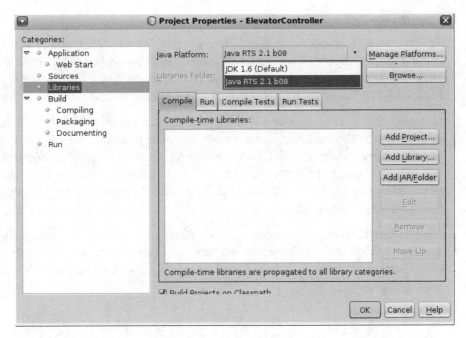

Figure 12-3 Your Java RTS project's Java platform.

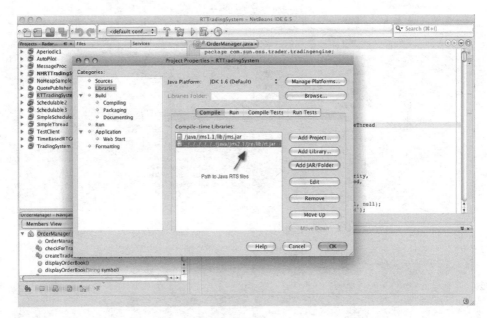

Figure 12-4 Adding the Java RTS files to your project.

Create an Eclipse Java Project

To add Java RTS as a development JRE in Eclipse, open the *Preferences* window, expand the *Java* entry along the left-hand list, and choose *Installed JREs*. Next, click the Add button on the upper right to display the *Add JRE* window (see Figure 12-5). Choose the path to the Java RTS installation, and provide a name.

However, this will only work on systems that support execution of Java RTS, such as Solaris or real-time Linux distributions. To make this work on other environments, simply add the Java RTS JAR files to your real-time project. You can do this in Eclipse in a similar way as with NetBeans. In the Eclipse *Project Properties* window (see Figure 12-6), select the *Java Build Path* entry in the list along the left-hand side of the window.

Click OK and you're ready to begin Java RTS development within Eclipse. Now that the development environment is ready, let's take a look at some tools that offer deep insight into the execution and scheduling of tasks within Java RTS and your application.

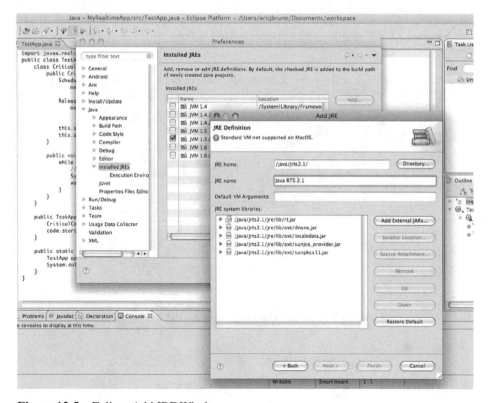

Figure 12-5   Eclipse Add JRE Window.

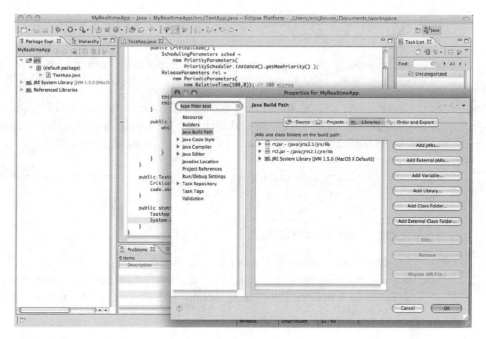

Figure 12-6 Adding JAR files to an Eclipse project.

The Thread Schedule Visualizer (TSV)

The Sun Thread Scheduling Visualizer (TSV) tool records and subsequently displays the scheduling of all threads within the Java RTS virtual machine. TSV runs only on Solaris 10 as it depends on DTrace to collect the data while the application executes. While your application runs, DTrace collects thread-specific data and records it to a file with the `.jrt3` extension. The name of the file will be unique, and is displayed when TSV and your application terminates. After the log file is created—and your application has terminated—you can view the results with the TSV viewer, which we'll discuss in a little while. Let's explore the recording scripts a little deeper.

TSV makes use of the DTrace probe points specific to the Java RTS VM, which we'll explore later in this chapter. The TSV tool comes with several DTrace recording scripts, which reside within the `/bin` directory of your TSV:

drecord—this TSV script is the default script to be used in most cases to profile the thread scheduling within the Java RTS VM and your application.

hrecord—this TSV script is similar to `drecord`, except that it's written to work with Java SE, albeit with limited information. We're going to focus on the Java

RTS scripts for the remainder of this chapter, but it's good to know that you can use TSV with Java SE if you need to compare.

srecord—using the jstack tool, this TSV script adds information about call stacks within the TSV display.

crecord—this TSV script allows you to pass in a custom script with additional DTrace probes to be recorded and included within the log file. This data will subsequently be displayed in the TSV viewer if formatted properly.

Let's take a look at the format of the log file that each of these scripts produces, which is subsequently parsed by the TSV viewer.

TSV Log File Format

Each DTrace event is recorded as one line within the output .jrt3 log file. Each line begins with timestamp followed by a number of entries, each separated by spaces. Table 12-1 iterates all of the acceptable entry types and related arguments.

Table 12-1   TSV log file format

Timestamp	Entry	Argument 1	Argument 2	Argument 3	Argument 4
Timestamp	on-cpu	Thread ID	CPU ID	Priority	–
Timestamp	off-cpu	Thread ID	–	–	–
Timestamp	set-name	Thread ID	<Thread name>	–	–
Timestamp	change-pri	Thread ID	Priority		
Timestamp	call-stack	Counter	Thread ID	CPU ID	Priority
Timestamp	call-stack	Counter	<Stack frame>	–	–
Timestamp	call-stack-end	–	–	–	–
Timestamp	user-event	Thread ID	CPU ID	Priority	<Event>
Timestamp	async-begin				
Timestamp	asyn-end				

In the table, the "< >" bracket entries indicate that all text from that point onward (spaces included) will be considered part of that one argument. For instance, where you see <Thread name>, all of the remaining text on the line will be considered the thread's name. Take the line below:

```
15285108049758 set-name 3 Gang worker#1 (RTGC Threads)
```

In this case, the name of the thread with ID 3 is considered to be "Gang worder#1 (RTGC Threads)." The TSV viewer uses this information to associate this name with the thread whose ID is 3. The same applies to the call-stack, user-event, and async-begin and async-end entries.

An example of a call stack sequence of entries is within the TSV log is shown in Listing 12-1. The first entry, with a counter value of 0, indicates the beginning of a call stack for the specified thread, along with its executing CPU and priority.

Listing 12-1   A TSV log file call stack entry

```
15358866145372 call-stack 0 17 0 158
15358866145372 call-stack 10 libjvm.so'void
   ObjectMonitor::enter_interruptible(int,Thread*)+0x284
15358866145372 call-stack 11 libjvm.so'void
   ObjectSynchronizer::instance_slow_enter(
   Handle,BasicLock*,int,Thread*)+0x16a
15358866145372 call-stack 12 libjvm.so'void
   ObjectSynchronizer::slow_enter_interruptible(
   Handle,BasicLock*,int,Thread*)+0x37
15358866145372 call-stack 13 libjvm.so'void
   InterpreterRuntime::monitorenter(
   JavaThread*,BasicObjectLock*)+0x63
15358866145372 call-stack 14 java/util/Vector.add
15358866145372 call-stack 15
   synchronizedvector/Main$RealTimeProducer.run
15358866145372 call-stack 16 StubRoutines
15358866145372 call-stack 17 libjvm.so'void
   JavaCalls::call_helper(JavaValue*,methodHandle*,
   JavaCallArguments*,Thread*)+0x1a1
15358866145372 call-stack 18 libjvm.so'void
   os::os_exception_wrapper(void(*(JavaValue*,methodHandle*,
   JavaCallArguments*,Thread*),JavaValue*,
   methodHandle*,JavaCallArguments*,Thread*)+0x14
15358866145372 call-stack 19 libjvm.so'void
   JavaCalls::call(
   JavaValue*,methodHandle,JavaCallArguments*,Thread*)+0x28
15358866145372 call-stack 20 libjvm.so'void
   JavaCalls::call_virtual(JavaValue*,KlassHandle,
   symbolHandle,symbolHandle,JavaCallArguments*,Thread*)+0xa7
15358866145372 call-stack 21 libjvm.so'void
```

continued

```
   JavaCalls::call_virtual(JavaValue*,Handle,
   KlassHandle,symbolHandle,symbolHandle,Thread*)+0x5e
15358866145372 call-stack 22 libjvm.so'void
   thread_entry(JavaThread*,Thread*)+0x12b
15358866145372 call-stack 23 libjvm.so'void
   RealtimeThread::thread_main_inner()+0x154
15358866145372 call-stack 24 libjvm.so'void
   JavaThread::run()+0x163
15358866145372 call-stack 25 libjvm.so'void*_start(void*)+0x4c
15358866145372 call-stack 26 libc.so.1'_thr_setup+0x4e
15358866145372 call-stack 27 libc.so.1'_lwp_start
15358866145372 call-stack-end
```

The top of the stack begins with a counter value of 10, which increases with each step downward into the stack. The `call-stack-end` entry indicates that the entire stack has been output, one entry per line. We'll explore how this is displayed in the TSV viewer in a later section.

An example of a user-event entry, which requires a custom DTrace script where you output your custom event when it occurs, is shown here:

```
15360567766770 user-event 17 1 158 Deadline miss at iteration 27
```

The entry includes a timestamp, the thread's ID, the executing CPU ID, its priority, and then text that describing the event. All text after the thread priority, including spaces, is considered part of the event description. To generate a user event from within your Java RTS application, simply add this line to your code:

```
com.sun.rtsjx.DTraceUserEvent.fire("Your event message here");
```

When this method is invoked, it fires the user-event DTrace probe within Java RTS, and includes the `String` you pass as the parameter. This `String` will be displayed within the TSV viewer, which we'll explore later in the chapter.

Most of the entries in a typical TSV log file note threads as they go on and off a CPU, change priority, or have their names set (see Listing 12-2). Because of the high-resolution timer used to generate the timestamps, the TSV viewer can use this information to give you a precise view of the scheduling of task within your application and the Java RTS VM itself.

Listing 12-2   Part of a typical TSV log file

```
15345981083100 on-cpu 1 1 19
15345983767838 on-cpu 2 0 19
15345983776817 set-name 2 Gang worker#0 (RTGC Threads)
15345983779807 off-cpu 2
15345983829515 change-pri 2 19
```

```
15345983848343 on-cpu 2 0 19
15345983906137 change-pri 2 19
15345983933991 off-cpu 2
15345984034379 set-name 3 Gang worker#1 (RTGC Threads)
15345984036846 on-cpu 3 0 19
15345984042078 off-cpu 3
15345984044714 change-pri 3 19
15345984052962 on-cpu 3 0 19
15345984069828 change-pri 3 19
15345984078782 off-cpu 3
15345984124652 set-name 4 Gang worker#2 (RTGC Threads)
15345984126801 on-cpu 4 0 19
15345984132114 off-cpu 4
15345984134852 change-pri 4 19
15345984142698 on-cpu 4 0 19
15345984158602 change-pri 4 19
15345984167408 off-cpu 4
   .
   .
   .
15376631192323 on-cpu 2 0 59
15376631194759 on-cpu 4 1 59
15376631216326 on-cpu 1 0 100
15376631233901 off-cpu 1
15376631235244 on-cpu 8 1 59
15376631258964 on-cpu 1 1 100
```

With the TSV log file and viewer, you can discover situations where a critical thread may have been delayed in processing an event or was interrupted by another higher-priority thread. Next, you can determine which threads or events were involved, and then work to remedy the situation.

Working with TSV Log Files

After a TSV log file has been generated, you may need to work with it further before using it with the TSV viewer. For instance, you may wish simply to note the size of the log in terms of the number of records recorded, the duration of time the application executed, or the list of threads by name and ID contained within the file. Further, you may wish to search for a single event, or all events that contain a certain string, or split the log file into multiple files due to size. The TSV logfilt utility provides all of this functionality, and we'll discuss how to use it in this section.

For instance, Listing 12-3 shows the logfilt command used to display information about a given TSV log file. In the output, you will see the total number of records recorded within the script, the number of threads for which events were captured, the thread names and IDs, and the duration of time the script ran for.

Listing 12-3   TSV log file information

```
% logfilt -q -l log1112.jrt3
Number of records     : 3862
Filtered out records : 3862
First timestamp       : 7123329810451
Last timestamp        : 7157462471968
Duration              : 0 h 0 mn 34 s 132 ms 661 us 517 ns
Number of threads     : 19
Threads list          : {19=HighResTimerThread,
                          17=RealtimeServerThread,
                          18=DeadlineMonitoringThread,
                          15=NoHeapRealtimeServerThread,
                          16=RealtimeServerThread,
                          13=WatcherThread,
                          14=NoHeapRealtimeServerThread,
                          11=CompilerThread0,
                          12=LowMemoryDetectorThread,
                          3=Gang worker#1 (RTGC Threads),
                          2=Gang worker#0 (RTGC Threads),
                          1=main,
                          10=Signal Dispatcher,
                          7=Reference Handler,
                          6=VMThread,
                          5=RTGC Thread#0,
                          4=Gang worker#2 (RTGC Threads),
                          9=Surrogate Locker Thread (CMS),
                          8=Finalizer}
```

To search for a particular user-event entry, you can use the logfilt utility with the -s command. For instance, if you triggered a user event within your application whenever a deadline was missed, you can quickly search the TSV log file to determine how many deadlines were missed, as shown here:

```
% logfilt -s "Deadline miss" log1112.jrt3
15376631216326 Deadline miss at iteration 16
15376631258964 Deadline miss at iteration 23
```

Splitting Large Log Files

In many cases, the generated TSV log file may be too large to be reasonably displayed by the TSV viewer. This may be due to the sheer number of threads in your application, the amount of activity while the log is generated, or simply the amount of time the application is executed. Whatever the cause, the remedy is to use logfilt to split the single TSV log file into many smaller log files according to some parameters you specify. It's important to use the `logfilt` utility to do this splitting, as it ensures that needed data is maintained across all the split log files, such as thread names.

You have options for how you split the files; it can be based on timestamps, elapsed time, thread priority, thread names, or some combination. You can even split a TSV log file more than once to get multiple logs files according to the criteria you require. Here are the parameters you can specify:

`-tsbegin <long>`—a timestamp used as the starting point.

`-tsend <long>`—a timestamp used as the ending point.

`-hrbegin <[HH:]MM:SS>`—the starting point as elapsed time (from the beginning of the log). The hour field is optional, although you must always specify minutes and seconds.

`-hrend <[HH:]MM:SS>`—the ending point as elapsed time (from the beginning of the log). The hour field is optional, although you must always specify minutes and seconds.

`-evbegin <string>`—the starting point specified as a user event string.

`-evend <string>`—the ending point specified as a user event string.

`-pmin <int>`—include content only for threads that are at least the specified priority.

`-pmax <int>`—include content only for threads that are less than or equal to the specified priority.

`-select <pattern>`—include content only for the thread(s) whose names match the pattern.

`-exclude <pattern>`—remove all content for the thread(s) whose names match the pattern.

You have a lot of flexibility in how you use these parameters. For instance, you can specify either a starting point or and ending point, or both. By default, `logfilt` sets the starting point as the very beginning of the log file, and the ending point as the end of the file, unless you override the default with specific parameters. However, you cannot mix a time-related starting or ending point with a user event on a single use of the tool; to do that, you will need to run `logfilt` more than once on the sub-files it generates. Let's look at a few examples.

Split Using a Timestamp

Let's assume we know that deadline miss occurs after the timestamp 15346168638502, and since this occurs well after the start of the application run, we can safely remove all records before that time. To do this, execute the following command:

```
% logfilt -tsbegin 15346168638502 log.jrt3 > deadlinemiss.jrt3
```

Of course, you can specify any meaningful, legal, filename ending in .jrt3 to send the output to. Because we didn't specify an ending point, the default (the end of the log file) will be used. We can now either display this new file in the TSV viewer, and further filter out content as needed.

Split Using Elapsed Time

In some cases, you may wish to view only a sample amount of time that an application runs. For instance, perhaps your application is a real-time controller for an assembly line, or other physical device, where the same processing occurs over and over again for a long time. You may wish to limit the records you display in the TSV viewer to just first hour(s), minute(s), or second(s) that your application runs. Whatever the elapsed time period is that makes sense to you and your application can be specified as shown here:

```
% logfilt -hrend 01:00 log.jrt3 > firstminute.jrt3
```

In this case, we've created a file that contains only the records from the first minute's worth of execution. Because we didn't specify a starting point, the very beginning of the log file is used as default.

Split Using Thread Priority

Perhaps you're only interested in how the threads above a certain priority in your application affect one another. To filter out those threads higher than a specific Solaris priority (not an RTSJ priority), use a command such as the following:

```
% logfilt -pmin 129 log.jrt3 > highprithreads.jrt3
```

This statement filters out all but the threads that are set to execute above the default priority of the RTGC in boosted mode. You can use whichever minimum priority makes sense for your application. You can also specify a ceiling priority with the following statement:

```
% logfilt -pmax 129 log.jrt3 > highprithreads.jrt3
```

In this case, you will have filtered out (removed all records for) all threads that execute above the default RTGC boosted mode priority. This, for instance, will show you how the RTGC interacts with only those threads potentially impacted by RTGC.

Split for a Specific Thread

There are cases when you want to view the execution of just one thread, or one set of threads, that match a pattern. For instance, perhaps you've named all of your time-critical threads by type, or you wish to view when just the Java RTS JIT compiler runs, or when the RTGC and its worker threads run. In the first case, assume we have a pool or `RealtimeThread` objects that process incoming messages, and we've named each thread `MessageThread-1`, `MessageThread-2`, and so on. You can use pattern matching to select just those threads with the following command:

```
% logfilt -select "MessageThread-*" log.jrt3 > messagethreads.jrt3
```

You can view just the Java RTS RTGC threads with the following command:

```
% logfilt -select "RTGC*" log.jrt3 > messagethreads.jrt3
```

Or, you can exclude the JIT compiler threads with the following command:

```
% logfilt -exclude "CompilerThread*" log.jrt3 > messagethreads.jrt3
```

Although the `select` and `exclude` commands are mutually exclusive (they cannot be mixed on the command-line), you can specify multiple instances of either `select` or `exclude` commands. For instance, the following creates a log file that contains data for only RTGC and JIT threads:

```
% logfilt -select "RTGC*" -select "CompilerThread*" log.jrt3 >
messagethreads.jrt3
```

Although the example above has consumed two lines, it's actually typed as a one-line command in the shell.

So far we've explored TSV log files, what they contain, and how to filter them into smaller files if needed. Let's take a look at how to generate TSV log files.

Record Your Application's Events

The basic script to be used to record scheduling events within your application is `drecord`, which is located within the `bin` directory of your TSV installation. To use the script, simply call drecord in front of your normal command line to start your application. For instance, to run the elevator simulator we explored in an earlier chapter, the following command was used to start it:

```
/opt/SUNWrtjv/bin/java -jar dist/Elevator.jar Main
```

To run this with the drecord DTrace script to record scheduling events, execute the following command:

/opt/tsv/bin/drecord /opt/SUNWrtjv/bin/java –jar dist/Elevator. jar Main

Now, with this one addition, the application will run in the context of DTrace with the drecord script providing instruction on which events to record, and how to output it to a log file. We chose to place the TSV files in /opt, but you can place the TSV files in any directory you choose.

This script adds the -XX:+PauseAtStartup command-line parameter to your java command. As we discussed earlier in the section on DTrace, this pauses the Java RTS VM after all DTrace probes are ready (a VM internal operation), but *before* your application begins to execute. The drecord script (see Listing 12-4) continuously looks for the presence of the vm.paused.<pid> file (explained earlier), and deletes it to start your application with the DTrace commands.

Listing 12-4   The TSV drecord DTrace script

```
#! /bin/ksh
DTRACE=/usr/sbin/dtrace

script='
:::BEGIN
{
  system("rm vm.paused.%d",$target);
}

sched:::on-cpu
/pid == $target && self->on_cpu == 0/
  {
    printf("%d on-cpu %d %d %d\n",
           timestamp,tid,cpu,curthread->t_pri);
    self->on_cpu = 1;
  }

sched:::off-cpu
/pid == $target && self->on_cpu == 1/
  {
    printf("%d off-cpu %d \n",timestamp,tid);
    self->on_cpu = 0;
  }

sched:::change-pri
/pid == $target/
  {
    printf("%d change-pri %d %d\n",
           timestamp,args[0]->pr_lwpid,args[2]);
  }
```

```
jrts$target:::thread-set-name
{
  printf("%d set-name %d %s\n",
         timestamp,(int)arg0,copyinstr(arg1,arg2));
}

jrts$target:::thread-start
{
  printf("%d set-name %d %s\n",
         timestamp,(int)arg0,copyinstr(arg4,arg5));
}

jrts$target:::user-event
{
    printf("%d user-event %d %d %d %s\n",
           timestamp,tid,cpu,curthread->t_pri,
           copyinstr(arg0,arg1));
}
'

CMD=$1

CMD="$CMD -XX:+PauseAtStartup"

until [[ $# -eq 0 ]];do
   shift
   CMD="$CMD $1"
done

$CMD &

VM_PID=$!
VM_PAUSED_FILE="vm.paused.$VM_PID"

until [[ -a $VM_PAUSED_FILE ]]; do
   sleep 1
done

LOGFILE="log${VM_PID}.jrt3"

$DTRACE -Z -q -b 16m -w -p $VM_PID -n "$script" /
           | sort -n -k 1 >| $LOGFILE
echo "Log generated in file $LOGFILE"
```

In Listing 12-4, the section in bold outlines the portion of the script that waits until the VM has created the vm.paused.<pid> file, which indicates it's ready to execute the application. Just after the bold section, the TSV log file name is generated with the PID of the Java RTS VM process, and the DTrace script is executed. At this point, the `vm.paused.<pid>` file is removed using the BEGIN clause at the top of the file, which causes the VM to execute the application and the script to record the applicable events.

Using Custom Scripts

You can use the provided `crecord` script to specify your own DTrace script to be used, but still take advantage of the code in the `drecord` script to pause the VM at startup, and generate a `.jrt3` log file when the execution is complete. Of course, the events recorded within that log file are according to the entries and formatting within your specified script. For instance, the following generates TSV log file for the elevator controller sample application using the DTrace script, named `myscript`:

```
% crecord myscript /opt/SUNWrtjv/bin/java –jar Elevator.jar Main
```

Note that the resulting log file, although generated by your own DTrace script, must still conform to the accepted TSV log file format we explored earlier. Also, you need to provide the direct path to the custom script if it doesn't reside in the directory that you execute the `crecord` command from.

Custom scripts are useful when you want to capture events specific to your application, to highlight certain events, or to do advanced processing such as the output of stack traces when certain criteria are met. In fact, the `srecord` script is provided to help you with stack trace output in particular. Let's take a look at this file now.

Generating Call Stacks

The TSV script, `srecord`, works as `crecord` does, but it includes post-processing to format the output of the DTrace `jstack()` command. This is used to include and format call stack information within the TSV log file when certain events (specified by the custom script you provide) occur. For instance, including the DTrace code in Listing 12-5 in a custom script will cause call stack data to be output whenever a thread blocks on a shared lock.

Listing 12-5   DTrace script to generate a call stack

```
jrts$target:::monitor-contended-enter
{
    printf("%d call-stack 0 %d %d %d\n",
        timestamp,tid,cpu,curthread->t_pri);
    jstack();
}
```

The code in Listing 12-6 highlights the portion of the `srecord` script that performs the post-processing required to format the `jstack` output.

Listing 12-6   The jstack() post-processing code

```
#! /bin/ksh
TSV_HOME='dirname $0'/..
DTRACE=/usr/sbin/dtrace
CFILT=c++filt
.
.
.

LOGFILE="log${VM_PID}.jrt3"

$DTRACE -Z -q -b 16m -w -p $VM_PID -s $CUSTOM_DSCRIPT /
          >| /tmp/$LOGFILE
echo "Execution completed, post-processing in progress"
if [[ $CFILT_SUPPORTED -eq 1 ]]; then
    cat /tmp/$LOGFILE | $JAVA /
        -jar ${TSV_HOME}/lib/StackNormalizer.jar /
        | ${CFILT} | sort -n -k 1 >| $LOGFILE ;
else
        cat /tmp/$LOGFILE | $JAVA -jar
${TSV_HOME}/lib/StackNormalizer.jar | sort -n -k 1 >| $LOGFILE ;
fi
rm /tmp/$LOGFILE
echo "Log generated in file $LOGFILE"
```

This script requires that the c++filt utility be present on your system. This is used to reverse the C++ name mangling that occurs within classes and methods. It can be found and downloaded with the GNU C++ libraries and binary utilities. You'll need to update the srecord file to include the full path to the c++filt utility (shown in bold in Listing 12-6).

Generating TSV Log Files with Java SE

Although the TSV tool was designed to work with Java RTS, it can be used with an application that executes with Java SE. However, this requires the use of a different script, as the DTrace probes are named differently between the two VMs. TSV includes the hrecord script, to be used in place of drecord, when run with Java SE.

Working with the TSV Viewer

To display any TSV log file in with the TSV viewer, you simply execute the tsv script with the name of the log file as the parameter, such as:

```
/opt/tsv/bin/tsv log12345.jrt3
```

When you do this, you'll see the entire execution of the application, broken out by thread, as showing in Figure 12-7. At the top of the window is the main thread display, where each thread is broken out in timeline fashion. The bottom right of the window is the thread detail section.

When you hover the mouse pointer over a line on the thread timeline, information such as the thread's name, ID, priority, and scheduling class is displayed (see Figure 12-8). The bottom right of the window displays information about the TSV viewer itself, along with other time-related information we'll discuss later.

In the thread timeline section, each thread is displayed within its own line horizontally. A line indicates that the thread was executing at that point in time. Therefore, the broken lines for each thread indicate when each thread was running, or not (i.e. idle or blocked). You may need to scroll up and down in the display to see all of the threads, as only a certain number may be visible on the screen at a time according to your monitor's resolution.

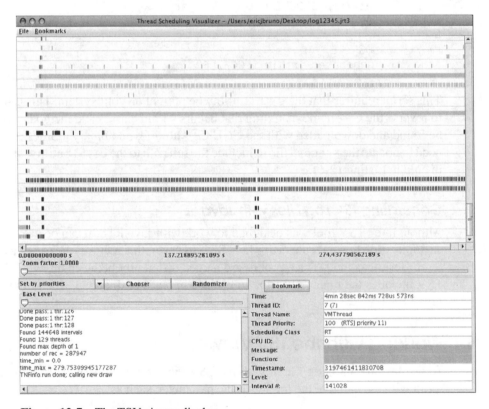

Figure 12-7   The TSV viewer display.

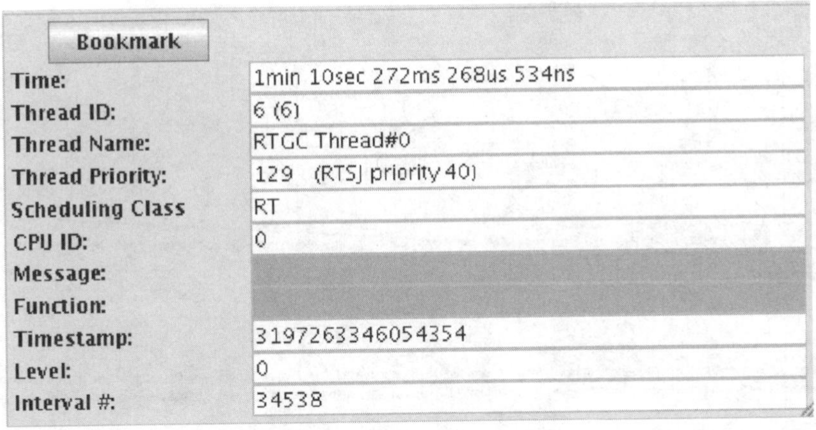

Bookmark	
Time:	1min 10sec 272ms 268us 534ns
Thread ID:	6 (6)
Thread Name:	RTGC Thread#0
Thread Priority:	129 (RTSJ priority 40)
Scheduling Class	RT
CPU ID:	0
Message:	
Function:	
Timestamp:	3197263346054354
Level:	0
Interval #:	34538

Figure 12-8 TSV thread detail section.

Although you cannot see the colors in this book, they are displayed with meaning in the viewer application. Threads are displayed according to a color scheme that summarizes its scheduling—specifically, thread priority. For instance, the following colors have the noted meanings:

Green: non-real-time threads executing within the Solaris Time Sharing, Interactive, or Fair Scheduling class of priorities.

Blue: threads running within the Solaris System class of priorities.

Red: threads running within the Solaris Real-Time class of priorities.

Within each color range, a darker color indicates a higher priority. User events, however, are colored randomly so as not to be confused with threads. Although the default is to color threads according to priority, you can change this by selecting the drop-down list box on the lower left-hand side of the viewer. For instance, you can re-color threads according to the CPU they execute on. This is useful to track time-critical threads that may be impacted as they migrate from one CPU to another.

Bookmarks

You can insert bookmarks at various points of the display simply by left-clicking anywhere on the thread display. For instance, in Figure 12-9, we've clicked on two points in the execution of the application, relatively close to one another. As a result, the TSV viewer will tell you the amount of time that elapsed between those two bookmarks.

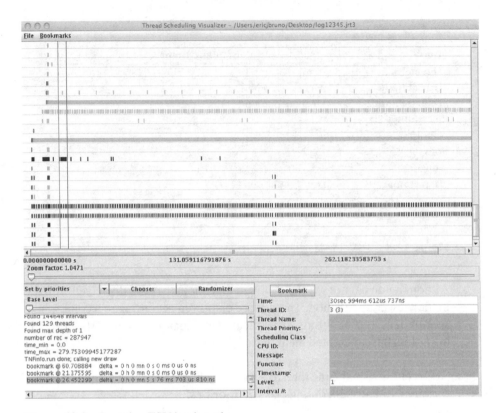

Figure 12-9   Inserting TSV bookmarks.

Looking at the bottom left of the TSV viewer shows that the time delta was 5 seconds, 76 milliseconds, 703 microseconds, and 810 nanoseconds (see the highlighted text). In the computer sense, this is a lot of time. As it stands, it would be very difficult to insert two bookmarks precisely enough to measure very small time intervals. Fortunately, the TSV viewer helps us by allowing us to zoom in, and thereby see more detail over smaller deltas of time.

Zooming In

To zoom into the display and change the elapsed time scale along the X-axis, left-click on any point in the display, drag to another point, left or right, and release the mouse button. The time scale increases in resolution, and you can see more detail for the threads within that period of time (see Figure 12-10). You can repeat this process to zoom in more, or simply use the Zoom Factor slider to increase or decrease the zoom.

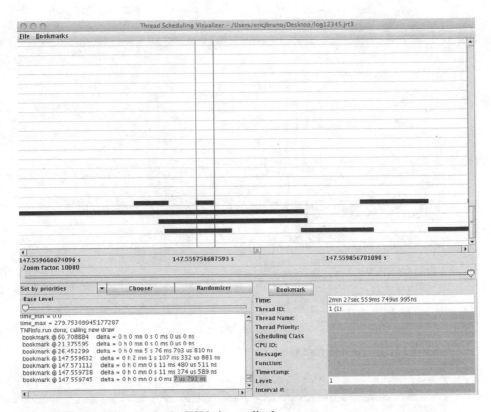

Figure 12-10   Zooming in the TSV viewer display.

In Figure 12-10, the zoom factor has been increased to the maximum. As a result, the time the top-most thread executed within the red and blue bookmarks is measured at around 8 microseconds. This detail was not visible before we zoomed into this portion of the display.

The power of TSV is the ease with which it allows you to study the execution of your application in terms of scheduling. By selectively zooming in and out of sections of the display, you can easily see how different threads interact. For instance, if you notice that a high-priority real-time thread is interrupted while it's executing (see Figure 12-11), you can zoom in and scroll up and down through the thread display to determine which thread may have interrupted it.

In the case shown in Figure 12-11, notice the high-priority thread is interrupted while processing. By setting bookmarks on either side of the interruption, we can then scroll through the display of threads until we match a thread of equal or higher priority that executed within that window of time. Figure 12-12 shows that that JIT compiler thread was elevated to the application thread's priority and executed for a small period of time.

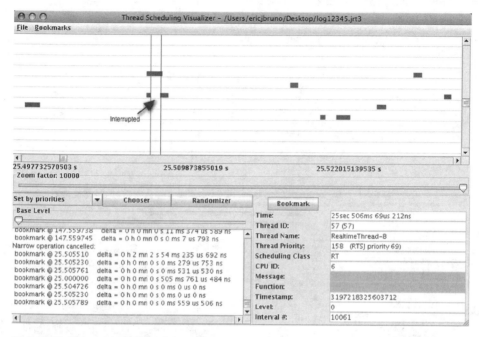

Figure 12-11   An interrupted thread.

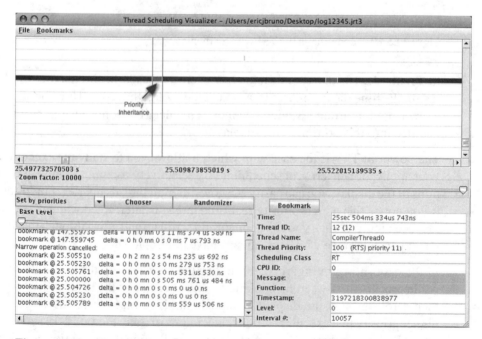

Figure 12-12   Compiler thread priority inheritance.

This is an example of priority inheritance (discussed in Chapter 1), where the JIT compiler locked a section of memory containing the code because it was actively compiling the application thread's class before the application thread began to execute. Once it executed the code for the class that was locked, the priority inheritance protocol boosted the compiler thread (the one that owned the lock at that time) so that it could complete its work and release the lock. The TSV viewer allows you see this type of detail in real-time thread scheduling.

User Events

User events are shown with the thread that generated them, at the time they were generated. Within the TSV viewer, this will appear as small boxes above the thread's boxes within the applicable thread's row within the window (see Figure 12-13).

Information about the user event is displayed within the thread detail view in the bottom right of the window. Hovering the mouse over each user event entry causes the user event message to display there.

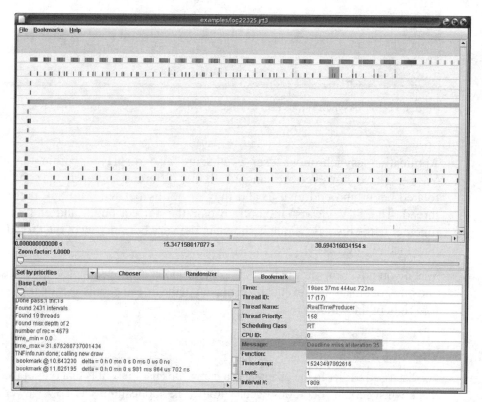

Figure 12-13   User events within the TSV display.

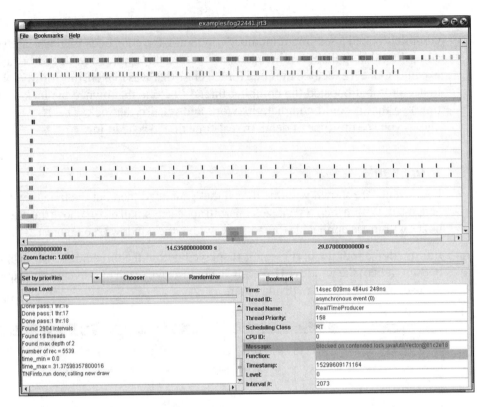

Figure 12-14   Asynchronous user events.

Application asynchronous user events are also displayed within the TSV Viewer. These, however, are handled slightly differently, as each one contains a related begin and end clause, and they're not associated with any particular thread. The TSV viewer attempts to pair the correct begin and end clauses together in the display, which is shown in the very bottom row of the thread display (see Figure 12-14).

When you hover the mouse over an asynchronous user event entry, the message and other details for the event are displayed in the thread details section in the bottom right of the window.

The Call Stack

As discussed earlier in the chapter, you can write custom scripts that output the call stack when certain conditions occur within your application. The TSV viewer displays a call stack with a series of small lines vertically stacked above the thread in

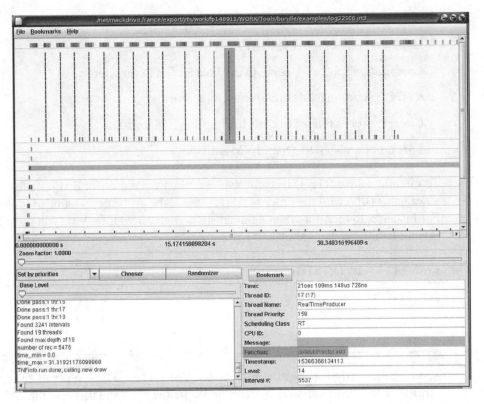

Figure 12-15 The call stack displayed

the thread display section when the associated condition occurs to cause the stack to be output (see Figure 12-15). Each vertical line corresponds to an entry on the stack.

Hovering over each vertical line shows the method at that stack position within the thread detail section at the bottom right of the window.

Java RTS DTrace Probes

The Java RTS virtual machine contains a DTrace provider named *jrts*, which allows you to monitor the internal activities of the VM. This includes thread scheduling, memory-related operations, compiler operations, the execution of the RTGC, and so on. The available probe types are:

***Schedulables*:** probes common to Schedulable objects (RTTs, NHRTs, and AEHs).

***Memory*:** probes related to RTSJ memory area operations.

Threads: probes related to JLTs, RTTs, and NHRTs.

Handlers: probes specific to AEH.

Compilation: probes specific to the Java RTS JIT compiler.

RTGC: probes related to real-time GC activity.

Classes: probes related to class loading and initialization.

VM: probes related to general VM activities.

To monitor a Java RTS DTrace probe, you must write a script that uses the provider name (jrts) with the process ID (PID), and the probe point name to monitor. For instance, to monitor when a thread starts in the Java RTS VM, you must add DTrace handler code as shown in Listing 12-7.

Listing 12-7   Java RTS DTrace probe

```
jrts1112::thread-start
{
...
}
```

To avoid the need to change the hard-coded VM PID each time you run a DTrace script, you can use a variable to locate and store the PID, and then use throughout your script, as shown in Listing 12-8.

Listing 12-8   Handling the PID in DTrace scripts

```
/*
 * Usage:
 *     <script> -p JAVA_PID
 */

:::BEGIN
{
  system("rm vm.paused.%d", $target);
}

jrts$target:::priority-change
/ arg1 == 1 /
{
  printf("%d : Thread %d is changing thread %d's priority to %d\n",
  timestamp,curthread->t_tid,arg0,arg2);
}
...
```

As described in the section on TSV, the Java -XX:+PauseAtStartup command-line option is used to ensure the VM is started, with probe points ready, before the DTrace script begins execution. The existence of a file named vm.paused.<pid> indicates the VM is ready, at which point the script begins. The first step is to remove this file (in the ::BEGIN section of the script) which causes the VM to begin execution of the application.

Let's take a look at all of the probe points available, by category. Much of this is taken from the Java RTS documentation set; specifically the *Sun Java Real-Time System DTrace Provider* document, available online at http://java.sun.com/javase/technologies/realtime.

DTrace Probes for Schedulables

The goal of the Schedulable probes is to provide information about thread priority changes, and thread blocking on lock contention. The following probes are available:

priority-change—This probe is triggered by an explicit priority change to an RTSJ Schedulable. The type of Schedulable (RTT, NHRT, or AEH) whose priority is modified is specified in args[1]. A value of 1 indicates RTT or NHRT, while a value of 2 indicates an AEH. If the modification applies to a thread, the thread ID is stored in args[0]. For a handler, args[0] contains the opaque ID for this handler. The requested new priority is provided in args[2].

priority-boost—This probe fires when the priority of the thread, args[0], is boosted to the priority, args[1], because of a contention on the lock, args[2]. Every time a thread's priority changes to a priority other than its default priority, perhaps due to priority inheritance, this probe fires.

priority-unboost—This probe fires when thread args[0] has its priority changed back to its default priority (args[1]) after boosting. There can be several boosts for a thread before an unboost, if there is a change in the boosting cause.

monitor-contended-enter—This probe fires when the current thread *attempts* to enter a contended monitor. An opaque ID identifying the monitor is stored in args[0]. The monitor's class name is provided in args[1], and the name's length in args[2]. If the monitor is not associated with a Java object, the args[1] argument is null and the args[2] argument is zero.

monitor-contended-entered—This probe fires when the current thread successfully enters the contended monitor identified by args[0]. The monitor's class name is provided in args[1], and the name's length in args[2]. If the monitor is not associated with a Java object, the args[1] argument is `null` and the args[2] argument is zero.

`monitor-contended-exit`—This probe fires when the current thread exits the contended monitor identified by the args[0] argument. The monitor's class name is provided in args[1], and the name's length in args[2]. If the monitor is not associated with a Java object, the args[1] argument is `null` and the args[2] argument is zero.

`monitor-wait`—This probe fires when the current thread calls `wait` on the monitor identified by args[0]. The monitor's class name is provided in args[1], and the name's length in args[2]. If the monitor is not associated with a Java object, the args[1] argument is NULL and the args[2] argument is zero. Arguments args[3] and args[4] provide the high 32-bits and low 32-bits of a 64-bit signed integer containing the wake-up time for the `wait` call.

`monitor-waited`—This probe fires when the current thread completes its call to `wait` on the monitor identified by args[0]. When this probe fires, the current thread owns the monitor identified by args[0] and is ready to resume its execution. The monitor's class name is provided in args[1], and the name's length in args[2]. If the monitor is not associated with a Java object, the args[1] is `null` and args[2] is zero.

`monitor-notify`—This probe fires when the current thread calls `notify` on the monitor identified by args[0] and at least one thread is waiting on this monitor. The monitor's class name is provided in args[1], and the name's length in args[2]. If the monitor is not associated with a Java object, the args[1] is NULL and args[2] is zero.

`monitor-notifyAll`—This probe fires when the current thread calls `notifyAll` on the monitor identified by args[0] and at least one thread is waiting on this monitor. The monitor's class name is provided in args[1], and the name's length in args[2]. If the monitor is not associated with a Java object, the args[1] is `null` and args[2] is zero.

DTrace Probes for Memory

The goal of the memory-related probes is to provide insight into the usage of the memory areas defined by the RTSJ, such as immortal memory and scoped memory areas. The following probes are available:

`memarea-change`—This probe is triggered every time a thread changes its current allocation context. The ID of the new allocation context is provided in args[0], and its type is specified in args[1]. The possible values for the memory type are in Table 12-2.

`memarea-enter`—This probe tracks each entry to a memory area. The ID of the memory area being entered is stored in args[0], and its type is specified in args[1] (see Table 12-2).

`memarea-exit`—This probe tracks each exit from a memory area. The ID of the memory area being exited is stored in args[0], and its type is specified in args[1] (see Table 12-2).

`scopedmem-creation`—This probe is fired when a new instance of Scoped-MemoryArea is created. An opaque ID identifying the new memory area is stored in args[0]. The name of the class used to create the ScopedMemory-Area instance is provided in args[1] and the name's length in args[2]. Arguments args[3] and args[4] are the high 32-bits and low 32-bits of a 64-bit signed integer containing the maximum size requested by the application in the ScopedMemory constructor. Arguments args[5] and args[6] are the high 32-bits and low 32-bits of a 64-bit signed integer containing the real size, in bytes, allocated from the backing store for this scoped memory area.

`scopedmem-first-enter`—This probe tracks the first enter to a scoped memory area. The first time a particular memory area is entered, this probe is triggered before `memarea-enter`. The ID of the memory area being entered is stored in args[0]. Because of the introduction of the "fireable" status, this probe may be fired even if no code actually enters the scope.

`scopedmem-last-exit`—This probes tracks the last exit from a scoped memory area. The ID of the memory area being exited is stored in args[0]. The amount of bytes in use in the scope before it was cleaned is specified in args[1]. The total memory in bytes available in the scope is specified in args[2].

Table 12-2   Memory area types

Value	Memory Area Type
1	Heap
2	Immortal Memory
3	Scoped Memory

On an exit, this probe is triggered after `memarea-exit`. Because of the introduction of the "fireable" status, this probe may be fired even if no code actually exits the scope.

`scopedmem-finalization`—This probe is triggered every time the VM detects that it has to execute finalizers before clearing a scoped memory area. The ID of the applicable scoped memory area is stored in args[0].

`immortal-alloc`—This probe is fired when immortal memory is allocated. The number of requested bytes is stored in args[0], and the actual number of bytes used after completion of the request is stored in args[1]. The address of the allocated object is available in args[2], which will be `null` if the allocation failed. Note: This probe is fired reliably only if the command-line option

`-XX:+RTSJEnableImmortalAllocationProbe` is set. If it's not set, the probe will not fire in many cases as the allocations are optimized for performance. Since this option is activated by default, it may lead to throughput loss during the startup phase.

Several of the probes indicate the memory area type as an argument. The values in Table 12-2 indicate the memory area type each probe is applicable to.

DTrace Probes for Threads

The DTrace probles for Threads are specific to JLT, RTT, and NHRT instances, and track events such as thread starts and stops, periodic execution, deadline misses, yields, and interruptions. The following probes are available:

`thread-set-name`—This probes fires when the current thread sets the name of the thread whose ID is in args[0]. The new name is available in args[1], and its length in args[2]. If the renamed thread is not alive, args[0] is zero. This probe also fires when a thread creates a system (for internal VM work) or a server thread (i.e., for AEH).

`thread-start`—This probe fires when the `start` method is invoked on a thread. The ID of the thread being started is available in args[0], and the thread type is specified in args[1]. The possible values for the args[1] are in Table 12-3. The thread's class name is provided in args[2], and its length in args[3]. The thread's name is provided in args[4], and its length in args[5].

`thread-begin`—This probe is fired just before a thread's run method begins to execute. A native thread fires this probe at the end of a successful call to the JNI

Table 12-3 Thread types

Value	Thread Type
-1	java.lang.Thread
1	javax.realtime.RealtimeThread
0	javax.realtime.NoHeapRealtimeThread

method `AttachCurrentThread`. A native thread creating a VM will also fire this probe at the end of the JNI method `JNI_CreateJavaVM`.

thread-end—This probe is fired after the completion of a thread's run method and, if it had an uncaught exception, the completion of the `uncaughtException` method of its `UncaughtExceptionHandler`. A native thread fires this probe when it calls the JNI method `DetachCurrentThread`.

thread-period-change—This probe is triggered when a thread's period is modified (not when the change takes effect). The thread's ID is stored in args[0]. Arguments args[1] and args[2] are the high 32-bits and low 32-bits of a 64-bit signed integer containing the value of the new period. This probe also fires when the thread's release policy is changed from periodic to aperiodic. In this case, arguments args[1] and args[2] are set to zero.

thread-deschedule-periodic—This probe fires when `deschedulePeriodic` is called on the thread identified by args[0]. If the `deschedulePeriodic` method is invoked on a non-periodic thread or a thread that's not alive, the method has no effect and the probe doesn't fire.

thread-schedule-periodic—This probe fires when `schedulePeriodic` is performed on the thread identified by args[0]. If the `schedulePeriodic` method is invoked on a non-periodic thread or a thread that's not alive, the method has no effect and the probe does not fire.

thread-aie-fired—This probe fires when an asynchronously interrupted exception (AIE) is generated. The ID of the thread that will receive the AIE is stored in args[0]. If the thread is not alive then args[0] will be zero.

thread-aie-delivered—This probe fires when a pending AIE is being propagated because the current thread is executing AI-enabled code.

thread-aie-cleared—This probe fires when an AIE is cleared by the current thread.

thread-wfnp-enter—This probe is fired when a thread invokes the `waitFor`
`NextPeriod` or `waitForNextPeriodInterruptible` method. If `waitForNext`
`Period` is invoked, args[0] is `false`; otherwise, it is `true`.

thread-wfnp-exit—This probe is fired when a thread returns from a `wait-`
`ForNextPeriod` call. The value returned by the `waitForNextPeriod` method is
available in args[0].

thread-deadline-miss—This probe fires when a thread's deadline miss
causes the release of its deadline miss handler. The ID of the handler to be
released is available in args[0].

thread-sleep-begin—This probe is fired at the beginning of the `Thread.`
`sleep` and `RealtimeThread.sleep` methods, before going to sleep.

thread-sleep-end—This probe is fired at the end of the `Thread.sleep` and
`RealtimeThread.sleep` methods, after the completion of the `sleep`.

thread-yield—This probe is fired when a thread performs a call to `Thread.`
`yield`.

DTrace Probes for AsyncEventHandlers

The DTrace probes for AEHs are meant to provide exposure to all phases of
events, when they're fired, how they're handled, and how server threads are pooled
and used internally to execute them. The following probes are available:

event-fire—This probe fires when the event identified by the args[0] is fired.

handler-creation—This probe fires after the creation of an AEH instance to
provide useful information about this handler. An opaque ID for this handler is
provided in args[0]. The class name of the handler is available in args[1], and its
length in args[2]. If the handler is allowed to access the heap, args[3] is false,
otherwise it is true.

handler-destruction—This probe fires just before the handler identified
in args[0] is collected. At this point, the handler can no longer be released or
executed.

handler-release-accepted—This probe fires when the release of a handler
has been accepted, perhaps due to an event, a timer, or a deadline miss. The ID
of the handler being released is specified in args[0]. Arguments args[1] and
args[2] are the high 32-bits and low 32-bits of a 64-bit signed integer containing
the time when the release request occurred, while arguments args[3] and args[4]
are the high 32-bits and low 32-bits of a 64-bit signed integer containing the

time the handler will actually be released. The real release time and the effective release time are different when the release of the handler has been delayed because of Minimum Interarrival Time (MIT) policy enforcement. In the other cases, the values are equal.

`handler-release-replace`—This probe fires when the release of a handler will replace a previously accepted release in the pending release queue. The ID of the handler being released is specified in args[0]. Arguments args[1] and args[2] are the high 32-bits and low 32-bits of a 64-bit signed integer containing the time when the release request occurred, while arguments args[3] and args[4] are the high 32-bits and low 32-bits of a 64-bit signed integer containing the time the handler will actually be released. The real release time and the effective release time are different when the release of the handler has been delayed because of Minimum Interarrival Time (MIT) policy enforcement. In other cases, the values are equal.

`handler-release-rejected`—This probe fires when the release of a handler has been refused. The ID of the handler being rejected is specified in args[0]. Arguments args[1] and args[2] are the high 32-bits and low 32-bits of a 64-bit signed integer containing the time of the release being rejected. The release policy being considered for this release is specified in args[3]. The possible values for args[3] are shown in Table 12-4.

Table 12-4 AEH release values

Value	Release Policy
1	Minimum interarrival time violation with ignore policy
2	Minimum interarrival time violation with except policy
3	Minimum interarrival time violation with replace policy
4	Minimum interarrival time violation with save policy
5	Arrival queue overflow with ignore policy
6	Arrival queue overflow with except policy
7	Arrival queue overflow with replace policy
8	Arrival queue overflow with save policy

handler-release-ignored—This probe fires when the release of a handler has been ignored. The ID of the handler being ignored is specified in args[0]. Arguments args[1] and args[2] are the high 32-bits and low 32-bits of a 64-bit signed integer containing the time of the release being ignored. The release policy being considered for this release is specified in args[3] (see Table 12-4).

server-thread-binding—This probe fires when a server thread is bound to the handler identified by args[1]. The thread ID of the server thread being bound is available in args[0]. Server threads executing a bound AEH fire this probe only once (when the handler is created).

server-thread-unbinding—This probe fires when a server thread (the current thread) unbinds itself from the handler identified by args[0]. Server threads executing a bound AEHfire this probe only once (when the handler is destroyed).

server-thread-creation—This probe fires when a new server thread is created, whose ID is available in args[0]. If the server thread is an instance of NoHeapRealtimeThread, args[1] is true; otherwise, it is false. This probe does not fire if the thread is intended to be associated with a bound AEH.

server-thread-destruction—This probe fires when a server thread (the current thread) is destroyed. If the server thread is an instance of NoHeapRealtimeThread, args[0] is true; otherwise, it is false. This probe does not fire if the thread is intended to be associated with a bound AEH.

server-thread-wakeup—This probe fires when the server thread with the thread ID args[0] wakes up. The priority at which this server thread has been awakened is specified in args[1]. If the server thread is a bound server thread, args[1] is zero.

handler-start—This probe fires when a server thread starts the execution of the main loop of the handler logic (not the handleAsyncEvent method, but an outer loop that tracks the fire count and any needed delay due to MIT violation). The handler ID is available in args[0].

handler-end—This probe fires when a server thread ends the execution of the main loop of the handler logic (not the handleAsyncEvent method, but an outer loop that tracks the fire count and any needed delay due to MIT violation). The handler ID is available in args[0].

handler-deadline-miss—This probe fires when a handler's deadline miss causes the release of its deadline miss handler. The handler ID of the handler to be released is specified in args[0].

When an AEH release is replaced or rejected, Table 12-4 outlines the values that indicate the reason.

DTrace Probes for Compilation

The compiler-related DTrace probes give you insight into the workings of the JIT compiler as it compiles classes and methods, and patches code due to late binding. The following probes are available:

`method-compile-begin`—This probe is triggered when the method compilation begins. Arguments args[0] and args[1] provide the class name and its length. Arguments args[2] and args[3] provide the method name and its length. Arguments args[4] and args[5] provide the signature its length. And argument args[6] indicates for which thread type this method will be compiled (see Table 12-3).

`method-compile-end`—This probe is triggered when method compilation ends. Arguments args[0] and args[1] provide the class name and its length. Arguments args[2] and args[3] provide the method name and its length. Arguments args[4] and args[5] provide the signature its length. Argument args[6] is set to `true` if the compilation was successful; otherwise, `false`. Argument args[7] indicates for which thread type this method was compiled (see Table 12-3).

`compiler-patching-klass`—This probe is triggered on runtime resolution of a class reference in compiled code. Arguments args[0] and args[1] provide the class name and the class name's length in which the symbol is unresolved. Arguments args[2] and args[3] provide the method name and the method name's length in which the symbol is unresolved. Arguments args[4] and args[5] provide the signature and the signature's length in which the symbol is unresolved. Argument args[6] provides the bytecode index where the symbol is unresolved in the method. Arguments args[7] and args[8] provide the name and the name's length of the resolved class. And argument args[9] is the type of the thread that triggered the resolution (see Table 12-3).

`compiler-patching-tablecall`—This probe is triggered on runtime resolution of a virtual/interface method call in compiled code. Arguments args[0] and args[1] provide the class name and the class name's length in which the symbol is unresolved. Arguments args[2] and args[3] provide the method name and the method name's length in which the symbol is unresolved. Arguments args[4] and args[5] provide the signature and the signature's length in which the symbol is unresolved. Argument args[6] provides the bytecode index where the symbol is unresolved in the method. Arguments args[7] and args[8] provide the class name and the class name's length of the resolved method. Arguments args[9] and args[10] provide the method name and the method name's length of the resolved method. Arguments args[11] and args[12] provide the signature and the signature's length of the resolved method. And argument args[13] is the type of the thread that triggered the resolution (see Table 12-3).

`compiler-patching-directcall`—This probe is triggered on runtime resolution of a direct method call in compiled code. Arguments args[0] and args[1] provide the class name and the class name's length in which the symbol is unresolved. Arguments args[2] and args[3] provide the method name and the method name's length in which the symbol is unresolved. Arguments args[4] and args[5] provide the signature and the signature's length in which the symbol is unresolved. Argument args[6] provides the bytecode index where the symbol is unresolved in the method. Arguments args[7] and args[8] provide the class name and the class name's length of the resolved method. Arguments args[9] and args[10] provide the method name and the method name's length of the resolved method. Arguments args[11] and args[12] provide the signature and the signature's length of the resolved method. And argument args[13] is the type of the thread that triggered the resolution (see Table 12-3).

DTrace Probes for RTGC

The following DTrace probes provide insight into the workings of the Java RTS real-time garbage collector (RTGC):

`rtgc-cycle-begin`—This probe fires when the RTGC starts a collection cycle.

`rtgc-cycle-end`—This probe fires when the RTGC ends a collection cycle.

`rtgc-change-priority`—This probe fires when the RTGC changes its priority. The new priority is provided in args[0].

`rtgc-worker-thread-start`—A RTGC worker thread fires this probe when it starts executing job args[0]. For the current GC cycle, the thread executing job 0 is called the Pacing Thread and the thread executing job 1 is called the Coordinator Thread. These two threads are used by the RTGC for internal purposes but are not part of the set of worker threads configured by the `RTGCNormal-Workers` and `RTGCBoostedWorkers` options.

`rtgc-worker-thread-stop`—A RTGC worker thread fires this probe when it completes the execution of job args[0].

`rtgc-policy-stats`—This probe fires at the end of each RTGC cycle and provides a number of counters related to the memory status during this cycle, as well as the parameters the RTGC will use for its next cycle. Argument args[0] provides the RTGC priority. Argument args[1] provides the `end_free_size` counter. Argument args[2] provides the `min_remaining_memory` counter. Argument args[3] provides the `mode_margin` counter. Argument args[4] provides the `critical_limit` counter. Argument args[5] provides the `normal_limit` counter. Argument args[6] provides the `RTGCCritical ReservedBytes` counter.

`rtgc-alloc-stats`—This probe fires at the end of each RTGC cycle and provides a detailed status of allocations that occurred during this cycle. The status is provided through an user structure (see Listing 12-9) pointed by args[0] with its size specified in args[1]. This structure may differ between releases of Java RTS.

`rtheap-tlab-alloc`—This probe fires every time a thread gets a new TLAB in the heap. The size of the allocated TLAB is provided in args[0].

`rtheap-mem-alloc`—This probe fires every time a thread successfully allocates memory in the heap without using the TLAB mechanism. The amount of memory allocated is provided in args[0].

`rtheap-mem-alloc-failure`—This probe fires every time a thread fails while trying to allocate memory in the heap without using the TLAB mechanism. The amount of memory the thread tried to allocate is provided in args[0].

`rtheap-split-alloc`—This probe fires every time a thread successfully allocates memory for a split object in the heap without using the TLAB mechanism. The amount of memory allocated is specified in args[0]. An opaque identifier of the split object being allocated is provided in args[1]. Because split objects are allocated in several pieces, this probe will fire several times for the same object.

`rtheap-split-alloc-failure`—This probe fires every time a thread fails while trying to allocate memory for a split object in the heap without using the TLAB mechanism. The amount of memory the thread tried to allocate is specified in args[0]. An opaque identifier of the split object being allocated is provided in args[1]. When such a failure occurs, all the previously allocated memory for this split object is freed.

`rtheap-total-alloc-quantum1`—This probe fires every time the total amount of memory allocated in the heap reaches a value which is a multiple of *quantum1*, which is set to 128KB by default. The current total amount of memory allocated in the heap is provided in args[0].

`rtheap-total-alloc-quantum2`—This probe fires every time the total amount of memory allocated in the heap reaches a value which is a multiple of *quantum2*, which is set to 1MB by default. The current total amount of memory allocated in the real-time heap is provided in args[0].

`rtheap-important-alloc-quantum1`—This probe fires every time the total amount of memory allocated in the heap by important threads reaches a value which is a multiple of quantum1 (128KB). The current total amount of memory allocated in the real-time heap by important threads is provided in args[0].

rtheap-important-alloc-quantum2—This probe fires every time the total amount of memory allocated in the heap by important threads reaches a value which is a multiple of quantum2 (1MB). The current total amount of memory allocated in the real-time heap by important threads is provided in args[0].

rtheap-critical-alloc-quantum1—This probe fires every time the total amount of memory allocated in the heap by critical threads reaches a value which is a multiple of quantum1 (128KB). The current total amount of memory allocated in the real-time heap by critical threads is provided in args[0].

rtheap-critical-alloc-quantum2—This probe fires every time the total amount of memory allocated in the heap by critical threads reaches a value which is a multiple of quantum2 (1MB). The current total amount of memory allocated in the real-time heap by critical threads is provided in args[0].

Listing 12-9   The RTGC Allocation Stats Structure

```
struct rtgc_alloc_stats {
// allocations by all threads in normal mode since VM startup:
      size_t normal_total;       // total for all GC runs
      size_t normal_worst;       // worst GC run
      size_t normal_average;     // average for all the GC runs
// allocations by all threads in boosted mode since VM startup:
      size_t boosted_total;      // total for all GC runs
      size_t boosted_worst;      // worst GC run
      size_t boosted_average;    // average for all the GC runs
// allocations by critical threads during this GC run:
      size_t critical_threads_cycle;  // total in all modes
      size_t critical_threads_in_deterministic;
                                 // in deterministic mode only
// long-term stats for RTGCCriticalReservedBytes:
      size_t critical_threads_worst;
            // worst case in deterministic mode since VM startup
      size_t reserved_field; // reserved for future use
      size_t critical_threads_total;
            // total allocations for critical threads
};
```

DTrace Probes for Class Loading

The following DTrace probes provide insight into which classes are loaded by which threads, how they are initialized, and which threads perform that initialization [Lindholm99]:

class-loaded—This probe fires when a thread loads a new class. Argument args[0] gives the name of the class being loaded, and args[1] its length.

Argument args[2] is an opaque ID for the class loader used to load the class. Argument args[4] is the type of the thread performing the class loading. Argument args[3] is undefined.

class-initialization-required—This probe fires when a class needs to be initialized, and the current thread proceeds to start that initialization. It comes before step 1 of the initialization process. Argument args[0] provides the name of the class being initialized, and args[1] contains the string length. Argument args[2] is an opaque ID for the class loader used to load the class. Argument args[3] is the current thread type (see Table 12-3).

class-initialization-recursive—This probe fires when a thread that needs to initialize a class discovers that it is already in the process of initializing that class. It corresponds to step 3 of the initialization process. Argument args[0] gives the name of the class being initialized and args[1] the class name's length. args[2] is an opaque ID for the class loader used to load the class. Argument args[3] is the current thread type (see Table 12-3). Argument args[4] is always `false`.

class-initialization-concurrent—This probe fires when the current thread discovers that another thread concurrently completed the initialization of the given class. It corresponds to step 4 of the initialization process. Argument args[0] gives the name of the class being initialized and args[1] the class name's length. Argument args[2] is an opaque ID for the class loader used to load the class. Argument args[3] is the current thread type (see Table 12-3). Argument args[4] is `true` if the thread had to wait at the beginning of the initialization process, otherwise `false`.

class-initialization-erroneous—This probe fires when the current thread discovers that the given class has already been marked as being in the "erroneous" state and cannot be initialized. It corresponds to step 5 of the initialization process. Argument args[0] gives the name of the class being initialized and args[1] the class name's length. Argument args[2] is an opaque ID for the class loader used to load the class. Argument args[3] is current thread type (see Table 12-3). Argument args[4] is `true` if the thread had to wait at the beginning of the initialization process, otherwise `false`.

class-initialization-super-failed—This probe fires when the current thread encounters an error trying to initialize the superclass of the given class. It corresponds to step 7 of the initialization process. Note the initialization attempt for the superclass would also have its own probe firings, with more information. Argument args[0] gives the name of the class being initialized and args[1] the class name's length. Argument args[2] is an opaque ID for the class loader used to load the class. Argument args[3] is current thread type (see Table 12-3).

Argument args[4] is `true` if the thread had to wait at the beginning of the initialization process, otherwise `false`.

`class-initialization-clinit`—This probe fires when the current thread commences execution of the `<clinit>` method of the given class. It corresponds to step 8 of the initialization process. Argument args[0] gives the name of the class being initialized and args[1] the class name's length. Argument args[2] is an opaque ID for the class loader used to load the class Argument args[3] is current thread type (see Table 12-3). Argument args[4] is `true` if the thread had to wait at the beginning of the initialization process, otherwise `false`.

`class-initialization-error`—This probe fires when the execution of `<clinit>` results in an exception being thrown (in response to which the class is marked as being in the "erroneous" state). It corresponds to steps 10 and 11 of the initialization process. args[0] gives the name of the class being initialized and args[1] the class name's length. Args[2] is an opaque ID for the class loader used to load the class. Argument args[3] is current thread type (see Table 12-3). Argument args[4] is `true` if the thread had to wait at the beginning of the initialization process, otherwise `false`.

`class-initialization-end`—This probe fires after successful execution of the `<clinit>` method and the class has been marked as initialized. It corresponds to step 9 of the initialization process. Argument args[0] gives the name of the class being initialized and args[1] the class name's length. Argument args[2] is an opaque ID for the class loader used to load the class. Argument args[3] is current thread type (see Table 12-3). Argument args[4] is `true` if the thread had to wait at the beginning of the initialization process, otherwise `false`.

DTrace Probes for VM Activity

The following DTrace probes expose events that occur within the VM that have potentially global impact:

`vm-creation-begin`—This probe fires at the beginning of the Java Virtual Machine loading and initialization.

`vm-creation-end`—This probe fires when the loading and the initialization of the Java Virtual Machine have successfully completed.

`safepoint-begin`—This probe fires at the beginning of a global safepoint performed by the VM.

`safepoint-end`—This probe fires at the end of a global safepoint performed by the VM.

Table 12-5   VM operation execution mode

Value	Mode	Requesting thread is...	VM Operation under safepoint?
0	safepoint	Blocked	Yes
1	no_safepoint	Blocked	No
2	concurrent	Not blocked	No
3	async_safepoint	Not blocked	Yes

vm-operation-request—This probe fires when a VM operation is added to the list of requested VM operations. Argument args[0] gives the name of the VM operation being added, and args[1] provides the length of this name. Argument args[2] describes the execution mode of this VM operation—possible values are shown in Table 12-5. Argument args[3] is `true` if this VM operation is to be executed before non-urgent pending VM operations, otherwise `false`. In case of a nested VM operation, this probe is not fired.

vm-operation-begin—This probe fires at the beginning of the execution of a VM operation by the VM thread. Argument args[0] gives the name of the VM operation being executed, and args[1] provides the length of this name. Argument args[2] describes the execution mode of this VM operation (see Table 12-5). Argument args[3] is `true` if this VM operation is to be executed before non-urgent pending VM operations, otherwise `false`.

vm-operation-end—This probe fires when the VM thread completes the execution of a VM operation. Argument args[0] gives the name of the VM operation that has been executed, and args[1] provides the length of this name. Argument args[2] describes the execution mode of this VM operation (see Table 12-5). Argument args[3] is `true` if this VM operation is to be executed before non-urgent pending VM operations, otherwise `false`.

The possible values of execution mode of the VM are shown in Table 12-5.

Application-Specific DTrace Probes

Via the Java RTS-specific `com.sun.rtsjx.DTraceUserEvents` class, you can fire your own `user-event` DTrace probes with application-specific text that you provide. This probe takes a `String` as args[0] as the message to be output, and that `String`'s length as an integer in args[1].

Bibliography

[Baker78] H. G. Baker, *List Processing in Real Time on a Serial Computer*, Communications of the ACM, Vol. 21, No.4, April, 1978.

[Bollella00] Bollella, Greg, et al., *The Real-Time Specification for Java*, Addison-Wesley Longman, January 2000.

[Brooks84] R. A. Brooks, *Trading Data Space for Reduced Time and Code Space in Real-Time Garbage Collection on Stock Hardware*, in Proceedings of the 1984 Symposium on Lisp and Functional Programming, Austin, Texas, August, 1984.

[Buttazzo05] Buttazzo, Georgia C., *Hard Real-Time Computing Systems*. Springer, 2005.

[Carnahan99] Carnahan, Lisa, and Ruark, Marcus, *Requirements for Real-Time Extensions for the Java Platform*, National Institute of Standards and Technology, September 1999 (Available at http://www.itl.nist.gov/div897/ctg/real-time/rtj-final-draft.pdf.)

[Detlefs04] Detlefs, et al., *Garbage-First Garbage Collection*, Sun Microsystems Research Laboratories, 2004 (Available at http://research.sun.com/jtech/pubs/04-g1-paper-ismm.pdf.)

[Henriksson98] Henriksson, Roger, *Scheduling Garbage Collection in Embedded Systems*, PhD thesis, Lund University, July 1998 (Available at http://www.cs.lth.se/home/Roger_Henriksson/thesis.html.)

[Jones08] M. Tim Jones, *Anatomy of Real-Time Linux Architectures*, IBM developerWorks, April 15, 2008 (Available at http://www.ibm.com/developerworks/linux/library/l-real-time-linux/index.html?S_TACT=105AGX03&S_CMP=ART.)

[Klein93] Klein, Mark, et al., *A Practitioner's Guide to Real-Time Analysis*. Kluwer Academic Publishers, 1993.

[Layland73] Liu, C. L. and Layland, James W., *Scheduling Algorithms for Multiprogramming in a Hard Real-Time Environment*. Journal of the ACM, 1973 (Available at http://portal.acm.org/citation.cfm?id=321743.)

[Lindholm99] Lindholm, Tim, and Yellin, Frank, *Java Virtual Machine Specification, 2nd Edition*. Prentice Hall PTR, 1999.

[Liu00] Liu, Jane W. S., *Real-Time Systems*. Prentice Hall, 2000.

[McCarthy58] McCarthy, John, *LISP: A Programming System for Symbolic Manipulations*, Communications of the ACM, 1958 (Available at http://portal.acm.org/citation.cfm?id=612201.612243.)

[McCarthy60] McCarthy, John, *Recursive Functions of Symbolic Expressions and Their Computation by Machine, Part I*, Communications of the ACM, 1960 (Available online at http://www-formal.stanford.edu/jmc/recursive.pdf.)

[McDougal07] McDougal, Richard, and Mauro, Jim, *Solaris Internals—Solaris 10 and OpenSolaris Kernel Architecture*. Prentice Hall, 2007.

[Pizlo04] Pizlo, F., et al., *Real-Time Java Scoped Memory: Design Patterns and Semantics*, Purdue University, (Available online at www.cs.purdue.edu/homes/jv/pubs/isorc04.pdf).

[Stoodley07] Stoodely, Mark, et al., *Real-time Java, Part 1: Using Java Code to Program Real-Time Systems*, IBM developerWorks, April 10, 2007 (Available online at http://www.ibm.com/developerworks/java/library/j-rtj1.)

Index

FREE Online Edition

Your purchase of **Real-Time Java™ Programming** includes access to a free online edition for 45 days through the Safari Books Online subscription service. Nearly every Prentice Hall book is available online through Safari Books Online, along with more than 5,000 other technical books and videos from publishers such as Addison-Wesley Professional, Cisco Press, Exam Cram, IBM Press, O'Reilly, Que, and Sams.

SAFARI BOOKS ONLINE allows you to search for a specific answer, cut and paste code, download chapters, and stay current with emerging technologies.

Activate your FREE Online Edition at www.informit.com/safarifree

> **STEP 1:** Enter the coupon code: TCOZGAA.

> **STEP 2:** New Safari users, complete the brief registration form.
> Safari subscribers, just log in.

If you have difficulty registering on Safari or accessing the online edition, please e-mail customer-service@safaribooksonline.com